Another City

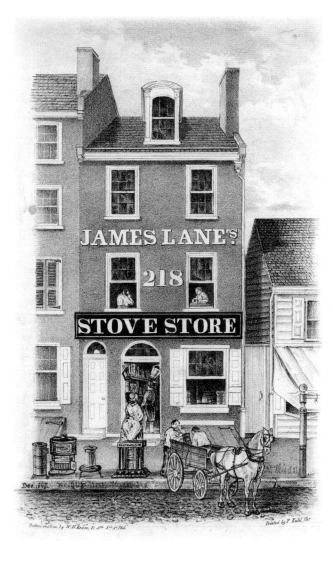

CRITTENDEN'S PHILADELPHIA

COMMERCIAL COLLEGE.

COLLEGE

BENKERT

BOOT MAKER

1856
JAYNE'S HALL

FARREL HERRING & CO.

SAFES

ARCADE H

ARCADE HOTEL

639   637   635   633   631   629   627   625   621   619

DELL UPTON

Another City

{ URBAN LIFE
AND URBAN
SPACES IN THE
NEW AMERICAN
REPUBLIC

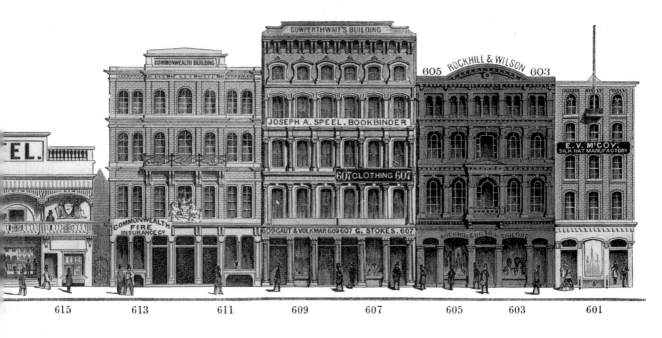

YALE UNIVERSITY PRESS   NEW HAVEN & LONDON

Published with assistance from the Ronald O. and Betty Miller Turner Publication Fund.

All photos by Dell Upton unless otherwise noted.

Designed by Richard Hendel

Set in The Serif types by BW&A Books, Inc.

Printed in China through World Print

Library of Congress Cataloging-in-Publication Data

Upton, Dell.

   Another city : urban life and urban spaces in the new American republic / Dell Upton.

      p.   cm.

   Includes bibliographical references and index.

   ISBN 978-0-300-12488-0 (cloth : alk. paper)

  1. Cities and towns—United States—History—19th century.   2. City planning—United States—History—19th century.   3. United States—History—19th century.   I. Title.

   HT123.U68   2008

   307.760973—dc22   2008001346

A catalogue record for this book is available from the British Library.

The paper in this book meets the guidelines for permanence and durability of the Committee on Production Guidelines for Book Longevity of the Council on Library Resources.

10 9 8 7 6 5 4 3 2 1

Cover illustration: *Market Street, from Fifth to Sixth, (South side.),* Philadelphia, 1860 (plate 8)

P. i: W. H. Rease, *James Lane's Stove Store,* Philadelphia, 1847 (fig. 1.6)

Pp. ii–iii: *Chestnut Street, from Seventh to Sixth (North Side.),* Philadelphia, 1859 (fig. 7.17)

Pp. vi–vii: *Stephens Plan of the City of Philadelphia,* 1807 (fig. 6.4, detail)

For Karen

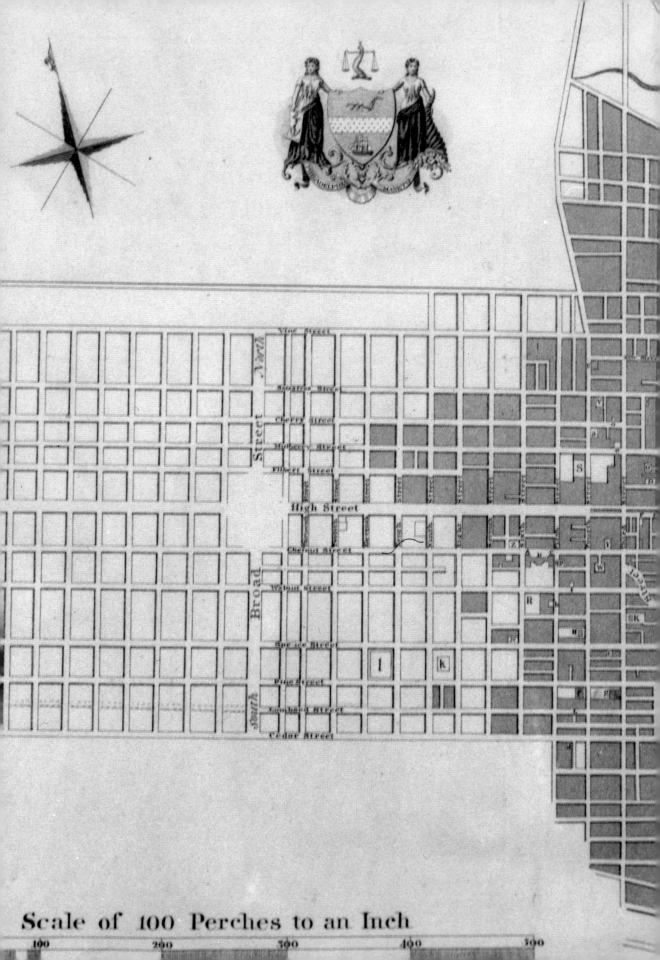

Vine Street

Sassafras Street

Cherry Street

Mulberry Street

Filbert Street

High Street

Chesnut Street

Walnut Street

Spruce Street

Pine Street

Lombard Street

Cedar Street

North Street

South

Broad Street

Scale of 100 Perches to an Inch

100   200   300   400   500

{ CONTENTS

{ **ACKNOWLEDGMENTS**

A book that has been as long in the making as *Another City* naturally accumulates many debts to friends, colleagues, and particularly archivists who made the work pleasurable as well as possible.

My first and deepest debts are to friends and former colleagues at Berkeley, where I taught during most of the years that I worked on this project. Paul Groth, Stephen Tobriner, the late Spiro Kostof, and the late Roger Montgomery taught me to love cities and gave me ways to think about them. Zeynep Kezer was both research assistant and valued interlocutor during the most critical years of the project. At various times, the longstanding Berkeley Americanists' reading group—Paul Groth, Mary Ryan, Margaretta Lovell, the late Larry Levine, Kathleen Moran, Dick Hutson, Chris Rosen, the late Jenny Franchot—gave encouragement and direction.

In Philadelphia, I logged countless hours in the Library Company of Philadelphia, where Jim Green, Phil Lapsansky, Denise Larrabee, Charlene Peacock, Susan Oyama, John Van Horne, Lynne Warren, and particularly Ken Finkel helped me to understand Philadelphia and its documentary and visual sources. Peter Parker, Linda Stanley, and the staff of the Manuscripts Reading Room at the Historical Society of Pennsylvania, Marty Levitt at the American Philosophical Society, and Bruce Laverty at the Athenaeum of Philadelphia also offered welcome assistance. Throughout my work on the Quaker City, Jeff Cohen generously shared his vast knowledge of its history and architecture. In recent years, Aaron Wunsch's insights and research skills have pushed me to sharpen my arguments a little more and to dig a little deeper in my own research.

In New Orleans, I was fortunate to have the assistance of the staff of the Historic New Orleans Collection, particularly Pamela Arceneaux, John Barbry, John Kukla, John Magill, Stan Ritchey, Jude Solomon, Sally Stassi, and Jessica Travis, as well as that of Wilbur Menary and the staff of the Rare Books and Manuscripts Room of the Tulane University Library, Ann Wakefield of the New Orleans Notarial Archives Research Center, and the staff of New Orleans City Archives at the New Orleans Public Library.

Most of the New York material derives from my work on the *Art and the Empire City* exhibition held at the Metropolitan Museum of Art in 2000. I am grateful to John K. Howat and the staff of the American Wing for their assistance.

Most of all I am indebted to the late Catherine H. Voorsanger for the opportunity to work on her show, for her great generosity of intellect and spirit, and for the opportunity to get to know her and Bart during the project.

Annmarie Adams, the late Robert L. Alexander, Nezar AlSayyad, Catherine Bishir, Dale Brown, Barbara Carson, Cary Carson, Tom Carter, Richard Cote, Betsy Cromley, the late James Deetz, Jay Edwards, Henry Glassie, Bernie Herman, Rhys Isaac, Jack Lesch, Bob St. George, Becky Shiffer, David Sloane, Daphne Spain, Abby Van Slyck, David Vanderburgh, Harry L. Watson, Mark R. Wenger, Shane White, and Mike Zuckerman offered welcome assistance, discussion, criticism, and simple encouragement over the years, and I am glad to be able at last to thank them in this way.

Sibel Zandi-Sayek, Tania Martin, and Tim Stokes all worked as research assistants on the project at one time or another, to its, and to my, benefit. Without Jennifer Reut's indispensable assistance the manuscript would never have been completed.

The lengthy research for this project was supported by fellowships from the Guggenheim Foundation, the Library Company of Philadelphia and Historical Society of Pennsylvania, and the Center for Advanced Study in the Visual Arts at the National Gallery of Art, as well as by a Getty Senior Research Grant, an NEH Travel to Collections Grant, a University of California Humanities Research Grant, and sabbatical leaves from the University of California and the University of Virginia.

Only Karen knows the whole story, and this book is for her.

INTRODUCTION

This book explores Americans' ambivalent attitudes toward their cities during the half century following the founding of the republic. My thesis is simple although my story is complex. Through *living* the city—through everyday experience in and of the material world of buildings, spaces, and people—American urbanites developed active senses of themselves as individuals and as members of a new republican society. In the process they created new kinds of urban spaces that were meant to propagate and accommodate these new roles.

Historians have examined socioeconomic structure and political ideology in the antebellum city, while architectural and urban historians have (to a much more limited extent) explored the ways that physical and demographic growth, new urban and aesthetic ideologies, and economic practices transformed American cities in the decades before the Civil War. My argument bridges these inquiries in an effort to understand how the effort of building and living in cities and of coping with one's neighbors in them shaped urban people's sense of selfhood and their understanding of what it meant to be the citizen of a republic.

In 1855, a New York journalist predicted that the greatest cities of the nineteenth century would be characterized by "civilization" and "urbanity" (as well as by Protestant Christianity and the English language). The first meant "'making a person a *citizen*;' that is—the inhabitant of a city," the second "the quality, condition, or manners of the inhabitant of a city."[1]

Above all else, *civilization* required a republican polity. As elaborated between the Revolution and the Civil War, the "protean concept" of republicanism came to mean many things to many people. At its core was a notion of political sovereignty vested in the people as a whole, understood as a collection of free individuals who were in some fundamental way essentially the same, therefore comparable, whatever their contingent differences in status or condition. Order in such a body politic arose from within, from the character of its citizens, rather than being imposed by a higher authority. Consequently, the political health of the republic depended on its (male) citizens' self-disciplined virtue, or moral vigor, which was thought to be lodged in a physical faculty susceptible to environmental influences.[2]

Urbanity had a more intimate focus. It was concerned with the individual as a member of an immediate community of neighbors and associates more than with an imagined political community. In the ballooning cities of the early nineteenth century, however, the intimacy of face-to-face community was increasingly as imaginary a concept as the all-encompassing political community of the nation. The possibility of distinguishing who one's neighbors appeared to be from who they "really" were diminished. The presentation of self and the assessment of others were increasingly sensory and performative. Thus deportment and visible self-presentation glossed identity. Appearance and action were assumed to be accurate indexes of character. They had to be if one were to traverse the new cities confidently.[3]

The concepts of civilization and urbanity, then, addressed those qualities that the anthropologist Anthony Cohen has called *selfhood*—the sense of one's internal coherence and independent, if circumstantially limited, agency—and *personhood*—the understanding of one's obligation to fulfill socially assigned and defined roles. Because civilization and urbanity were enacted in space, the nature of the urban artifact was of critical importance to antebellum city dwellers.[4]

Americans made their cities but in many cases treated them as creatures not of their own making. There was often good reason for this. The conscious act of city-building almost always has unwanted, or at least unexpected, consequences: roofs leak, windows reflect a blinding glare, noises bleed from one space to another, too much or too little air enters the building, views are cut off, iron wheels on stone pavements drown one's words and sometimes one's thoughts, living and working produce solid, liquid, and gaseous wastes. What did these "relics of civilized life" bode for civilization and urbanity? In Part I, "The Lived City," I examine the sensory encounter with early-nineteenth-century cities. The growth of enormous, complex, commercial (and later industrial) cities in the decades after 1790 sensitized city people to the chaos around them. Insistent and importunate sights, sounds, and smells surpassed anything previously known in the new nation, and they continued to multiply beyond control through the political, economic, and technological resources available to antebellum Americans. To the kinds of men and women who wrote the travel accounts, diaries, letters, and local ordinances and drew the architectural plans, maps, and prints that provide much of the evidence for this study, sensations that their forebears and many of their contemporaries took for granted seemed oppressive and worrisome in their new intensity. If, as the anthropologist Edward Hall argued, perception is as much a matter of what can be screened out as of what can be taken in, then the sheer volume of new stimuli demanded that city people change their modes of perception or that the city be changed to engage the senses in an acceptable manner.[5]

As the city's insistent multisensuality encroached on its residents' daily lives, making them feel besieged and in danger of succumbing to overstimulation, they tried to resolve contradictions among the testimonies of eye, ear, and noise—to bring the city into "focus" so that the visual order could be a true representation of the urban community. Urban opinion makers advocated a city organized to suit a consciously narrowed order that favored vision, with hearing muted and echoing the evidence of the eye—smell and touch suppressed, and taste hardly considered. They sought quieter surfaces for streets, attempted to outlaw vendors' use of noisemakers and vocal cries to attract business, built (or thought about) sewers, and removed cemeteries from built-up areas. And they built new kinds of buildings, set in new—or revitalized—street plans to channel their fellow citizens into the proper kinds of interaction, at once civilized and urbane. Although these efforts were rarely successful, they did affect the form of antebellum cities and American expectations of urban life since.

Certain people, especially among the political and economic elite, devoted vast physical, imaginative, and economic resources to inventing physical settings appropriate to the new models of urban life. So in Part II, "Metropolitan Improvements," I turn to the many large-scale projects for developing, embellishing, and reordering American cities in the early republican years. Wherever one turned, workmen were constructing public and private buildings, "regulating" streets (leveling them and defining a building line), improving the waterfront, and replanting parks and squares, all projects directed toward the twin goals of civilization and urbanity. Others were building new civic, cultural, charitable, and therapeutic institutions.

These projects were driven by a powerful desire to create a city that was regular—visually and spatially uniform. Most conspicuously the colonial cores of the old ports as well as newly established coastal and inland cities were fitted with expansive grids to define space in easily legible ways. New York's Commissioners' Plan of 1811 is only the most famous of many such additions, and not even the first gridded addition to that city (fig. 1). Urban grids were often projected far beyond current needs and took decades to fill out, or in most cases even to be surveyed, but they conveyed a vision of a modular framework that could "separate" and "classify" the people and the daily life of a city.

As streets were made uniform, so were the buildings that lined them. Freestanding mansions surrounded by gardens and warehouse-residences alike began to disappear, replaced by closely set rows of identical houses and waterfront wholesale stores. Houses for well-off people, as well as houses for the less well-

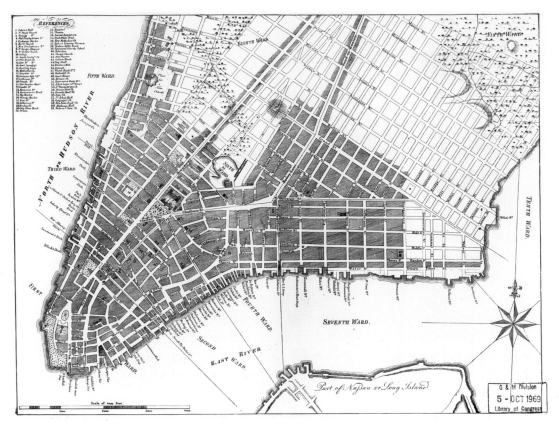

FIGURE 1. *Map of the City of New-York in 1808*, showing gridded additions to the original city before the 1811 Commissioners' Plan. (Library of Congress, Maps Division)

off, were built as sets of standardized units. In Philadelphia, William Sansom was thought to be the first to construct such a block-long row "with strict attention to uniformity." The (partly extant) row of twenty houses he built in 1799 on Walnut Street between Seventh and Eighth Streets, backed by twenty-two on George (now Sansom) Street, exemplified the modular uniformity that Philadelphians would seek to impose on their city in the coming decades (figs. 2, 3). Julia Row, a block-long row of such houses put up in the Crescent City by the New Orleans Building Company in 1832–33 was popularly known as the Thirteen Sisters (fig. 4). Nicknames of that sort were common in many American cities and testify to the novelty of their uniform appearance.[6]

Builders of such houses chose bricks that were smooth-surfaced, straight-edged, and uniformly colored. They laid them with a minimum of mortar between joints to give the impression of a single unbroken wall surface, one that couldn't have been more different from the rough-faced, broad-jointed walls of colonial houses, many of which had patterns picked out in bricks of contrasting colors and textures. Uniform facades masked increasingly uniform interiors.

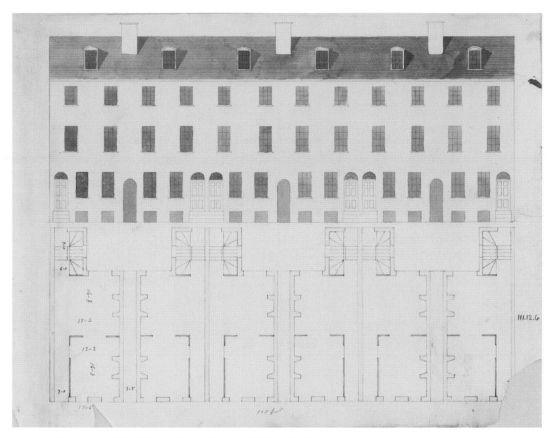

FIGURE 2. Proposed 200 block Spruce Street Row (att. William Garrigues, 1824), Philadelphia, plan and elevation. (Girard Papers, Girard College)

A standard row-house plan with a side passage (hallway) running from front to back on each floor, containing a stair and opening onto two rooms, one behind the other, had emerged from varied colonial practices by the beginning of the nineteenth century. Even the "back buildings," or rear service ells, of urban houses were standardized (see fig. 2).[7]

Uniformity's appeal was evident in the number of houses that were remodeled to fit it. Almost 10 percent of the new structures reported in Philadelphia in 1833 were back buildings. The architect-builder Thomas S. Stewart, who survived on small-scale projects, recorded a number of such jobs in his ledger, including the undated commission to remodel a house on Race Street above (west of) Seventh Street for a Mr. Proll. Stewart extended the half passage of the existing house to run the full depth of the house and replaced the original back buildings with ones of the new standardized plan.[8]

Entire business districts created de novo along the interior "streets" of the shopping arcades, built in the 1820s and 1830s, were the commercial equivalents of the uniform domestic rows. The new office buildings (first for the fed-

FIGURE 3. 202 Spruce Street, Philadelphia. Survivor of the Spruce Street row (fig. 2)

FIGURE 4. Julia Row ("Thirteen Sisters") (James Dakin and Alexander Wood, 1832–33), New Orleans

eral government), with rows of identical offices lining corridors, the hospitals, the houses of refuge, the prisons, and the asylums were organized in the same way, their interior plans resembling those of the cities that they served (fig. 5).

Each of the new types had its own peculiar history, and each might seem to have been a rational response to some aspect of urban economic growth, merchandising strategies, therapeutic programs, or social interaction. For each one it would be possible to construct the kind of formal and intellectual genealogy that constitutes so much of architectural history. Collectively, however, they take on a different aspect as propositions about the proper relationships among people and institutions—about civilization and urbanity. Although many of these new building types appear in retrospect to be commonsense or even "natural" expressions of social relationships in space, they were the results of years, even decades, of experimentation.

For these reasons the new urban landscape of the early nineteenth century cannot be understood as a simple reflection or unconscious manifestation of a cultural synthesis. Rather, it was a critical response to the city as its builders understood it. Some of the new types, such as schools, prisons, and various types of asylums, were designed to mould new citizens or to remould faulty ones. Others, including the new commercial and shopping spaces, as well as parks, squares, and other places of public recreation, responded to what some writers called the "promiscuous" mixing of crowded streets and public spaces. So while the everyday life of the city shaped urbanites' senses of selfhood and personhood, their behavioral and architectural responses might be read as *critiques* of that everyday life.

The prime movers of the most impressive metropolitan improvements were, necessarily, urban elites, and it is they whose concepts of a harmonious society and a systematically ordered landscape were most clearly articulated in public and private documents and in structures built and imagined. More modest metropolitan improvements, motivated by diverse viewpoints and assuming

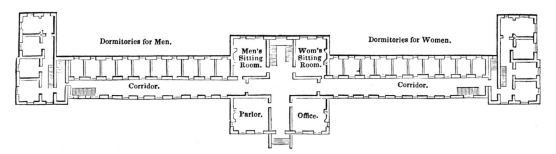

FIGURE 5. Friends Asylum for the Relief of Persons Deprived of the Use of Their Reason (William Strickland, 1815), Philadelphia, plan, 1855, after 1830s additions. (The Library Company of Philadelphia)

FIGURE 6. Merchants' Exchange (William Strickland, 1832–34), Philadelphia

a wide variety of forms, were undertaken by varied middle- and upper-class urbanites. All hoped that their projects would alleviate the abrasive aspects of the exploding city and reorder human relationships within it. These new environments were aimed at shaping personhood, with the conscious production of selves left to homes and religious institutions.

Among the most conspicuous of the urban projects were the headquarters of new commercial and cultural enterprises, such as merchants' exchanges, first-class hotels, libraries, tradesmen's associations, and fraternal orders, as well as the proliferating Christian churches. These were scattered throughout the built-up portion of the city, as were the smaller asylums and other therapeutic institutions. Most of these new institutional buildings, even the hospitals, asylums, and prisons, were housed in architecturally ambitious structures intended to stand out against the uniformity of the urban domestic and commercial fabric (fig. 6). Libraries, scientific and technical societies, and fraternal orders often established their presence on the street by erecting structures larger and more sumptuous than they could use or afford, then rented portions of their buildings to other institutions to defray the costs of their civic display.[9]

Such "monumental structures," wrote a correspondent to the *New-York Mirror* (who thought there were too few of them in Philadelphia), were "aspiring evidences of American enterprise." They were necessary symbols of the collective success of American urban life, the "metropolitan improvements" that proud city fathers and merchant entrepreneurs featured in books and lithographs, and even illustrated on the wallpaper and dinnerware that furnished their homes.[10]

A republican spatial imagination shaped arcades, office buildings, cemeteries, prisons, and entire cities, but it achieved mixed results. While it provided a clear way to organize urban space and urban spaces, it was much less successful in shaping the life that went on inside them. It failed to tame and rationalize the messiness of urban life along the lines that their builders predicted. The inherent ambiguities of the republican spatial imagination were particularly evident in conflicts over the ways that the systematized city would be used. What were the proper roles of urban governments and private citizens in shaping and using the new urban landscape? How were rights to use the city to be decided and determined? In the first half of the nineteenth century, the meaning of public space in American cities was defined on two parallel fronts—in legal and political battles over the use of the public domain for private economic purposes, and in legal and cultural conflicts over the political and social uses of streets and urban open spaces. They are the subjects of Part III, "Public Spaces and Private Citizens."

The raw materials of my account come mostly from Philadelphia and New Orleans, but I turn freely to other American cities, particularly New York, since this is not a comparative study. Nevertheless, Philadelphia and New Orleans offer useful complements that make them appropriate as prime examples. Many of the new urban and architectural forms and practices of the early nineteenth century first appeared in the United States in Philadelphia, and Philadelphians often articulated their purposes most clearly. New Orleans was for outsiders an exoticized magnifying mirror of their own preoccupations. They compared their expectations with New Orleans's management of racial hierarchy, gender conventions, commercial practices, urban order, moral standards, and even linguistic facility. Although most observers tended to raise the same kinds of questions in the same locations—the market, the levee, the slave auction, the cemeteries—their conclusions were as varied as their home experiences and their preconceptions. New Orleans was "good to think," as Claude Lévi-Strauss once said in another context.

There were personal ties, as well. In the years after the American Revolution, New Orleans attracted a host of Americans who expected to make fortunes there. Many of them were Philadelphians, such as the merchants Benjamin and Thomas Morgan and the architect Benjamin Henry Latrobe. Others helped form both cities, even though they were primarily associated with one or the other. Architect William Strickland, for example, designed the U.S. Mint in both cities, although he never went to New Orleans. The irascible, enigmatic, immensely wealthy merchant Stephen Girard spent a brief time in New Orleans in his younger days but lived his public life in Philadelphia. Yet he was involved in Louisiana's Ouachita land schemes, and both his philanthropic activities and his famous will clearly influenced New Orleans's enigmatic, immensely wealthy merchant, John McDonogh. Mercantile and some manufacturing firms maintained a foothold in both cities. Wood and Perot, the great Philadelphia ironworkers who made the cornstalk fences for which New Orleans is renowned, operated a Crescent City agency, Wood and Miltenberger.

The transformation of cities and elites' attempts to come to grips with them were not universally accepted in any city, but in Philadelphia elite voices spoke the loudest, and opposing opinions were often faintly expressed. By contrast, New Orleans after the Louisiana Purchase was the home of a colonial population of both elite and humble standing who acutely resented their involuntary subjugation to the United States and were proud of their indigenous lifeways. Measures for urban reordering that were applied both in the North and in New Orleans (often by émigrés from Philadelphia or New York) and that might be resisted inconsistently or without explicit explanation in the North sometimes encountered opposition in New Orleans that was vocal, articulate, and ready to challenge the fundamental assumptions of such projects.

This work will strike some readers as an odd sort of architectural history, if they see it as architectural history at all. It is certainly not an old-fashioned effort to "describe and perhaps account for the visual or stylistic differences between one building and another," but few architectural historians of any stripe do that exclusively any more. Still, much current architectural history is concerned with what might be called the "insider" aspects of architecture. It accepts as the groundwork of analysis the premises and canonical visual forms set by a particular architectural tradition's "hierarchies, . . . axiomatic and derivative principles, or . . . classificatory and axiological criteria," whether derived from high culture or from traditional sources. This discourse is self-referential and usually self-conscious. It is an exercise in intellectual history in that it deals with the dissemination and permutation of received systems of ideas. It is most interested in makers' intentions, and it deals best with users' reactions when reception is evaluated in terms of disciplinary assumptions.[11]

This book is also an intellectual history of architecture, but it differs from others in several ways. First, when I use the term architecture, I mean the entirety of what is sometimes called the built environment or the cultural landscape, whether or not it is made by people professionally trained in design or the building crafts. I do so because the practice of building—of imagining, shaping, and interpreting a material world—is integrated at all levels. Buildings exist and are used in the physical, psychological, symbolic, and utilitarian contexts of other buildings and of other categories of artifacts.

Second, if buildings exist in heterogeneous physical contexts, they are also made and used in the course of varied human activities, only a few of which address architecture in its narrowest sense. Consequently, builders and designers work from underlying assumptions common to many aspects of human life. As the folklorist Henry Glassie said of architectural design, "Before they have been burdened with [formal] knowledge about architecture, [architects'] eyes have seen, their fingers have touched, their minds have inquired into the wholeness of their scenes. They have begun collecting scraps of experience without regard to the segregation of facts by logical class." So even the most self-consciously theoretical and aesthetically ambitious building cannot be understood adequately on insider, intradisciplinary terms alone. Makers' and users' understanding of their enterprise is never purely architectural.[12]

One implication of this statement is that an "intellectual history" of architecture cannot be restricted to analysis of the development and reception of formal systems of thought. Common or popular political, social, economic, religious, and even medical beliefs are also intellectual in the sense that they use received ideas to make judgments about the world and the ways one ought to act in it. They affect architects', builders', and clients' ideas about how the built environment should be made and used.

Moreover, just as "architecture" is a heterogeneous category, so the life of formally systematic ideas is not restricted to their official or trained expositors. All acquire outside audiences who use them in unexpected ways. And systematic ideas themselves often rely on metaphors and modes of thought shared with, and sometimes derived from, extradisciplinary channels, meaning that ideas do not flow in one direction only. Thus it seems reasonable to call this exploration an intellectual history of architecture, even though it is much more porous and open-ended than most such histories. Mine is an outsider's intellectual history of architecture, rather than an insider's one, or rather one in which the distinctions of insider and outsider are of only marginal interest.[13]

This intellectual history differs from older ones in another way. The ideas that interest me rarely have lineages that can be tracked in a quasi-genealogical manner. While one might speak of the *causes* of the Civil War or the *influence* of Frank Lloyd Wright on European architecture, it is much more difficult to track changes in informal intellectual realms, where connections and transformations are often oblique, multiple, and even unrecognized by their agents. The intellectual history of architecture that I am examining is linguistically and experientially, rather than logically, based. It is linguistic because architecture was most often imagined metaphorically and analogically rather than worked out according to formal rules of logic or rhetoric. It is experiential because metaphors and analogies acquire their force through our corporeal participation in our surroundings.[14]

In his study of twentieth-century microphysics, the historian of science Peter Galison rejects the traditional view of scientific change as a single unbroken strand of progress, but he also challenges the more recent account of the history of science as a series of decisive ruptures or "paradigm shifts," as Thomas S. Kuhn called them. For Galison, scientific change is defined by the shorter trajectories of independent but related scientific subcommunities, each with its own preoccupations, goals, language, and procedures. These subcommunities' paths intersect irregularly but fruitfully with one another. There is no neat chain of causes and effects, no single arc of progress, but "many traditions coordinate with one another without homogenization." Galison offers the image of a cable, whose strength derives from the intercalation of many short, entwined strands, rather than from a "single, golden thread" that runs the length of the cable. "It is the *disorder* of the scientific community—the laminated finite, partially dependent strata supporting one another; it is the *dis*unification of science—the intercalation of different patterns of argument—that is responsible for its strength and coherence."[15]

As Galison points out, the cable metaphor carries one only so far. Intercalation makes a cable strong simply by the friction between adjacent strands, whereas the connections among scientific communities arise from "coordinating different symbolic and material actions." That is, the rich symbolic language and material practices of the subcommunities, rather than the mere friction of a cable, are responsible for the intercalation of scientific enterprise.[16]

Intercalation is a fruitful way to think about urban cultural change. Architecturally, for example, the physicians who founded hospitals and insane asylums, the merchants and developers who commissioned shopping arcades, the surveyors who laid out cities and subdivisions, the board members who oversaw public schools, and the theorists of "prison discipline" who promoted penitentiaries all had particular goals and made varying but specific demands on architecture. Yet they produced remarkably similar buildings. In part this was the result of what we might call "interlocking directorates": the merchants, developers, physicians, school-board members, and penologists were often the same people, and even when membership in these groups did not overlap significantly they often hired the same small group of architects and contractors to build their streets, buildings, parks, and wharves. Nevertheless, ad hominem explanations alone are not adequate. Merchants, politicians, scientists, physicians, or theologians might stand as the equivalent of Galison's scientific subcommunities: each group had its own language, practices, and goals, as well as its own universe of "symbolic and material actions," to borrow Galison's phrase, but these were intercalated.

The process that Galison calls intercalation is sometimes called transversality, another term borrowed from science, which implies "convergence without coincidence, conjuncture without concordance, overlapping without assimilation, and union without absorption." In the humanities, transversality is used to describe cultural phenomena that coexist, that even cooperate, that are pretty much the same without being absolutely identical. The philosopher Calvin Schrag, following Paul Ricoeur, calls this similarity ipse-identity. Ipse-identity describes sameness for the moment, for the task at hand, to all intents and purposes, as opposed to idem-identity, which describes things that are demonstrably the same according to objective and unchanging criteria. In terms of cultural practices, transversality, "lying across and extending over surfaces, accelerating forces, fibers, vertebrae, and moments of consciousness is not grounded in a universal telic principle but proceeds rather as an open-textured gathering of expanding possibilities." As an image of cultural change, the metaphor of transversality reinforces the point that adjacencies and transferrals are more relevant than sources and derivatives or causes and effects.[17]

How is this possible? In the natural world, transversality is sometimes the result of very specific virus-borne migrations of genetic traits between species, which stimulates change outside the genetic ancestral tree. There are no cultural viruses, of course, but visual and verbal similes and metaphors can play a similar role. By definition, metaphors and similes propose ipse connections; their malleability makes them portable. Antebellum urbanites, for example, were enamored of metaphors of system, order, and articulation, of "separation" and "classification" (two ubiquitous watchwords of the era), of enumeration, tabulation, and comparison, and they sought out kinds of information amenable to such operations. The distribution of repetitive cells along circulation spines seemed to be the spatial correlate of separation, classification, tabulation, and enumeration. Although this language was born in mathematics, the sciences, and economics, the vocabulary of these fields had not yet calcified, as it later did, into a specialized language that allowed the sciences and the social sciences to achieve precision at the cost of their words' metaphorical power. In early-nineteenth-century America, technical language remained figurative. As such, it was well suited to move transversally among fields as disparate as politics, moral economy, and architecture. The metaphors carried their associated modes of thought with them, by which I mean habits of mind that often operated below the surface of explicit argument but that shaped the narrative structures eventually shared by a variety of scientific, economic, and social discourses.[18]

In using intercalation and transversality to convey the messiness and multi-dimensionality of historical change, I have worked transversally myself, since both are ipse metaphors that converge without becoming identical. But the metaphorical aspects of the intellectual history of architecture I am constructing are inextricable from its experiential aspects. Galison's science progresses through "symbolic and material practices," and both are equally important to my story. The urban cultural landscape was lived and inhabited even as it was spoken or described. In the end it was *narrated* more often than it was analyzed by its makers and users. By that I mean that architecture was rarely discussed or criticized as a discrete object. Instead, it was most often treated as an actor in narratives of real or potential human interaction. The sociologist Henri Lefebvre emphasized the distinction yet inseparability of individual experience—the lived aspect—and socially learned responses—the narrative aspect—in everyday life. He argued that the "concrete, practical and alive" experience of every-day life determined the "discreteness yet inclusiveness of the individual and the social. . . . This unity is the foundation of all society: a society is made up of individuals, and the individual is a social being, in and by the content of his life and the form of his consciousness."[19]

In the early republican city the individual and the social, the metaphorical and the material found their common nexus in the body, where the socio-cultural and the perceptual, or what Schrag calls the "we-experience" and the "I-experience," met. As embodied beings with mass and extension, people co-habit the same material realm as buildings, clothing, and their neighbors. Our bodies are artifacts as much as our chairs or our weapons are: we shape, use, and interpret them according to learned ideas just as we do our gardens or our buildings. We are part of the cultural landscape. A history of the urban land-scape must also encompass the bodies that built and used it.[20]

Received ideas filter lived experience, and they may blunt or redirect our perceptions, but at the same time language acquires specificity and changes meaning in its encounter with the specificity of material existence. We know the landscape and we know each other through perception and we know our-selves that way as well. We anchor selfhood in our own and others' presence *in* the landscape and in its presence *to* us. But these ecological aspects of bodily ex-perience are mediated through language, and here the issue of metaphor comes back into play. Bodily metaphors, widely used in the early American republic to discuss many aspects of social life and the experience of the built environment, naturalized the links between the two.

So the study of the built environment and the way it was lived are insepa-rable aspects of the same project. In city streets, in their confrontation with the roaring tide of vehicles and manufacturing and building construction and particularly in their immersion in the undertow of their fellow human be-ings, antebellum Americans developed a lived sense of their new society. In the embodied experience of urban life, the abstractions of political ideology, plan-ning ideas, and personal identities were tested and absorbed specific content. The city artifact shaped and annotated this experience and was shaped by it. An understanding of the embodied immersion in urban life thus can help us to understand how the more abstract and intangible values, mores, concepts, and modi operandi that we gather under the rubric "self" are realized: the self is always a self in space. In turn it can help historians of material culture find the culture revealed in the material in performative ways that transcend static statements of intention and belief.

All that I have said so far implies that this study cannot be constructed as a linear narrative with a clear, chronologically fixed beginning and end or origin and result. Nor do I pretend to offer a comprehensive survey of urban history or of the architectural history of the new building types that appeared in my period. Instead, it seems more appropriate to employ a series of case studies that illuminate the ways common figures and metaphors cut through and or-dered the lived landscape, linking buildings and builders in loose-jointed but unmistakable ways. One might make the same points, with different details, by investigating hospitals, schools, hotels, asylums, or even houses, but enough is enough.

PART ONE

The Lived City

CHAPTER 1 { **CITIES OF PERPETUAL RUIN AND REPAIR**

As cashier of the Bank of Germantown and then secretary of the Germantown and Norristown Railroad, historian John Fanning Watson was immersed in Philadelphia's transformation from a modest-sized commercial port to a large industrial center. Yet, despite his own role in changing the city, Watson was overwhelmed by the result. Shortly before he died he added an urgent coda to the second edition of his *Annals of Philadelphia,* a work that celebrated the "olden time"—meaning the years around 1800, the period of his own youth and the twilight of the Quaker City's preeminence as a seaport. "*Our People are fast changing,*" Watson declared in his "Final Appendix of the Year 1856." "All is now self-exalted and going upon stilts." Telegraphing his agitation in staccato phrases that mimicked the mounting urban frenzy, Watson denounced the "*rivalship of grandeur in houses,*" the "general clatter from crowds of people and confusion now along the streets—no room now to turn or look about—once it was peaceful—pleasant and safe to walk the streets,—now tall houses, are crowded with numerous working tenants—formerly, they were in smaller houses and in bye places.—'Tis terrible now to sicken and die at [*sic*] crowded streets, where the rattle of omnibuses is unceasing." Watson the railroad executive was dismayed by the anonymity of railroad and steamship travel where "people must go by hundreds [and] where they can only stare at, and scan each other without speaking" and by hotels "where all must keep aloof, and look askance at each other." "To my eye," he wrote, "the whole aspect is changing.—It is indeed, already, another City—*A city building on the top of the former!* All the houses now, above *three* stories—present *an elevation* so manifest, as to *displease the eye;*—and particularly, where several, *go up* so exalted, as to break the former *line* of equality, and beauty. Even such edifices, lately constructed, as the Bank of North America, [and the] Philadelphia and Western Bank, are struck down by the still later, *towering* business houses and hotels, &c., near them." The new Philadelphia offended his senses and his sense of propriety and revealed "Our anti-social character."[1]

Yale University president Timothy Dwight saw things much differently. He marveled at the electric atmosphere of New York in the years after the War of 1812. A vibrant energy "spreads through all classes and is everywhere visible. The bustle in the streets, the perpetual activity of the carts, the noise and hurry at the docks which on three sides encircle the city; the sound of saws, axes, and hammer at the shipyards, the continually repeated views of the numerous buildings rising in almost every part of it, and the multitude of workmen employed upon them form as lively a specimen of 'the busy hum of populous cities' as can be imagined." New York was the most prodigious of the new urban centers, but all other major American cities experienced boisterous growth on a lesser, but still notable, scale during the fifty years after 1790. Many smaller towns, such as New Orleans, metamorphosed from insignificance to national importance during the same era (table 1). "This city, which we thought so beautiful and large when we arrived in the year 1809, was a mere suburb" compared to the New Orleans of 1831, Jean Boze reported to his former employer.[2]

The new cities were scenes of "perpetual ruin and repair," the *New-York Mirror* reported. "No sooner is a fine building erected than it is torn down to put up a better." The urban architecture of every antebellum decade was taller and more voluminous than that of its predecessors, with striking changes of scale around 1830 and again in the late 1840s and 1850s. At the same time, builders undertook massive projects of "regulation"—cutting down hills, filling low places, draining swamps, building levees, widening streets, and reorganizing their plans—to push urban boundaries outward.[3]

Table 1 Population of Five Major American Cities, 1790–1860

	1790	1800	1810	1820	1830	1840	1850	1860	Rank in 1860[a]
Baltimore	13,503	26,514	46,555	62,738	80,620	102,313	169,054	212,418	4
Boston	18,320	24,937	33,787	43,298	61,392	93,383	136,881	177,840	5
New Orleans[b]	5,037[c]	8,056[d]	17,242	27,176	46,082	102,193	130,565	168,675	6
New York	33,131	60,515	96,373	123,706	202,589	312,710	515,547	813,669	1
Philadelphia[e]	44,096	61,559	87,303	98,193	147,877	198,009	286,087	565,529	2

Sources: Campbell Gibson, *Population of the 100 Largest Cities and Other Urban Places in the United States: 1790 to 1990*, Population Division Working Paper No. 27 (Washington, D.C.: Population Division, United States Census Bureau, 1998), www.census.gov/population/www/documentation/twps0027.html, downloaded Nov. 22, 2006; Kimberly S. Hanger, *Bounded Lives, Bounded Places: Free Black Society in Colonial New Orleans, 1769–1803* (Durham, N.C.: Duke University Press, 1997), p. 22.

[a] Brooklyn, N.Y., third in 1860.

[b] Includes Lafayette (Garden District), 1850–60.

[c] 1791.

[d] 1803.

[e] Includes Northern Liberties and Southwark to 1820; add Spring Garden and Moyamensing, 1830–40; add Kensington, 1850; includes all of Philadelphia County, 1860.

Early republican cities ballooned with growing, diversifying populations. Alongside the western Europeans and Africans and their descendants and the (ever-present but rarely noted) Native Americans who had lived in them since before the Revolution, Irish, German, and West Indian immigrants poured into the coastal ports, accompanied by a smattering of people from more exotic locations. "We have Turkish saloons, and Turkish baths, French coffee houses and French theatres, German Gardens, large bier saloons, opera houses, and reading rooms, Spanish hotels, Italian churches, and Italian newspapers, Chinese boarding houses, inhabited only by the Chinese, and in the lower part of the city, there is a gambling place, we are told, supported principally by natives of Portugal. The Celts, the English, and the natives of 'bonnie Scotia,' have also their especial resorts; so have the descendants of the Africans," boasted a New York journalist in an article entitled "The World in Little."[4]

The frenzy of everyday urban life can distract one from the relatively straightforward order of the largest American cities at the beginning of the nineteenth century. Although their formal plans varied, those cities that had been formed during the colonial period exhibited remarkably consistent patterns of urban development. Most assumed a bell shape draped around an inverted T-shaped armature where the waterfront intersected with a perpendicular axis defined by varying arrays of public buildings, parades, markets, and wharves.[5]

The T-armature was an "informal" (some might say vernacular) practice that may have been implicit but was no less real for that. It was produced by shared principles of siting and orientation, inflected by social and occupational preferences for location near (or apart from) other people or other trades, and the resulting gradients of land and rental values that affected individuals' and institutions' choice of location within the urbanized area. This planning strategy guided colonial port builders no matter what the formal plans of their cities, organizing cities without formal plans (such as Boston) as well as those with pre-established plans (such as Charleston), and it continued to influence American city builders through the early decades of the new republic. Indeed the often-dissonant relationship between formal plans and everyday city-building practices was a central theme of American urban thinking during those decades.[6]

Philadelphia exemplified these patterns clearly. William Penn and his surveyor Thomas Holme intended their new city to fill its grid evenly from the Delaware to the Schuylkill River, but urbanization clustered predictably along the Delaware, the principal access for oceangoing vessels (plate 1). High (now Market) Street, which runs west from the Delaware, accommodated the market sheds built and continually extended from 1693 until they were finally removed in 1859. The Court House (1708), the principal government building, stood above the first shed, with the Quakers' largest meetinghouse (1696) adjacent to it. The densest urban development followed High Street inland. The renowned Clarkson-Biddle map of 1762 clearly illustrates the bell-shaped settlement pattern that the T-plan generated, with development extending along the river north and south of the city limits long before the original grid had filled, and density dropped radically as one moved away from the center.

By the late eighteenth century this rough-hewn working city was urbanized at a scale and density previously unimaginable in the American colonies. In 1750 Philadelphia's population was slightly fewer than 13,000 people, with about 2,000 more people living just outside the city limits. During the next half century the population of the "city and districts" (Philadelphia plus Southwark and the Northern Liberties) doubled. When the first federal census was taken in 1790, the city proper was home to 28,522 people, while the city and districts together sheltered 44,096. By 1800, over 20,000 of the city's 62,000 residents lived in the districts. When all was said and done, the city's population had grown more than five times in half a century, or about 3.4 percent per year.[7]

While a few more than 2,100 houses were sufficient to accommodate the city's residents in 1750, the city and districts required 6,784 dwellings and more than 400 shops and stores forty years later. By the middle of the nineteenth century, there were an estimated 60,000 houses in the city, a number that had recently been growing by about 3,500 per year. The expansion of the built-up area is evident in the 1794 map published by the geographer A. P. Folie. Folie's work depicted an urbanized area at least two blocks (or "squares," in Philadelphia parlance) deep stretching from Prune Street in Southwark to Brown Street in the Northern Liberties (fig. 1.1). In the city proper, urbanization penetrated to Sixth Street for the entire north-south extent of the city and to Ninth Street in a four-block swath from Race to Walnut streets. Six years later bits of development were beginning to reach the Center Square. Although the urbanized population was nearly three times as large in 1830 as in 1800, and dense settlement reached up High Street three squares past Center Square with outliers stretching to the Schuylkill River, the city retained the bell shape[8] (fig. 1.2; see fig. 6.5).

Within the urban bell, Philadelphia's land use, social composition, and density were heterogeneous. It was very much a "walking city," meaning that it was possible to travel on foot easily from any part of the city to any other part. It had the familiar characteristics of a pre-industrial (or mercantile) city, in the sense that it was not rigidly segregated by social class, economic status, or urban function. Wealthy and poor people, blacks and whites lived relatively close to one another. In 1800, for example, most free blacks lived in white households. Elizabeth and Henry Drinker, who were among the wealthiest Philadelphians in the late eighteenth century, shared their square (between Front and

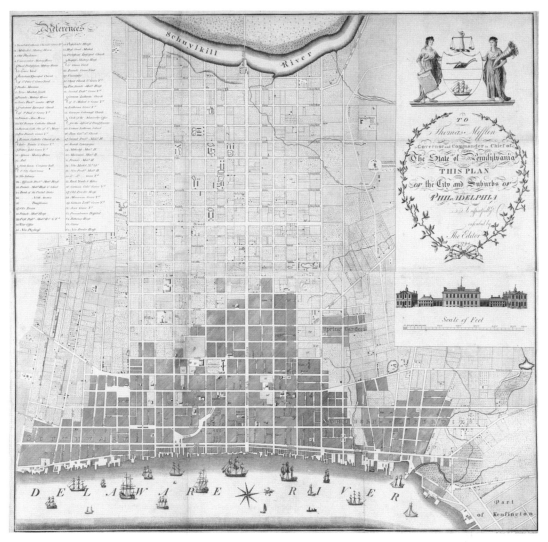

FIGURE 1.1. A. J. Folie, *Plan of the City and Suburbs of Philadelphia,* 1794.
(The Library Company of Philadelphia)

Second, Arch and Race streets) with a German couple named Pantlif who were
in the habit of fighting with their neighbors' African American servants and
who had trained their dog to attack black people. They were eventually caught
with a house full of stolen goods. The Drinkers' neighbors also included "French
people" (impoverished refugees from Saint Domingue) and several other poor
families.[9]

Nevertheless, the growing city's landscape already showed visible signs of
occupational sorting and the hardening of social and economic divisions. During the early nineteenth century, well-off people began to move away from
their places of work. Great eighteenth-century merchants such as the Drinkers usually lived behind or above their warehouses, but by the beginning of

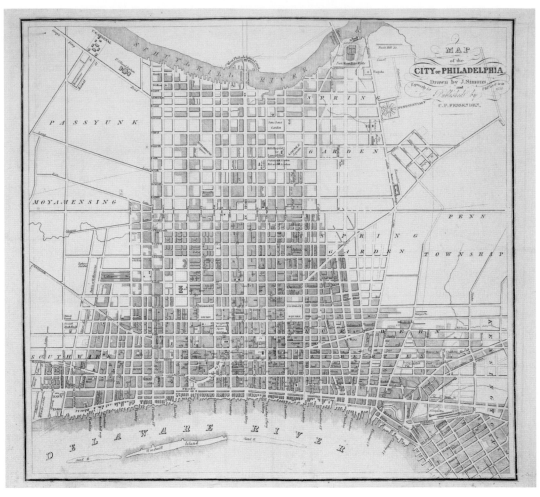

FIGURE 1.2. J. Simons, *Map of the City of Philadelphia*, 1830. (The Library Company of Philadelphia)

the nineteenth century they and their neighbors had begun to move inland, away from the waterfront. "Peggy Wharton came this morning to take leave of us as next-door Neighbours," Elizabeth Drinker wrote in 1796. "They leave us this day, and remove to their new-house in third, near Spruce Street." As the fugitive merchants moved progressively west, John Fanning Watson reported, "Houses . . . of grand dimensions were running up for dwellings above Fifth and Sixth streets even while stores were following close after from Fourth street." All along the urban edge, old and "inconvenient" buildings were replaced by "stately and modernized houses."[10]

The Drinkers lived near lower-class people but not adjacent to them, for while the merchant family's house stood on Front Street, their impoverished neighbors resided in Drinker's Alley on the interior of the block. This was a familiar pattern. Poor Philadelphians inhabited Coombe's Alley, Elfreth's Alley, Loxley's

Court, and a myriad of other spaces hidden off the main streets and behind the residences of their better-off compatriots. As settlement expanded, a clear hierarchy appeared. The largest houses were built on the major east-west streets. Most were three stories tall, but by 1830, four-story houses could be found, "many after the modern style of building," with marble basements. North-south streets also contained impressive houses, but few exceeded three stories. The alleys sheltered small houses of one and two stories, as well as three-story "trinity" houses with a single square room on each floor (fig. 1.3). Many of these were built of wood long after better-off Philadelphians' houses were routinely built of brick. Older-type structures that combined artisans' workshops and living quarters remained scattered throughout the city but were particularly common near the waterfront.[11]

By the end of the eighteenth century some neighborhoods had begun to assume distinctive social characteristics, although none was dominated by a single social class or ethnic group. Poor people were scattered relatively uniformly throughout the city, but they were most conspicuous in the Northern Liberties and especially in Southwark, where few of their economic betters chose to settle. This pattern held throughout the first half of the nineteenth century, as differential tax assessments and the location of mid-century soup kitchens indicated. The northern edge of the city was also the home to many of Philadelphia's Germans. Blacks who did not live in the homes of the whites for whom they worked were likely to be found north of Arch Street and west of Fourth Street or, increasingly, along the southern and southwestern edges of the city. South and Lombard streets were established early on as heavily black districts, and they remained so throughout the nineteenth century. Knowing this, Elizabeth Drinker's daughter and grandchildren "went in our Waggon to South street, to look after a maid."[12]

To house Philadelphia's growing population, developers erected hundreds of new dwellings. At the beginning of the new century James Mease estimated that 500 new houses had been built in the Quaker City every year since the Constitution went into effect, but historian Carole Shammas calculated an average of 228 per year between 1760 and 1800. The Philadelphia City Council formally counted 345 in 1833. Many of these were built by single developers such as William

FIGURE 1.3. 800 block of North American Street, Philadelphia. Small early-nineteenth-century houses in the Northern Liberties

Sansom, who Mease claimed had built 200 by 1805. The great rows of houses that line Philadelphia's main streets are the best known and most conspicuous visual evidence of this frenzied house construction, but most developers and landlords built smaller numbers on scattered sites.[13]

Most of the new houses were intended for the upper and middle strata of the population. The 1833 City Council inventory noted that three-story buildings were by far the most numerous; 286 were built in Philadelphia that year. Four-story buildings accounted for 26 houses, and two-story houses for 33 new buildings. Some of the two- and three-story buildings were undoubtedly the tenements (rental houses) that one finds in alleys and, in Southwark particularly, in the back yards of row houses.[14] These tiny houses, with a single square room on a floor, were built by speculative developers and intended for working-class tenants, but not for the poorest among them (fig. 1.4).

Many of the poorest Philadelphians continued to occupy small one- , two- and three-room houses as they always had.[15] By 1790, most Philadelphians resided with 6 other people; workers shared their much smaller residences with 6.5 others. Some were family members, others were outsiders taken in to help meet the rent. Increasingly, poor Philadelphians lived in the cast-off houses of their betters, which had been subdivided into tiny tenements, a pattern established by the time of the Revolution. When Benjamin Loxley assumed the management of two houses that the Carpenters' Company had bought and intended to demolish, he found that they were shared among many tenants (fig. 1.5). One was a four-room house with a shop in the first-floor front room and an office and privy in the yard behind it. The other had a single room on each floor and a hyphen (Philadelphians called it a "piazza") connecting it to a two-room ell or "back building." These spaces were rented to eleven different tenants. Five lived in the main houses: Joseph Alstein and four others "gone or poor." There was one tenant living in each of the two shops (presumably the ground floor of the one-room house was the other shop) and the two kitchens and two in the office. In an era when many workers could hope to make little more than £60 a year, these tenants combined to pay an annual rent of £66. Similarly, among the Drinkers' neighbors were "four families in [a] small house, where are but 4 rooms, one of them the kitchen." A survey of the area east of Front Street between Vine and Sassafras streets, taken for the Councils in 1833, the same year as the census of new buildings, found 92 families living in 64 rental properties, with 55 families, totaling 253 people, living in 30 of them, with no privy to serve any of them. In 1837, "a collection of six or seven" black men and women was found living in a cellar in Mary Street with "no kind of furniture . . . and a heap of shavings was the common bed of the whole party."[16]

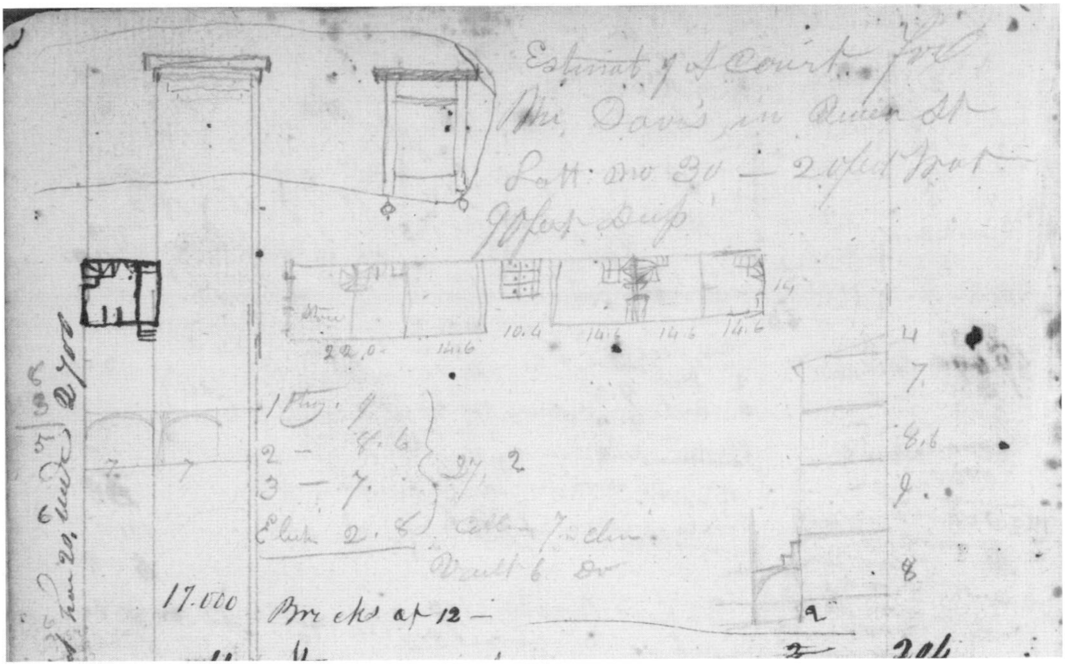

FIGURE 1.4. Thomas S. Stewart, *A Court for Mr. Davi's [sic] in Queen Street Lott no 30*, Philadelphia, ca. 1835, sketch plan. These drawings, typical of the crude sketches found in Stewart's day book, illustrate four 14-by-14 ½-foot single-room, three-story houses, and a three-room building at the alley entrance. The latter includes a store on the street side. The development, which occupies the entire depth of a 90-foot-deep lot, is divided into two blocks, with a six-hole privy between them. (Athenaeum of Philadelphia)

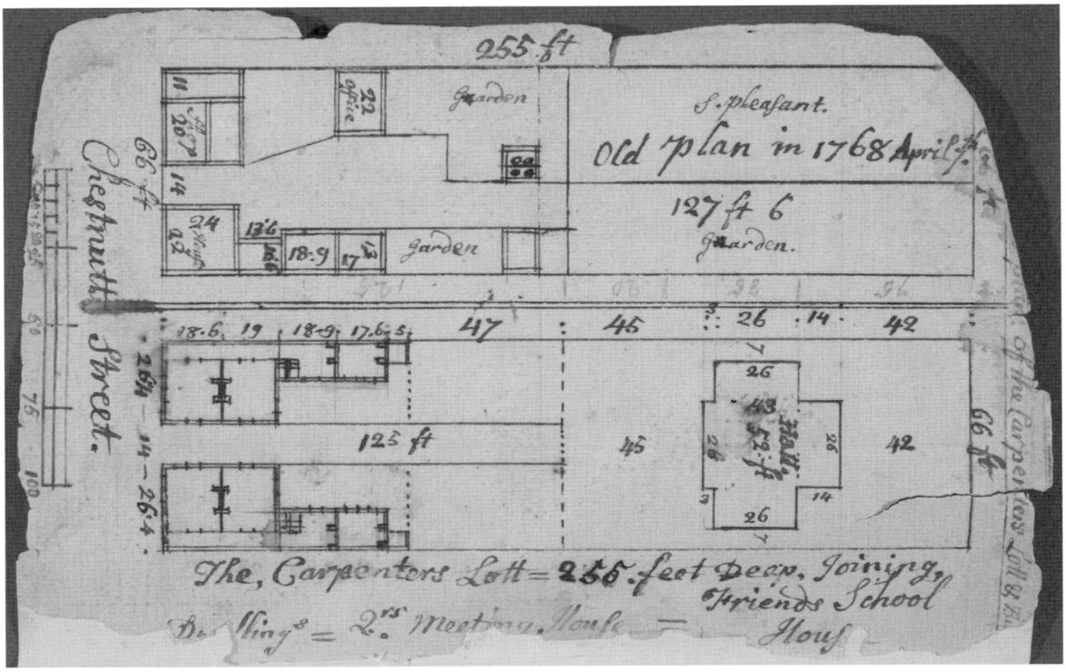

FIGURE 1.5. Benjamin Loxley, Carpenter's Court, Philadelphia, plans before and after redevelopment, 1768. (Benjamin Loxley Papers, Uselma Clark Smith Collection, The Historical Society of Pennsylvania)

Philadelphia's T-shaped armature was reinforced by the city's food-distribution system. Until the public market sheds along High Street were demolished in 1859 and replaced by a system of privatized neighborhood market houses, most Philadelphians obtained their food from the markets that stretched west along High Street, eventually reaching Seventeenth Street, with others running north and south along or adjacent to Second Street. Some durable goods were also sold in the markets, but most were offered by wholesale merchants along Front and Second streets and by artisans whose shops abutted the market area.[17]

In 1794 Joseph Cook erected an elaborate new building at the southeastern corner of Market and Third streets (plate 2). The Shakespeare Building was not the first purpose-built group of retail stores, but it was the first architecturally ambitious one, a three-story structure containing three shops, occupied at first by jewelers, with residences above and below. It was a financial failure that came to be known as "Cooke's Folly." After a few years this "grand Edifice" was stripped of its decoration and let to humbler tenants, but it made a deep impression on Philadelphians, who recognized in it the beginnings of a new kind of merchandising that led to the emergence of separate wholesale and retail districts. By the middle of the century, wholesale businesses could be found as far west as Third Street. Fashionable retail businesses had pushed out High Street, then shifted a block over from Market to Chestnut Street, Philadelphia's tamer version of New York's Broadway.[18]

Nevertheless, the center of the growing city had not lost its mixed character. People still lived in and around commercial buildings. Exclusive shops stood near ordinary ones. Many sellers of clothing, household items, and luxury goods made and sold their merchandise in the same building or on the same lot, so that one was never far from the sights and sounds of small-scale manufacturing (fig. 1.6). Beginning early in the century, heavy industry—ironworks, brickyards, stone works, textile mills, the U.S. Navy Yard—formed a deepening band around the edges of the city.[19]

From the middle of the eighteenth century, Philadelphia's landscape was punctuated by larger-scale buildings that housed hospitals, almshouses, and prisons. Like the monasteries, almshouses, hospitals, orphanages, and other large religious institutions of medieval European cities, which were sited on vacant land just inside or outside the walls, the builders of their secular American counterparts clung to the fringes of the built-up area, where large tracts of cheap land were available. The first such institutions, including the Pennsylvania Hospital (1754–56 and 1794–1804), the Old Almshouse (1760–67 and 1814–15, dem. ca. 1835), and the Walnut Street Jail (1773–74, dem. 1836), were constructed when the urban edge at the head of the bell was Sixth Street, the site of the mid-eighteenth-century State House (Independence Hall) (fig. 1.7; see plate 13). Smaller institutions, such as the Asylum for Indigent Widows and Single Women (1819–20) and adjacent the Orphans' Asylum (1816; burned and rebuilt 1823–24), the St. Joseph's (Roman Catholic) Orphans' Asylum (1807), the Pennsylvania Institution for the Deaf and Dumb (1824–26), and the Institution for the Blind (1834), continued to be built within the city, but by the second quarter of the nineteenth century urban development had engulfed the larger ones (fig. 1.8). Major new institutions, as well as new buildings for older ones, were sited just outside the new urban edge. Now it was not just cheap land that builders sought. They wanted to be near enough to the city for convenience, but far enough away to promote a salutary, contemplative atmosphere separated from the distractions of urban life.

A glance at a nineteenth-century map of Philadelphia would show an arc of large-scale institutions that recalled the circle of fortifications found on maps of Renaissance cities. Beginning at the north with the first-built of these structures, the Friends' Asylum for the Relief

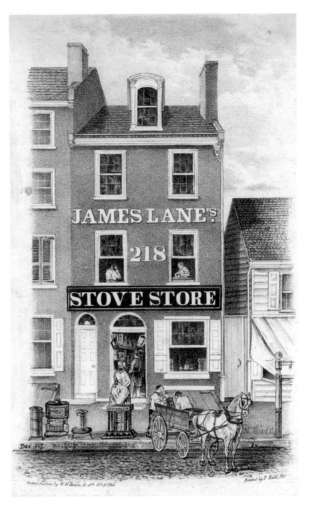

FIGURE 1.6. W. H. Rease, *James Lane's Stove Store*, Philadelphia, 1847. An early-nineteenth-century commercial building. (The Library Company of Philadelphia)

of Persons Deprived of the Use of Their Reason (1814–17), the ring ran southwest to the Pennsylvania Hospital for the Insane (1835–41) and the Blockley Almshouse (1829–34) on the west side of the Schuylkill River, facing the U.S. Naval Asylum (1826–29) on the east side, then back southeast to the Moyamensing Prison (1832–35) south of the city (fig. 1.9). The arc was anchored by a significant cluster northwest of the city. There a careful observer would spot the Girard College for orphans and the white (1827–28; replaced 1854) and colored (1848–49) houses of refuge (juvenile detention centers), all gathered in the shadow of the Eastern State Penitentiary (1823–36), or Cherry Hill Penitentiary (so-called after the orchard that had formerly occupied its site) (plate 3; see fig. 10.1, plate 12). Although most of these institutions were not directly connected to religious organizations, they exemplified, as their medieval forebears did, the most cherished

FIGURE 1.8 Pennsylvania Institution for the Deaf and Dumb (now University of the Arts) (John Haviland, 1824–26), Philadelphia

values of the society that created them. And like the Renaissance fortifications, they offered the city a formidable line of defense, but one directed toward internal rather than external enemies.[20]

Philadelphia's pattern was similar to those of other northern cities. In many ways it also resembled that of another of the focal cities of this study, New Orleans, a city laid out on the banks of the Mississippi in 1721 (fig. 1.10). This grid, later known as *le carré de la ville* or the Vieux Carré (old or original square), was

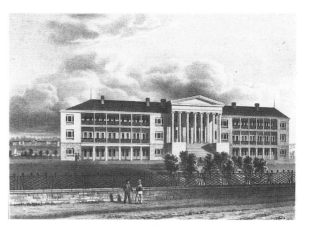

FIGURE 1.9. J. C. Wild, *U. S. Naval Asylum* (Marine Asylum) (William Strickland, 1827–33), Philadelphia, 1838. (The Library Company of Philadelphia)

only about one mile wide by half a mile deep—a quarter of the size of Philadelphia's plan. The engineer-planmaker Pierre le Blond de la Tour and the surveyor Adrien de Pauger set the cathedral, priests' residence, and prison at the back of

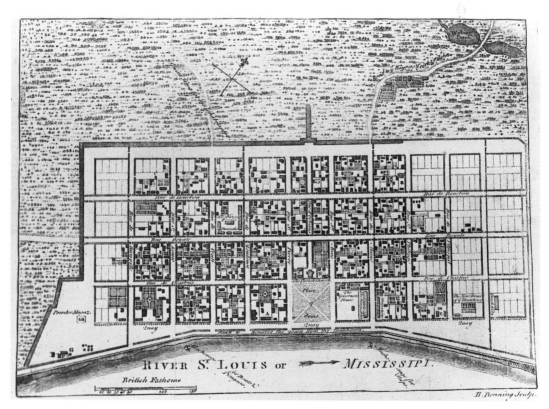

FIGURE 1.10. New Orleans (Adrien de Pauger, surveyor; Pierre le Blond de la Tour, planner/engineer, 1721), 1764. This map shows only the four ranges of blocks initially occupied. (Courtesy Historic New Orleans Collection, Museum/Research Center, acc. no. 1774.25.18.25)

the *place d'armes,* a square that abutted the waterfront at the center of the long side of the grid. The residences of the principal officials, as well as military and governmental barracks and storehouses, flanked two other sides of the square and extended out from them along the river in both directions, creating an urban front whose indented facade resembled that of Louis XIV's near-contemporary palace at Versailles, with its recessed central court of honor. The quay and the place d'armes also accommodated the city's public markets. By the middle of the eighteenth century the urbanized portion of the city had assumed the familiar bell shape, with the apex cut off by a drainage canal and fortifications that ran along the back side of the city. The imaginative power of the armature is evident in Orleans Street, an axial street that runs inland from the rear of the cathedral, giving the T its body but originally dead-ending at the canal.[21]

New Orleans's peculiar topography and its French origins skewed subsequent urban development. The city was laid out on the narrow natural levee of the river, a relatively "high" ground created by centuries of alluvial deposits. As one moved away from the river the land fell away into swamps broken only by the Metairie and Gentilly ridges, about halfway between the river and Lake Pontchartrain. Thus, until twentieth-century drainage systems made the interior inhabitable (by New Orleans standards), urban growth clung closely to the banks of the Mississippi.[22]

As the city grew it was strained through the long-lot or arpent system of land grants. The French and some other European colonizers distributed land in long strips that stretched inland from a river. This ensured that each grantee received some of the best as well as the worst land, although the widths of the strips and thus the size of individual holdings varied according to grantees' wealth or social standing. Since New Orleans occupies an S-shaped curve on the Mississippi River (the source of its nickname Crescent City), the long-lot strips assumed wedge shapes that expanded and contracted like a Victorian woman's fan.[23]

Late in the eighteenth century plantation owners upriver and downriver from the Vieux Carré began to subdivide their plantations into faubourgs, or suburbs. The first was the upriver Faubourg Sainte-Marie, immediately adjacent to the Vieux Carré. It was laid out by Maria Josefa Deslondes and her husband, Bertrand Gravier, in 1788, following a disastrous fire in the old city a few weeks earlier. In 1795 Claude Tremé created a de facto Faubourg Tremé just behind the Vieux Carré when he began selling lots there. After a series of disputes with Tremé, the city purchased his land and formally surveyed it in 1810. In the meantime, the guardians of Bernard de Marigny, then a minor, secured permission to subdivide his downriver plantation into the Faubourg Marigny in 1805. As the nineteenth century wore on, other landowners laid out faubourgs, not

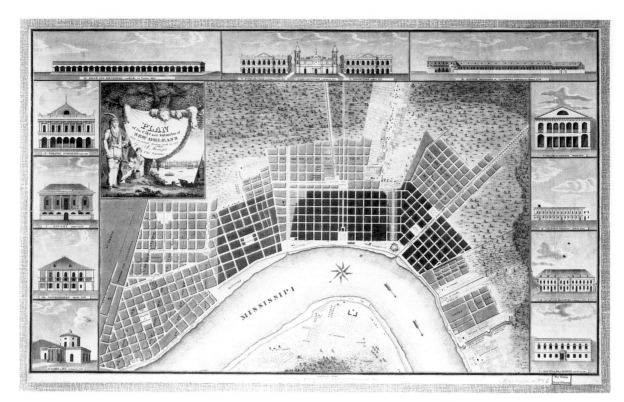

FIGURE 1.11. Jacques Tanesse, *Plan of the City and Suburbs of New Orleans*, 1815. (Library of Congress, Maps Division)

necessarily in order of proximity to the urbanized area. Their grids zigged and zagged at the property lines, fossilizing the old agricultural land divisions in the new city (fig. 1.11).[24]

Unlike Philadelphia, where urban settlement flowed seamlessly into the Northern Liberties and Southwark, New Orleans began as a fortified city, if a haphazardly fortified one. When the faubourgs were laid out the wooden palisades, ditches, and earthen forts at the riverside corners of the Vieux Carré still existed, although all were in ruinous condition. Nevertheless, they stood as barriers to the easy flow of traffic between the old city and its outliers, and after the American acquisition of Louisiana the municipality claimed "the terrain belonging to the City, on which are put forts and batteries constructed under the Spanish Government." Suburban residents also began to agitate for "the continuation of the streets parallel to the river as far as the faubourg." The first American governor, William C. C. Claiborne, refused, declaring the fortifications federal property. After the palisade finally came down, the city council found that it had to defend "the right of the Corporation to the Commons," the wedge of common land that wrapped around the downriver end of the Vieux Carré to the Faubourg Tremé, not only from the federal government but from appro-

FIGURE 1.12. Meat Market ("French Market") (Jacques Tanesse, architect; Gurlie & Guillot, builders, 1813), New Orleans, as restored and enclosed in the 1930s

priation by interlopers such as Daniel Clark, whose ropewalk obstructed the connection of the city streets to the Faubourg Sainte-Marie. These struggles over the nature of public space paralleled the decades-long and more notorious battle over the public's right to the batture, the alluvial soil that accumulated on the water side of the levee.[25]

In the late Spanish-French years, New Orleans was devastated by several major fires. After the March 21, 1788, conflagration, which was estimated to have destroyed a third of the city at the heart of the Vieux Carré, there was another disastrous one on December 8, 1794, that may have destroyed as many as six hundred buildings—possibly half of the existing city. Thus a visitor to the city at the time of the Louisiana Purchase would have seen a townscape that was, on the whole, quite new.[26]

The main market, later known as the French Market, stood on the levee adjacent to the place d'armes. Its 1808 building was destroyed in a hurricane and rebuilt in 1813 (fig. 1.12). The city was still small enough that this market could serve the entire population. When the faubourgs expanded, a vegetable market was added in 1822, but the city began to erect a series of neighborhood markets in the faubourgs, unlike Philadelphia, which held on to its central markets until 1859.[27]

In the late eighteenth century Francophone merchants began to build characteristic kinds of shop houses along Chartres and Royal streets, the second and third streets from the river, respectively. They contained residences above one or two rooms of commercial space, with a lateral carriageway leading to a rear courtyard bracketed on two sides by their own service buildings and enclosed on the third by the adjacent property. This urban type gradually replaced the "low browed dwellings" that John H. B. Latrobe found still standing in parts of the city in 1834. The latter, long, raised houses cloaked by *galeries* (porticoes) and called by architectural historians "Creole houses," were the homes of well-off residents of the eighteenth-century city (fig. 1.13). At the rear of the Vieux Carré and in the adjacent faubourgs Tremé and Marigny there were "entire Squares . . . without a single two story building but composed of rows of one storied dwellings with sheds projecting from the eves over the pavements" (plate 4). As Latrobe observed, these "Creole cottages" (as present-day historians and geographers call them) were set right at the street line, with flared eaves projecting over the sidewalk, or *banquette*. Their four facade openings, often all louvered doors, opened right onto the sidewalk, hence the traditional name "banquette houses." As in the larger merchants' houses and the earlier Creole houses, service buildings set along the rear of the lot or occasionally at right angles to the Creole cottage sheltered slaves and work spaces and delineated rear courtyards that were important elements of

FIGURE 1.13. Madame John's Legacy (late eighteenth century), New Orleans

the New Orleans cityscape (fig. 1.14). Creole cottages were Afro-European syntheses brought to New Orleans from the Caribbean. A different combination of the same cultural elements, the shotgun house, built for poorer occupants, came to the Crescent City after the Haitian Revolution, but the surviving architectural evidence suggests that they did not catch on until the mid-nineteenth century.[28]

FIGURE 1.14. Rear courtyard, 917 St. Ann Street, New Orleans. Pre–World War II photograph. The arcaded entry marks an open gallery between rear rooms called cabinets, which were common features in Creole cottages. There are service buildings to the left and right. (Courtesy Historic New Orleans Collection, Museum/Research Center, acc. no. 1978.55)

FIGURE 1.15. Row houses, 921–19 Dumaine Street, ca. 1840. These houses mark the edge of the mid-nineteenth-century expansion and densification of the Vieux Carré. A Creole cottage, a survivor of the houses they replaced, interrupts the row three houses from the right of the photograph

Anglo-American immigrants brought a new repertoire of urban buildings. A few tall, narrow, side-passage houses similar to the rows in Philadelphia and New York were built in the Vieux Carré, but most were constructed in the Faubourg Sainte-Marie as that suburb became the favored site of Anglophone residence and work (fig. 1.15). In addition, northerners brought the characteristic commercial buildings that were found in great numbers in cities such as Philadelphia, New York, and Boston. Multistory wholesale stores with arcaded (later granite-piered) ground stories replaced older French and Spanish government and commercial buildings along the levee (now Decatur Street) in the Vieux Carré, and they lined New Levee Street in the Faubourg Sainte-Marie. Up-to-date retail stores were mixed among granite-piered wholesale stores along Canal Street, the dividing line between the old and new cities that split the former Common (fig. 1.16)

New Orleans was very small until "Americans" began to arrive in the 1790s, but like northern cities it was socially mixed from its inception, with people of all stations living in close proximity to one another. However, the Crescent City's mixture took on a distinctive quality owing to the city's racial order. On the eve of the Louisiana Purchase New Orleans was home to 8,056 people, including 1,048 who lived in the upriver and downriver faubourgs and an additional 700 listed as "white persons not domiciled." (Transient seamen and soldiers in the government barracks were not counted.) Of the 8,000 residents,

FIGURE 1.16. Jay Dearborn Edwards, 500 block of Canal Street, New Orleans, late 1850s.
(Courtesy Historic New Orleans Collection, Museum/Research Center, acc. no. 1982/167.1)

1,335 were free people of color and 2,773 were slaves.[29] With the post-1803 influx of white Anglophone outsiders (called Americans throughout the antebellum period) and of free and enslaved blacks from the north and from the Caribbean, the racial mix changed, but New Orleans always had a significantly higher proportion of black residents than northern cities did. In 1820, for example, Philadelphia's population was 10.7 percent black and New York's 8.8 percent black, while New Orleans's was half black. Twenty years later the proportions were 11.2 percent, 5.23 percent, and 39.63 percent, respectively (tables 2, 3). A majority of New Orleans's black population was always enslaved, but the proportion both of slaves and of free people of color in the total population declined during the first half of the nineteenth century, partly as a consequence of whites' conscious efforts.[30]

The high proportion of blacks, free and unfree, might seem to distinguish New Orleans's urban landscape radically from Philadelphia's. For example, the racial order might affect the typical residence patterns we observed in the Quaker City. Although there is no estimate of the number of houses in New Orleans at the time of the American accession comparable to the Philadelphia numbers for 1790, if we assume the same ratio of inhabitants to total population as in Philadelphia, there would have been slightly fewer than three thou-

Table 2 Free and Enslaved African Americans in
Urban Populations, 1800–1850

	1800	1810	1820	1830	1840	1850
Baltimore	5,614	7,681	14,683	18,910	21,166	28,388
Boston	1,174	1,464	1,683	1,875	1,977	2,424
New Orleans	3,000	10,911	13,592	26,038	33,280	26,916
New York	6,367	9,823	10,866	13,977	16,358	13,815
Philadelphia	4,265	6,354	7,582	9,806	10,507	10,736

Source: Leonard P. Curry, *The Free Black in Urban America, 1800–1850: The Shadow of the Dream* (Chicago: University of Chicago Press, 1981), pp. 244–45.

sand houses in New Orleans and its suburbs in 1803. In fact, it was estimated that there were only around one thousand. The number of "houses"—separate properties—was relatively small because many enslaved people lived in houses and outbuildings belonging to their masters, although enough slaves lived separately from their masters to provoke the city council to outlaw the practice. Some lived with whites or free people of color to whom they were hired, as did many of Philadelphia's African Americans at the same time.[31]

Blacks made good use of the landscape of domestic courtyards. On the one hand, these spaces were hidden domains within which a lover, a family member, or a colluding white person could effectively conceal a runaway slave only a few yards from a master's own dwelling. On the other hand, urban residents often rented portions of their service quarters to slaves, free blacks, and whites alike, so that the courtyard was a place where the three groups interacted freely and often in ways not legally countenanced. "Salomon negroman" was the slave of a Mr. Dubourg but rented a courtyard room from the sheriff, Mr. Quarles. We meet Salomon in court testifying about a violent encounter between Charles, a slave belonging to a nearby tavern owner, and Joseph Pichon, a Portuguese man. They were rivals for the affections of Sally, a black woman who lived in the same yard as Salomon and Pichon. In short, the relationship between the main house and the back buildings often resembled that between the Drinker house and its alley neighbors more than it did a plantation house and its outbuildings. The institution of slavery and the southern racial order inflected the urban landscape of New Orleans when compared with northern cities, but it did not create a completely different urban world.[32]

The same can be said of ethnic and linguistic differences in the city. New Orleans was always a cosmopolitan place, even when it was tiny. In 1835 the city struck visitor Joseph Holt Ingraham as having been "built by a universal

Table 3 Percentage of Free and Enslaved African Americans in Urban Populations, 1790–1850

	1790	1800	1810	1820	1830	1840	1850
Baltimore	NA	21.17	21.6	23.4	23.46	20.69	16.79
Boston	NA	4.71	4.4	3.97	3.05	2.6	1.46
New Orleans	63[a]	35.29	63.28	50.01	56.5	39.63	23.13
New York	10.47	10.53	10.19	8.8	6.9	5.23	2.68
Philadelphia	19.5	9.2	10.5	10.7	9.8	11.2	8.8

Sources: Leonard P. Curry, *The Free Black in Urban America, 1800-1850: The Shadow of the Dream* (Chicago: University of Chicago Press, 1981), p. 246; W. E. B. DuBois, *The Philadelphia Negro: A Social Study* (1899; rpt. New York: Schocken, 1967), p. 47; Kimberly S. Hanger, *Bounded Lives, Bounded Places: Free Black Society in Colonial New Orleans, 1769–1803* (Durham, N.C.: Duke University Press, 1997), p. 139; James Oliver Horton, *Free People of Color: Inside the African American Community* (Washington, D.C.: Smithsonian Institution Press, 1993), p. 129; Kenneth T. Jackson, ed., *The Encyclopedia of New York City* (New Haven: Yale University Press, 1995), pp. 921–22; Gary B. Nash, *Forging Freedom: The Formation of Philadelphia's Black Community, 1720–1840* (Cambridge: Harvard University Press, 1988), p. 143.

[a] In 1795, 55.5 percent of black population (35 percent of total) was free (Hanger, *Bounded Lives*, p. 139).

subscription, to which every European nation has contributed a street, as it certainly has citizens." When the Americans arrived they found French, Spanish, and African people and their Creole descendants. New Orleans was second only to New York as an antebellum port of entry, and by 1840 almost half its population was foreign born. It had a large Irish population, boasted enough Germans to support German periodicals and a German theater, and constantly exchanged people and goods with the French and Spanish Caribbean islands. Thus the ethnic mix was not unlike that of a northern city such as Philadelphia. Yet the colonial status of the French and Spanish populations and the clash of legal traditions between Americans and Louisianans made language a point of social rupture. Most white Anglophones and Francophones refused to learn one another's language. They sat separately in public assemblies. They maintained their own theaters, their own publications, their own merchants' exchanges, their own first-class hotels, their own business districts, their own cemeteries, their own voluntary associations, and, of course, their own churches.[33]

For a time they even had their own city governments. In 1837 the city was split into three separate "municipalities," each with its own laws and government. The First Municipality, the old Vieux Carré, was dominated by the French and headquartered in the Cabildo on the place d'armes. The Second Municipality encompassed the Faubourg Sainte-Marie, which by that time was often referred to as the American Sector. Its government was eventually housed in the monumental new Municipal Hall (now Gallier Hall) erected just two years before the dissolution of the three municipalities. The Third Municipality, the Faubourg Marigny, was home to a multiethnic population, including white and black Creoles, Irish, enough Mexicans (called "Spanish") to support a bull ring in Washington Square, Germans, whose neighborhood came to be known as Little Saxony, and free people of color.[34]

By mid-century ethnic and racial divisions were intercut by economic differences. The adjacent blocks of the Vieux Carré and the American Sector were the wealthiest part of the city, but the Anglophone population was beginning to build suburban villas in the upriver city of Lafayette, now known as the Garden District, which was annexed to New Orleans when the three municipalities were dissolved in 1852. The Francophone elite built large houses along the Esplanade, the street that separated the Faubourg Marigny from the Vieux Carré. Modest householders dominated the "downriver lakeside" quarter of the Vieux Carré and the adjacent faubourgs Tremé and Marigny. A contractor laying a sidewalk along Barracks Street in the lower Vieux Carré stopped work because most of the residents there were too poor to pay their assessments. The city agreed to accept their taxes in installments to avoid forcing them out of their "small properties." A few blocks farther downriver one came to the Faubourg Marigny, dismissed by a French resident as the "faubourg of poverty." Upriver from the Faubourg Sainte-Marie, near where flatboats were broken up at the end of their journey, close to employment on the levee and in slaughterhouses, cotton presses, and ironworks, another faubourg of poverty formed and became known as the Irish Channel.[35]

CHAPTER 2   {   **THE RELICS OF CIVILIZED LIFE**

Early-nineteenth-century New Yorkers called Broad Street, one of the city's principal thoroughfares, Smell Street, while Beaver Street was Slaughterhouse Lane, nicknames that acknowledged the oceans of fetor that flooded antebellum American cities. Tanneries, distilleries, slaughterhouses, fat-rendering plants, and other industrial enterprises belched forth distinctive stenches, to the disgust of their neighbors. The most offensive of these were traditionally exiled to the edges of cities, but not always. A soap house near the waterfront in Philadelphia was a "disagreeable surcumstance" to its neighbors, the wealthy Drinker family. Similar industries operated in the middle of large nineteenth-century cities, where they frequently attracted lawsuits. Even restricting these industries to the edges of cities was not a solution, for then they lay in the path of expanding residential development, as in "Gentilly, Metairie and neighboring places" outside New Orleans, whose residents complained to that city's council about the unlicensed slaughterhouses near their homes.[1]

Although such industrial stenches often drove urban dwellers beyond the limits of tolerance, they were accents in a stew of odors endemic to everyday life. The most pervasive of all urban smells were those that the New Orleans physician Edward H. Barton called "the relics of civilized life": the odors arising from human and animal wastes and refuse. Food spoiled in the markets, particularly in warm weather, perfuming the air for blocks around. Decaying and fermenting grain filled warehouses and ships on the waterfront. Animal odors were everywhere. Cattle, goats, swine, and other live animals lived in town—in addition to the ever-present horses—to supply food and to act as scavengers. Even a city as large as Philadelphia was compelled in 1821 to pass an ordinance barring free-ranging goats from streets, alleys, public squares, and the State-House Yard (the grounds of Independence Hall). Although the city fathers endorsed an act of the state legislature in 1789 to prevent residents from allowing pigs to roam the city, they refused to appropriate funds to enforce it, and nearly forty years later James Ronaldson still found cause to complain about the "increasing practice of feeding swine in the streets." New York's public porkers roamed free until the middle of the nineteenth century.[2]

Nineteenth-century cities had no comprehensive drainage systems. In 1849, Boston was one of the best served, with approximately twenty-five miles of sewers, while Baltimore had only one mile. In Philadelphia, there were eleven miles of sewers, which were beginning to replace the earlier system of gutters that fed into open sinks, where liquids evaporated or were absorbed into the earth. Other cities, such as Louisville and Cincinnati, followed the example of New Orleans, where ditches so deep and wide that footbridges were required to cross them lined the streets and drained into the Mississippi River. These ditches were minimally cleaned and maintained by chain gangs of slaves taken from the city jail or rented to the city by their masters.[3]

In densely built-up sections of the city, outhouses (usually called privies or necessaries) were shared among several households. Some Philadelphians' privies, particularly in older neighborhoods of the city near the Delaware River, were located in their basements in the manner of medieval urban houses in Europe. Only the best houses and businesses were supplied with individual backyard necessaries, and even these backed so closely onto neighboring properties that they sometimes collapsed during cellar excavations for new buildings.[4]

Unlike rural outhouses, which were small and could be relocated as they filled, urban privies were quite sizable pits. They were periodically dusted with lime to sanitize them and to suppress their foul smells, but they were cleaned out only at ten- or twelve-year intervals. Privy cleaning was a disgusting operation conducted at night and in winter to reduce the pollution of whole neighborhoods: "Tho Necessary, yet very offensive," punned Elizabeth Drinker about a privy cleaning next door to her house. During the removal of forty-four years' waste from her own family's outhouse, the Drinkers burned incense in the kitchen to ward off the stench. For a similar operation in 1831, Stephen Girard hired Stephen Bill to empty a six-foot-diameter privy at one of his rental properties on Spruce Street in Philadelphia, "depth of filth taken out 13 feet."[5]

Many poor people and some who were not so poor had no privies at all. They dumped their excreta directly into the street, where it mingled with the urine of male passersby who customarily relieved themselves there, or they had it removed by nocturnal "tubmen" who often spilled as much in the streets as they succeeded in carrying to the river for disposal. Urbanites also threw their garbage and other domestic and commercial offal into the streets. In New York, this rotting refuse accumulated in the center of the streets and became known as "corporation pie" (fig. 2.1). Cities hired scavengers to cart it away—but not often and not very far. They usually dumped it into a convenient vacant lot or at the edge of the city.[6]

Inevitably, growing populations created more "offal" and "filth" than urban authorities could manage. In most American cities, streets, rivers, creeks, and gutters were informal, illegal, but widely used depositories of convenience for everything from household trash to dead animals. Thomas Condie and Rich-

A cheil's amang ye takin' notes; and faith he'll prent it. Burns.

NEW-YORK AS IT IS.

Respectfully dedicated to the Corporation of the City of New York by Serrell & Perkins

FIGURE 2.1. *New-York as It Is, Respectfully dedicated to the Corporation of the City of New York by Serrell & Perkins,* ca. 1850. (The Library Company of Philadelphia)

ard Folwell reported in 1798 that the open sinks into which Philadelphia's gutters flowed "exhale the most noxious effluvia; for dead animals and every kind of nausea, are thrown into them, and there remain until they become putrified," even as they assured readers that "there are few cities that can vie with Philadelphia in point of elegance or even cleanliness." James Pitot complained of "garbage and dead animals lying all over the streets" of New Orleans in 1802. Possibly as a dramatic letter to the editor, some brazen parties in New Orleans dumped "some dozen or fifteen, or more, cartloads of filth" into the downtown streets near the offices of the *Daily Picayune,* creating "a most abominable stench" in 1854.[7]

Waterfronts were the most popular dumping grounds. Some Philadelphia merchants used the Delaware River near their stores as privies, while the Drinkers disposed of spoiled food there, including two barrels of tainted salt fish, which Elizabeth Drinker assumed would "probably be taken up by some one" and eaten. New Orleans's levee and batture were littered with the "contents of privies, decayed or putrefying fish, flesh and fowl, from the markets; damaged flour, potatoes and fruit, rotten hides,—to which we may add, as an occasional incident, dead horses, mules, etc." Lighters, barges, and keelboats loaded with horses, cattle, hogs, and victuals "fermented or damaged, . . . emitting inconvenient odors [and] offensive vapors," moored next to steamboats and oceangoing ships. These vessels dumped their garbage and raw sewage into the water at their moorings, where it joined the sewage of upriver settlements, the run-off from the city's drainage-ditch sewers, and the contents of household chamber pots emptied there by passersby. The stench was so powerful that Louisiana's first American governor, William C. C. Claiborne, claimed that it often disturbed him "even when in my chamber."[8]

Early in the American regime the city council proposed to build three floating bridges along the Mississippi "upon which the negroes will be compelled to go in order to throw all cesspool filth and other refuse into the current and not on the banks of the river, as is now practiced . . . to the greatest displeasure of those who frequent the levee." This project failed. A decade later the engineer-architect Benjamin Henry Latrobe specified that the intake pipe for his water-works would run far out into the river's channel "by which he would escape the vast impurities which were near the shore, where every species of filth was hourly deposited." Nevertheless, as late as 1834 Latrobe's son John observed men along the batture filling hogsheads of drinking water from the river. Dip a glass into the "dirty, gurgling mass" of the river "as it rolls along, and constantly boiling up from the bottom," wrote one disgusted commentator. "Dip a tumbler full, each of which is thick with what you may call '*mud*,' if you please. . . . Yet those who live here, . . . drink it, and say they '*like it.*'"[9]

Climate, poor drainage, unpaved streets, and air pollution rendered the urban environment palpable as well as fragrant. Benjamin Latrobe claimed that in Pittsburgh "the Earth is a rich mould that melts in the Rain, and after a hour's shower is an unfathomable quagmire. The mud is incredible. Besides its depth, i[t] sticks and slips, and has all the possible qualities of well tempered brick earth, to which the muddiest State of the Washington common, is a well carpeted drawing room." Such conditions were common in the badly and incompletely paved streets of even the largest cities.[10]

In some cities heavy industry compounded the problem. Industrial smoke that contributed to stenches also covered cities with soot, which could not be restricted to certain neighborhoods as, to a limited degree, industrial odors could be. The notorious pall that hung over Pittsburgh in the early twentieth century began a century earlier. The city's glass works and ironworks and its steam engines generated a "thick cloud of smoke, impenetrable to the rays of the Sun" in 1813, and dusted the city with a "fat blacking, which lights upon every thing and every body. White clothes are inadmissible[,] white skin not less so. Every body wears a black Mask. You see the most beautiful women walking about in this fashion. So much for the Sky." In New York, according to one journalist, wherever buildings were being constructed, the "air in their neighborhood is so loaded with clouds of lime and dirt, that people of irritable lungs should not attempt it. Macbeth might justly call such passage, 'the way to dusty death.'"[11]

Even without industrial assistance, the intense heat and humidity that afflicted most eastern and Gulf Coast American cities for large parts of the year made the sea of stench palpable.[12] The climate was most oppressive in New Orleans, of course. Diarist Luther F. Tower frequently complained of summer heat that was "intolerable." "The hottest day yet," he wrote in September 1846. "The sun is actually Scorching. People engaged in business on the Levee Complain bitterly. Deaths by Coup du Soleil [sunstroke] are frequent." Yet northern cities could be equally oppressive. In July 1797 Elizabeth Drinker recorded a "very warm yea hot day" in Philadelphia: "I fear we shall hear of many who have suffer'd by the heat, it may be called intense . . . great complaints of the heat." In July 1834 New York City's temperature hovered between 86 and 94 degrees for eleven days running, resulting in the deaths (attributed to "drinking cold water") of twenty-four people on the tenth alone, and the expiration of several horses pulling the Greenwich Street and Broadway stages. Even on ordinary summer days, daily life in a northern city was uncomfortable. Harrison and Holms promoted their New York daguerreotype studio as "the coolest rooms in town to have a Likeness taken." In rivals' shops, they facetiously claimed, "several respectable citizens disappeared lately. . . . They suddenly fell into a melting mood, and nothing had been seen of them but sundry coats, hats, boots, wigs, &c."

Heat brought other bodily afflictions, including bedbugs, "those filthy insects" who arrived with the spring, and, even worse, the swarms of mosquitoes endemic in cities with open sewers and watercourses of all sorts. For most visitors and residents, as for Harriet Martineau, they were a "great and perpetual plague." While mosquito bars (netting around beds) served well enough during the night, one had to fight the pesky creatures all day and all evening. Women wore gloves, wound loose muslin around their throats and ankles, and draped nets over their heads, while men resorted to loose pantaloons and boots and sometimes draped netting around their work spaces as well (fig. 2.2). One man claimed to have invented a full-body net that hung from his hat brim. But most people grew accustomed to the bites and preferred to put up with them "rather than bear a little additional warmth" from the extra clothing.[13]

Mosquitoes added yet another dimension to urban life: "Splendid Serenades." Their drone was a continuo in a fractured symphony of sounds and noises that

FIGURE 2.2. Benjamin
Henry Latrobe, *Colonel
Blackburn's Specific against
Muskitoe bites in the Month
of July*, 1796, Rippon
Lodge, Virginia. (The
Maryland Historical
Society)

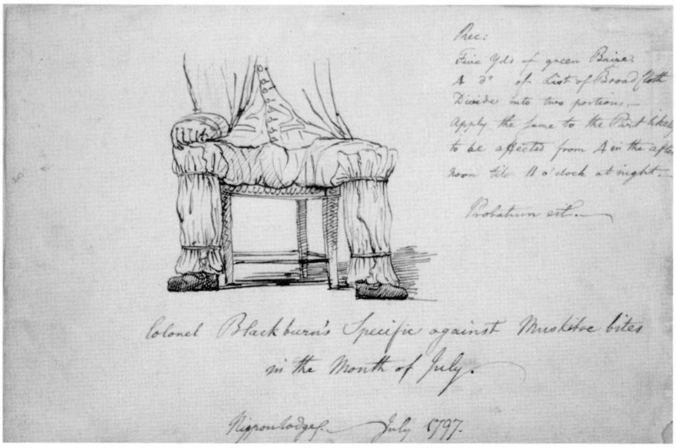

filled the city day and night, growing louder as the nineteenth century wore on. American city streets were stone-paved (when they were paved at all) with cobbles or Belgian blocks. Carts, wagons, and omnibuses clattered over them on wooden- and metal-rimmed wheels. "Ungreased and screaming cartwheels," a legacy of Spanish-era attempts to suppress smuggling, grated on sensitive nerves in New Orleans. "The very air [of New Orleans] howls with an eternal din and noise," wrote Alabama visitor Albert J. Pickett. Under such conditions, merchants were forced to relocate their clerical offices to the rear of their buildings to escape the din. Courts found it difficult to conduct business over the clamor of the street, so the first experiments with noise-reducing pavements such as wooden blocks, asphalt, and macadam were conducted around public buildings in Boston, New York, and Philadelphia, although many New Orleanians opposed the first proposals to pave Crescent City streets, fearing that it would simply add to the noise.[14]

Small-scale manufacturing in the upper stories, cellars, and back- and side yards of shops and residences in the heart of the city showered noise upon neighbors and passersby (fig. 2.3). This cacophony was intermittently pierced by more distinctive sounds. "Loud and repeated cries of fire" disturbed urban visitors' sleep, but they were so common that residents ignored them. During the day, the "universal clanking" of church bells tolled deaths, holidays, and the arrival of distinguished visitors. At the beginning of the nineteenth century Philadelphia still had a bellman, or town crier, and New Orleans a town drummer. Philadelphia's auctioneers hired bell ringers to announce auctions and to advertise all sorts of other goods (fig. 2.4). The curmudgeonly historian John Fanning Watson complained about the employment of "a bell-man to keep the neighbourhood in irremediable distress, for an half hour together." The bell man's instrument punctuated the distinctive cries of street vendors adver-

opposite
FIGURE 2.3.
William
H. Rease,
*Melloy & Ford
Wholesale Tin
Ware Emporium*,
Philadelphia,
1849. (The
Library
Company of
Philadelphia)

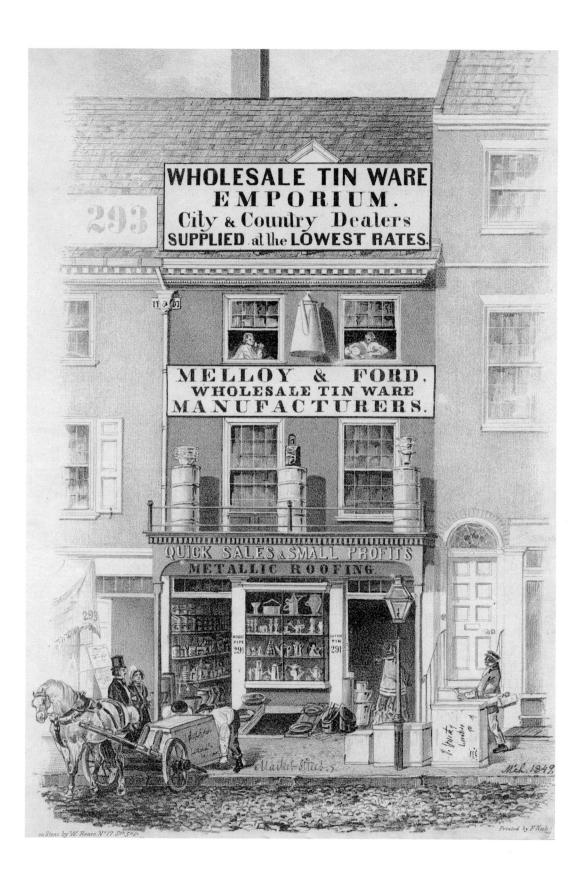

FIGURE 2.4. W. H. Isaacs, *Life in Philadelphia: A Crier Extraordinary*, Philadelphia, ca. 1825. Auctions were traditionally announced by a bellman who cried the items for sale. (The Library Company of Philadelphia)

tising their wares and services: "Hot Muf–fins!" "Sweep, O-O-O-O!" "Messieurs, amateurs, connoisseurs de toutes couleurs, venez, venez, achetez de moi!"[15]

These accounts offer a vivid, if repulsive, image of the dizzying sensory ambience of antebellum American cities. Sensory overload was as old as urban life, but in the decades after the establishment of the nation, inadequate infrastructure and weak governmental regulation in rapidly expanding cities immersed urbanites in an ever-deepening ocean of sights, sounds, smells, and textures that was trying, even overwhelming.

Most present-day Americans would find such environments difficult to tolerate and, more and more often, so did their nineteenth-century ancestors. One warm May day in 1863, General Benjamin Butler, commander of the Union forces occupying New Orleans, set out with his wife to view the city that his troops had captured a few months earlier. A short way into their drive, the couple came to the turning basin of the New Canal, which drained the city and provided access for cargo boats coming from Lake Pontchartrain.

> As we approached the "basin," the air seemed filled with the most noxious and offensive stenches possible,—so noxious as almost to take away the power of breathing. The whole surface of the canal and the pond was covered with a thick growth of green vegetable scum, variegated with dead cats and dogs or the remains of dead mules on the banking. The sun shone excessively hot, and the thermometer might have been 120°. We turned to the right and went down along the canal as far as Lake Pontchartrain, finding it all in the same condition until within a few rods of the lake. We drove back by a very different route.[16]

Returning to his office, Butler summoned the city official who oversaw the canals and streets, and demanded to know what was wrong. The man professed ignorance. "Did you observe anything special" when you last visited the canal, Butler asked.

"No, General."

"Not an enormous stink?"

"No more than usual, General; no more than there always is."[17]

The Butlers' and the commissioner's conflicting reactions to the canals of New Orleans invite us to take a critical look at these accounts, to push past the picturesquely disgusting by asking whether they were more than ever-present annoyances. Faced with early republican cities in all their manifestations, visitors and residents reacted in ways that were neither random nor entirely predictable. They had a history and an anthropology, as well as a psychology and a neurology, that are sometimes evident in the written and visual records left by nineteenth-century urbanites. Consider Alexander Graydon's recollection of his walk to school through the streets and byways of prerevolutionary Philadelphia, then English North America's largest city.

> I had my choice, indeed of different streets, and sometimes varied my course; but it generally led me through what is now called Dock street, then a filthy uncovered sewer, bordered on either side by shabby stables and tan-yards. To these, succeeded the more agreeable object of Israel Pemberton's garden

(now covered in part by the [first] bank of the United States) laid out in the old fashioned style of uniformity, with walks and allies nodding to their brothers, and decorated with a number of evergreens carefully clipped into pyramidal and conical forms. Here the amenity of the view usually detained me for a few minutes: Thence, turning Chesnut street corner to the left, and passing a row of dingy two story houses, I came to the Whale bones, which gave name to the ally, at the corner of which they stood. These never ceased to be occasionally an object of some curiosity, and might be called my second stage, beyond which there was but one more general object of attention, and this was to get a peep at the race horses, which in sporting seasons were kept in the widow Nichols's stables, which from her house (the Indian Queen at the corner of Market street) extended perhaps two thirds or more the way to Chesnut street.[18]

Few of the monuments of Philadelphia's broad main streets celebrated by early-nineteenth-century printmakers, strangers' (travelers') guide authors, and travelers appear in Graydon's anecdote. He zigzagged through side streets, alleys, and back lots, taking note of curious landmarks along the way. At the same time, Graydon's written memories were colored by his persona as an author. He was a former Pennsylvania politician and a prominent but disillusioned revolutionary looking back on the colonial city of his youth. As Graydon told it, the schoolboy and his city were one: the kinds of homely and unsophisticated landmarks that might attract a boy's attention epitomized homely and unsophisticated Philadelphia itself. His own growth was transparently intertwined with the city's. Graydon used a common early-nineteenth-century technique for ordering his childhood recollections: studding his account with literary allusions that help give it shape and significance. The description of Israel Pemberton's garden, for example, paraphrased Alexander Pope's description of seventeenth-century formal gardens—"Grove nods at Grove, each Alley has a brother"—and Joseph Addison's complaint about trees that rose in "Cones, Globes, and Pyramids" as a way emphasize to readers the old-fashioned quality of a city that was rapidly losing the landmarks of its founders. The decline of the unpretentious city paralleled the decline of the new republic, in which upright citizens such as Graydon were pushed aside by pretenders and self-promoters.[19]

At the same time, another kind of progress shaped the tale: from the foul smells of sewage, poorly kept stables, and tanneries in and around Dock Creek—from the relics of civilized life—to the visual pleasures of Pemberton's garden, the whale bones, and the race horses. In his walk to school, Graydon enacted the phylogeny and ontogeny of selfhood. Students of human development and the psychology of perception write of the ways that the human animal has come to favor the so-called "distance receptors," especially vision and hearing—forms of perception that one can practice at a distance—over the more immediate systems of touch and taste on which other animals rely. Smell lies somewhere between the two—it has lost much of its practical function in humans but remains an important emotional and memory stimulant, as we will see in the next chapter.[20]

The changes that have occurred over the course of human evolution are repeated to some extent in the development of individuals. Infants use taste and touch (direct contact with the environment) as important orientation tools, but early on, visual observation and bodily imitation supersede tactile exploration as key developmental strategies, even in newborns. After infancy, most people rely on the other three senses, particularly hearing and sight, which embody varying degrees of spatial separation between stimulus and receptor.[21]

Reliance on listening and especially seeing allows a person to distinguish a self from its surroundings and to distinguish elements of the surroundings from one another. This ability—"field independence," or the capacity to separate perceived items from their contexts in a "structure of space"—is critically important in shaping the elementary sense of selfhood, as a finite object in a world of objects. At a more advanced level, it permits a person to see him- or herself as an entity apart from the family or other social group, for selfhood is developed in the context of other selves: "To know oneself is to know oneself as a person among others," in the words of psychologist R. Peter Hobson. One learns that one is a being similar to but different from other beings. The achievement of a degree of field independence and "intersubjectivity" is part of the developmental process of infants, but it is also explicitly encouraged by cultural values that modify and reinforce this general human tendency to favor distance receptors.[22]

In other words, while we all share these biases and patterns, as self-conscious beings we are not the prisoners of our physiologies. Neurological and psychological properties shape the human orientation to the world, but to the universal characteristics of all animate beings and to the common developmental trajectory of individual members of our own species humans add a cultural dimension, an element of learned behavior that fine tunes, interprets, and sometimes redirects these instinctual patterns. As a result, the particular mix, or "ratio," of our perceptual faculties varies over time, across cultures, and according to the gender, age, and physiological and psychological constitutions of individual people (as, for example, in the commonplace pattern through which people who have lost the use of one or another sense often develop the others more highly to compensate for the impaired faculty).

Graydon portrayed his boyhood walk as this sort of journey, from the raw sensory experience of Dock Creek to the absorption of the cultural pleasures of art, science, and sport—the garden, the whale bones, and the race horses—as he moved toward school. So his anecdote points us to the deeper significance of the relics of civilized life. Early republican urbanites were anxious to discover what their near contemporary Immanuel Kant called a "fixed and abiding" self: a personal and social identity that would remain stable in the face of great political and urban changes. Graydon's *Memoirs* painted him as just such a person, holding to principle when others in the new republic abandoned theirs.[23]

The relics of civilized life were troubling because city people understood how much their selves were contingent on their connection to their surroundings: the self was inevitably a self in space. Elizabeth Drinker was reminded of this during a walk with her son through Philadelphia one spring day in 1798. "On our way home, I was quite deranged, or in other words lost myself—leaning on Williams Arm we walked on for a considerable time without speaking, my thoughts were employ'd" in thinking about a legal deposition. "When we had just past the market in second Street, and William spake to me, and interrupted my revery I was fairly lost, knew not where we were, nor could I find it out 'till we came to the Church, nor then could hardly reconcile that we were in second street, we had intended when we sett off to go another way. I believe I am not the first that has for a short space of time forgot themselves, tho' not apt so to do: I never was so before in my life, nor can I account for it altogether[.] I did not fully recollect myself 'till we were near front [street], in Arch street."[24]

Like Graydon and most of her other contemporaries, Drinker assumed that a "single real and authentic essence," a "decision-making agent ultimately responsible for the actions of the whole person" governed each individual. When she lost contact with that pilot Drinker lost her *self*. The incident so troubled her that she wrote about it defensively and at length in her diary, even though she recognized that it was a common type of mental lapse. It unnerved her.[25]

In a society that was growing and fluid, city people in the early republic depended on the evidence of their senses to anchor themselves in the scene. John H. B. Latrobe conveyed this vividly in his account of a visit to New Orleans in 1834 to trace the steps of his father and half-brother, both architects and both victims of yellow fever there two decades earlier. Latrobe's path through New Orleans suggests that he may have been using his father's manuscript journal as a guidebook, but his tourist's itinerary quickly dissolved in the Crescent City's sensory intensity. The ship that brought him had moored near the vegetable market, and Latrobe set off upriver along the levee toward the meat (now French) market, his ears regaled by the cries of vendors, "shouting forth in French English and the negro patois," competing with the seven church bells calling worshippers to prayer. As he crossed the place d'armes heading toward his boarding house on Canal Street, he was struck by the "full and noisy custom" of the cafés and saloons, whose patrons drank "Rum and gin, Monongahela, and Tom and Jerry" prepared from an "army of bottles, with contents of all colors" and served on marble- or mahogany-topped bars fitted with "shining brass works." On the street, soldiers in "gay and tasteful uniform" passed by, as their "sundry thumps upon a bass drum [spoke] martially to the ear." Snatches of inconsequential conversation drifted toward his ears as he passed the shopkeepers lounging in their doorways, men and older mixed-race women sitting on their balconies, smoking cigars, and beautiful young quadroon women pedestrians, admired but then snubbed when their racial identity was revealed ("dont let her hear you").[26]

Latrobe's account was a highly self-conscious effort to record his sensory immersion in the city. As he discovered, his multiple levels of awareness did not always mesh. The path from sensation to enlightenment through perception was not as direct as Graydon's account suggested. In his encounter with the quadroon woman, Latrobe responded positively to the human signs she showed, to signs that we recognize instinctively as human social signals. At the same time, he was also attracted by more limited cues learned from the gender norms of his native culture—"a fine figure, a beautiful foot, an ankle like an angels—an air quite distinqué [sic], and then so strange, and characteristic—so Spanish." However, his response was quickly reproved by his unnamed companion, for he had missed even more subtle, more narrowly defined, local racial signs: "A Quadroon! Well, I'll know better next time."[27]

The relics of civilized life appropriately emphasizes the human aspect of the urban sensory world. While the new sensory intensity of visual chaos, cacophony, stench, heat, humidity, and filth created real discomfort and disorientation, it acquired additional alarming connotations in antebellum American cities, where rapid social diversification, economic transformation, and new ideologies of selfhood and personhood prompted anxious scrutiny of one's own and others' place in society. Intrusions on individual comfort were described as intrusions on spatial order, and intrusions on spatial order were in turn interpreted as disruptions of social relations. Of all the sensations that grated on city people's nerves, the ones that other people created were most offensive. Surrounded by industrial noises, animal stench, climatic oppression, and human beings, they allotted most of their energies to scrutinizing their neighbors.

CHAPTER 3

{ **THE SMELL OF DANGER**

One day during New Orleans's devastating 1853 yellow fever epidemic, the Reverend Theodore Clapp returned to the city. Although he had lived there for three decades, Clapp was overpowered by the "offensive effluvium which filled the atmosphere for miles around, resembling that which arises from putrefying animal fat or vegetable matter. As I rode upwards towards the heart of the city, I became quite ill, and on reaching my residence was seized with fainting and vomiting."[1]

It seems odd that Clapp, a man celebrated as one of the few clergy courageous enough to remain in the city during the first great cholera epidemic of 1832, should be so unnerved by the simple odor of a city renowned for its stench. Part of the explanation can be found in the peculiar mechanics of the human sense of smell. Odors are processed through an organ of the brain called the amygdala, which by evolutionary accident has accumulated a miscellany of apparently unrelated functions. It controls the autonomous nervous system, and it moves data from short-term to long-term memory. In doing so it also attaches emotional content to these data, so that particular odors can stimulate vivid, emotion-laden memories evoking distant, rarely contemplated events in a person's past. As a result, the amygdala is the primary organ of conditioned fear and anxiety, controlling active and passive responses to danger. In this light, Clapp's reaction appears to have almost a rat-in-a-maze kind of inevitability—almost, but not quite. We also need to know something about Clapp's and his contemporaries' understanding of the meaning of odors to understand the fears that these smells evoked.[2]

American urbanites recognized the interpenetration of the body and its surroundings. While we appear to be securely bounded by our enclosing envelope of skin, we absorb the environment as we breathe, eat, and drink, and our metabolic processes release our bodily products into the atmosphere at the same time. Thus we are entwined with our physical environment in the most intricate and inextricable ways. Many nineteenth-century people, including most of those who wrote urban commentaries, medical treatises, and memoirs, understood this in some way. Its significance for them was colored by a common eighteenth-century belief in a material basis of morality: our morals are grounded in a corporeal "moral faculty" that is as susceptible to environmental attack as physiological health is. If environment affected both bodily health and the integrity of self, so it was shaped by both. The relics of everyday life were inescapable aspects of the environment, but in other, equally critical ways their character was determined by people's responsible and irresponsible acts. To Theodore Clapp's contemporaries, the smell of danger threatened more than individual lives and health. A common language was used to assess the health of bodies, morals, and the republic. A healthy body, a morally responsible self, and a successful republic were all characterized by "constitutions" that were "balanced," so a threat to one was a threat to all. The smell of danger threatened the very foundations of republican society.[3]

Early-nineteenth-century physicians and laypeople shared a longstanding belief in a direct connection between fetor and disease. The dangers of the landscape were readily detectable by the senses because any disagreeable smell was dangerous. Even the smell of a candle melted on a hot stove was as "unhealthful" as it was unpleasant. Professionals and laypeople differed in their understanding of the process, however. Popular belief held that odors themselves caused illness, a lesson conveyed by innumerable cautionary tales and incorporated into a variety of preventive practices. For example, it was said that while burying a victim of the 1793 epidemic Philadelphia gravedigger Sebastian Ale, who had "lost his sense of smelling [and] fancied he could not take the disorder," accidentally broke open the coffin of a recent yellow fever victim, releasing "such an intolerable and deadly stench" that he soon died of the disease. Benjamin Henry Latrobe's widow attributed her husband's death from yellow fever to a similar misfortune. He had been felled by the "insupportable" stench created when a trench was cut through New Orleans's levee to lay the intake pipe for the city's waterworks. That same city's council worried that the "putrid odors" of corpses carried through the streets to the cemetery endangered those they passed.[4]

If smells could cause illness, powerful but not repulsive smells might ward it off preemptively. To combat yellow fever, Americans lit bonfires, burned tar, fired guns in the streets, burned gunpowder or nitre in their houses, sprinkled vinegar on themselves and their possessions, and carried garlic in their pockets and shoes. Mathew Carey reported that in Philadelphia in 1793 tobacco smoke was considered to be such an effective protection against yellow fever that "many persons, even women and small boys, had cegars constantly in their mouths."[5]

Many physicians and other scientifically inclined people attributed illness to an atmospheric corruption called miasma, which was responsible for all sorts of ailments but particularly for epidemic diseases such as yellow fever and cholera. Miasma, an odiferous substance defined by one layman as "putrid atoms," was the agent of disease, as opposed to a medium that *carried* agents of disease, as, for example, we accept that polluted water carries microbes. The New Orleans physician Edward H. Barton, who struggled to recast prevailing medical theories into a more rigorously scientific form, rejected the prevailing conception of miasma as "a 'secret agency'—a 'peculiar something,' productive of, or rather constituting the epidemic principle." He declared this view "devoid of plausibility" and instead chose to understand miasma as a "class of chemical actions." Miasma was produced by putrefaction, a "process of fermentation in organic substances containing nitrogen and sulphur, which gives rise to the formation of products of a disagreeable odor." In Barton's judgment, disagreeable smells were by-products of miasma rather than its essence.[6]

Miasma caused disease, while qualities of the landscape—the *topographie physico-médicale*—generated miasma. For example, there was general agreement that a hot site surrounded by swamps and marshes, such as New Orleans's, was inherently deadly. In addition, some experts believed that the deltas of rivers—again, sites such as New Orleans's—were dangerous, as were such disparate atmospheric conditions as excessive sunlight and cool, humid night air. In this view, epidemic diseases were geographical phenomena: they could be described spatially, in terms of landscapes conducive to illness.[7]

Miasma required a "medium of conveyance" to activate it: noxious effluvia produced by human bodies and everyday urban activities. Together the environment and its human occupants formed a so-called epidemic constitution or tendency of a population to unhealthiness under the influence of its surroundings. An epidemic constitution was a pathological form of a medical constitution, defined as the product of "such a combination of climatic and terrestrial conditions as influence the constitution of man."[8]

These medical theories and popular beliefs were not offered casually: they were formed in the face of an extended public-health emergency. As cities outgrew the economic resources, technical knowledge, and political will of municipalities to cope with the relics of civilized life, they were wracked by wave after wave of devastating diseases, notably yellow fever and cholera. The famous outbreaks, such as Philadelphia's yellow fever epidemics of 1793 and 1798 and the national cholera pandemics of 1832 and 1848, were merely the most spectacular examples of visitations that arrived in nearly every city nearly every year.[9]

Medical theorists were unable to explain the appearance of epidemics to everyone's satisfaction, and practitioners were unable to devise any effective cures for epidemic diseases, so civic leaders and ordinary citizens undertook a frantic, extended search for those environmental qualities of American cities that generated epidemic constitutions. The inquiry pointed toward urban stench. The smells of open sinks and stagnant water, the "noxious and acrid gases" of industry, privies, stables, slaughterhouses, and cow barns; and putrefying vegetable and animal matter of all sorts were the cause of epidemics (in popular opinion) or clues to its breeding places (from the scientific point of view). A columnist in the *Illustrated Magazine of Art* added gas lighting, which produces "vapours which, after being carried along with the gas in the pipes, issue through the escapes, and spread in the earth, giving it a fetid smell that betrays itself when there is any digging for repairs, making trees wither and perish by poisoning the roots, and taint[s] the water in wells." Danger also lay in badly tended urban cemeteries, with their open graves and cracked tombs. The New England cleric Timothy Dwight argued that "even in cases where [no offensive smells are] perceptible . . . effluvia, too subtle to become an object of sense . . . ascend in sufficient quantities to affect with disease, or at least a predisposition to disease, those who by living in the neighborhood are continually breathing this mischievous exhalation." Beyond all these extraordinary circumstances, though, danger lay in the inevitable by-products of everyday life—in human "emanations, in the form of insensible perspiration and animal heat" that had an "effect on the air [that] is most prejudicial."[10]

Thus discussion of epidemic constitutions inexorably turned from topography to the role of human action in forming and destroying disease-generating conditions. During and immediately after epidemics city people energetically, if briefly, guarded urban and personal hygiene. The air of afflicted cities was full of the smells of the whitewash and lime used as disinfectant, while water trucks washed the streets. A New York journalist urged the necessity of bathing during the 1849 cholera epidemic as a way of washing off the "miasmic and infectious vapors" that "impregnated" the atmosphere and were "detained" by the skin which was "coated with the unctuous matter which exudes from it" unless it was frequently washed. The winter following Philadelphia's 1798 yellow fever visitation, Elizabeth Drinker observed, witnessed a campaign of privy cleaning, even among those "who would, otherwise have neglected it."[11]

The precise human role in fomenting disease was unclear to physicians and their patients alike. Miasmatic theorists distinguished infectious diseases, passed through the effects of atmospheric agents on the tissues and therefore caused by local conditions, from contagious diseases, which were passed by germs through physical contact between a sick person and a healthy one and were therefore capable of being carried from place to place. In practice, though, they conflated the two, denying contagion while speaking vaguely of such secret agents as the "fomites" that might cling to the garments, bedclothes, and furniture of victims of epidemic disease. So laypeople began to identify people as well as practices that they ought to avoid. They burned the clothes of the dead, and they avoided touching the living. When they fell ill they used every available ruse, from flight to the adoption of aliases, to elude public-health authorities seeking to commit them to hospitals where they would encounter other sick people. When they were captured and died in the hospital, their friends attributed their demise to contact with, even proximity to, corpses. The particularly fearful avoided even second-hand contact with contaminants. Mathew Carey noted that during the great yellow fever epidemic of 1793 subscribers to Philadelphia newspapers often made their servants sprinkle each issue with vinegar, while out-of-state postmasters used tongs to dip letters mailed from the Quaker City into the same liquid.[12]

By the middle of the nineteenth century, the Enlightenment postulate of a physically based moral faculty had lost its persuasiveness, but the connection between the physical and the moral had become a commonplace. Edward Barton pronounced disease and crime "twin sisters: as exists the one so flourishes the other." He argued that "the most effective means of advancing the cause of morals and religion among us, would be the establishment of sanitary measures," concluding, inevitably, that "cleanliness is next to godliness."[13]

One could protect one's health by living a clean, moral life and by maintaining a thoughtful, optimistic frame of mind, for any mental or temperamental weakness weakened the body's physiological defenses. In general, "great distress . . . gives an epidemic character to diseases." A gloomy, pusillanimous, or nostalgic disposition, or "a depressed, anxious state of mind," were dangerous. The Philadelphia Board of Health concluded that because "excessive fear has always increased the liability to cholera," the best defense was a "composed and confident state of mind." The dominant "faculty psychology" taught that sensation and reason were at odds, so strong minds and strong characters resisted the data of senses such as smell that provoked irrational or nonrational responses and were avenues for invasion and the erosion of health and morals.[14]

"The connection of the body with the mental and moral faculties," which one late-eighteenth-century commentator matter-of-factly assumed, implied not only that a healthy person was likely to be a moral person, but also that an immoral person was particularly susceptible to bodily infirmity. Lax moral standards were among the universally cited preconditions for susceptibility: "excessive dissipation, in every manner prompted by human passion," "*les excès vénériens*," "indulgence in . . . gross intemperance." The Roman Catholic Mathew Carey observed, in words with theological undertones, that the "inhabitants of dirty houses have severely expiated their neglect of cleanliness and decency, by the numbers of them that have fallen sacrifices."[15]

From human complicity in the creation of epidemic constitutions, then, the discussion shifted to people's culpability for their own illnesses and, ultimately, to their guilt in endangering others. During every epidemic before 1860, including all the great yellow fever and cholera outbreaks that decimated cities from New York south, urban publics were assured that those whose lives were disordered by poverty, immorality, or lack of discipline were the principal, even the only, victims of infection. In Carey's judgment, middle-aged and robust men were likely to contract yellow fever because they engaged the infected atmosphere more vigorously, but tipplers and drunkards, high-livers, fat men, prostitutes, servant maids, the poor, and residents of dirty houses were in the most danger. In 1832 the College of Physicians of Philadelphia characterized the likely victims of cholera as "the poor, the ill-fed, the ill-clothed, and the intemperate." The anonymous author of *New Orleans as It Is* thought it necessary to look no farther for explanations of that city's epidemics than its socially mixed character: "Go to that part of the city where you would certainly expect neatness and order, and . . . look for a desirable dwelling, but none can you find, unless on one side or the other is a miserable shanty or hovel, filled with the most degraded human beings, either black or white." When the majority of sufferers were also non-Anglo-American immigrants, their moral and physiological stamina were scrutinized even more critically. These newcomers shared the moral faculty common to all people, but it was viewed as weaker in them. Older, theologically based moral explanations for epidemics, which attributed them to widespread social immorality, were given a scientific veneer, and epidemics were redefined as the products of widespread personal immorality.[16]

Strong voices disputed this claim. A correspondent of the *Home Journal* argued that immigrants who died of disease did so in "about the same proportion" as natives, while the idea that yellow fever's importation was "all a farce" was at least as prevalent as the common opinion that it had been introduced to American cities by outsiders. The fate of African Americans in particular warned against too great a certainty on this subject because empirical observation often conflicted with theoretical and racial suppositions. It was widely argued that black people were immune to yellow fever, if not to cholera. Most blacks were routinely employed in arduous manual labor. In New Orleans it was their particular task to clean the filth from the streets, gutters, batture, and levee. By all the lights of medical theory they should have died en masse, for people exposed to urban putrefaction, especially young men engaged in strenuous occupations, were supposed to be most at risk. Yet medical writers denied that Negroes were susceptible. The Medical Society of New Orleans claimed that none had died during the 1817 epidemic, and it classified those few who contracted the disease in 1819 among newcomers recently arrived from the north.[17]

By the prevailing moral-faculty theory, these data implied that African Americans were either morally superior to those whites who succumbed to disease or that they lacked a moral faculty that would make them suffer for their sins. Neither possibility was acceptable in the context of prevailing racial and medical ideas, so they were not entertained in the medical or journalistic literature. In fact, the claims of black immunity were disingenuous, as many contemporaries recognized. If blacks could not become ill, they could be expected to do the dirty work of epidemics uncomplainingly. During the early yellow fever outbreaks in Philadelphia, African Americans were told they were immune to persuade them to remain in town and nurse the sick after most white residents had fled. Yet while they accepted these duties, black people recognized the assertions of their immunity as a cynical lie. Absalom Jones and Richard Allen, founders of Philadelphia's two preeminent African American churches, pointed out that they had nursed their neighbors from charity, even though they knew they were in as much danger as anyone else, only to be repaid with accusations of stealing from the sick and the dead.[18]

Discerning whites understood that Africans and their descendants were not immune to yellow fever (although Mathew Carey thought that fewer African Americans were taken sick and that they were cured more easily than whites, even though his own statistics showed that fifteen of twenty blacks admitted to the Bush Hill fever hospital died). Lay people such as Elizabeth Drinker assumed that Negroes were likely to be carriers because they were poor, not because they were black. Nevertheless, during the 1798 epidemic the Philadelphia College of Physicians again recommended that post-death purification should be performed by blacks, "native Africans, if possible."[19]

There can be no doubt that the poor and the disadvantaged were hard hit by epidemics. The spatial economy of the antebellum city placed them in the cast-off portions of the city, which were likely to be near the watery breeding places of the *Aëdes aegyptii* mosquitoes we now know to be carriers of yellow fever. Since Aëdes aegyptii have a flying range of only one hundred yards, the nearer one lived to their breeding grounds, the more likely one was to be infected. Urban political economy also denied the poor the kinds of sanitary arrangements that would have kept them safe from cholera, which we now attribute to the *vibrio comma* bacillus that lives in food and water contaminated by other victims' feces. A petition from people residing near Rittenhouse Square in Philadelphia, then a thinly populated section of the city, complained about the "effluvia from neighboring ponds, and especially from the street dirt deposited in the square, which being in heaps, occasions numerous ponds of stagnant or putrescent water in the intermediate spots, which in summer send forth pestilential vapours." They were especially aggrieved because, "being of the working class," their health was their only asset, yet they were condemned to live in an environment that threatened "loss of health and loss of life." They pointedly told the Philadelphia City Council that their exposure to disease was one "from which the wealthy are more exempt by your better care of the purity of the air around their dwellings."[20]

By raising the issue of ethnic and economic difference in the context of discussions of epidemic disease, medical experts and journalists turned the debate irrevocably from empirical to qualitative judgments. Investigators began to map disease by mapping the diseased. Dangerous districts were those inhabited by dangerous residents: neighborhoods and neighbors were equally and inseparably hazardous. Looking back on a Philadelphia epidemic of 1762 from the perspective of the 1793 yellow fever season, John Redman recalled that the earlier outbreak had been traced to the neighborhood east of the New Market on South Second Street, "in which, after some considerable search and tracing it, it was found to have originated in a number of small back tenements forming a kind of court, the entrance to which was by two narrow alleys from Front and Pine-streets, and where sailors often had their lodgings." Frederick Augustus Tallmadge, president pro tem of the New York Board of Assistant Aldermen called the Board's attention to the public health risks posed by Laurens Street (now West Broadway), between Canal and Spring streets, which was littered with heaps of garbage and offal, "constantly undergoing fermentation," and pools of stagnant water. "It was also tenanted in a manner very prejudicial to the health of the neighborhood," he added. Summoned to Laurens Street to help quell a riot, he took an informal census and found the street's houses crowded with both black and white tenants: 280 whites and 173 blacks were packed into ten adjacent houses. In Tallmadge's view, the social and physiological evils of crowding blacks and whites together created a public-health hazard.[21]

In short, the domain of disease was projected onto the city as the realm of certain kinds of people. The preindustrial city, where alleys and other zones of poverty interpenetrated even the most elite residential pockets, formed an unnerving network of peril as the physical geography of disease became a human geography of fear. Elaborate statistical tables were compiled to demonstrate the connection empirically. In 1794, Philadelphia's so-called Fever Committee published street-by-street tables of the epidemic's toll, tallying the total number of houses and the number which were still inhabited, the number of people (broken down by race) who had fled or remained, and the number of deaths in each street. As one might expect, the greatest number of deaths were in the principal, and most heavily populated, streets. Nevertheless, rumors that cir-

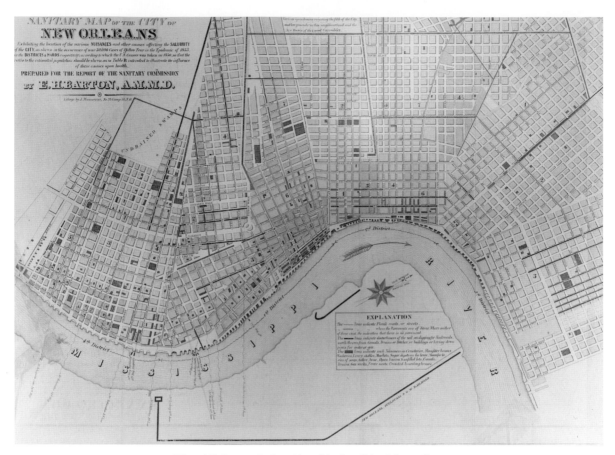

FIGURE 3.1. Edward H. Barton, *Sanitary Map of the City of New Orleans*, 1857. (Tulane University Library, Louisiana Collection)

culated by word of mouth and through the newspapers emphasized the alleys, the northern and southern edges of the city, and the waterfront, areas dominated by the lower sort.[22]

In the hands of the contrarian physician Edward H. Barton, the question of the human geography of disease took an unnerving turn. In 1857 Barton published the most elaborate of the epidemiological geographies, his *Sanitary Map of New Orleans,* which showed those parts of the city most likely to propagate yellow fever (fig. 3.1). Barton constructed his map of environmental conditions by plotting the location of cases, as the 1794 Fever Committee had done in Philadelphia, but he directed his readers' attention to topography and away from fever victims' character. Since New Orleans's topography remained constant, human action was the variable that determined the geography of epidemics. Consequently Barton's map analyzed the human-made landscape of New Orleans.[23]

The *Sanitary Map* made complex physiological and social phenomena visible and deceptively simple to those who would understand and control them. When Union General Benjamin Butler took command of the captured city five years after Barton published his work, he used it as an epidemiological tourist's map and prescription for action. "I found a map showing the localities of the city," he recalled, "the portions where the yellow fever usually raged being indicated by heavier shading." He went immediately to the French Market and other places that the map suggested were the origin of most epidemics, "and I thought I detected why it raged in those spots; they were simply astonishingly filthy with rotting matter."[24]

The deeper lesson of Barton's map was not so quickly grasped. Although he railed against immorality, filth, and other traditional enemies of public health, Barton identified the most dangerous places in New Orleans's landscape as those where people dug into the earth, exposing eons of putrefying matter to contact with human effluvia. He declared flatly that "no epidemic has occurred that has not been preceded and accompanied by a local disturbance of the original soil of the country, (in digging and clearing out canals, basins, &c.), although other local causes doubtless had their influence." The first epidemic, in 1797, had coincided with the digging of the Carondelet Canal. Others were "simultaneous with extensive exposures in the streets for pavements—large fillings up and enclosures of the batture, and the cleaning out and deepening" of the Carondelet Canal. "This has been so unequivocal and so constant, and without exception, that it seems to the [Sanitary] Commission to bear the relation of cause and effect." Barton supported his claims with a detailed ward-by-ward analysis of sanitary conditions, and he summarized his findings in the map: the unhealthiest sections of New Orleans were those where people were working hardest to improve the city. The canals, fills, and paving necessary for survival in a city that lay below the level of its river, and for economic growth in a city whose principal livelihood was waterborne commerce, provoked yellow fever epidemics.[25]

In shifting his gaze from human failings to the city's most forward-looking acts, Barton wrapped a tragic message in the language of scientific empiricism: people inevitably caused their own demise. It was an unalterable rule of urban living. Barton thus complicated the nexus of urban life and landscape, revealing the threat that the best-intentioned acts of citizenship posed to life itself.

CHAPTER 4

{ **NOISE AND GABBLE**

Wave after wave of noise broke in the streets of nineteenth-century American cities, growing louder as the century wore on. The "ceaseless rush of the tide of life" engulfed city people in closely built-up city streets that resembled "magnificent canals, deep but narrow," through which traffic flowed like water, in New York physician Frank Johnson's memorable image. "Surging masses of beings and objects, man and beast and vehicle, are promiscuously slipping, scrabbling, and jolting, rattling, and thundering along, with nought whereon to tread or roll but endless piles of stones." In New Orleans's market, Alabamaian Albert Pickett was overwhelmed by the "cursing, swearing, whooping, hollowing, cavilling, laughing, cry-screams of parrots, the music of birds, the barking of dogs, the cries of oystermen, the screams of children, the Dutch girl's organ, the French negro humming a piece of the last opera. . . . The people engaged in building the tower of Babel, whose language was confounded and confused for their presumptuous undertaking, never made a worse jargon or inflicted a greater blow upon harmonious sounds, than is to be found here." On the adjacent levee, once the promenade of fashionable people, Pickett found, the "very air howls with an eternal din and noise."[1]

Even domestic life was awash in cacophony. Johnson described the plight of the imaginary mistress of a Fifth Avenue mansion. Her costume and her demeanor complemented her carefully decorated parlor, filled with the finest goods, including beautiful carpets to "render all movements . . . silent and sylph-like," the whole calculated to create a pleasant retreat, carefully insulated from the hurly-burly of the city outside. "Yet one coal cart alone rattling along the stony way interrupts all conversation, and destroys half the comfort and pleasure" of this palace, Johnson lamented.[2]

Darkness brought no relief, for an unnerving cacophony erupted in American cities at night. A Newark, New Jersey, woman complained in 1798 that "noise in the streets" had left her with "no sleep for several nights," as did a Florida clergyman who wrote in 1860 that "although excessively fatigued I could not sleep because of the noise & disturbance in the streets." Philadelphian Elizabeth Drinker often lay awake at night listening to the city: "screaming in the Street, howling of Dogs, and a thumping as I thought in our house." Even placid neighborhoods took on a different tone after dark. A visitor to New Orleans who remarked on the quiet of his street was told by a black resident that "you neber here in de night, I reckon, massa."[3]

Sound is profoundly corporeal. All sound is vibration—a shaking of the body by environmental forces. An earthquake and a spoken word are variants of the same phenomenon. Both convey information through their inherent qualities— through variations and irregularities in pitch, timbre, volume, and duration. Our auditory system detects an astonishing range of these variations. Because it also links our ears stereophonically, the minute differences in the times that sounds reach each ear helps us locate their source. At night noises seemed menacing because they came from everywhere and nowhere, without apparent relationship to landscape or listener. "I never was much disturb'd by common noises in the night as many are," Elizabeth Drinker explained, "if they were such as I could account for and not excessevely loud." Using her ears, she calculated the sites of nocturnal disturbances near her home and her children's (not always accurately: "It always appears much nearer than it really is," Drinker realized). When fires, deaths, and other noteworthy events were announced by bells and alarms, she mapped them aurally, then confirmed her judgment by reports solicited from visitors, family members, and, often, servants dispatched to investigate: "This evening about 8 o'clock fire was cry'd. . . . [S]ent John to enquire where it was."[4]

Like odors, then, sounds cross architectural boundaries, and their sources and meanings may be uncertain. Urban noise invaded churches, courtrooms, offices, homes, and one's own thoughts, disrupting carefully fashioned theaters of social action. New Orleans's founders aligned the city offices, the Roman Catholic church, the headquarters of the City Guard (watchmen), and the prison along one side of the place d'armes. This made for an impressive visual display of authority, but it also had unintended, disturbing consequences. As townspeople sat listening in the city council chamber, attended mass in the Church of St.-Louis, or simply passed on the street, their tranquility might be destroyed by the sounds of torture in the jail yard. At one city council meeting, Benjamin Latrobe "was excessively annoyed for nearly an hour by hearing successive cracks of a Whip, each followed by a scream, and as the tone of the Screams varied, I presume it was a day of execution at the Jail." In the early 1830s, the city government finally agreed to move the jail to the back of the city (adjacent to Circus or Congo Square, the principal African American gathering place) after repeated complaints from clerics about the "unpleasantness of being daily disturbed, during prayers in Jesus Christ's temple, by the crack of the whip and the screams of its victims." The priests didn't object to the whippings themselves, but the delicate sensibilities of Christians were unsettled by their intrusion into the church.[5]

In early-nineteenth-century American cities, the diffuse quality of sound when compared with the relatively fixed nature of visible landmarks made audibility and silence a useful way to talk about urban presence. The discussion of audibility bore on questions of personal and social identity. Who had a right to be heard and who did not? Which sounds should one be allowed, or forced, to hear, and which not? Because sounds invade our thoughts as much as they do the spaces we occupy, they can undermine our sense of personal agency, even our self-possession, if they are relentless enough. As the British philosopher Edmund Burke noted in 1757, "Excessive loudness alone is sufficient to overpower the soul, to suspend its action, and to fill it with terror. The noise of vast cataracts, raging storms, thunder, or artillery, awakes a great and aweful sensation in the mind, though we can observe no nicety or artifice in those sorts of music. The shouting of multitudes has a similar effect." According to present-day psychologists and anthropologists, sounds, particularly when they are divorced from the reassuring context of vision, stimulate nonrational emotional responses and memories. Owing to the peculiar structure of the human brain, the intrinsic physical properties of sounds can calm or aggravate a listener, apart from any information they might convey. Burke feared the political consequences of cacophony: "By the sole strength of the sound [of the shouting multitude, which] so amazes and confounds the imagination, that in this staggering, and hurry of the mind, the best established tempers can scarcely forbear being born down, and joining in the common cry, and common resolution of the croud." Unstable selves made for unstable societies.[6]

So although complaints about the aural city—the spoken, declaimed, shouted, screamed, sung, drummed, rattled, hammered, heard, overheard, and endured city—began in reaction to the rapid crescendo of urban noise and the nerve-wracking discomfort that accompanied it, rapid social diversification, economic transformation, and new ideologies of selfhood and personhood prompted anxious scrutiny of one's own and others' audible presence in antebellum urban society. Intrusions on personal peace of mind were often described as violations of spatial order, and violations of spatial order were in turn interpreted as disruptions of social order.

Unfortunately for those who believed that self and society were threatened by urban noise, it was impossible to define an ideal, unitary sonic order. For example, while city people reeled in the growing din, they could not suppress it entirely. Some sounds of every sort were useful, although many were not. Even traffic noise had practical value. The thunder of iron-wheeled vehicles on cobblestones was disruptive and unsettling, but a street that was too smooth encouraged drivers to speed and prevented pedestrians from hearing vehicles in time to avoid injury. Wooden pavements had made Broadway near City

Hall "very quiet & peaceful" but "a perfect race course," complained the diarist and one-time mayor Philip Hone, so that "hardly a day passes without an Accident." Wooden pavements "render our streets quite as unsafe as would a heavy fall of snow, with vehicles passing and re-passing without bells," another New Yorker wrote. To replace the "thundering," "deafening" city with a silent city was wrong-headed. What was wanted was an active "humming" city that conveyed useful information unimpeded by noise.[7]

Human sounds were even more problematic. As with mechanical sounds, no simple embrace or rejection of vocal expression was possible for early-nineteenth-century Americans, as they found out when they attempted to regulate street vendors. These men, women, and children attracted business with cries or with the sounds of bell, horns, and ratchets, each trade with its characteristic sound, which varied from city to city (fig. 4.1). James Stuart heard "Corn piping hot" cried in the streets of New York, while in Philadelphia he would have heard "Hot Corn, Hot Corn" hawking the same product—corn boiled on the cob and sold at curbside. In New Orleans, Joseph Holt Ingraham reported that "Black women, with huge baskets of rusks, rolls and other appurtenances of the breakfast table, were crying, in loud shrill French, their 'stock in trade,' followed by milk-criers, and butter-criers and criers of everything but tears."[8]

A special genre of books for middle-class youngsters in many American and European cities described the distinctive cries and sounds of watchmen and firemen; vendors of fruit, pepper-pot, roast corn, pastries, muffins, gingerbread, and matches; knife grinders; oyster men; and chimney sweeps—all of whom children could see and hear daily in the streets around their homes but whom they were not permitted to meet in person. *The Cries of Philadelphia* conceded that the "ears of the citizens are grated with this uncouth sound"—the chimney sweeps' "Sweep-O-O-O"—but reminded children that sweeps were a "necessary and suffering class of human beings" and congratulated the city burghers for tolerating the "unpleasant and merciless bawling of those sooty boys ... in such a noisy place as this, where every needless sound ought to be hushed."[9]

FIGURE 4.1. Nicolino Calyo, *The Oysters man*, New York, ca. 1840–44. (Collection of the New-York Historical Society, neg. no. 57585)

The *Cries* books treated street sounds as picturesque representations of urban social interdependence. They were sympathetic to poor urban workers, who were as necessary and inevitable in the city as the streets themselves. "Every comfort we enjoy is produced in part by the labour of the poor, who are entitled to much humanity and no ill-nature," *The Cries of Philadelphia* taught

its young readers. Suffering these noises was the price prosperous people paid for their comfort.[10]

Many adults rejected this claim. In New Orleans as in New York, roving oyster vendors announced themselves by trumpets—an intolerable intrusion on the public peace, according to a city councilman named Palfrey. Palfrey's claim outraged a colleague. Oyster sellers were poor men, he said: "They must live!" Besides, how could people who made their living from steam engines and cotton presses (which, we all know, make no noise at all, the colleague added) object to a simple trumpet?[11]

A few years later the residents of Mulberry (Arch) Street in Philadelphia complained about trumpet-blowing charcoal sellers in their neighborhood. In refusing to suppress these vendors, the city council noted that there were so many equally nerve-wracking sounds in the city that to stamp them all out was neither possible nor desirable. To forbid sellers' "calling the attention of the people to their occupation or business, by the blowing or sounding of any horn, trumpet or other wind instrument, by the ringing of bell or bells, or by crying aloud the articles they have for sale, within the limits of the city" would end business in Philadelphia. The council recommended the traditional market nostrum: the charcoal sellers would disappear if no one patronized them.[12]

Although some urban residents condemned street cries and calls in even harsher terms than they did mechanical and accidental noises, others found much in ambient vocalizations to sweeten the cacophony. Philadelphians thought the watchmen's cries "peculiar and musical." The New Orleans market was filled with a cheerful, lively chatter. Music was everywhere. A black coachman's song in Cincinnati, "ringing clear and full above the noises of the street," caught the ear of an aspiring minstrel performer. Stevedores on the waterfront in Savannah and elsewhere in the South sang and chanted as they worked. Worshippers spilled out of New Orleans churches and immediately commenced "singing, dancing, and all kinds of sports . . . in every street" accompanied by violins and fifes. A drunk strolled along a Crescent City street singing, "I keep a good look out I am a smart fellow I am Singin fol de rol." More accomplished street musicians—Tyrolese organ grinders, Scots bagpipers, black banjo players—enlivened the air in New York. Lydia Maria Child counted such serenaders among the "things that cheer this weary world" and scolded city authorities for banning them.[13]

Human sounds were the ligaments of the social body. Silence dismembered society, sometimes intentionally. Antebellum prison theorists advocated unbroken silence as a way of dispersing criminal society and reconstructing criminal selves by breaking off human communication and (in theory) forcibly reorienting the self to the divine. In Quaker meetings, absolute silence implied the suspension of human relationships in the presence of something higher. But eventually the silence was dispelled as one Friend sought to communicate a spiritual insight to the others, and individual seekers were once more a Society.

Under ordinary circumstances, the antebellum city was silent only in times of calamity. During epidemics, when most activity was suspended, the customary ringing of bells to announce deaths was forbidden, and a foreboding silence hung over the city. The Swedish visitor Frederika Bremer intended to convey something of the same sense of dread in her account of a slave sale in the basement of a large house in New Orleans. The black men and women offered for sale were "silent and serious. The whole assembly was silent, and it seemed to me as if a heavy gray cloud rested upon it. . . . The gentlemen looked askance at me with a gloomy expression, and probably wished that they could send me to the North Pole" for witnessing their evil business.[14]

But misplaced sounds—noise—deformed the social body. One winter Sunday's evening, Elizabeth Drinker reported an alarm that broke up several religious services, raised because "some took delight in Alarming the Inhabitants for every triffling matter." "The boys are very fond of noise and hubbub," she wrote on another such occasion. At Philadelphia's Second Street Market, neighbors complained in 1805, "the Butcher Boys, dissipated men, and idle women collect, and the Market during the whole night is the scene of every species of riot and debauchery; the people in each side of the street are not only molested by their wicked and vulgar noise but even are prevented from sleeping" on Saturday evenings.[15]

The language is important. The market rowdies' noise was not merely vexatious, it was "wicked and vulgar." Descriptions of nocturnal noise always invoked lower-class indiscipline and hinted, openly or covertly, at criminal conspiracies. In St. Louis in 1856, a local newspaper reported, "blood-thirsty fiends, desperate rogues, coarse rowdies and brutal ruffians" shattered the night with their "hellish orgies. . . . Hardly a night passes in which one, if he listened and watched, could not see the glittering dagger flash in the air, hear the shriek or groan of the assassin's victim."[16]

Visiting Philadelphia in 1849, Lady Emmeline Stuart Wortley came to hate the city's "unearthly nightly noises, and the rumors of war which seemed unceasing and ever-increasing in the City of Brotherly Love. . . . All night a sound as of a masque and procession of one hundred menageries let loose, filled one's ears. The deserts of Africa seemed to have disgorged half their denizens on the beautiful streets of fair Philadelphia: while bells, horns, gongs, and rattling fireengines, helped to swell the hideous chorus." The next morning she learned that "it was the fashion" of people in Moyamensing, a working-class district just beyond the southern boundary of the city, "to regale the ears of the inhabitants of that city frequently with such harmonious serenades.... The Moyamensingists, in short, seem to look upon a riot or a row, or something resembling it, as the first necessary of life: they also would seem to entertain a new theory with regard to sleep, and to consider it a wholly needless indulgence."[17]

Wortley's text shows that she knew about the deadly riots of the 1840s that had rocked Moyamensing and Kensington, south and north of the city proper, and she also knew about the gang warfare in Moyamensing during the time of her visit. This violence was directed against blacks, Roman Catholics, and those few public officials who tried to restrain the rioters. Yet she attributed the tumult to the African American residents of the district and used metaphors of masques (allegorical dramas featuring fantastic and grotesque beings), zoos, and African deserts, of "hideous" cacophonies brought to "fair Philadelphia." Nighttime in Moyamensing evoked a child's nightmare for her: it was a Sendakian jungle of racial fantasies. In a city that was already growing beyond the possibility of intimate personal knowledge by the end of the eighteenth century, the dark removed the last vestige of individuality and even humanity from one's servant, one's apprentice, one's junior clerk, or the worker who lived in the back alley. All that was left was a junglelike, uncivilized cacophony of subhuman sounds that threatened mayhem.

In New York's almshouse, Edward S. Ely heard the "dialect of almost every nation . . . for the English, Scotch, Irish, Dutch, German, French, Spanish, and Italian, as well as American poor, have met" there. Albert Pickett found that most of these same languages—French, English, Spanish, Dutch, Italian, as well as "Swiss"—could be heard in New Orleans's markets. There was also a large antebellum German-speaking community with its own theater and publications, and many blacks spoke a Creole (Africanized) French that outsiders usually dismissed as "negro patois," dialectical evidence of African Americans' inability to speak properly. Just as the dark cloaked antisocial behavior, so did such opaque language. Among the sounds of the humming city—the "perpetual murmur of a hive," in Lydia Maria Child's image—anything obscure or false was potentially dangerous. Criminals' "flash" language, also called cant or the patter, came to stand for the linguistic chaos and subterfuge that Americans heard in the variety of languages, unintelligible to the monolingual, that enlivened active commercial ports.[18]

In the flash language, *flash* means "in the know." Those who wrote about this slang painted it as a secret language, comprehended only by initiates, that allowed criminals to recognize one another and to communicate "so as not to be understood by honest men." Massachusetts State Penitentiary guard William Going was celebrated for his command of the flash language, which he claimed to have learned during a stint as a kind of undercover policeman. At the penitentiary one day Going happened to be standing next to the warden, Major Daniel Jackson, and a couple of convicts. He heard one of the latter "say he could ciff the swell cove, for he had as lief die as not; and knowing him to be a bad-tempered fellow, and understanding the flash language, I called the Major to me, and told him that Collins had threatened to stab him with a knife." A search produced the weapon and Collins's confession. "These proceedings broke the convicts from using the flash language," Going boasted.[19]

In truth, the flash language was hardly secret. Anyone who cared to understand it could easily do so, for dictionaries had been published in Europe since the sixteenth century, and new ones—often plagiarized from older examples rather than based on original research—appeared regularly thereafter. Still, writers about the flash language continued to insist on its impenetrability. They argued that cant was an unchanging international language of criminals, impossible to understand fully unless one had learned it from birth yet transparent to any criminal in the world. Its universality created a single vast criminal nation that threatened to overpower the linguistically splintered nations of the respectable. Unlike respectable speech, early scholars believed, the flash language originated among rootless outsiders. At first Jews were blamed, but by the early nineteenth century the flash language was most commonly attributed to Gypsies.[20]

The flash-language literature presented a hysterical caricature of the linguistic cacophony of antebellum American cities. Post-1803 New Orleans, with its audible ethnic diversity, became the testing ground for these anxieties about linguistic fragmentation and its associated loss of authority and social order. To Anglophone outsiders French seemed universal. John H. B. Latrobe encountered people of all races and nationalities on the levee, but "French was the language that principally met my ear. Sometimes Spanish and rarely English." He speculated that this was because "the French Men talked the loudest." Samuel J. Peters, an English Canadian raised in Connecticut, took the unusual step of working in a French firm's New York countinghouse to prepare for a move to New Orleans, for he had been told that no one could find work in the Crescent City who could not speak French. Nearly thirty years after Peters settled there, the newcomer Rollin Fillmore wrote to one of his relatives that not only was French widely spoken, but "on some of the Streets the signs are all in french[.] So you see it would be an advantage to me if I could 'parlez vous.'"[21]

Those who tested their French in New Orleans found that whites spoke the language rapidly and with an accent that was very different from the Parisians'. Most Americans declined even to try to understand, dismissing French as unintelligible noise: "jabber" was the most common verb for the act of speaking it. Even Benjamin Latrobe, who had learned French as a child and checked into a French-speaking New Orleans hotel to relearn the language, referred to the conversation there as "noise and gabble."[22]

Language became a weapon in the struggle between the English- and French-speaking factions in New Orleans. English speakers ("assuming somewhat the manner of conquerors—and an intellectual superiority which they did not always merit," according to Samuel Peters's son) insisted on the exclusive use of English as a means to understand and control what was happening around them. In 1822, the American-dominated state supreme court nullified legal documents written in French, which were the basis of the land titles of the entire pre-American elite. The Francophone-dominated New Orleans city council searched frantically for a translator to render its minutes into English. Then Bernard Marigny, a wealthy New Orleans landowner and state legislator, introduced a so-called "French bill" into the legislature to quiet the titles, dubbing himself the "savior of the French language." Two decades later he oversaw the introduction of a clause into the state's constitution of 1845 protecting the French language and requiring that employees of the legislature be bilingual. Both languages were spoken in the statehouse until the mid-nineteenth century.[23]

After the Louisiana Purchase, French was commonly understood in New Orleans to be a language of resistance to the American presence. James Pierpont, an officer in the U.S. Navy, complained to the city council in 1821 that police officers had invaded his Conti Street room in pursuit of black people fleeing a raid on a funeral in the back yard. Pierpont went to the guard house and asked "in a civil and respectful manner" whether anyone there could speak English. A Captain Cardineaud said no. Pierpont then tried to lodge a complaint against the commander of the group who had entered his room. Cardineaud responded, apparently in English, that "he should not tell me, and turning to the Guard said something to them in french, which I did not understand. It was not long, however before I learned the purpose of his Speech, for it was no sooner ended than the whole of the guard rushed upon me—and with the greatest violence thrust me out of the Guard house—several of them struck me with their guns and it was with the greatest difficulty that I saved myself from falling."[24]

Americans found French particularly offensive when blacks spoke it. Joseph Mason, an Anglophone, encountered eight or nine French-speaking black men gathered at the corner of Poydras and Levee streets in the Faubourg Sainte-Marie in 1811. According to witness David Shields, Mason marched up to the group and demanded to know what they were talking about. One of the men "answered very insolently . . . in broken english which Deponent understood 'it is none of your business.'" Enraged, Mason and Shields seized two of the men and attempted to take them to the guard. Shields's captive escaped, while Mason's "kept on Cursing the Deponent both in english & french, and would not march." Several French-speaking whites watched but would not assist the Americans.[25]

New Orleans blacks took advantage of the openings linguistic fragmentation afforded. Enslaved and free people of color used the French language as a double-edged tool against American control and white domination generally. While the American and French elite were arrogantly monolingual, the records suggest that many blacks were bilingual—trilingual if one adds Creole French. A few, like the slave Célestine, who escaped in 1828, spoke all three of the principal European languages of New Orleans—English, French, and Spanish. Their linguistic facility gave them the power to hear and understand much more of what was happening around them than most of the whites and so to turn the situation to their own advantage.[26]

In spite of their mastery of several tongues, New Orleans's African Americans were routinely characterized by whites as barely human beings for whom spontaneous outbursts and inarticulate noises substituted for speech. A traveler referred to blacks' "joyous and unthinking laughter," which strikes the heart of the matter: black sounds issued directly from animal emotions, unmediated by reason. The nearly universal use of dialect in quoting black speakers reinforced the point. As rendered by whites, the mispronunciations and malapropisms of black dialect showed that African Americans were incapable of expressing themselves rationally through language. So to Joseph Holt Ingraham, the lively verbal give-and-take of the black vendors in the Crescent City's market—"sounds stranger and more complicated than any I ever imagined could be rung upon that marvellous instrument the human tongue"—was nevertheless meaningless chatter and its speakers were social voids. The market offered "nothing to gratify the spirit of inquiry or observation, in the ignorant, careless-hearted slaves, whose character presents neither variety nor interest." Ingraham cautioned his readers that "they cannot be ranked among the class of their fellow-beings denominated citizens, and consequently, are not to be estimated by a stranger in judging this community."[27]

At issue was a conception of human vocal expression as an existential act. This Euro-American belief, stretching back at least to classical Greece, categorized people by the sounds they made. It heard speech as a special kind of sound that communicates controlled, reasoned, civilized thought, conveying a carefully mediated view of the speaker's inner state, or self. In this respect language was qualitatively different from other human sounds, which were unmediated and unsocialized, revealing aspects of the self that ought properly to be hidden.

Articulate speech was a sign of a speaker's social power. Humans were superior to other animals, the articulate to the inarticulate, men to women, whites to nonwhites. Those who could not speak must be, in antebellum terms, "dumb," a word that already carried the double meaning of mute and stupid. Deaf mutes, people incapable of forming or hearing spoken language, were widely believed to be inherently childlike, uncivilized, socially inept, and morally suspect. They needed some alternative form of discipline to make up for that provided by trained speech. These assumptions were reinforced by the early modern European concept of civility, in which the "natural"—a category that included children, "primitive" people, the wilderness, and, often, women—was divinely ordered to be brought under the control of legal, moral, and religious authorities, to be made civil, or civilized, by the disciplines of reason and revelation exercised in public and in private.[28]

Through the complex interplay of making noise and making sense, speaking and listening, hearing and being heard, one defined oneself as human in an inanimate landscape and as an autonomous member of society. To have a voice, to speak, was both to exercise independent agency—selfhood—and to claim a place in society—personhood. In antebellum America, a new popularly based politics and elaborate public ceremonies of all sorts during the early republic provided opportunities for lengthy, forcefully delivered oratory of a new sort—directed to popular values and employing popular modes of speech. The fiery oratory of politicians and reformers; the impassioned rhetoric of speakers at the mass public meetings that characterized the politics of antebellum cities; the speechifying at building dedications, public holidays, and other gatherings; the many new varieties of popular theater; the psychological calculation of the "new measures" used by evangelical preachers—all gave Americans the opportunity to appreciate the power of the spoken word, and they "enshrined the art of oratory," appreciating it in all of its varieties but hearing it through sharply critical ears.[29]

According to historian Kenneth Cmiel, traditional rhetorical standards promoted a precise, eloquent mode of argument that appealed to an elite, rational public. As audiences grew larger and more diverse in the nineteenth century, public speakers increasingly changed their tactics, appealing to their publics by using popular, colloquial diction and by evoking structures of feeling rather than of logic, resulting in a style that Cmiel called "middling rhetoric." Recent ethnographers of speech have pointed out the widespread appeal of this tactic in many times and places. The goal of this kind of rhetorical performance is not to persuade through logic but to "seal a position" by closing off objections to it in a more intuitive manner. Audiences typically construct the speaker's meaning as being like their own, rather than being swayed to a new position or action of the speaker's chosing. The orator's task is immediate and performative, to move the audience to "swing along" emotionally. The ability to do so manifests personal power.[30]

William C. Preston's performance before the U.S. Supreme Court did just that for fellow attorney Sidney George Fisher. Although Preston was awkward and unfashionable in appearance and repeatedly dipped snuff throughout his oration, "daubing it in his haste all over his sweaty face," he had a powerful voice, "loud & rough," that he used effectively. "Broad views, close reasoning, luminous arrangement, illustrated and adorned by fine thought & poetic imagery, and clothed in language clear, chaste, appropriate, glowing & rich. Tho he spoke with the utmost vehemence & rapidity, he never hesitated for a word, never reconstructed a sentence, but rolled out his sounding & harmonious periods as complete & highly finished as tho they had been elaborated in his study." Preston was less learned and less effective a reasoner than Horace Binney, Fisher thought, but Binney lacked Preston's "glow of feeling & the sunset radiance of imagination." Preston's performance "threw me into a fit of enthusiasm for my profession." Fisher had swung along.[31]

The right to speak is unevenly distributed through any society. In antebellum America social power was measured by how well one spoke, with inept or misplaced speech framed as cacophony, and by whether and in what situations one was allowed to speak. So public oratory, a performance that was ostensibly devoted to public ends, was an exercise of personal power, an assertion of self, while the verbal assertion of self in turn translated back into social power. The authority to speak presumed the speaker's credibility and carried the obligation to use it honorably. Although the concept of honor was defended most vociferously in the South, conservative elites in both the North and the South accepted the notion that the honorable man spoke truthfully. His words were free of the noise and distraction of untruth. To put it another way, the authority of speech to order human society derived from its grounding in a worthy self.

The danger of popular speech, to those who remained loyal to older rhetorical standards and older conceptions of personal authority, was that a speaker might adopt an inauthentic persona to appeal to an audience. After attending the courtroom performance of attorney David Paul Brown, Thomas Pym Cope pronounced him "fluent, verbose, scurrilous, but not esteemed a well read lawyer." He "so pleased the crowded audience that, on the close of his argument, they caused the court-room to ring with cheers for Brown, contrary to usage & propriety." Brown offended Cope because his speech assumed authority without fulfilling its prerequisites: he was ill educated and so had a shaky grasp of truth, and in any case he played to the crowd rather than to truth. He said scurrilous things about the Quakers, Cope's own denomination, and he used "language referring to mind & soul, strongly bordering on impiety."[32]

Those without authority, including nonwhites, women, and the poor generally, could not be trusted to speak honorably, and (circularly) those without honor could not speak authoritatively. But for every writer who found the torrent of unrestrained public speech "obscene and infamous," there were a hundred people in the street who stood alongside Walt Whitman, "not a bit tamed." "I too am untranslatable," he declared. "I sound my barbaric yawp over the roofs of the world." The snide diarists' sarcasm and the mobs' violence masked an open-endedness about the urban soundscape and an evolving assertiveness among those whose voices were often categorized by their betters as noise. Many elite and middling urbanites listened and found themselves curious about, even moved by, kinds of speech of which they disapproved in principle.[33]

Willing to listen, Lydia Maria Child was surprised to find herself swinging along with the Methodist preacher Julia Pell. On a friend's recommendation, Child interviewed Pell one day in 1841 then went to hear her preach at New York's Elizabeth Street Methodist Church. Pell confused Child by her failure to conform to accepted categories. The illiterate daughter of a fugitive slave, Pell was nevertheless "lady-like" in person. In the pulpit, her dress was "tastefully appropriate," but it seemed ill-matched to her "voice like a sailor at mast-head, and muscular action like [the actor] Garrick in Mad tom." Pell's sermon was an "odd jumbling together of all sorts of things in Scripture," but delivered so dramatically that Child "was almost prepared to have seen her poise herself on unseen wings, above the wondering congregation." The sermon, Child noted condescendingly, must have terrified her humble audience, but after rousing them to an agitated pitch, she brought them back down again to shouts of "That's God's truth!" "Glory!" and "Hallelujah!" The congregation had swung along, but so had Child, who found herself excited by a description of resurrection and judgment that she rejected theologically: "Combined as my religious character is, of quiet mysticism, and the coolest rationality, will you believe me, I could scarcely refrain from shouting Hurrah for that heaven-bound ship! And tears rolled down my cheeks."[34]

Child defended Pell's right to speak publicly against those who thought she should be silenced for her youthful "missteps" and against those who questioned Pell's authority as a woman to do so. She was curious about Pell and delighted by her performance, but even she did not quite know how to respond to a powerful sermon by an illiterate African American woman. Others were even more puzzled, for women's public speech contradicted long-established religious, rhetorical, and political beliefs.[35]

FIGURE 4.2. Ronaldson's Row, ca. 1830, Philadelphia. As the first, third, and fourth houses illustrate, the original doors were all on the right sides of the facades, rather than being paired in the customary fashion (cf. fig. 2)

Women who spoke were derided by the ancient Greeks as leaky jars. To antebellum Americans, they were gossips: as the weaker sex women inevitably revealed what they should not, conveyed information without regard for truth, and wasted time better spent more productively. A contributor to *Godey's Lady's Book* declared that "those think most who speak least—as frogs cease croaking when a light is placed on the banks of the pond. . . . All sedentary artists, tailors, shoemakers, weavers, have, in common with [women], besides hypochondriac fantasies, this habit of gossip." The Philadelphia type-founder, developer, and lifelong bachelor James Ronaldson constructed a row of houses with an unusual arrangement of the front entries, reputedly "'to prevent tattling women from gossiping on the door-steps,'" a variation of the patriarchal fantasy of putting doors on female mouths that, the classicist Anne Carson notes, has persisted since antiquity (fig. 4.2).[36]

Quaker meetings were among the few public assemblies in which women were accorded the privilege and the authority of speech, or as a hostile listener put it, where "any female can allow any holiday to her tongue." Observers customarily compared female preachers to male speakers, as Philadelphia diarist William B. Davidson did in his account of two Quaker sermons he heard at an 1825 meeting. One was delivered by an elderly male Friend and the other by the esteemed traveling minister Anna B. Braithwaite. Davidson was struck by the style of the sermons. The old man began haltingly then "proceeded faster until he was reasonably fluent and then commenced a slight sing song which increased to a regular tune much like a man crying clams." By comparing the man's sermon to a street vendor's cry, Davidson assigned it to the category of noise. Braithwaite "spoke much more naturally than is usual among the friends and had but little sing song." Davidson thought her performance "quite equal to that of a middling clergyman, perhaps shewing more natural talent."[37]

Another renowned Philadelphia Quaker preacher, Elizabeth Evans, was a tart-tongued orator whom Thomas P. Cope could not abide. Cope ascribed a forcefulness to her speech that was proper only to men and so unauthorized in Evans. "She is probably the most finished female orator belonging to the Society [of Friends]," he conceded, "but she would be none the worse for indulging a little less vanity & ambition & a little more charity & less self-importance." On another occasion, he remarked that "if this ambitious woman had the power, she would make some of us a head shorter in quick time or cause the *auto-da-fé* to send our bodies off in vapour and smoke. Masculine in body & mind she exercises uncontrolled sway in our assemblies & knows well how to wheedle submissive necks to her purposes." Evans's speech lacked authority both for her sex and for her social origins, for she had been "raised . . . from the dregs of society to a giddy eminence." Cope disingenuously confided to his diary that he had often written of Evans, but "never in malice," nor written anything about her and her husband "which I cannot conscientiously abide by." His language was honorable because it was grounded in truth. Evans did not act so honorably, he suggested. She intimidated any critic by "attack[ing] him publicly from the gallery, not the name, but in a manner sufficiently pointed to mark him to the audience." Since she had spoken under the cloak of religion and had not named her target, however, "he cannot, of course, reply."[38]

As the century wore on, women spoke in public and published their words in increasing numbers. They participated politically by debating politics with male relatives and acquaintances, by discreet gestures of public support for male political action, and by occasional open public demonstrations. By mid-century these efforts had achieved a measure of acceptance, but women's right to a public voice was still limited.[39]

White women's right to speak publicly was challenged most often in formal settings such as religious services, mass meetings, and publications. For African Americans such formal public speech was physically dangerous. Rioters, such as those who destroyed Philadelphia abolitionists' Pennsylvania Hall in 1838, were intent on silencing black voices and the voices of those who spoke on behalf of African Americans. The Hall, the anti-abolitionist Sidney George Fisher wrote angrily, "was deliberately opened & burnt, in broad day, by a mob of well-dressed persons, the police scarcely interferring & the firemen not being allowed to play on the fire." After Pennsylvania rewrote its constitution in 1838 to cancel black men's franchise, aggrieved petitioners to the state legislature described the consequences of silencing their political and personal voices. They had been subject to all manner of "injury, insult, and outrage." Their churches and houses had been burned, their persons attacked and some of them murdered by people emboldened by the new state constitution, which classed them with "paupers, vagabonds, and fugitives from justice," the only other people excluded from citizenship. They were "assaulted on the public streets, our wives, mothers and daughters insulted, and upon the slightest resistance, dragged before a magistrate, incapable of speaking our language correctly" (a slur against the Irish). Disfranchisement had reduced free black men to the status of women, silent and helpless.[40]

As the black men's petition pointed out, the authority to speak affected everyday life in countless ways. African Americans addressed whites undeferentially, as equals, at great personal cost. Sometimes the speech was heated and probably not calculated, as when the New Orleans free man of color John Reeves was "generally very insolent to whites" when drunk, or when a J. Cornen, an official at a New Orleans horse race, was insulted by a group of black men when he tried to break up a fight. On another occasion, the widow Robin of the Faubourg Marigny complained to the court that a "supposedly" free man of color named Estevan, who believed that she was concealing a weapon that had wounded him a short time before, had appeared at her door and insulted her and threatened her with a dagger, "in contempt of the laws of the State concerning slaves and free people of color." The New Orleans slave Jacques was arrested in 1816 when, returning home to discover that his door had been broken in by men searching for a runaway slave, he "allowed himself to say some very injurious things against whites in general."[41]

At other times the assumed equality was deliberate and aggressive. A "stout black man" pushing through a New York crowd was heard to mutter, "Damn these white people, there's no getting along for them." A brief account in the *New-York Herald* detailed the more calculated self-assertion and consequent legal troubles of a mulatto Baltimore oyster seller named Dixon, "such as he called himself, for negroes have, by right, no surnames." The newspaper reported that someone had signed Dixon's name (the reporter assumed) to a letter to the editor of another newspaper, "in which every body, almost, was libeled." Dixon was imprisoned. To the anonymous author of the article, the idea that Dixon could have written the paper himself—that he could have "spoken" publicly—was as absurd to contemplate as his arrogating to himself a surname, a social existence. The writer assumed that the absurdity was part of the libel, in suggesting that a mixed-race nonentity had uttered these insults against important people.[42]

With a name, which "confers socialness," one assumes a social existence and can define one's own social role. It follows that to control the way one is addressed is an important first step to claiming a voice, as Dixon did in choosing a surname. So did Philadelphia's black citizens in retitling themselves. "Once they submitted to the appelation of servants, blacks, or negroes," complained John Fanning Watson, "but now they require to be called coloured people, and among themselves, their common call of salutation is—gentlemen and ladies." In the same spirit, a former slave in Mississippi demanded of a white planter, "Call me Mister," not "Uncle" or any of the other patronizing titles whites often assigned blacks.[43]

In antebellum cities, speaking and listening were intertwined but never equal. Was it better to be a good speaker or a good listener? From the point of view of the elite white men who shaped most definitions of acceptable speech and speakers, speaking and hearing were complementary. They spoke. Others were expected to listen and adapt themselves to the order they proclaimed. Confrontations over black speech in New Orleans arose when white men found their master-y, their authority, challenged by blacks' unauthorized or unintelligible "secret" speech. Critics of the flash language feared that cant would create relationships that the uninitiated—the unsuspecting honest citizen, the policeman—could not control. Elizabeth Evans offended Cope because, as a woman, she reversed the roles of speaker and hearer. Those who ridiculed evangelical stump preachers and the leaders of the new Mormon religion also emphasized unauthorized speech (fig. 4.3). These religious leaders' social origins did not grant them the authority they assumed, as one Ohio mob made clear when it tarred Joseph Smith's mouth shut. In all cases, the proper relationship of speaker and hearer was inverted.[44]

Anthropologists tell us that cultures that treat speech as a marker of intelligence tend to be self- and mastery-oriented, seeking self-expression and the imposition of the will on reality. Those that equate the ear, or hearing, with the seat of reason tend to be "reality-oriented," using aural evidence to adapt the self to the situation. In antebellum American cities, the reliance on speaking or hearing did not distinguish cultures but exposed rifts within the new national culture. Those who claimed the authority of speech and who created the

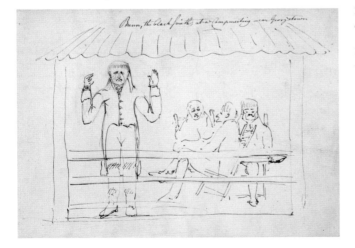

THE NIGHT WATCH-MEN.

FIGURE 4.4. *The Night Watch-Men*, Philadelphia, 1839. The watchman stands outside his watch house. He carries a torch to light the street lamps and a ladder to help him reach them. (The Library Company of Philadelphia)

new urban spaces discussed in Part II were motivated in both cases by an effort to create an ideal urban order, an urban landscape and urban society "in focus," where all the senses told the same story, where each portion was in harmony with every other portion.

The musical metaphor is significant. Musical theorist Jacques Attali argues that the kinds of sounds a society deems harmonious or discordant characterize—even prefigure—the kinds of social qualities it values. In antebellum America the connection was explicit. Musical rituals and metaphors helped urbanites to link sounds, spaces, and social order. Rhythm—time manifest as interval and duration—connoted movement through modularly ordered space. The anarchic regime of night noises was offset by the comforting routine of the city watchman, who emerged at intervals from his small, octagonal watch box, placed at a major intersection, called the hours, lit the street lamps, announced the weather, and walked his beat (fig. 4.4). The watchmen of New Orleans's Night Guard carried staves that they tapped on the pavement at each intersection, aurally clicking off the city's grid as they paced off its divisions. It was Elizabeth Drinker's nocturnal "amusement" to "hear how the time passes" as the Philadelphia watchman cried the hours. Although Quaker City watchmen were forbidden to disturb sleepers after Drinker's time, they panto-mimed the same rhythmic relationship as their New Orleans colleagues. Twice hourly "each watchman goes in a direct line for four squares, turns no corners except into alleys &c. that lead from the street allotted to him," timing his trav-els to intersect at each intersection with the watchman patrolling the crossing street.[45]

Similarly, harmony evoked social integration, for it organized multiple sounds into systems of dominance, subordination, and cooperation. Together, rhythm and harmony heralded the fusion of individual comfort and social order. Cope was delighted to discover in 1805 that rather than ringing a cur-few bell as in New England (or firing a curfew cannon, as in New Orleans), the Alexandria, Virginia, watchmen gathered before they set off for their nightly rounds and performed a horn serenade "in a steady, soft strain which strongly resembles the sweet melody of an aeolian harp."[46]

Elite dreams of harmonious social interaction were often thwarted by au-diences, who understood that the ability to listen allowed them to evade or at least to bend their assigned roles, as the multilingual black population of New Orleans, as well as many white women, were able to do. As attentive listeners they understood the situation more thoroughly than self-involved speechifiers. Attentive listening could be a way to form an alternative mode of being, a real-ity oriented strategy that sought momentary advantage and freedom of action rather than an ideal order or enduring "harmony."[47]

The dazzling rhetoric of men of power stood at one end of a continuum that spanned the range of urban sounds all the way to clanging bells and booming fireworks, linking language and noise in a single rushing stream that immersed all city people. The crescendo of urban noise was matched by the crescendo of urban speakers. "The great phenomenon of the Age," declared *Putnam's Monthly Magazine,* "is the growth of great cities." "Excluding Paris," the journal assured its readers, the greatest of these were "those in which evangelical religion, and the English language are prevalent and dominant." Even Paris was great only because it was intimately connected to the Protestant, Anglophone world. Meta-phors of communication and music, of transparency and harmony, bespoke a yearning for a unitary order in which a few voices spoke clearly and authorita-tively, while others hummed along.[48]

Other observers recognized the energy that cities derived from the variety of their inhabitants—not only street vendors with their cries, but immigrants from many parts of the world. Another New York journalist, writing a few months before the *Putnam's* piece was published, celebrated the city's "Babel-like confusion of tongues. . . . One may walk through Wall Street or Broadway, and hear French, Spanish, Italian, English, German, Turkish, and almost every other language used in the known world, spoken at the same moment." This linguistic polyphony was part of the city's "noise—its hurry, its bustle," he wrote. "The haste with which every body moves, and acts, and speaks, is another characteristic of New York that I admire. It is contagious, and it has a good effect upon the spirits and health of an idle man."[49]

CHAPTER 5

{ **SEEING AND BELIEVING**

In "Starting from Paumanok," Walt Whitman associated his own birth with that of the United States, a nation founded by

> Dead poets, philosophs, priests,
> Martyrs, artists, inventors, governments, long since,
> Language-shapers on other shores,
> Nations once powerful, now reduced, withdrawn, or desolate. . . .

He named the

> Okonee, Koosa, Ottawa, Monongahela, Sauk, Natchez, Chattahoochee,
>   Kaqueta, Oronoco,
> Wabash, Miami, Saginaw, Chippewa, Oshkosh, Walla-Walla

who had once peopled the continent, but who were rapidly giving way to

> . . . the wigwam, the trail, the hunter's hut, the flatboat, the maize-leaf,
>   the claim,
> the rude fence, and the backwoods village. . . .

In this and many other of his poems, Whitman transformed a cliché of popular culture—the catalogue of disparate people, places, or things—into art. He did not have to look far for inspiration. Whitman began his career as a journalist for the *Brooklyn Eagle* newspaper while living across the East River in New York, a growing metropolis whose harbor, a fellow journalist wrote, was filled with the "Yorker," the "substantial representative of Old England," the "Dutchman," the "clumsy Dane," the Norwegian polacca, and the "'long-limbed' brigs and schooners that come from 'down east.'" Other journalists chronicled streets lined with a "confused assemblage of high, low, broad, narrow, white, gray, red, brown, yellow, simple and florid," their "glories . . . rather traditional than actual," and teeming with a "river deep & wide of live, perspiring humanity."[1]

   On the street passersby were surrounded by buildings whose surfaces were covered with the names of merchants and tradesmen and lists of their wares, and by fences and other unguarded surfaces thickly plastered with posters touting plays, political candidates, circuses, patent medicines, lectures, minstrel shows, and public meetings (plate 5). When they opened their newspapers or glanced at the bills thrust into their hands, they scanned long lists of goods for sale at the retail stores, shopping arcades, dry-goods stores, large-scale "emporiums" and "warehouses," and ever larger department stores that came to line city streets. On stepping into one of these, shoppers found the lists transformed into three-dimensional reality. The first fancy retail stores in late-eighteenth-century Philadelphia displayed "buck-handled 'Barlow' penknives, . . . gilt and plated buttons, and . . . scissors, curiously arranged on circular cards, (a new idea)" as well as "fine mull mull and jaconet muslins, . . . chintses, and linens suspended in whole pieces, from the top to the bottom, and entwined together in puffs and festoons, (totally new)." Fifty years later, when the New York dry-goods merchant A. T. Stewart opened his vast "Marble Palace," its walls were hung with paintings and goods—"every variety and every available style of fabrics in the market"—piled on every surface and hung from the ceilings and even from the dome, he surpassed his predecessors only in scale. Stewart's was the most prominent of a long procession—a three-dimensional list—of "palaces" that lined New York's Broadway and pressed in from adjacent streets. In any one of them customers would find counters "heaped in wild profusion with every imaginable dainty that loom and fingers and rich dyes and the exhausted skill of human invention have succeeded in producing—drawn together by the magic power of taste and capital."[2]

Wherever they turned, then, urban Americans and their visitors were struck first by number and variety, and they resorted to lists to encompass what they could not adequately characterize. Whitman's lists expressed the generous, celebratory, all-embracing voice of his poetry. A similar generosity seems to underlie the popular-culture inventories, which extended beyond inanimate objects to places and the people who inhabited them. By setting the most disparate people and things into the closest possible proximity, early-nineteenth-century writers and artists transformed the rational, classificatory catalogues of eighteenth-century science into dramatic, kaleidoscopic impressions of the antebellum street. New York's were thronged with "French and German dry goods jobbers, Bremen merchants, Jew financiers, southern, eastern, and western speculators and peculators, auctioneers, men of straw and men of substance; New York, New Orleans, Hamburg, Liverpool, San Francisco, Boston, and Cincinnati . . . huddled together in a six cent omnibus pélé-mélé with St. Louis, Lyons, Charleston, Manchester, and Savannah; all rushing to—Wall street, Broad street, Pearl street, Front street, South street." In New Orleans's market James Stuart discovered "Negroes, Mulattoes, French, Spaniards, Germans, and Americans, . . . all crying their several articles in their peculiar languages," where Benjamin Latrobe had marveled at "White Men and women, and of all hues of brown, and of all Classes of faces, from round Yankees, to grisly and lean

Spaniards, black Negroes and negresses[,] filthy Indians half naked, Mulattoes, curly and straight haired, Quateroons of all shades long haired and frizzled, the women dressed in the most flaring yellow, and scarlet gowns, the men capped and hatted."[3]

These lists testified to an insatiable need to *see* the city, to take in, record, and assign a meaning to every aspect of it. But they also intimate an equally insatiable need to *be seen*. In the antebellum street surging masses of all sorts of people grew increasingly, assertively visible. All, even those whose personal codes of behavior prescribed reticence, required an audience for their performances. The most explicitly articulated of these codes were espoused by respectable and would-be respectable middling- and upper-class people. Most of our evidence for seeing and being seen comes from their pens, crayons, and occasionally from their cameras. However, if we read their comments or view their images against the grain, it is possible to glimpse several other ways of seeing and being seen.

Self-defined respectable people measured one another according to a canon of behavior that recent historians have labeled gentility, refinement, or civility. First articulated in the late seventeenth century among the western European elite and introduced to North America by a segment of the colonial ruling classes soon afterward, genteel standards of behavior were adopted in the nineteenth century by a growing company of aspiring middle- (and some lower-) class people. Gentility was described, analyzed, promoted, and defended in countless nineteenth-century popular publications, ranging from etiquette books to newspapers, all aimed at up-and-coming urbanites. Defined by one contemporary as that "ease and freedom of manners which distinguish persons in the higher walks of fashionable life," gentility was a performance art choreographed according to exacting rules of self-presentation. It was at once a means of claiming social position and of lubricating social frictions among people.[4]

Gentility prescribed standards of conduct, association, and consumption. One had to act in the proper way, to associate with the proper people (and, more importantly, to avoid the wrong ones), and to equip oneself with the proper accouterments. Unlike, say, models of piety or intellect, which described intangible, inherent qualities and might even (as in the case of Protestant piety) deny the reliability of visual evidence, the code of gentility was necessarily a self-consciously acquired, readily perceptible trait. One could only assess gentility by the eye, the ear, and the nose. So when Elizabeth Drinker encountered an old friend, the lapsed Quaker Richard Nesbett, after an absence of some time, "his appearance flutter'd me a little, not having heard of the change, his hair powder'd, his language quite altred, to Mr., Madam &c. [from the Quaker practice of avoiding honorifics] rather janteé [genteel] in his manner: poor Man! . . . he is much altred in his word and action."[5]

Genteel self-presentation played a double role in the early-nineteenth-century city. In its original guise as a code of conduct among elites and aspiring elites in the mobile commercial world of the eighteenth century, it was a kind of fraternal handshake that allowed the refined to recognize social equals who were not personally known to them. In the new city, expanding beyond any possibility of comprehensive personal acquaintance even among the gentry of a single city, it served a similar end. But it also served a more private purpose, as a mode of self-definition for those adrift in the city's social ebb and flow, as well as for those seeking to reinvent themselves in a fluid society. To the extent that the genteel bodily ideal was internalized, it offered the possibility of a fundamental transformation of self. Although gentility existed only in visible performance, it was more than a mere show; it also had an inward-turning aspect. A mannered posture, a carefully cultivated tone of voice, fine clothes, expensive furniture, could be more than signs of identity: they might *become* identity. Act like a genteel person long enough and you were that person. Outward appearance became the self herself.[6]

As a public performance, gentility was founded on, and always referred to, the individual body. Civil people operated within a tight spatial envelope that governed behavior and movement and contained bodily processes and their by-products. No evidence of a person's presence beyond his or her conversation and carefully regulated appearance ought to escape into the social environment, much less impinge on others, nor should any be left behind. Neither should a self-respecting person tolerate any intrusion on her own boundaries.

The ideal early-republican genteel body was a discretely bounded form disciplined to remain within a narrow but impenetrable shell of personal space. Fashion plates from the second quarter of the nineteenth century were peopled by relatively thin, erect men and women (fig. 5.1). Both sexes have impossibly narrow waists and prominent hips. Even in the customary casual poses with legs abow—known in the visual arts as contrapposto—personal space remains closely confined to the envelope defined by the men's exaggeratedly large chests and the women's equally inflated hips.

Most cultures and most eras celebrate a handful of ideal bodily types that represent desirable human qualities. Yet bodies are relatively nondescript, highly varied entities. The eighteenth-century English author Charles Varlo remarked that the diversity of human temperament and human bodies was part of a divine plan to make people dependent on one another. If so, bodies must be altered—changed from objects to artifacts—to make them match the ideal.[7]

Costume, sometimes supplemented by dietary control, physical exercise,

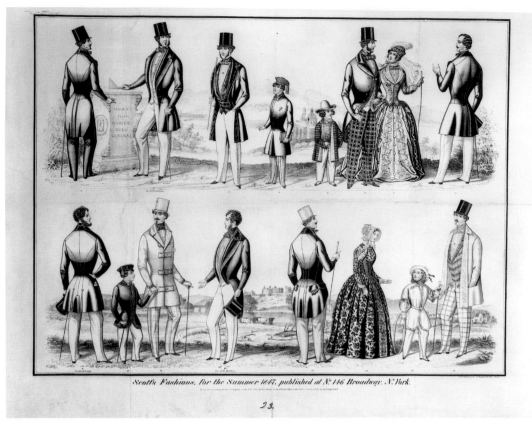

FIGURE 5.1. *Scott's Fashions, for the Summer 1847.* (Library of Congress, Prints and Photographs Division)

posture training, and even surgical reconstruction, is the most common means of making ordinary bodies approximate such ideal ones. In the genteel code it was carefully fitting clothes that emphasized the desirable aspects of the body and deemphasized the others. In both male and female costumes the tightly fitted upper portion contrasted with a more capacious lower body encompassed by women's dresses and the skirts of men's jackets. Both coyly emphasize the hips while modestly concealing them. The women's floral prints and (in other styles) ruffled sleeves or skirts added a softness appropriate to the sex, yet the overall impression in both men and women was of a body that could be contained only through concentrated self-discipline (fig. 5.2; see fig. 5.1).[8]

The confidence man Algernon Fitz-Cowles, a central character of George Lippard's mid-nineteenth-century Gothic novel *The Quaker City*, assembles (a parody of) just such a body using a costume chosen with the aid of his servant Endymion's discerning eye.

[T]he handsome colonel Fitz-Cowles, stood revealed in the light, his dark face looking somewhat worn and haggard, around the eyes, while his slen-

FIGURE 5.2. Edward W. Clay, *Philadelphia Fashions, 1837.* (The Library Company of Philadelphia)

der form, attired in the rainbow morning-gown and close fitting drawers, though well proportioned, and graceful in its outlines, by no means displayed that perfection of symmetry, which distinguished the person of the millionaire in broad daylight, along Chesnut street. For instance, the Colonel was thicker around the waist, thinner about the hips, smaller in the region of the calves, than was usual with him, when arrayed in full dress. His face was very pale and his cheeks lacked that deep vermillion tint, which gave such life to his dusky countenance at the evening party, or the afternoon parade. . . .

"Here—help me to dress Dim [Fitz-Cowles's Creole servant Endymion]. My corsets, Dim—"

"Here they are Massa—" cried Dim, throwing open, one of the drawers of the dressing bureau—"New pair Massa—"

"Lay that Morning gown on the chair. Now lace me. Tighter I say—that 'ill do. That's about the waist we want—is n't it Dim?"

"Yes Massa. Dat's de wasp [waist] *com*-plete!"

"Hips, Dim—"

"Which hip you want, Massa? Big hip or little hip?" cried Endymion, rummaging in the open drawer—"Dis pair do?"

"More subdued, Dim, more subdued. Just large enough to make my frock coat set out in the skirt. That's the idea—"

With a careful movement Endymion strapped certain detached portions of padding, around his master's form below the waist, and in a moment, this part of the ceremony was finished, giving quite a voluptuous swell to the outline of the Colonel's figure.

"Calves, Dim—"

"Which boots Massa wear to-day? Hab dis big calf or de toder one?"

"We want a good calf to-day, Dim. A large, fat calf. That pair will do. Tie it round the leg—there, there. Draw the stocking over it—gently—gent-ly! That's about the outline—eh?"[9]

The bounded body hinted at the possibility that it might escape the envelope and fly off in all directions. The point was conveyed in the popular images of those whose bodies *did* elude their control. One of the best known was the stock minstrel-show character Zip Coon, an urban black man dressed in fashionable costume whose body was so large and misshapen that he appeared to be bursting out of his clothes (fig. 5.3). Zip affected an awkward, knock-kneed pose, getting the elegant contrapposto of the fashion plates exactly backward. His arms stretched a prodigious distance from his body as he fumbled with his lorgnette, and his undisciplined, curly hair defiantly spilled out from under his hat. Zip

Coon was the best known of a wide-spread genre of white antebellum humor that ridiculed blacks' genteel self-presentation as inherently ridiculous.

Zip Coon was a dandy, and dandies of any race were popular targets. The dandy was a figure who distorted the conventions of gentility in an effort to be seen. Benjamin Henry Latrobe observed in New Orleans that "most rational men feel it to be of importance that their dress should not attract particular notice by its extravagance of fashionable cut, or by its defiance of all fashion. And yet there are others, I think they are called dandies . . . who subject themselves to pain and ridicule to attract notice in their dress." The dandified Philadelphian in 1819 wore "pads on his breast and shoulders, corsets around his waist, and

plaints on his hips, to say nothing of the precise rotundity of that part of his collar over-topping his cravat." This was exactly the figure that Fitz-Cowles assembled a decade and a half later. (*The Quaker City* was set in 1832.) As the finishing touch to his costume, Dim urges Fitz-Cowles to "Turn de collar down and tie up de scarf wid dis gole pin—dat's de ticket!" The corseted dandy was so tightly bounded that he lost the ease of movement that is part of gentility (fig. 5.4). His limbs, out of control, started off in every direction: he was at once too confined in his clothing and not confined enough in his behavior, for dandies rejected boundaries of all sorts, refusing to remain within their own or to respect others'. The dandy carried a lorgnette on a chain or ribbon around his neck, "which he whips from his bosom, and applies to his eye, as often as he is introduced to a stranger of either sex, and as often as he sees a female who has any pretension either to youth or beauty." The popular name "quizzing glass" emphasized the intrusive use to which dandies put lorgnettes: to make visual inspections they had no right to make.[10]

As these lampoons of faux gentility demonstrate, the spatialized body implied a particular relationship to urban space. The bounded, genteel body demanded a roomy cushion of social space around it. A Quaker family walking to meeting on a Philadelphia Sunday morning exemplifies this ideal urban

St JOHNS PARK.
Sept. 28. 1829.

Inconveniency of tight lacing.

oh! oh! ah! ah! I shall communicate
this to the morning Courier & N.Y. Enquirer.

FIGURE 5.4. Anthony Imbert, *Life in New York: Inconveniency of Tight Lacing. St. John's Park, Sept. 28, 1829.* St. John's Park was New York's most fashionable residential district in the beginning of the nineteenth century. (The Library Company of Philadelphia)

FIGURE 5.5. John Lewis Krimmel, *Sunday Morning in Front of the Arch Street Meeting House, Philadelphia,* late 1811–early 1813. (Metropolitan Museum of Art, New York, Rogers Fund, 1942 42.95.17)

proxemics (fig. 5.5). Closely ranked, their eyes downcast, their attention turned inward, they navigate the public space of the street as though there were no one else in the city. In effect, they walk the streets as though they are in private. The high wall around the Arch Street Meetinghouse, behind them, connects this social space with a parallel conception of the urban landscape as a series of discrete properties buffered by the neutral framework of the streets. It is no surprise, then, that antebellum urban views intended to present positive images invariably showed the streets and public places of even the largest cities as relatively empty, with people passing by alone or in pairs. William Birch's early view of High Street, Philadelphia's main thoroughfare, depicts a tranquil scene with widely spaced single and paired strollers going about their business apparently unaware of other pedestrians (fig. 5.6). Even a street vendor and a troop of horsemen seem subdued, and the city's busiest market house is confined to the distant background. The scene could not be more starkly different from Edward W. Clay's claustrophobic image of a smoky New York sidewalk (see fig. 12.1). They

FIGURE 5.6. William Birch, *High Street, from Ninth Street, Philadelphia*, 1799, looking east toward the High Street market houses in the distance. (The Library Company of Philadelphia)

are equally exaggerated utopian and dystopian views based on the same assumptions about the proper relationship of personal and urban space.

It is not surprising that particular modes of self-presentation should serve to distinguish urban groups. A more interesting question is, why these? Why the emphasis on the perimeters and extremities of the human body? Some of the answer lies in the deepest recesses of human psychology. Like other animals, we are territorial. Our daily round occupies a limited and predictable range, and we tend to maintain a relatively constant personal distance—"a small protective sphere or bubble"—between ourselves and others of our species. This territorial buffer serves not only to protect our bodies, as it does for other kinds of creatures, but is also an important stage in the process of self-definition. Our earliest glimmers of self-awareness come as we realize that we are bounded objects in a space that extends beyond us. By differentiating self and non-self in this elementary way, we gain a sense of agency, understanding that some but not all of what happens around us can be attributed to our own wills. Taken together, our bodies and their protective bubbles help to define our selves by giving us an idea of "self-coherence" as physical entities with the power to act and be acted upon, within limits.[11]

Yet these limits are remarkably fluid. The anthropologist Anthony Cohen makes a useful distinction between borders and boundaries. Borders are facts. The formal line dividing two nations is a border. Boundaries, on the other hand, are normally permeable and imprecise; they divide only to the extent that they are allowed to. National boundaries are continually crossed by people, languages, ideas, and goods. The body appears to be defined by a clear border, the enclosing envelope of skin. But the closer one looks, the more our borders appear to be boundaries, and very permeable ones at that. The environment penetrates the body as a person breathes, eats, and drinks. The skin itself is a boundary, constantly "exchanging matter with energy." The body in turn extends into space in the cloud of vapor every living animal gives off.[12]

Our "egocentric space" further blurs our borders and extends our boundaries. We tend to perceive anything that moves with our bodies—our tools and our clothes, for example—as part of ourselves, as our metaphorical speech shows. We say "she touched me" when we mean that she touched the sleeve of my coat or "he hit me" when we mean that his car ran into my car. Prosthetics such as canes or tools stretch us even farther into the environment, but they are still "me." Then our "sensorimotor space" and our "receptive field"—the areas within our immediate grasp and within reach of our perception, respectively—colonize an even larger territory beyond our bodies proper.[13]

Consequently, our extremities–the tops of our heads, our arms and legs, our shoulders, our hands and feet and whatever they contain—are critical points of intersection of our selves and our surroundings. Perceptual psychologists have observed that people judge whether they can pass through a door by the scale of their shoulders and register their (unconscious) conclusions by turning their shoulders to various degrees in passing through narrow openings. More abstractly, our bodies are invested with our intellectual, sensate, and emotional senses of ourselves as three-dimensional objects, and the ways we project ourselves can say much about our sense of presence to others.[14]

What it might say varies, for culture shapes and amends and gives significance to the raw psychology of agency and territory. It defines the practical limits of our territory and the social meanings of the personal colonization of space. A "big" perimeter, for example, might embody aggressive self-confidence or bald-faced pretense, a small one fear or quiet self-sufficiency. In the early republic, genteel codes fastened on compact, painstakingly learned postures as signs of agency, of *self* control. They idealized a body drawn in on itself and at rest, creating a distinctive and unambiguous iconography of self. In an urban setting where other sorts of visual cues were ambiguous and fluid, the genteel body's tight, predictable perimeters were easily identifiable to the eye. The care-

FIGURE 5.7. Jim Crow (University of Virginia Library)

fully limited, closely controlled territory repelled intrusions by sight or touch. It spoke of self-possession, of a clear sense of identity and a powerful agency.[15]

We can understand this if we look at the fictive opposite of the genteel white urban male: the untutored rural black man as stereotyped in "Jim Crow," Zip Coon's country cousin on the minstrel stage (fig. 5.7). In the many images of Jim Crow, his clothes are a ragged parody of genteel dress, his body is contorted rather than straight, parts of his costume fly off on their own, and his feet burst through the toes of his shoes. The song's refrain captures Jim's unconstrained locomotion:

> Weel about and turn about and do
>   jis so,
> Eb'ry time I weel about and jump
>   Jim Crow.

Promenade in Washington Square

FIGURE 5.8. Edward W. Clay, *Promenade in Washington Square*, Philadelphia,
ca. 1829. (The Library Company of Philadelphia)

Like black speech, the black locomotion parodied by Jim Crow suggested that
African Americans lacked the self-possessed agency idealized in the genteel
code. Any attempt to learn it resulted only in Zip Coon.[16]

Aside from their racial denigration, the Jim Crow images teach a broader lesson that is conveyed more gently in *Promenade in Washington Square,* which depicts a couple in Philadelphia's favorite genteel promenading spot (fig. 5.8). The
man's shoulders are enormous, his chest puny, his hat towers over him, and his
neck assumes giraffe-like proportions. His companion's shoulders are equally
outsized, her hat is as tall as his and as wide as her shoulders, and it is trimmed
with a flamboyant pennant of crepe and bows. That is, their clothes expand
their egocentric spaces at all the sites that present-day psychologists identify as critical to body image. The couple transgress other boundaries as well,
for the woman carries a conspicuous purse, a sign in the nineteenth century

that one was well-heeled but a vulgar boast in the eyes of the genteel, who believed money should be possessed and used in abundance but never explicitly acknowledged.[17]

Another lithograph, *Two of the Killers,* illustrates both the power and the limits of genteel readings of the body (fig. 5.9). As depicted in this lithograph, the Killers, a Philadelphia street gang, clearly violate all the canons of gentility. Their clothes are made of fabrics in contrasting patterns (and presumably colors), violating ideals of fitting in, of occupying one's niche just so, of being restrained but not inconspicuous, of manifesting a self-respect that stopped short of self-promotion. Rather than standing erect in a small envelope of space, each man leans against the street furniture, arms akimbo, hat and cigar at a jaunty angle. They exhale clouds of cigar smoke. They take up too much space. But rather than seeming clueless and awkward, as Jim Crow does, or parvenu and self-promoting, as the couple promenading in Washington Square do, they are self-possessed and indifferent: they own the street and they know it.

While some urbanites may have been ignorant of or uncaring about the rules of refinement, many others evaded, improvised upon, and even parodied them. In other words, genteel representations of the ungenteel—the only evidence we have—might be read as descriptions of alternate modes of dress and self-presentation that, like the genteel ones, were performances to be witnessed. These alternate modes sometimes escaped gentry notice, at other times left them puzzled, and at certain moments deeply disturbed them. Given the resources available in the market society of the early nineteenth century, one cannot expect these forms of self-presentation to hearken back to primal cultural or ethnic roots—to be completely different from those of genteel urbanites. Rather, they played off the same raw materials of costume and posture, psychological structures, and cultural expectations that the genteel did.[18] They exemplified counter-gentility rather than its absence, but the similarities of reference laid them open to the misreadings and ridicule that we have been examining.

For example, while gentility encouraged circumspection on the street and an avoidance of (obvious) attention-getting, the increasing numbers of lower-class native-born and immigrant urbanites who thronged the streets invited scrutiny (see figs. 5.2, 5.8). Whereas gentility stressed "taste" rather than "fashion," these urbanites luxuriated in fashion. As Valeria, a pseudonymous correspondent to the conservative magazine *Port Folio,* argued, "We have freedom of the press, and freedom of religion, and why should we not enjoy a freedom of fashions?" Fashion was an expression of republican liberty, and lower-class urbanites' adopted dress emphasized a glittering surface and perimeters that claimed as much street space as possible.[19]

FIGURE 5.9. *Two of the Killers*, ca. 1848. (The Library Company of Philadelphia)

This assertiveness took varied forms that shared similar strategies of visibility. In New York in the 1840s and 1850s the semi-legendary street gang the Bowery Boys were apotheosized as the types of "the Democracy"—native-born, worldly, lower-class urbanites determined to have their say in the degentrified politics and civic life of post-Jacksonian America (fig. 5.10). Far from confining himself to a spatial bubble, the "b'hoy," as he was known in the popular press, strode the Bowery arm in arm with his "g'hal," his "black silk hat, smoothly brushed, sitting precisely upon the top of the head, hair well oiled, and lying closely to the skin, long in front, short behind, cravat a-la-sailor, with the shirt collar turned over it, vest of fancy silk, large flowers, black frock coat, no jewelry, except in a few instances, where the insignia of the [fire] engine company to which the wearer belongs, as a breastpin, black pants, one or two years behind the fashion, heavy boots, and a cigar about half smoked, in the left corner of the mouth, as near perpendicular as it is possible to be got."[20]

Both free and enslaved African Americans used some of the same techniques to attract attention, and sometimes they shared the b'hoys' and g'hals' defiant command of the street, even

A "BOWERY BOY" SKETCHED FROM LIFE.

FIGURE 5.10. *A Bowery Boy,* New York, 1857. (Courtesy, American Antiquarian Society)

when it was dangerous to do so. For example, while gentility stressed constricted boundaries, eighteenth-century black men often styled their hair in ways that emphasized height and bulk. At other times, they combined African practices such as head shaving with queues and bunchings that alluded to the wigs that were fashionable among whites. In the nineteenth century, with the advent of shorter hairstyles among both whites and blacks, strikingly colored and shaped clothes gained favor among both free and enslaved African Americans. Since slaves often wore their best clothes to market, it is no surprise that the market folks in New Orleans's market appeared to dress "in the brightest hues imaginable." Women chose brightly colored cloth for the legally required tignons, made them appear larger with great combs ("African taste and Parisian as well," as one white New Orleanian recognized), and completed their costumes with large hoop earrings and rabbit-skin shawls. Dressed in this striking manner, the free and enslaved black women who worked in the market sat at their stalls bantering loudly with each other and with prospective customers.[21]

William Grimes, a coachman in Savannah during his years of enslavement, related that, dressed in the fine costume that was a perquisite of his office, he often strolled the city's streets at night. "I would walk as bold as I knew how, and as much like a gentleman." Denmark Vesey, a self-freed black man who was executed for organizing a slave conspiracy in Charleston, was said by his prosecutors to have dressed in a striking manner in public, rather than inconspicuously as blacks were expected to do, and to have looked directly into the eyes of whites rather than diverting his gaze in the customary fashion. Felicité Fouché, a black New Orleans woman, took the same approach. Passing down St. Louis Street one day, she encountered the attorney Etienne Mazureau and his wife, who "believ[ed] that the said Woman of Colour as soon as she would know them would as it was her duty to do, take the other side of the banquette & yield to them, instead of disputing them the said banquette & compell them to keep aside themselves." But Fouché did just that, announcing "in the french language the following expressions to Wit . . . 'I never yield to any body. the Street is for every body. [Y]ou might have passed some where else by deviating a little.'"[22]

In this light, the black dandies who excited so much contempt among white commentators in northern cities appear even more strikingly as conscious transgressors of the genteel manner. A fictional Philadelphian in Francis J. Grund's *Aristocracy in America* complains that a black man "actually eyed my sister through a quizzing-glass as she was walking in Chestnut-street." The man in *Philadelphia Fashions, 1837* was equally bold, fearlessly staring back at the white man who looked him over (see fig. 5.2). Rather than being reticent, these people were expansive. Rather than respecting boundaries, they challenged them.[23]

American Indians were regular visitors and occasional residents in most cities and were particularly numerous in the lower Mississippi Valley. They traveled the streets and sat in the markets of New Orleans selling roots, herbs, game, produce, prepared foods, and souvenirs such as baskets and miniature bows and arrows. On market days, the levee next to the market was the site of fast-paced, violent ball games called *toli* or *raquette,* a pre-contact Indian sport played by most indigenous southeastern groups and attracting large audiences and multiracial participants.[24]

Nineteenth-century Indians in the New Orleans region adopted a carefully composed, conspicuous self-presentation. Men typically had long hair bound in two braids, while the women's hair, rather than flowing free, was usually tied at the back, their extremities ornamented with brass anklets and bracelets. Both sexes painted their faces and occasionally tattooed or scarred their cheeks, shoulders, and limbs. Indians of the region wrapped themselves in blankets. Men draped them over their shoulders and wrapped a piece of coarse stuff (a type of fabric) around their upper legs. Women made a kind of knee-length skirt of their blankets. Leggings, shell-covered belts, flamboyant feathers, and face paint added to their striking appearance. Bright colors—blue, red, yellow, and green—were favorite facial colors. Scarlet leggings, "brilliant ribbons," and other equally bright clothing complemented faces and jewelry (plate 6).[25]

Indians' costumes marked them as participants in the growing economy of the Euro-American world. Indeed, they were exacting consumers who knew precisely what they wanted. Amos Stoddard, reporting on Louisiana early in the American regime, cautioned that the "Indians are much more particular in the color and quality of their goods than is generally suspected." Each nation had its own taste in trade goods that was recognizable to others. Indian adherence to their own notions of fashion, Stoddard believed, would lead them to freeze in the winter "rather than cover their bodies with a blanket too large or too small, or which is deficient in a border, or has one too many, or the color of which is not suited to their taste." Native people of the region preferred British to American manufactured goods, and they demanded "several different articles at the same time, so as to complete what may be called a suit," or they would refuse to purchase any. Indians' mannered appearance was designed to be conspicuous and attention-getting, but in romanticized descriptions and visual images, native dress conveyed no logic and appeared to signify nothing but savagery. Indians were shown wearing simple and unornamented clothing that shrouded their bodies without offering a clue to their shape or contributing to the effects of posture (fig. 5.11). Their hair was similarly unfettered and unshaped.[26]

It begins to be apparent why nineteenth-century observers found street life so engrossing, but also why the human lists were often tinged with ambivalence as much as celebration. Those who watched the growing, increasingly disparate crowds on antebellum streets wanted to know who they were. Where did they fit into one's own social universe, economic world, or polity? So in addition to reveling in variety, listers sought to fit people into manageable categories. The art historian Elizabeth Johns has called this practice *typing*, a process that tamed the complexity of the antebellum city by assigning its denizens a limited number of generic characters. If it was hazardous to be exposed to certain

FIGURE 5.11. Native American vendors, New Orleans. (Courtesy Historic New Orleans Collection, Museum/Research Center, acc. no. 1974.25.20.53)

smells or certain sounds, it was equally so not to be able to see what one needed to see or to believe what one did see. The legibility of people and spaces became conflated in popular culture, as urbanites found increasing numbers of both puzzlingly, and sometimes ominously, obscure.[27]

As he did so often, Edgar Allan Poe placed his finger on this anxiety in "The Man of the Crowd" (1840). Sitting with cigar and newspaper, looking through a plate-glass window at the passing crowd on a London street (mirroring the window-shopper's activity), Poe's narrator seeks to make sense of what he sees. At first, "my observations took an abstract and generalizing tone" as he classified—typed—the passersby according to their "aggregate relations." Then the narrator becomes absorbed by the details of "figure, dress, air, gait, visage, and expression of countenance." The crowd includes "noblemen, merchants, tradesmen, stock-jobbers"—or rather, it includes people who are "undoubtedly" members of that class. Intrigued, he chooses one old man and follows him all evening and through the night until he seems to flag, only to be revived by throngs who emerge in the morning. The narrator realizes that his prey is a "man of the crowd . . . the type and genius of deep crime. He refuses to be alone." Having no individuality or even existence except as part of a mass, he is a book that "does not permit itself to be read."[28]

Herman Melville's confidence man is the era's best-known fictional man of the crowd, a figure of contingent, unstable identity who was dangerous to anyone he encountered. But early-nineteenth-century popular literature and the popular arts were full of similar figures who pretended to be what they were not. They ranged from minstrels, whites who purported to enact the culture of plantation slaves for urban audiences, to the dandies, poseurs, sorcerers, unknown strangers, and impostors who strode the city streets of novels, plays, and popular prints.[29]

Even more than the fear of crime, middling and elite urbanites' fascination with urban variety revealed even deeper anxieties about the dissolving boundaries between selfhood and personhood. At a time when notions of inherent social hierarchies were eroding, how was one to be sure even of glimpsing, much less of being able to evaluate, a stranger? Behind the question Who are you? lay the question Who am I?

Two widely held assumptions exacerbated these doubts. First, nineteenth-century theories of identity posited a Cartesian separation between the true self and its fleshly vehicle. The body was often at odds with the higher aspirations of the self. Its unruly, even forbidden, impulses and passions had to be disciplined for the good of the inner being. But the body was also the medium of social interaction, the vehicle of personhood. As the English visitor Edward Abdy observed, "Where no distinction is attached to rank or birth, it is natural that other 'outward and visible signs' should supply their place and be proportionably valued." Those outward signs, he said, were money and dress. Using such criteria, another Briton, James Flint, decided that "on Sundays it would be difficult to discriminate betwixt the hired girl and the daughter in a genteel family, were drapery the sole criterion." He read this as evidence of the "general diffusion of comfort and competence," one of the "symptoms of republican equality" in Philadelphia. Others attributed the same pattern to pretense and deception. Abdy told of a family living in a garret, forced to borrow money even for tea, "while the daughters were vying in the Broadway with the wives of wealthy merchants, and 'fishing' for admiration with silk and ribbons, and all the arts of the toilette."[30]

This family, like the couple in *Philadelphia Fashions, 1837* or like Algernon Fitz-Cowles in *The Quaker City,* took advantage of the visual nature of gentility. The mannered ease of refinement was the product of an arduous learning process, but it *was* a learning process. Furthermore, gentility implied a materialist notion of the role of possessions in shaping and expressing identity: you were what you wore, rode in, sat on, lived in. Genteel possessions were essential to the performance of gentility, and they also acted as instructors in refinement. Such goods were available to anyone with the money to purchase them. Clark's Broadway Tailoring in New York advertised men's clothing "made to fit and decorate the body, and impart ease and elegance to the figure," virtually a definition of gentility. "THOSE WHO HAVE NO TASTE" need not worry: the establishment offered "quick and ready directions in the gentlemanly assistants of Mr. Clark."[31]

However, the code of gentility also professed an ideal of transparency or truth and a concomitant abhorrence of "pretending" or "pretense": one ought to be what one *appeared* to be. Contemporary assessments of gentility tended to turn on the authenticity with which a person inhabited his material world. A cartoon such as *Philadelphia Fashions, 1837* assured its intended audience that the true person would be visible through any disguise, however skillful (see fig. 5.2). But the assumption that authenticity of some sort underpinned gentility or that the visible manifestation of gentility revealed a worthy inner being is incompatible with the notion that gentility can be bought or learned. That both views were held at once emphasizes the extent to which gentility's appeal to aspirants lay as much in a quest for self-definition as for social advancement. But it also highlighted the ambiguity of the genteel code and its limited usefulness on the streets of the antebellum city.

As we have seen, the genteel ideal of transparent, authentic self-presentation had a spatial dimension. The genteel street was sorted and easily legible to passersby. Gentility's nightmares of deception and obscurity also had a spatial dimension, which was mapped and exploited by popular writers and artists who made explicit what had been implicit since Elizabeth Drinker's days: the night—the invisible—epitomized all that was uncontrollable and unknowable in the city. Writers and artists conjured a second, sinister city that had infiltrated the shadowy recesses of urban life. The shadow landscape flourished during the night, when its inhabitants colonized such familiar spaces as the marketplace. During the day it receded into the alley dwellings, taverns, oyster cellars, brothels, and docks, territories over, under, behind, and at the edges of the everyday city, places that were unfamiliar to respectable society. These spaces were not simply neglected urban fringes and backsides, but they formed an aggressive, morally and medically subversive landscape inhabited by shadowy figures determined to victimize the unwary. By the late 1840s sensationalist journalists had seized on the association of darkness and invisibility with disorder and danger. The physical metaphors of light and dark were too obvious and too easy to be passed over by publishers and authors eager to exploit the increasing social and spatial divisions of the commercial city. Books such as *New York by Gas-Light* and *Sunshine and Shadow in New York* manipulated the fantasies of bourgeois Americans, acting as tour guides to the exotic nocturnal landscape of the poor and the dissolute. These books would not have been credible before the social and functional sorting of growing cities rendered more and more places and people unfamiliar to the middle-class public.[32]

George Lippard skillfully conflated invisible spaces and illegible people in narratives that mixed dramatic current events with scenes drawn from his own charged imagination. His works evoked an evil shadow landscape that permeated respectable society but that was unbound and unbounded by the landmarks and spatial organization of everyday life. In his best-known novel, *The Quaker City,* much of the action takes place in Monk-hall, a den of criminals and a clubhouse for the debauched business, social, and religious leaders of Philadelphia. Monk-hall is an eighteenth-century country mansion now engulfed by urbanization but closed off to the outside world, its windows blocked, its entrances guarded. Its three visible stories are mirrored by three subterranean levels, including a vandalized crypt in which the book's most dastardly deeds transpire. Monk-hall's former gardens and grounds have been filled with modern houses and commercial buildings, but tunnels lead to former outbuildings scattered among the modern buildings. To Lippard the shadow landscape and the honest landscape were inseparable: corruption was the hidden face of respectability.[33]

The Quaker City is full of confidence men and women, people who for bad *or* good reasons shift from one identity to another. Nearly every major character has more than one. The confidence man and forger Algernon Fitz-Cowles

" **A cry at once arose that a white man was shot,** and the attention of the mob was directed to the California House, at the corner of Sixth and St. Mary street."—page 30

FIGURE 5.12. The Killers' attack on the California House, Oct. 9, 1849.
(The Library Company of Philadelphia)

manipulates his identity to gull his marks but is ultimately revealed to be Juan Larode, the illegitimate son of a "*Personage* [who] was either a Canadian Statesman, or a British Lord, or a *Mexican Prince!*" Long-Haired Bess, one of the criminal gang, was originally the innocent Emily Walraven, while Gustavus Lorrimer, the seducer whose boasts to a drinking party set the plot in motion, presents himself to his victim under the softer name of Lorraine Lorrimer. Luke Harvey, the morally ambiguous hero, operates undercover as Brick-Top to foil the tangled criminal conspiracies that form the plot. Harvey's assistant, the buffoonish policeman Easy Larkspur, ingratiates himself with Fitz-Cowles disguised as the braggart southern planter Rappahannock Mulhill.[34]

The Quaker City's shadow landscape was largely an imaginary one, but five years after that novel's publication Lippard mapped the shadow landscape onto the existing city in accounts based on a real-life election-night riot. On October 9, 1849, the Killers attacked a black-owned bar in St. Mary's Street, a small alley lying near South Street and the Philadelphia-Moyamensing line that was occupied mostly by African Americans (fig. 5.12). They set fire to the bar and prevented firemen from extinguishing the blaze. The incident so intrigued Lippard that he published three different versions of the story under three different titles.[35]

In Lippard's highly fictionalized accounts, the story centers around the Killers' leader, variously named Charles Anderson Chester or Cromwell D. Z. Hicks. The spoiled son of a prominent but unscrupulous Philadelphia merchant, Chester/Hicks steals from his father and absconds to Cuba. After his return he passes a bad check in his father's counting house then disappears into the shadows of Moyamensing. Meanwhile, the elder man plots to abduct and rape Ophelia Thompson, a poor but virtuous young actress, with the help of the barkeeper Black Herkles. As it happens, Herkles's alley tavern is the Killers' haunt, and a disguised son overhears his father's plan. He determines to thwart it, from spite more than from benevolence. In the ensuing fracas, both men die, Ophelia is rescued, and the tavern burns to the ground.

All of the action in *The Killers* unfolds above, below, and out of sight of decent people. To drive the point home, Lippard included maps in both *The Life and Adventures of Charles Anderson Chester* and *The Killers* (fig. 5.13). Ophelia lives in Runnell's Court, "one of those blots upon the Civilization of the Nineteenth Century, which exist in the city and districts of Philadelphia, under the name of Courts. It extended between two narrow streets, and was composed of six three story brick houses built upon an area of ground scarcely sufficient for the foundation of one comfortable dwelling. Each of these houses comprised three rooms and a cellar." (In other words, it was what is now called a "trinity" house [see fig. 1.3].) In Lippard's story, as so often in real life, the three rooms and the cellar of the house were each rented separately. "Whites and blacks, old and young, rumsellers and their customers, were packed together there, amid noxious smells, rags and filth, as thick and foul as insects in a decaying carcase." The Killers, on the other hand, live in a boarded-up, unfinished house—"(unfinished on account of the numerous riots which have so long kept the District of Moyamensing in a panic)"—which they enter through the cellar. Their smoke-blackened "den" is adorned with signs reading "THE KILLERS FOR EVER!," "GO IT KILLERS!," and "DOWN WITH THE BOUNCERS [a rival gang]!" Herkles's bar is a "low and narrow room, filled with stench and smoke, with negroes, men, women and children huddled together in one corner." The father operates from a counting room "hidden away at the far end of a large gloomy" warehouse and has a room in an "odd out-of-the-way corner" of his house for his "most secret thoughts." He attacks his victim in Black Herkles's tavern and plans to carry her off to an isolated house on the banks of the Schuylkill River.[36]

Like fire alarms in the night, the Killers signified the dangers that surrounded law-abiding citizens but were invisible to them. The point was made most explicitly in Lippard's best passage. A shapeless heap on the barroom floor rises

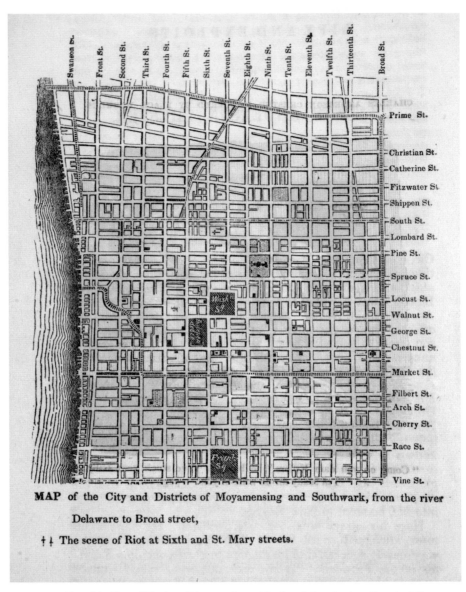

FIGURE 5.13. *Map of the City and Districts of Moyamensing and Southwark, from the river,* 1849, depicting events in Lippard's *The Killers.* South is at the top. (The Library Company of Philadelphia)

and assumes the form of the sinister Dick Hellfire, chief of the Killers, unrecognizable even to the elder Chester as his son. Later, Hellfire

> passed from the Court into the street, where a couple of ruffian-like men stood beneath the light of the street lamp. As he approached them, he made a sign with his right hand, and the two ruffians followed him like dogs obeying the whistle of a master. Along the dark and deserted street the loafer [Hellfire/Chester] pursued his way, until he came to the corner of a well known street leading from the Delaware to the Schuylkill; a street which, by the bye, was lighted at every five yards by a groggery or a beer-shop. At the corner and near the door of every groggery stood groups of men or half-grown boys—sometimes two and sometimes three or four in a group. The loafer passed them all, repeated the sign which he had given to the first two ruffians. At the sign the men and half-grown boys fell quietly into his wake; by the time he had gone half a square he was followed by at least twenty persons; who tracked his footsteps without a word.

This spectral society was everywhere and nowhere at once. The Killers could materialize like ghosts or demons.[37]

The villains and even some of the wilier protagonists in all of Lippard's works share Dick Hellfire's power to become shapeless and therefore completely invisible until it is too late. The arch-villain of *The Quaker City*, Devil-Bug, uses this ruse repeatedly: "The gal's [*sic*] will come trampin' down the alley for dear life—they'll see a black lump on the ground—they'll rush on thinkin' it a stone, but that black lump will rise on its feet and it will stretch out its arms and grasp 'em." In a similar manner Brick-Top is unrecognizable as Luke Harvey because his red wig hangs down over his eyes and a bushy red beard covers the lower portion of his face, while his clothes have no shape at all: they are "not ragged clothes, nor damaged clothes, nor shabby genteel clothes; but absolute and unconditional rags."[38]

Here Lippard manipulated the central psychological element on which both gentility and countergentility turned. Shapelessness rendered Dick Hellfire and Devil-Bug invisible and an indistinct form also made Luke Harvey invisible as Brick-Top because a clearly defined shape was essential to conveying one's identity in public. Lippard's insistence that Brick-Top was dressed in rags, pure and simple, rather than ragged or shabby genteel clothing meant that his costume defined no recognizable body.

The relics of civilized life that bombarded the senses, and the mixed throngs that crowded the streets of antebellum cities, were the crucible within which city dwellers formed a sense of what it meant to be a citizen of a republican city. The tension between the two—between too much information, too much sensation, and too little—informed the processes of self-formation and city building in the first half of the nineteenth century. Self-construction and self-presentation depend on context. Our perception guides us in forming a sense of agency, of that corner of the material world that we can call a self, while human interaction—"intersubjectivity" in the psychologists' jargon—contributes to agency or selfhood and also to defining our personhood, or social existence. We learn to be ourselves in the context of others. We learn from observing others and from their instruction. As we begin to learn that other people are different selves, with minds, feelings, and intentions different from our own, we begin to project ourselves into others' places, to try to see the world through others' eyes. To the extent that we experience what others experience and understand that we do, we develop a sense of ourselves as part of a human community. To do so, however, requires a fundamental respect for others as subjects of their own experiences that can never be fully known, rather than simply as objects of ours. It is significant, then, that for many urbanites the kaleidoscopic sight of people, things, and spaces in early-nineteenth-century American cities—the forms too many to encompass except in lists—appeared amorphous, as a shadow landscape inhabited by inscrutable people. Viewed in this light, gentility assumes a harder edge, one that has at least as much to do with exclusion as with recognizing eligible social partners. Equally important, the loud, stinking, filthy, crowded, disorganized early-nineteenth-century American city set the conditions within which some Americans sought to imagine new ways of urban living and working, with the assistance of political and cultural ideas inherited from the revolutionary generation. That is the subject of the following chapters.[39]

PART TWO

Metropolitan Improvements

{

CHAPTER 6

THE GRID AND THE REPUBLICAN SPATIAL IMAGINATION

In 1789, after a conservative counterrevolution reversed many of the democratic reforms of the revolutionary years, the Pennsylvania legislature restored Philadelphia's charter, which had been revoked under the 1776 state constitution. The "Act to incorporate the city of Philadelphia" defined the city corporation's task in republican terms: it was to be dedicated "to the advancement of public health and order; and to the promotion of trade, industry, and happiness." In honor of Philadelphia's revived government, the new council redesigned the city seal (fig. 6.1). In the new version, two female figures supported a central shield. The left-hand figure was meant to represent "the City of Philadelphia wearing an olive Crown, and bearing in her right hand an unfolded Scroll, displaying the Ground plot of the City, between the Rivers Delaware and Schuylkill." After discussion, the Common Council accepted the design, "except, that instead of an Olive Crown on the head of the Dexter Figure, a wreath of Flowers was substituted." They paid Robert Scot £8.12.6 to engrave the new emblem.[1]

Just as their new charter represented a slightly remodeled version of a prerevolutionary institution, so the councilors drew on familiar symbols for their new coat of arms. Most of its elements were borrowed from the city's colonial-era seals. The inclusion of the city's gridded plan, however, was strikingly novel. Following a century of indifference, elite Philadelphians began to celebrate William Penn's and Thomas Holme's now-famous plan of Philadelphia and to call for the restoration of its neglected elements. From the time of the

FIGURE 6.1. Pre- and post-1789 seals of Philadelphia. (The Library Company of Philadelphia)

new charter until the Civil War, and particularly in the decades before 1830, the "ground plan of the said city as laid out by the worthy founder and proprietor thereof" was a rallying cry for urban reformers. Their new appreciation had a forward- and a backward-looking aspect. For the city councilors of 1789, it stood as a reminder of a mythical past of consensus and civic harmony and as a beacon of disinterested virtue in a city that had just turned back "mob" rule. The moral force of Penn's plan was augmented by the rediscovery in 1827 of the "Instructions" that Penn had sent to the first colonists in 1681—the now-famous description of the "greene Country Towne, wch will never be burnt, and allways be wholsome"—in the Hamilton family papers.[2]

Nostalgia alone cannot account for the movement to restore the city's grid. For a brief period, Philadelphia's plan offered hope of a rational reconstruction of urban life similar to the republican reconstruction of national government and to the ongoing Enlightenment reconstruction of human knowledge. Many Philadelphians had been actively involved in both projects, and they hoped to achieve similar success in reforming their city. Eventually, though, the plan's reputation faded once again. In 1874 the Penn-Holme map (which represented only a portion of the late-nineteenth-century city) was replaced by an anchor on the left figure's scroll. In the early nineteenth century, though, it spurred the imagination as it never had in Penn's own day.

Penn and Holme's *Portraiture of the City of Philadelphia in the Province of Pennsylvania* of 1683 (which was never the definitive plan of the new city) depicted a gridded town structured around two major, intersecting streets and anchored by five open squares, one in the center surrounded by a constellation of four others (fig. 6.2). It promised port facilities on both the Delaware and the Schuylkill rivers and showed the location of available lots. But Philadelphia never grew in the way Penn hoped, and the distinctive qualities of Holme's plan were forgotten.[3]

By the third quarter of the eighteenth century, when Philadelphia was British North America's largest city, urbanization extended west on High Street to Eighth Street and stretched along the Delaware River the entire length of the municipality and into the liberty lands to the north and south (see plate 1). The densely built-up area was even smaller. A continuous line of building ran along both sides of Front and Water streets from Pine to Race streets. The squares (as both Philadelphians and New Orleanians still call the rectilinear tract that most other Americans call "blocks") between Walnut and Race streets and Front and Third streets were completely built up, and those on either side of High Street from Third to Fourth streets were nearly so. In other words, after nearly a century of building, 10 squares out of the 176 delineated in Holme's map had

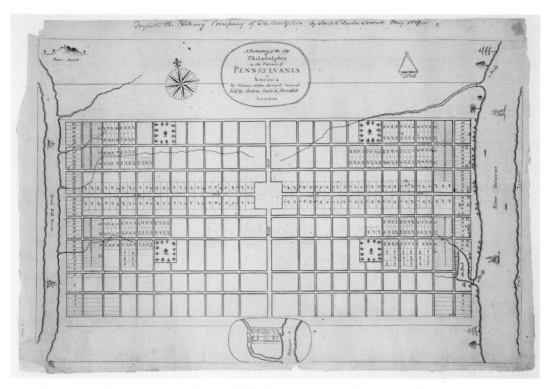

FIGURE 6.2. Thomas Holme, *A Portraiture of the City of Philadelphia in the Province of Pennsylvania*, 1683. A facsimile published in 1812 reflects the renewed interest in the Penn-Holme plan. (The Library Company of Philadelphia)

been fully developed in the largest and most prosperous city in English North America.

Within this urbanized sector the plan had been altered. Philadelphia sat on a plateau above the Delaware River. There was a two-story drop from the lots on Front Street to the river's edge. By 1705, King (Water) Street had been inserted at the foot of the bank, and houses and warehouses were built to exploit the difference between the two levels, standing two or three stories high on Front Street and four or five stories on Water Street, with entrances from both levels (fig. 6.3). By the early eighteenth century, as well, private wharves extended into the river, despite Penn's insistence that the waterfront be common land for the use of all Philadelphians.[4]

Equally striking were the secondary streets, alleys, and courts that penetrated the interiors of the larger squares, as property owners subdivided their lots (fig. 6.4). Although these interpolations are often described by urban historians as unfortunate perversions of Penn's green country town, they were part of the process of "building here after Streets" on individual holdings that Penn anticipated. In the days of the walking city they were essential to the creation of a vital urban landscape.[5]

FIGURE 6.3. John Moran, 114–16 North Water Street, Philadelphia, 1868.
(The Library Company of Philadelphia)

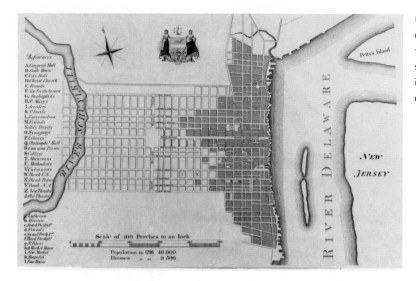

FIGURE 6.4. *Stephens Plan of the City of Philadelphia*, 1807. Of the five original squares, only Center Square is shown. (Historical Society of Pennsylvania)

The five open squares never amounted to much in the eighteenth century. Center Square was so far out of town that it had little potential urban use until the nineteenth century. Of the four satellite squares, two lay even farther west of urbanization, their sites occupied by brickyards and farmers' fields. Property owners on the two easternmost squares complained that although they had "paid more for their grounds in expectation of the original design being executed," those squares had also been relegated to marginal uses. The Proprietary (the title adopted by the Penn family) had leased part of the northeast (now Franklin) square to the German Calvinists for a graveyard in 1741. A powder house also stood there. By the end of the eighteenth century, it had become a pit of "stagnant waters, of dung, human excrement and . . . of filth." It was not set off from the grid as the Penn-Holme plan indicated; instead, Seventh Street passed straight through it. The southeast (now Washington) square was rough, sloping ground slashed by a gully. It was enclosed by a post-and-rail fence, a rural type of fence commonly used for gardens, paddocks, orchards, and other working spaces near houses, but never for formal settings. A post-and-rail fence was appropriate for this square, which served as a pasture, private burying ground, and potter's field. Soldiers were interred there during the Revolution, as were yellow-fever victims in 1793, the latter dumped into a common grave kept open until the epidemic subsided. There were also some squatters' houses on one corner. On the south the square abutted the Holy Trinity Roman Catholic graveyard, and it faced the Walnut Street Jail on the east. Most strikingly, this southeastern square, then lying at the edge of urbanization, was used on Sundays as a dancing ground and gathering place for black people, in a manner similar to the more famous Congo Square in New Orleans. The four subsidiary squares were of such little consequence that eighteenth- and early-nineteenth-century mapmakers sometimes omitted them (see fig. 6.4).[6]

Although the profession of city-planning was not formally organized in the United States until the early twentieth century, one must look to the very beginnings of the republic, to the revival and rehabilitation of the urban grid in cities such as Philadelphia and New York for its beginnings, if one defines city planning as the establishment of a formal physical order intended to integrate social, economic, and aesthetic goals. Orthogonal (gridded) planning acquired a new life in the early republic as a model for new towns and as a tool for extending old ones both in ad hoc forms and in grand, all-encompassing schemes. As the British traveler Francis Baily observed, the grid was a "plan of which the Americans are very fond, and I think with reason, as it is by far the best way of laying out a city. All the modern-built towns in America are on this principle."[7]

The story of New York's renowned (or notorious) Commissioners' Plan of 1811, the last of a series of gridded additions to the colonial city, illustrates the renewed devotion to orthogonal planning. When the city sold off five-acre portions of its commons in the 1780s and larger parts in the 1790s, City Surveyor Casimir Goerck prepared gridded plans of the tracts. Private developers laid out orthogonal subdivisions on the outskirts of town, as well (see fig. 1). Faced with this welter of small additions, the Common Council ordered its street commissioner in 1804 to prepare a "plan on paper for new streets hereafter to be laid out and opened." When this project was thwarted by landowner opposition, the council submitted a bill to the state legislature in 1807 calling for state-appointed commissioners to produce a comprehensive map of the city. The resulting plan, which subsumed and in some cases overrode private developers' grids, projected the city's urban development 155 blocks north of Goerck's additions.[8]

The "grand manner" of baroque planning, which emphasized major urban landmarks sited on squares and circles that were linked by diagonal avenues cutting across a city's fabric, offered New York's planners the principal alternative to gridded planning. Late-seventeenth-century Annapolis was a small-scale grand-manner plan, but the first large-scale example was Pierre Charles L'Enfant's plan for the new national capital at Washington. L'Enfant's baroque scheme was chosen despite Thomas Jefferson's preference for a simple grid "as in Philadelphia," and it proved to be a seductive precedent for town builders in the new nation. Diagonal streets and squares appeared in such early-national-period plans as those for Detroit, Indianapolis, Baton Rouge, and the idiosyncratic Jeffersonville, Indiana. Even Philadelphians flirted with the idea. An 1802 map by Peter Charles Varlé projected an extension of the city across the

Schuylkill in which a succession of two squares and a circle, the first a market square built above the river, lay on the Market Street axis. Four diagonal streets (some following preexisting roads) radiated out from the central, or Washington, square, two of them intersecting subsidiary squares that echoed the four squares of the Penn-Holme plan.[9]

The New York Commissioners considered but rejected diagonal avenues, believing that a grid was superior for those purposes for which L'Enfant chose baroque planning. As the commissioners noted in their report,

> one of the first objects which claimed their attention, was . . . whether they should confine themselves to rectilinear and rectangular streets, or whether they should adopt some of those supposed improvements, by circles, ovals, and stars, which certainly embellish a plan, whatever might be their effects as to convenience and utility. In considering that subject, they could not but bear in mind that a city is to be composed principally of the habitations of men, and that strait sided, and right angled houses are the most cheap to build, and the most convenient to live in.

The commissioners went on to note that "the price of Land is so uncommonly great [that] it seemed proper to admit the principles of Economy to greater influence than might under circumstances of a different kind have consisted with the dictates of Prudence and the sense of Duty." A grid would make the city's "situation in Regard of Health and Pleasure as well as . . . the Convenience of Commerce peculiarly felicitous." They concluded that the "effect of these plain and simple reflections was decisive. . . . The present plan [was] adopted . . . because, after taking all circumstances into consideration, it appeared to be the best; or, in other and more proper terms, attended with the least inconvenience."[10]

Such appeals to custom and economic constraint were common. In addition, the grid was promoted as an inherently salubrious and comfortable urban order. Thomas Jefferson recommended it to Orleans Territory Governor William C. C. Claiborne on this basis as an ideal way to extend New Orleans. (Private developers of faubourgs had anticipated Jefferson's suggestion as early as 1788.) Claiborne responded enthusiastically: "As this City promises to have a rapid increase (& the havoc of Disease is at present so evident) I must confess, I entertain sanguine hopes of introducing this favourite Scheme." Grid plans were healthy, their advocates believed, because they conducted breezes to all parts of the city, an advantage that both Jefferson and the New York Commissioners emphasized.[11]

The disadvantages of grids, on the other hand, included their maladaptation to irregularities of terrain and their clumsiness for diagonal travel across the city. In the 1840s Alexander Mackay marveled that "there is but one short cut that I could discover in all Philadelphia, and that is in the neighbourhood of the Exchange. So unlooked-for an oddity in such a place put me on inquiry; but nobody could tell me how it got there. It is found so useful, however, that many wish it multiplied to an indefinite extent." (Mackay's shortcut was Dock Street, created when Dock Creek was filled just before the Revolution.) Moreover, the absolute regularity of gridded streets made a town "at first embarrassing to a stranger," who would find it difficult to navigate through its undifferentiated streets, particularly given the haphazard labeling of streets and buildings.[12]

Among travelers, who were the most frequent commentators on America's urban grids, visual qualities were more interesting than practical ones. The grid's regularity was its most striking visual attribute, but people disagreed whether that was good or bad. The orthogonal plan was "beautiful," "regular," "symmetrical," and "neat" to those who liked it. To those who did not, it made for a city that was "mediocre" and "tiresome" in its "unbroken uniformity," a criticism that, Jefferson claimed, "all persons" made against Philadelphia. A trip through Philadelphia, the "Quaker paradise," at first delights the visitor, said the British traveler Thomas Hamilton, but "before he has got through half the city, he feels an unusual tendency to relaxation about the region of the mouth, which ultimately terminates in a silent but prolonged yawn." To overcome his boredom in Philadelphia, Hamilton longed "for the mere sake of variety, to encounter a row of log huts, or get immersed in a congress of dark and picturesque closes, such as delight all travellers—without noses—in the old town of Edinburgh." In a similar frame of mind, Charles Dickens "would have given the world for a crooked street" during his visit to the city.[13]

Americans were less inclined to indulge in such easy jibes: the form of their own cities was an urgent matter. While foreign travelers' opinions of the grid were usually unconditional, Americans tended to be more ambivalent—never more so than when confronted with a city such as Boston, which was crowded seemingly at random onto a small, hilly peninsula. As the New Haven cleric Timothy Dwight noted at the beginning of the nineteenth century, "The settlers appear to have built where they wished, where a vote permitted, or where danger or necessity forced them to build. The streets strike the eye of a traveler as if intended to be mere passages from one neighborhood to another, and not as the open handsome divisions of a great town; as the result of casualty, and not of contrivance." As a result, "the streets, if we except a small number, are narrow, crooked, and disagreeable." In the same spirit, the austere Philadelphia merchant Thomas Pym Cope dismissed New York for its "twining, narrow & filthy avenues." Cope "always thought large, airy, straight streets preferable to narrow, crooked and confined ones."[14]

Yet the same qualities struck others very differently. Cope's traveling companion, the novelist Charles Brockden Brown, found "something to admire in every step" in New York, declaring that "there is a certain indescribable something in the streets which gives them an appearance very beautiful & superior in taste & excellence to the streets of Philadelphia." Cope himself eventually changed his tune. In Boston a few years after Dwight, he decided that the "inequality of the ground on which the City stands, the various twinings of the streets, the different materials used and opposite taste displayed in the formation of their buildings, present to the eye of a stranger a continued novelty." Job R. Tyson, another Philadelphia Quaker, praised the cleanliness and "agreeable variety" of Boston's "narrow and winding" streets, but wrote of his "embarrassment in attempting to find my way from one part of the city to another, from the numerous intersections and variations of names which the same street undergoes from particular points.—The best private dwellings are of an elegant and spacious fabric, surpassing in extent & grace of architecture any buildings in Philadelphia. . . . I cannot imagine a more magnificent spectacle than the disposition of the houses of certain streets in Boston along Walnut, Chesnut or Arch Sts. [in Philadelphia]. But the narrowness and curvatures of the streets, is in a good degree removed by the civility of the people to a stranger."[15]

Tyson appreciated the picturesque aspects of Boston's irregular street pattern and hilly site, but he also liked full, axial views of fine houses, which were not available in Boston. Tyson's preference was close to the aesthetic of the grand manner, with its direct and unambiguous vistas. His confusion allied him with Dwight, who thought Boston's site "most agreeably varied," but he regretted that the city had not been laid out along a 120-foot-wide north-south street that would form the spine of a grid of smaller streets. By virtue of their terminating at the waterfront, the small streets would have "assumed the appearance of vistas" on the water and the surrounding countryside.[16]

Tyson, a practical man of business, worried about the difficulty of getting around Boston. As Philadelphian John Fanning Watson noted in comparing New York's picturesque old town with its gridded additions, "I might prefer for convenience of living, straighter and wider streets, as their new built ones in every direction are; but as a visiter, it added to my gratification, to wind through the unknown mazes of the place, and then suddenly to break upon some unexpected and superior street or buildings, passing in another direction. It gives entertainment to the imagination, to see thus, the lively tokens of the primitive Dutch taste for such streets; and the narrow lanes, aided the fancy to conceive, how, the social Knickerbockers, loved the narrow lanes for their social conveniences, when setting in their stoopes in evenings, on either side the narrow pass."[17]

Dwight's, Tyson's, and Watson's ambivalence revealed a deeper tension between aesthetic preferences absorbed from education and popular culture and a sense of spatial possibilities that was ingrained in Euro-American culture. The latter overcame aesthetic misgivings. The grid's power in the years after 1790 derived from diffuse assumptions about the spatial qualities of order and human behavior. Tyson's principal interest in Boston, for example, was in its orderly society, where a "decent stranger, they think, is entitled to attention & respect." Most of his letter described institutions such as schools, asylums, jails, and houses of correction that reinforced Boston's social order and compensated for its faulty physical order. Philadelphians believed that the grid gave their city the advantage.[18]

Planners and scholars commonly dismiss grids as commonsense artifacts, useful only for "the *buying*, and *improving* real estate, on streets, avenues, and public squares, already laid out and established on the ground by monumental stones and bolts, *at the cost of the city*," in the words of John H. Randel, Jr., the surveyor of New York's Commissioners' Plan. Yet the value of the grid even for such utilitarian purposes was based on political ideology and social values. If we look closely, it is apparent that to those who came to appreciate orthogonal planning in the early republican years, its value for citizenship and urbanity encompassed but was not limited to mundane commercial transactions. The grid's seductive power was grounded in widespread beliefs in essentially spatial qualities of social, political, and economic order that might be labeled the spatial imagination.[19]

By *spatial imagination* I mean to indicate a way of thinking about the city that surpasses the simple instrumentality attributed to the grid by Randel and by modern commentators. Imagination fascinated eighteenth- and early-nineteenth-century philosophers, psychologists, and critics. Although their definitions varied in detail, most centered on a quest for fundamental continuities that might synthesize the varied data of experience into a grander order. For David Hume, the imagination was "naturally sublime," at once feebler than sensory experience but also more vigorous in its "unlimited power of mixing, compounding, separating, and dividing" the material of experience. In another place he described it as a "gentle force" that seeks a "uniting principle" among ideas, meaning the data of experience. Immanuel Kant likewise conceived the imagination as a synthetic power capable of perceiving hidden connections and organizing them into "general procedures," or schemata, for relating the abstract logical categories of the mind and the diverse sense data of experience. The poet Samuel Taylor Coleridge, who proclaimed his deep affinity for Kant's ideas, described the imagination as "'a law of our nature' . . . by which 'we gradually represent as wholly like' whatever is 'partially like.'" It was a "shaping" and "ordering" power that "dissolves, dissipates, in order to create; or where this process is rendered impossible, yet still at all events it struggles to idealize and to unify." Both ultimately assigned the imagination a constitutive role in our world. In Kant's philosophy, imagination mounts an endless campaign of self-positing or self-making that creates the categories of self, space, and time within which we exist. Coleridge eventually identified the imagination as "the living Power and prime Agent of all human Perception, . . . a repetition in the finite mind of the eternal act of creation in the infinite I AM. . . . It is essentially *vital*."[20]

I define the *spatial imagination* in this spirit. It was an attempt to order and unify, to "represent as wholly like" social and spatial phenomena that were "partially like" by translating nonspatial goals and categories into spatial terms. Based on a sense of the proper relationships among people or institutions, it fused physical and nonphysical attributes into a kind of Platonic space that ordered and unified all connections, all relationships, all hierarchies at once. This fusion of the material and the nonmaterial cannot be achieved in the "real," Euclidean world, although we often act as though it can be. The spatial imagination, then, is a synthetic process. When it succeeds, the results seem obvious, but even spatial arrangements that in retrospect seem to be "natural" or commonsense fusions of the social and the spatial often take years or centuries of experimentation to emerge. More often, the synthesis never gels, exposing its underlying assumptions to examination.

In the early republic, the urban spatial imagination seized on the grid as its schema. I call it a schema because the reinvigoration of the grid in the early national period entailed a reconceptualization of its qualities. The project to revive the Penn-Holme plan of Philadelphia, for example, disguised a revolutionary new urban vision as the restoration of an old one. Penn had conceived his gridded city as a closed, hierarchical community. Holme's *Portraiture* depicted a limited number of lots lying along the two main axial streets and occupying the areas between the riverfronts and the subsidiary squares (see fig. 6.2). They were graded in size and in desirability of location and were to be distributed to the First Purchasers, the wealthy men expected to buy large tracts of land in the new colony. The rest of the map was left blank; this represented land retained by Penn to be given to later purchasers. The plan illustrates the multiple qualities of the spatial imagination very distinctly. Penn's and Holme's Philadelphia was really several cities in one. It was a land-based city centered on its public squares, but it was also a water-based city facing its port (originally, its *ports*: the distribution of the First Purchasers' lots in the *Portraiture* emphasizes its dual-fronted nature). The purchasers of the largest tracts were to receive lots in both "cities." The land-based city was divided into neighborhoods, each focused

on a local open space set off from the hurly-burly of city life by the simple device of making it larger than a single block, so that traffic did not flow easily
around it. These four open spaces, now called Franklin, Washington, Logan, and
Rittenhouse squares, were to be available to the public "for the like use as Moor
Fields in London," that is, for public recreation, rather than to be reserved for contiguous property holders. The main square was likewise intended for "Houses
for Public Affairs" in Philadelphia, but no effort was made to establish the seat
of government there until the nineteenth century. Penn and Holme assumed
that the city's residents would be evenly distributed throughout Philadelphia's
east-west expanse, so the central square was initially given over to a Friends'
meetinghouse, but even that was gone by 1702. So the proprietor and his surveyor had already assigned what they thought were the best spaces in the city
to the "best" people and had named the major streets after them. It was only
after a falling out between Penn and the First Purchasers, who wanted to priva-
tize parts of the city that Penn had intended for public use, that he removed the
Purchasers' names, declaring that henceforth the streets of Philadelphia would
be named after "things that Spontaneously Grow in the country."[21]

Nineteenth-century Philadelphians imagined the Penn-Holme plan in a very
different way. The grid's spaces no longer diagrammed a specific, closed community with fixed places in the landscape. Instead, they offered a template for
the relationships of a diverse, more loosely ordered citizenry. The new spatial
imagination envisioned urban society and the urban landscape as a set of relationships ordered from within rather than from without, from the inherent
qualities of humanity manifested by freely acting, self-disciplined individuals
rather than from the contingencies of social structure, but it left unresolved
the nature of public action and the relationship of the public to the private.

This new spatial imagination appealed most vividly to the mercantile elite,
and it was continually challenged by the spatial and social practices of other
segments of the urban population. But it *was* the loudest and most explicitly
articulated of several competing models of urban spatial order, therefore it is
the most thoroughly documented one in the written and built records. Those
who shared it were impelled to reform and reorganize both cityscape and society into a single, centralized, rational order—a systematic landscape. Although
they never succeeded in creating a total order, they did introduce significant
changes to American cities in the years between 1790 and 1840.

The new spatial imagination was grounded in that late-Enlightenment
habit of mind that historians of philosophy and science call the "systematic"
or "geometrical spirit," the "passion to order and systematize as well as to measure and calculate." The desire to describe, categorize, and organize the world
based on "degrees of identity and difference" first bore fruit in the world of bot-

any, and particularly in the work of Carl Linnaeus. It spread to other sciences and mathematics and then into political administration and social thought through chains of metaphor and analogy. Logical assumptions that helped to explain the natural and social worlds were eventually turned onto the city. Systematic thinking assumed the existence of inherent relationships—"immanent connection," to borrow Ernst Cassirer's phrase—within various natural and human phenomena. It often assumed that these inherent qualities were visible to the careful observer, holding out the possibility of knowing and ordering the world systematically. The "systematic spirit" was the scientific manifestation of Kant's imaginative self-constitution of the world.[22]

Systematic modes of thought were broadly available to educated Americans in the eighteenth and early nineteenth centuries through the literature of science, economics, and human nature distributed by the many learned societies, libraries, schools, and public and private museums founded during the late-colonial and early-republican years. These institutions were particularly thick on the ground in Philadelphia, the intellectual as well as the commercial capital of the new republic. The Quaker City was home of two important prerevolutionary scientific organizations, the American Philosophical Society, "held at Philadelphia for promoting useful knowledge," and the College of Philadelphia (later University of Pennsylvania) medical school, the nation's first. After the Revolution these were augmented by such renowned institutions as Charles Willson Peale's museum (1786), the Academy of Natural Sciences (1812), and eventually the Franklin Institute (1824), whose attention was devoted to practical technology as the American Philosophical Society drifted toward pure science. The Library Company of Philadelphia (1731), the city's original subscription library, was joined in the early nineteenth century by another, the Athenaeum, and then by occupationally oriented libraries geared toward mechanics, merchants, apprentices, and others. By underwriting institutions such as these, Philadelphia's elite strove to promote a kind of systematized, scientificized thinking that they hoped would have practical consequences for their day-to-day existence.[23]

Natural history—botany, zoology, and paleontology—enthralled educated Americans in the late eighteenth and early nineteenth centuries. Botany, the science that defined the main characteristics of the systematic mindset, was particularly popular in Philadelphia, where John Bartram had established his famous botanical garden in 1730 as the first of several similar gardens in the Quaker City. These included the Pennsylvania Hospital's garden, planted in 1774, and William Hamilton's Woodlands, which was begun in 1779 and which, like Henry Pratt's early-nineteenth-century Lemon Hill, served both scientific and aesthetic purposes. Hamilton's garden was reputed to contain eight thousand species of plants, including specimens brought from the West by Lewis and Clark, and others imported from Australia.[24]

Nonbotanical scientists and, increasingly, a large segment of Philadelphia's general public were drawn to botany. Benjamin Franklin told Manasseh Cutler that "He delights in natural history," and showed him "a huge volume on Botany." The merchant Thomas P. Cope found the Woodlands a "place of much public resort" in 1803, "owing to [Hamilton's] having that rare curiosity—an Aloe in bloom," while diarist Charles Thomson likewise encountered a "considerable company" on hand to see a night-blooming cereus at Joshua Longstreth's botanical garden in 1820.[25]

Late-eighteenth-century botany and zoology (another field in which Americans were especially active) remained grounded in the enumeration and classification of the plant and animal kingdoms, which had been the central obsession of the "classical" age of science in the seventeenth century. Taxonomists assumed that a definitive description could be created by examining a limited number of specific characteristics. The method was based on an assumption of comparability: a classification must arise from counting those qualities that an organism shared with others, rather than from identifying its unique attributes. It was based as well on externally observable similarities rather than on a search for underlying structural or phylogenetic patterns.[26]

A classification of this sort might be created by any trained observer. It yielded results that could be enumerated and that were often summarized in tabular form. Thomas Jefferson's *Notes on the State of Virginia* (1780), with its lists of plants and animals, tables of meteorological conditions, population, militia, and Indian tribes exemplified the systematic worldview, as did Meriwether Lewis' 1803 invitation to William Clark to join his expedition. Lewis told Clark that the purpose of the mission was

> scientific . . . such as ascertaining . . . the names of the nations who inhabit [the country to be explored], the extent and limits of their several possessions, their relations with other tribes and nations; their languages, traditions, and monuments; their ordinary occupations in fishing, hunting, war, arts, and the implements for their food, clothing and domestic accommodation; the diseases prevalent among them and the remidies they use; the articles of commerce they may need, or furnish, and to what extent; the soil and face of the country; its growth and vegetable productions, its animals; the mineral productions of every discription; and in short to collect the best possible information relative to whatever the country may afford as a tribute to general science.[27]

Newtonian natural philosophy, which included mathematics, physics, and astronomy, offered a different kind of systematization. While classical botanists and zoologists classified according to a few visible traits, Newtonians sought to uncover the immanent connection among apparently discrete bodies. Newton argued that all matter was originally the same, and he advanced the concept of an aether or aethers, "each very subtle and elastic, and 'some secret principle of unsociableness' and the reverse, whereby particles, both of aether and of grosser bodies, selectively flee and approach one another," and whose actions could be described systematically through mathematics. Although Newton eventually rejected this theory of the universe's operation in favor of a belief in direct divine intervention, it remained current among his followers. The work of the Newtonians was certainly less widely known in America than that of botanists such as Linnaeus, but Newton's works circulated among Philadelphia's merchants throughout the eighteenth century, and popularizations were available in print and from itinerant lecturers who offered experimental demonstrations of Newtonian principles. From the Newtonian postulate of an invisible aether that linked the entire physical world, Benjamin Franklin developed his concept of an electrical fluid and a unitary theory of electrical action to explain it.[28]

Lessons that late-eighteenth-century Americans of many classes learned in their daily working lives reinforced the precepts of science in sparking the systematic spatial imagination. A seventeenth-century revolution in economic consciousness moved high-level Anglo-American economic theory toward a naturalistic image of inner system and regulation comparable to that presented in scientists' writings. The commercial network that grew throughout England in the sixteenth and seventeenth centuries showed anyone who cared to notice it the interdependence of all members of the economy. Economic actions "were undirected but patterned, uncoerced but orderly, free but predictable." Many laypeople understood economic principles as analogues of the "operation of systems in the physical universe." These laypeople included several eighteenth-century Philadelphia merchants who argued that "credit has its own laws, as unalterable in themselves, as those of motion or gravity are, in nature."[29]

Some people believed that one could catalogue and tabulate economic relationships just as scientists did elements in the natural world. In *The Gentleman Accomptant,* the English popularizer Roger North (who also wrote about architecture) celebrated double-entry bookkeeping as an art comparable in beauty and elegance to oratory or dancing. North contrasted the systematic economic understanding of great merchants with the shortsighted and impressionistic thinking of small tradesmen and farmers. To the merchant, double-entry bookkeeping offered a concrete image, complete and true, of the abstract system of relations underlying commercial transactions. It was both precise and systematic, "so comprehensive and perfect, as makes it worthy to be put among the Sciences, and to be understood by all Virtuosi, whether they intend to make use of it or no, even for pure Speculation, Curiosity, or rather Admiration." North likened well-kept accounts to "the Branches and Leaves of a Tree, in a perpetual Series, all hanging to each other, no less but rather more essentially than [branches] do; for of those, many may be prun'd off, and the Tree left integral and sound; but here not one Accompt, or Line of it can be spared."[30]

North's confidence in great merchants may have been misplaced. Until the late eighteenth century, even those wealthy traders who appeared to keep double-entry accounts rarely used them in a systematic manner to compute profit and loss or to balance accounts. Yet the merchant, whose generalized trading was conducted at every economic scale from the local to the international, was in an ideal position to appreciate the interdependence of commercial relations. As an eighteenth-century guide to the professions noted, "Commerce, the Sphere of the Merchant, extends itself to all the known World, and gives Life and Vigour to the whole Machine" of trade. At the same time, experience of the economy's system was widespread. Eighteenth-century Americans of many classes were intensely involved in production for the market and participated in one fashion or another in the international economy. As a result, the sense of the economy as a system was even more vivid in the nascent United States than it had been in England, even if few large- or small-fry were familiar with formal economic theory or possessed the precise mathematical understanding of their own affairs that North advocated.[31]

But what moved the system? Why was it that apparently chaotic decisions formed a pattern? For followers of the new political economy, the answer lay in yet another form of immanent connection, this one grounded in human nature. Economic writers proclaimed a universal human impulse, arising from the instinct for self-preservation, to seek the maximum personal gain from any economic transaction. As a result, the chaotic, self-seeking decisions of individuals would generate predictable, orderly patterns of behavior. Just as the essence of the natural world was inaccessible to direct observation but could be detected by its effects and described through chemical or physical formulas, so the essence of human nature could be discerned in merchants' accounts and in enumerations of many other sorts. Adam Smith's *The Wealth of Nations,* one of the primary tracts advocating this new view, was available in Philadelphia soon after its 1776 publication, and Philadelphia merchants quickly made use of liberal arguments. Smith bolstered his thesis with language intended to evoke Newton's physics. His American readers took the hint. In opposing artisan-radical attempts to regulate prices in the face of widespread speculation, for example, some Philadelphia merchants wrote that hoarding and price gouging "have their foundation in the laws of nature, and no artifice or force of man can prevent, elude, or avoid their effects."[32]

The vision of voluntary but coordinated action, of which Smith's invisible hand is the most memorable image, lay at the heart of the systematic spatial imagination and pervaded writings about cities and city life. It synthesized the physicists' sense of immanent connection and the botanists' (apparently contradictory) demand for visible resemblance with the economists' understanding of human nature.

Although specific precepts about the natural world and about economic behavior helped urban Americans understand their environment, their common efforts to enumerate, tabulate, and compare, and their preference for kinds of information that were amenable to such operations, were the most enduring lessons that systematizers took from science and economics. In the late eighteenth and early nineteenth centuries "numeracy," or the ability to manipulate numbers, flourished as the pervasiveness of commercial relations inspired a newfound belief in the universal necessity of arithmetical skills in a republican society. As with the botanist's classifications or the physicist's formulas, to reduce something to numbers, as Patricia Cline Cohen has noted, was to make it seem uniform and finite, patterned, related—systematic and, hence, manageable. To tame the chaos of a growing nation, Americans resorted to "political arithmetic": to counting, tabulating, and comparing the intangible qualities of their own society. Statistical manuals, gazetteers, and even city directories, novel genres for early republican America, were the *Principia Mathematica* of social life. The energy that Europeans turned to inspecting and categorizing their colonies a century later was, in the United States, devoted to a great national project of self-knowing, self-classification, and self-fashioning. Because he viewed his work as a record of the progress of his city, for example, Clement Biddle appended a discussion of the history of Philadelphia's plan and a statistical overview of its population to the city's first directory. It was a project to reduce a wide-ranging and potentially chaotic life to a manageable system. But in toting up the refulgent facticity of their new nation, Americans had in mind more than mere utility: "political arithmetic" was an introspective discipline on a par with Puritan diary-keeping.[33]

The systematic imagination could project the precision, enumeration, and hard data of mathematics onto a variety of human fields because system was less a method than a mode of thought, a mental habit that often operated below the surface of explicit argument. It was based on congruities of nomenclature and visual presentation that organized scientific, economic, and social texts using similar narrative patterns. Even scientists worked out their problems using models based on other sciences. They attempted to construct Linnaean classifications of other living things, of minerals, even of geometrical forms. Much of the immanent connection they sought was invested in their subject matter by the language that they employed. Thus the idiom of system spread far beyond the boundaries of individual disciplines or fields of inquiry through a chain of metaphors that linked the material and immaterial worlds in ever larger and more encompassing networks, making it possible to connect, for example, biology and morality or, in the case of cities and buildings, spaces and behavior.[34]

As an illustration of this transversality, consider the famous museum that the painter Charles Willson Peale established at his home at Third and Lombard streets, Philadelphia, in 1786. Driven, as he told George Washington, to "collect every thing that is curious in this Country," Peale amassed an ever-expanding inventory comprising several hundred quadrupeds—some alive—over 1,600 birds, 200 reptiles and amphibians, thousands of insects, 8,000 minerals, fossils, fishes, and 11 wax figures representing ethnographic types, along with the skeleton of a mastodon he had excavated in 1801. These natural history specimens were added to his existing portrait gallery of famous American patriots, a collection that grew to nearly one hundred paintings as Peale added politicians, American and European scientists and artists, and (as he grew older), Americans famous for their longevity.[35]

Peale's Museum was distinguished from old-fashioned cabinets of randomly selected curiosities by the organization of his exhibits: "The several Articles will be classed and arranged according to their several species," he noted in his first advertisement. His ambition was to create "a world in miniature" within a single all-encompassing taxonomic system ostensibly derived from Linnaeus but in fact cobbled together from the hodgepodge of conflicting variants available to amateur naturalists of the early republican era. An 1824 strangers' guide entry probably written by Peale claimed that the "system of Linnaeus has been adhered to in the arrangement of the mammalia and birds; . . . that of Cleaveland in mineralogy. . . . Lamarck's system has been the guide in conchology." Peale meticulously worked out the nomenclature for each specimen in blank books he bought for the purpose, then posted the names in guides attached to the wall in each gallery.[36]

The naturalist's emphasis on the visible guided Peale's presentation of his specimens. He created large, quasi-natural landscapes in his first museum building at Third and Lombard streets that were meant to appear "natural," meaning as they appeared to the eye in the wild. Thus, they were "real," although both the setting and the groupings were highly stylized and selectively grouped—

they were nature condensed and ordered by artifice. When Peale moved his museum to the State House (Independence Hall) in 1802, the fusion of artificial and natural was even more striking. In the hundred-foot Long Room on the second floor, Peale came closest to achieving his ideal classification scheme (plate 7). Rather than group all his animals in a single artificial environment, he distributed them among the several rooms that were at his disposal. On the longest wall of the Long Room, Peale showed his birds, arranged according to Linnaeus' system, in 140 equal-sized cases stacked twelve feet high. While the overall arrangement was gridded and taxonomic, the interior of each case had a painted background and three-dimensional props "to represent appropriate scenery, Mountains, Plains or Waters, the birds being placed on branches or artificial rocks, &c." Above the cases was a double-row of equal-sized portraits of the "Animal Man," set close together in a gridded arrangement similar to that of the cases below. The juxtaposition of birds and portraits equated the physical taxonomy of lower animals with a human moral classification based on character or behavior. The difference was further blurred by including physically as well as morally exceptional human "specimens" and by posing the zoological specimens to suggest their characteristic behavior, for Peale argued that an accurate description of an animal ought to include "its manners, disposition and general character," as well as its visible bodily attributes. Thus humans, distinguished by their behavior, were also interesting for their physiology, while animals, ordered by their physiologies, also deserved attention for their behavior. By finessing the difference between human essence (character) and visible animal characteristics, Peale alluded to the more encompassing and ultimately divine system that he wished his visitors to discover in his museum. Some did. According to Peale, Constantin-François Volney declared on entering the museum in 1797, "This is the House of God! Here is nothing but truth spoken."[37]

As a highly skilled popularizer rather than a trained scientist, Peale illustrates the ways the systematic outlook might shape nonprofessionals' modes of thought. Among professional physicists and chemists, an interest in system and essence—innate connection—precluded the possibility of visibility. Among botanists and zoologists, system and visibility downplayed essence, although the most advanced taxonomic research, to which some Americans, including Peale, contributed data, was beginning to probe beyond external surfaces. While Peale alluded to innate connection in his museum, the whole was based on the act of seeing.[38]

The intellectual structure of Peale's museum blurred the distinction between the literal and the metaphorical, as his juxtaposition of birds and portraits suggests. It was a characteristic elision among early republican systematizers. Similarities and metaphors easily slipped over the line into concrete, precisely describable relationships across and within the moral, economic, and material realms.

The juxtaposition of the human and natural worlds at Peale's museum was a republican civic gesture. Republicanism emerged from the turmoil of the American Revolution as the central ideology of the new nation. As elaborated between the Revolution and the Civil War, this "protean concept" came to mean many things to many people, but all agreed that fundamental political rights derived from common membership in the human race. As humans we bequeath power to the state rather than deriving our rights from membership in a class, estate, or other subgroup dependent upon the state. Sovereignty, that is, emanates from citizens who are in some essential way the same, therefore comparable, whatever their contingent differences in status or condition. Republicans argued that the health of the state depended on citizens' sharing common values rationally discovered and on their vigilance and self-discipline in enforcing them. As in the natural world, political order arose from within rather than being imposed from without. In other words, republicanism was yet another manifestation of the search for innate connections. It assumed the same essentialism, comparability, and articulated relationships that characterized Linnaeus's plants, Newton's universe, and Peale's natural and human specimens.[39]

Early republican writers emphasized the importance of visibility and transparency in properly articulating individual and society. A sense of context, a view of the whole within which the self was situated, maintained perspective and maximized social effectiveness. A republican society worked best when nothing was hidden, when every citizen's choices were supported by equal access to essential information and to the means to understand it. Ignorance reduced a republic's productivity while private knowledge unbalanced commonality by affording some people an unfair advantage. It followed that all citizens should be educated and that practices that favored insider knowledge, such as irregular or needlessly complex customs that required arcane skills to understand, should be eliminated. To achieve this, republican enthusiasts sought to reform the most fundamental categories of information and inquiry. One author predicted that the regularization of weights and measures would lead to the elimination of compound numbers from mathematics because they would no longer be needed in commerce, while mathematics instruction would be accessible to a wider audience. Decimalization of the currency was even more necessary for republican transparency because it ensured equitable economic life and made for the smoothest integration of individual transactions into the economic system. Erastus Root, the author of an arithmetic text, pleaded for the speedy acceptance of the new decimal currency in the United States, urging his "Fellow-Citizens, no longer meanly [to] follow the British intricate mode of reckoning.—Let them have their own way—and us, ours.—Their mode is suited to the genius of their own government, for it seems to be the policy of tyrants, to keep their accounts in as intricate, and perplexing a method as possible; that the smaller number of their subjects may be able to estimate their enormous impositions and exactions. But Republican money ought to be simple, and adapted to the meanest capacity."[40]

Articulation in the economic world depended as much on the sameness of commodities as on the essential sameness of human motivation. Material goods and immaterial services were rendered comparable by their essential attribute, value, which was described and rendered visible by money. Money was a "medium of commerce to estimate the value of other things," according to the Philadelphia merchants, and thus, in Samuel Blodget's words, a "labour-saving machine... intended to save the trouble of barter." The decimalization of American currency aimed to remedy the "unequal values allowed in different parts of the Union to coins of the same intrinsic value." Much of Secretary of the Treasury Alexander Hamilton's report on the subject was devoted to the methods to determine the comparative value of monetary media as a step toward specifying a single standard.[41]

Philadelphian John Dorsey's proposal to decimalize the weights, measures, and monetary system of the United States at a single stroke, and thus to reduce the entire material and economic worlds to simple equivalences, exemplified both the republican impulse to transparency and the conceptual elision that the systematic mindset encouraged. Beginning from the mundane empirical observation that a cubic foot of water at 60 degrees Fahrenheit weighs 1,000 ounces Avoirdupois, Dorsey, Philadelphia's keeper of weights and measures, a former state senator and sometime architect, proposed to "establish an uniform System—and by it to reconcile the Unit of Weight, the Unit of Lineal Measure— the Unit of measure of Capacity & the Money Unit of the UStates." Seduced by the idea of comparability, Dorsey wished to legislate a universal, fixed relationship between mass, dimension, and monetary value that would be applicable to all commodities at all times.[42]

Politics and economics intersected in republican citizens in a second way: a new fondness for statistics assigned numerical values to outwardly disparate individuals and thus defined their status as atoms of a unified republic. Occasionally these values were, literally, values. Samuel Blodget, an amateur architect and the author of America's first statistical manual, figured that if each U.S. citizen was worth about $400, the total value of the American population in 1801 was $2 billion. He used this sum to construct an elaborate calculus of population, land, and movable goods that would predict the increase in the nation's value that might be expected in coming decades. While his legerdemain confuses the naked eye, Blodget defended such calculations as contributions to republican transparency: "national arithmetic" of this sort helped to "guard against imposition on the minds of our uninformed citizens for the purposes of election." Blodget's immediate concern in valuing the public, however, was to estimate the country's net worth and its likelihood of retiring the national debt. Not only sovereignty but the government's credit rating emanated from the people.[43]

The assumptions that lay so close to the surface in Dorsey's proposal and Blodget's national arithmetic are essential for understanding the systematic landscape, for they expose the interpenetration of language and artifact that is indispensable to the spatial imagination. By casting the parallel, discontinuous physical, moral, and commercial worlds into a single discursive system, metaphors of system and essence, of innate connection, bridged the chasm between the physical and the mental, investing metaphor with concreteness and specificity. In American cities the systematic spatial imagination was a *republican* spatial imagination. These metaphors encouraged urban elites to imagine a landscape infused with and promoting the necessary physical, intellectual, moral, and economic aspects of republican society, or, more accurately perhaps, it encouraged them to act as if such a landscape already existed. The republican spatial imagination was an act of speaking, building, *willing* human relationships and urban space into a living, self-posited republican "I AM." The grid was its schema. Its attributes were *transparency,* or the openness of the landscape to examination and understanding by all comers; *classification,* or the visible representation of relationships; and *articulation,* or the creation of relationships that were flexible and individually manipulable.

The republican city was unified through being visible and accessible to its residents; vistas and lines of sight stressed the commonality of the enterprise, as did ease of movement within the city. These assumptions were apparent in a petition presented to the city council in 1827 by residents and landowners living west of Penn (Center) Square in Philadelphia. They explained that "inasmuch as by interrupting the prospect and entirely Shutting out the view between the Eastern and Western sides of Market Street a line of demarcation appeared to be created; which even supposing it to be merely ideal was nevertheless detrimental; and altho' when closely considered was perhaps only imaginary became notwithstanding a substantial grievance; . . . This barrier being considered as removed by an intended demolition of the Centre building [Benjamin Henry Latrobe's Center Square Pump House], the view will no longer be intercepted nor the direct communication by foot passengers interrupted;

But the Eastern and Western Inhabitants may [once] more regard themselves as connected with each other as well in point of Interest as feeling."[44]

Transparent space permitted *classification* of urban life the way visibility permitted classification of plant species. Classification described each citizen, each piece of ground, each land use in relation to every other. It allowed a ready assessment of their value—that is, it permitted a ready comparison and statement of relationships. At the same time, while the early republican spatial imagination emphasized visibility and the mapping of the self in place, it set off permanency and clarity of place against flexibility—*articulation*—of the self in space. Classification in early republican space described not a fixed hierarchy but a relational order, a single framework within which many overlapping, even ephemeral, suborders might coexist. One of the advantages touted for grid planning over grand-manner planning was that the latter identified certain sites or users as inherently significant. L'Enfant noted that in designing Washington he had "determined some principal points to which I wished to make the others subordinate." In a republican plan, all spaces, all locations must be potentially equal. Hierarchies, emphases, differences in value arise from the choices of its occupants rather than being predetermined by planners. Republican space thus emphasized equal access, equalization of potential value, the maximization of the number of potential uses. In a sense, the republican spatial imagination sought to equalize spatial opportunity by conquering space, as John C. Calhoun put it, eliminating inherent differences to provide a clear field for the construction of intentional ones.[45]

No urban form inherently possesses the qualities embodied in the republican spatial imagination. Everything depends on how one interprets particular models. Thus, both advocates of the grid and advocates of baroque planning could claim visibility and spatial equalization as attributes of their plans. Even L'Enfant bolstered his defense of his baroque plan of Washington, D.C., by arguing that the principal purpose of his avenues was "to connect each part of the city, if I may so express it, by making the real distance less from place to place, by giving them reciprocity of sight, and by making them thus seem connected, promote a rapid settlement over the whole extent, rendering those even of the most remote parts an addition to the principal." However, it was the grid that was most commonly selected and that was invested with the qualities of republican space.[46]

The very monotony that was often cited as the grid's greatest fault might be said to render it transparent. There were no surprises, no dramatic revelations or sudden discoveries to be had in an orthogonal plan as there were in a baroque town; any part could in theory be imagined by extrapolation from any other part. Arthur Singleton told his readers that in Philadelphia "after you have walked one square, you have seen the whole." That this was never really true in any early republican city was frustrating to many urban leaders, and it was a central problem in understanding and reforming cities, for while the sameness of the grid made it easily comprehensible as a whole, it was more difficult to understand on the ground. As Jacques-Pierre Brissot de Warville observed, Philadelphia's regularity, "which is a real ornament, is at first embarrassing to a stranger; he has much difficulty in finding himself, especially as the streets are not inscribed and the doors not numbered. It is strange that the Quakers, who are so fond of order, have not adopted these two conveniencies." A baroque plan offers clues to the locations of major monuments at least. Even these are not evident on the ground in a grid plan.[47]

The grid's order presumes a bird's-eye, or plan, view. Seen from above, without perspective, the entire order of the city is clear—"a two-dimensional record of solids and voids," in Spiro Kostof's words—its divisions absolute, its relationships obvious. The grid permits easy classification because every part is clearly distinguished from every other part. Indeed, *separation* and *classification,* almost invariably paired, were the ubiquitous watchwords of early republican urban space and society.[48]

Here the systematizers' use of metaphoric language to assert inherent connection is particularly striking. Latrobe characterized grid planning as "lay[ing] down streets after the pattern of a multiplication Table." Like a mathematical table, orthogonal planning permitted ready comparison, since relationships could be quantified in terms of distance and area. Linnaeus's classification tables were modeled on mathematical tables, and he also compared them to maps. Early republicans likened their maps to mathematical tables and hoped to use them to classify urban spaces and urban people as Linnaeus had done with plants.[49]

The British traveler Thomas Hamilton also used a mathematical image in referring to Philadelphia as a "city laid down by square and rule, a sort of habitable problem—a mathematical infringement on the rights of individual eccentricity,—a rigid and prosaic despotism of right angles and parallelograms." But Hamilton's metaphor pointed in the opposite direction from those of American defenders of the grid. He assumed the essential incompatibility of individuality and social order. In the republican spatial imagination, the grid seemed precisely suited to promote individuality by providing for a nonspecific general order within which individual, but presumably similar, ends could be pursued. Hamilton was not blind to this. "Philadelphia is par excellence a city of mediocrity [moderation]," he wrote. "Its character is republican not democratic. One can read the politics of its inhabitants in the very aspect of the streets. A coarse and vulgar demagogue would have no chance among a people so palpably observant of the proprieties, both moral and political. The Philadelphians are not traffickers in extremes of any sort."[50]

In the grid, as in John Dorsey's proposed system of weights, measures, and money, then, the very different qualities of space, value, and people were articulated into a republican spatial order. Virtue and commerce seemed to emanate from the space itself, Charles Dickens noted. As he walked through Philadelphia's streets, "the collar of my coat appeared to stiffen, and the brim of my hat to expand, beneath [the city's] quakery influence. My hair shrunk into a sleek short crop, my hands folded themselves upon my breast of their own calm accord, and thoughts of taking lodgings in Mark Lane over against the Market Place, and of making a large fortune in speculations in corn, came over me involuntarily." In other words, the republican, capitalist character of the grid was so powerful that it transformed Dickens' body, mind, and clothing into those of a Quaker merchant.[51]

By inscribing Philadelphia's grid on their new city seal in an age when the power of images to shape public life was widely accepted, the city council adopted a talisman that promised future republican virtue and commercial prosperity. In this spirit, vast grids were platted on paper, even as the survey of land crawled along block by block to keep pace with private development. Both New Yorkers and Philadelphians published plans showing the contrast between the existing city and its grid (fig. 6.5; see fig. 1.1, plate 1). These images implied that the promise of future prosperity would be fulfilled. Thomas Twining found that in the United States it was customary "to reckon as streets such as were only *contemplated* and not yet begun."[52]

The grid was more than a utilitarian or self-evident planning strategy, as the legal historian Hendrik Hartog has noted. It was an intellectual program for the subordination of the landscape to republican life. The seductive power of the grid for the republican spatial imagination is evident in the many practical and impractical projects designed to reduce the gridded city to the transparency and legibility of its mapped representation. So most of all the creation of the new Philadelphia seal marks the beginning of a period of a widespread effort in American cities and towns in the decades after 1790 to "regulate" their cityscapes, a term used for the meticulous ordering of both the human and natural environments. The regulation projects of the early republic constituted an aggressive new campaign to subdue the environment, creating a landscape that would embody republican values and that would promote republican modes of citizenship and selfhood.[53]

Just as John Dorsey's project for reforming weights, measures, and currency revealed the conceptual elisions hidden in metaphors of system, D. B. Lee's and

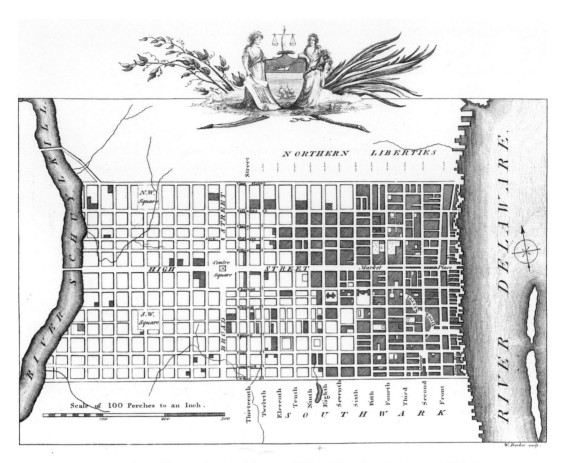

FIGURE 6.5. William Birch, plan of the City of Philadelphia, 1800. Birch has embellished the map with the city seal, which connects the gridded plan to urban prosperity. (The Library Company of Philadelphia)

W. Beach's 1834 project for illuminating Philadelphia exposed the same kinds of elisions in thinking about space. Lee and Beach proposed to build a centrally located three-hundred–foot brick tower with a perpetual coal fire on top. It would cast a light "nearly equal to that produced by a full moon" on all the streets, alleys, yards, and into all the houses within a three-quarter-mile radius. The result "would be an even regular light throughout the city and districts . . . sufficient for almost any purpose for which light is required." Householders would be protected from falls in the dark, and they would save money on candles and oil. Abroad, the light would serve as a beacon for travelers and, best of all, there could be "no dark places, in which a person walking would fall over curb stones, or into gutters—and there would be no dark corners, or hiding places, in which thieves or midnight robbers might secrete themselves, to evade the watchman." The city's space would be as equal and transparent at night as during the day.[54]

Although the Lee-Beach proposal seems as laughable as Dorsey's in its naiveté, the same assumptions guided post-1790 attempts in many American cities and towns to regulate their surroundings. The desire for urban order was not new. From the very beginnings of European town-building in North America, rulers tried to give their settlements an orderly appearance by laying out streets, enforcing building lines, and enacting building regulations, such as those requiring corner lots to be built first to define corners and to make fledgling settlements seem more populous than they were. The Lords Proprietors of the Carolina Colony ordered their governor in 1679 to "lay out the Streets [of Charleston] broad and in straight lines and that in your Grant of the Towne lotts you do bound every ones Land toward the Streets and in an even line and to suffer no one to incroach with his buildings upon the streets," while the surveyors of New Orleans made similar, sometimes bitterly resisted efforts to clear preexisting houses from the lines of their new streets.[55]

On the whole, however, the colonial plans of the major cities had been shaped by the peculiarities of topography. The precise siting of Boston's T-shaped core of wharf, which extended into the harbor perpendicular to a major street that ran along the harbor, and of its Common were governed by the locations of the Town Cove, a large, relatively unusable triple-peaked hill called the Trimountain, and the narrow neck connecting the city to the mainland. New Amsterdam/New York also grew along its harbor. A 1625 plan for a regular town within fortifications was superseded by development facing the East River, with three major streets running back from the river front. Attempts to create an evenly settled, canal-laced Netherlandish city never proceeded beyond customary admonitions to build up the open lots in the city and the construction of one canal, named after Amsterdam's Prinzengracht, in 1657. It was quickly filled and converted to a street by the English conquerors.[56]

Philadelphia's site was originally a hilly plateau, slashed by ravines and rising toward an "abrupt" bluff above the Delaware River and falling into swamps on the Schuylkill River side. Thomas Holme's *Portraiture*, which seems at first glance to be an idealized plan for the city, made concessions to topography: the northern rank of squares was eliminated because a creek named Pegg's Run made too much of the land unusable (see fig. 6.2). The intervals between the east-west streets were adjusted to avoid ravines and take advantage of ridges. During the site survey after the *Portraiture* was published, the ideal grid continued to be adjusted. The Schuylkill streets were pulled back from the river and the central square was moved west to occupy the true high point of the tract rather than the map's central point.[57]

As cities grew and land values rose, colonial municipal governments began to alter topography in minor ways to accommodate their cities' plans. Philadelphians built an arched bridge to carry Front Street level over Mulberry (now Arch) Street where it dropped off toward the Delaware River. Just before the Revolution they covered meandering Dock Creek to create Dock Street, the only winding thoroughfare in the antebellum city limits, as Alexander Mackay and Charles Dickens noticed.[58]

Some postrevolutionary urban regulators continued colonial practices—for example, in Wilmington, Delaware, where the "Regulators of Streets" policed encroachments on the town plan just as the surveyors of New Orleans had done a century earlier. More commonly, however, regulation after 1790 involved comprehensive, sometimes heroic efforts to eradicate topographical irregularities, to create a landscape as much like its two-dimensional mapped image as possible. The exponential increase in scale of ambition and expenditure on these projects created qualitative differences between colonial- and federal-era cities.[59]

The most heroic early-republican regulation was the demolition of Boston's Trimountain following the 1795 purchase of one of the hills, Mount Vernon, from John Singleton Copley by a syndicate known as the Proprietors of Mount Vernon (fig. 6.6). The architect Charles Bulfinch proposed leveling the entire crest of Mount Vernon to make a huge square nearly two hundred by five hun-

FIGURE 6.6. *Beacon Hill, from the Present Site of the Reservoir Between Hancock & Temple Streets*, 1858, after J. C. Smith drawing of 1811–12. Charles Bulfinch's monument commemorating the Revolutionary-era beacon that once stood on the spot still perches precariously on the peak. (Library of Congress, Prints and Photographs Division)

dred feet. The final plan was not quite as ambitious, but it did involve lowering the hill's summit fifty to sixty feet so that "all its roughnesses and irregularities [were] removed at prodigious expense, its steep western declivity cut down, and a field of nearly thirty acres converted into one of the most beautiful building grounds in the world." Within a few years, the city decided to create new land in the Mill Pond, a small bay on the Charles River side of the peninsula, and began demolishing Beacon Hill, another of the Trimountain's peaks, for soil.[60]

Boston's alterations stood out among similar, only slightly less arduous efforts in other cities. In New York, "as the buildings proceed, the ground is levelled," so that by 1828, James Stuart claimed, there was "little inequality of ground in any part of the island" of Manhattan, which had been a rugged and rocky terrain. Even tiny Newcastle, Delaware, sought Latrobe's help in "regulating the levels of Streets, and furnishing to the corporation a correct Plan of the town."[61]

Regulation, a continuous process in Philadelphia, gradually converted the site into a nearly level plain. Despite some colonial grading, the historian John Fanning Watson evoked the still-varied topography of the late-eighteenth-century city:

What was emphatically called "the hill" in the olden time, extending from Walnut street in a course with the southern side of Dock street, presented once a precipitous and high bank, especially by Pear street and St. Paul's church, which might have been cultivated in hanging gardens, descending to the dock, and open to the public gaze. Thence crossing beyond Little Dock street you ascended to "Society Hill," situate chiefly from Second to Front street, and from Union to the summit of Pine and Front streets. From that cause, buildings on Union street, north side, might have shown beautiful descending gardens on their northern aspect.

Watson opposed "the 'system of levelling' [a word that also connoted social leveling] the once beautiful natural inequalities of the city ground plot," which he attributed to "bad taste and avidity for converting every piece of ground to the greatest possible revenue." He then recorded in great detail, street by street, almost block by block, the progress of regulation in the city, as street levels were raised or lowered as much as twelve feet.[62]

Once it was leveled, the space of the grid needed to be made transparent, or easily legible, and articulated, or readily accessible. Traditionally, for example, way-finding in the city depended on familiarity with its inhabitants. In New Orleans, the French visitor C. C. Robin discovered that it was fruitless to ask people for addresses, since no one knew the names of the streets, even of those on which they lived. Instead, Orleanians named streets, "like neighborhoods, by the name of some prominent person who lives there."[63]

Local naming customs depended on knowledge available only to a few people and so contradicted the ideal of republican space. A system was needed that anyone could understand, such as the public display of street names and numbers that New Orleans ordered in 1805. Street numbers made the Crescent City intelligible to natives and visitors alike, and they were also a way of tabulating political arithmetic spatially. By matching the inhabitants to their residences, the city council realized, house numbering (which failed in 1805 and was tried again in 1811) would also "facilitate the collection of the taxes imposed upon the inhabitants of the city and faubourgs."[64]

Philadelphia first tried numbering a few years before New Orleans did. Odd numbers were allocated to the north and east sides of Philadelphia streets, and even numbers to the west and south sides early in the colonial era, but neither street name nor number was usually posted until the city ordained in 1790 that street "names [be] painted on boards, with an index hand pointing to the progression of the numbers." Even posting street names and numbers was not enough. Individual street numbers were assigned in Philadelphia as construction proceeded, so there was no way of telling in which block a given address would be found. Pictorial business directories show that half-numbers were common and residences on business streets were often unnumbered.[65]

Beginning in 1830, several different suggestions were offered to rationalize street numbers according to a single universal principle. The first anchored the street numbers at Center (by then called Penn) Square and ran north, south, east, and west from there. The city council was to "establish permanent numbers to the corner of each street, letting the same numbers be found to correspond at all the principal streets, running north and south; so that one part of the city would be a complete index for the other." In this way, the observer on the ground could make the same judgment of relative position as the user of a map. By fixing the intervals between street numbers on each block arbitrarily, allowing six or seven numbers for every hundred feet regardless of the actual density of development, the city fathers revealed that conceptions of equal urban space informed their spatial imaginations: the street grid was turned into an algebraic grid, with evenly graduated x and y axes. Uniform street numbering on the present system, with each block beginning a new hundred but no fixed intervals between numbers, was not enacted until 1858. At that same time the city also rationalized street naming by eliminating duplicate names in the old and newly annexed parts of the city, leading to new complaints of confusion as traditional local knowledge became obsolete.[66]

To articulate the city, the circulation network was improved by widening streets and making new connections to peripheral areas. The early-nineteenth-century New Orleans petitions to connect the old street grid to that of Faubourg Sainte-Marie demonstrated that residents wanted multiple, easy communications to all parts of the city (see Chapter 1). Watercourses separated other cities from their hinterlands or one part of a city from another, and large, multiple bridges were built in the early nineteenth century. A revolutionary-era pontoon bridge spanning the Schuylkill at Gray's Ferry in Philadelphia was supplemented in 1805 by the wooden "Permanent Bridge" at Market Street and seven years later by the so-called Colossus, or Lancaster-Schuylkill bridge, near Fairmount.[67]

In addition, elaborate public works projects of other sorts aimed to equalize and articulate space in the republican city. Philadelphia's waterworks are a case in point. The city's reliance on inadequate and polluted well water and a belief that unusually dirty parts of the city were responsible for the annual yellow-fever epidemics prompted the corporation to investigate means of rendering the entire city healthy. A contract was eventually made with Benjamin Henry Latrobe, who argued that his system would supply adequate clean water to every neighborhood through public hydrants, while providing water to clean the streets, extinguish fires, and cool the air. In Latrobe's scheme, water was conveyed through a brick tunnel from a basin on the Schuylkill River to a pump house on Center Square, from which it was distributed through wooden pipes to individual subscribers and public hydrants. Since development was only then reaching the grid's midpoint, the location's advantage was symbolic more than real. Like the plan itself, the waterworks promised that Philadelphia *would* develop in an orderly east-west fashion, and the Center Square pump house's distribution box accordingly contained hookups for future mains.[68]

New York's Croton Waterworks, finished in 1842, also relied on a subterranean network that knit together the urban spaces of New York and its citizens. At the same time the system linked the city to its hinterland, for unlike the Philadelphia or New Orleans waterworks, which drew water from rivers that flowed past the city, Croton water came from the Croton River, forty-one miles away. It traveled down a lengthy aqueduct and across High Bridge to a receiving reservoir in the middle of the present Central Park, then finally to a distributing reservoir on the site of the present New York Public Library.[69]

Individually, each of these improvements might be interpreted as a pragmatic effort to make exploding cities work. But although instrumental motives were central to city building, they were imaginatively recast and raised to a more allusive plane that might not seem obvious in the physical city. Only by examining the patterns—the continuities of language and analysis, the similarities among solutions to disparate problems—can we recognize an underlying analytical thread, a way of seeing that chooses the phenomena that are defined as problems and then points the directions that solutions take. It is this way of seeing, the tendency to imagine the city as a system of systems drawn from disparate registers of human life and landscape, and the desire to integrate them into an embodied republican society, that I have called the *republican spatial imagination*.

The systematic city was above all a dynamic city. As the French artist Jacques Gérard Milbert observed, Philadelphia's order was saved from monotony by the "lively traffic." Transparency, articulation, and classification promoted a useful familiarity with urban space. The republican spatial imagination envisioned that space as a scaffolding that specified no uses and emphasized no sites in advance, one that could accommodate and articulate the maximum number of disparate uses. Each person's purposeful movements through the streets connected otherwise independent spaces in a network of personal significance. The street was the negative between the positives of private values; it traced the boundaries and described the location of parcels with no fixed relationships to one another aside from their shared essential comparability. The fundamental order grew from within, shaped by the value of the parts. By 1820, a quarter-century of discussion and experiment had produced a characteristic republican spatial vocabulary that invested schemes for urban planning and infrastructure with the new social and environmental ideas, ideas that also reshaped familiar building types, transforming the marketplace and commercial street into the arcade, the counting room into the office building, the burying ground into the cemetery, and the jail into the penitentiary.[70]

{

Pedestrians ambling along Philadelphia's Chestnut Street in the late 1820s encountered a building unlike any ever seen in the United States—the Philadelphia Arcade (fig. 7.1). Midway along the north side of the street between Sixth and Seventh streets, the marble-faced brick building stood only as high as the conventional three-story brick structures on each side of it, yet its monumental scale and appearance overshadowed its neighbors. Four tall arches clustered at the center of the facade, flanked by a pair of empty semicircular niches. At the springing of the arches the entablature bridged the openings as a balustrade that marked the level of the second floor. A heavy blocking course bore the inscription "Philadelphia Museum." By descending exterior stairs at either end of the facade the intrigued passerby could reach a pair of large cellar rooms, one housing David Gibbs's Franklin Eating House and the other Michael O'Rourke's Shades Refectory. The arches led into the ground floor, where a pair of fourteen-foot-wide stone-paved passages or "avenues" separated three blocks of identical stores, twelve on each of the outside walls and twenty set back-to-back in the center (fig. 7.2). In these shops, each fitted with a "plain show window on each side and sash door in two parts, lifting shutters, square transom and sash over the door and windows," shoppers could buy confections, ladies' shoes, books, dry goods, and minerals. Ascending the marble stairs, elegantly fitted with iron balusters and mahogany rails, curious wanderers would find another group of stores that were approached along cantilevered galleries encircling a light well that illuminated all three floors through the full-length skylights set above each avenue (fig. 7.3). A final climb led to a large, open third-floor room built especially to accommodate the renowned Philadelphia Museum, the former Peale's Museum, which had been moved here from Independence Hall shortly after its founder's death in 1827 (fig. 7.4).[1]

The Philadelphia Arcade was conceived in 1825 by attorney and real estate speculator Peter A. Browne and English émigré architect John Haviland. Browne and Haviland offered investors fifteen hundred shares of stock in their fledgling enterprise at $100 a share, to be paid in $20 installments as the work progressed. Although they sold only a thousand shares, they agreed to cover the remainder of the issue themselves, then moved swiftly to accomplish their project. For $50,000 the newly formed Philadelphia Arcade Company purchased

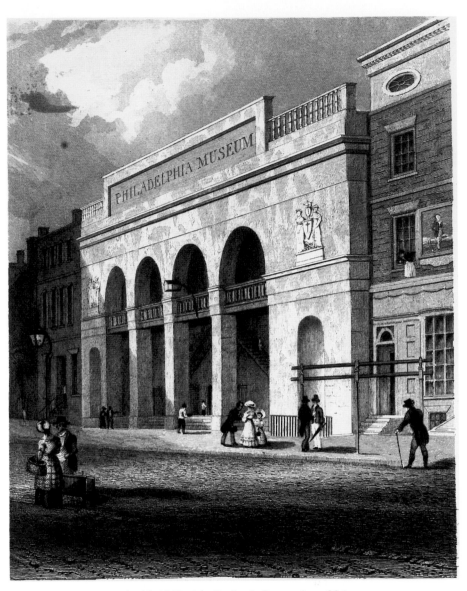

FIGURE 7.1. C. Burton, *Arcade, Philadelphia* (John Haviland, 1825–27; dem. 1860), ca. 1830. (The Library Company of Philadelphia)

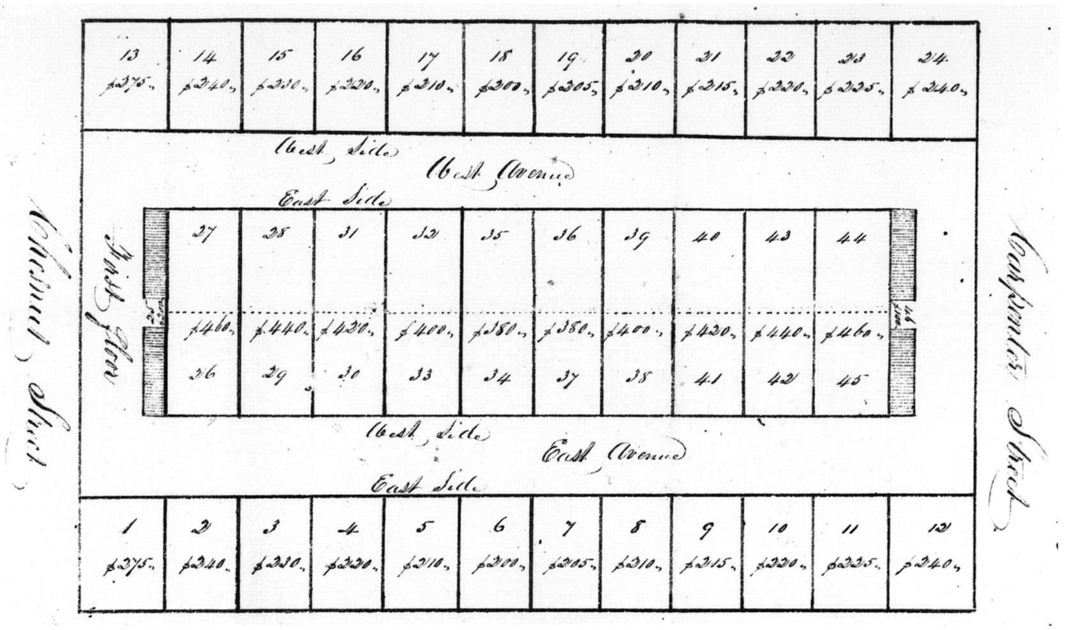

FIGURE 7.2. Philadelphia Arcade, first-floor rental plan, ca. 1827.
(Edward Shippen Burd Papers, The Historical Society of Pennsylvania)

the early-eighteenth-century Carpenter mansion from William Tilghman, who became a shareholder.[2]

As a building type that offered luxury shopping in a refined environment, the commercial arcade was, as its principal historian notes, a significant milestone on the road from the freestanding neighborhood shop to the department store. Like early luxury retail shops, arcades were designed to attract a genteel, exclusive clientele. Some European arcades even charged admission to exclude riffraff. Like the shopping malls of the twentieth century, they were conceived as improved, microcosmic cities but also as tools for enlarging and reforming the cities they graced. But to treat arcades as simple stages in the evolution of retailing overlooks a significant point: almost every antebellum American arcade, including Philadelphia's, failed. To understand their failure it is necessary to consider their peculiar, untenable position at the intersection of new modes of retail sales, rapid urban development, and challenges to traditional ideas about the ethics of business enterprise.[3]

In the late-eighteenth-century United States, the dissemination of genteel standards of behavior transformed retail sales as merchandisers based their sales strategies on the desire of a self-defined gentry to avoid its inferiors. Sellers appealed to an illusory scarcity to stimulate demand. Goods that were in fact available in great numbers to anyone who could pay were promoted as

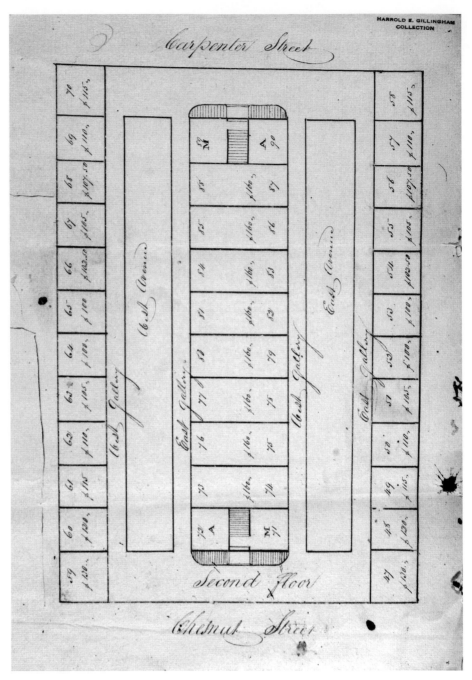

FIGURE 7.3. Philadelphia Arcade, second-floor rental plan.
(Edward Shippen Burd Papers, The Historical Society of Pennsylvania)

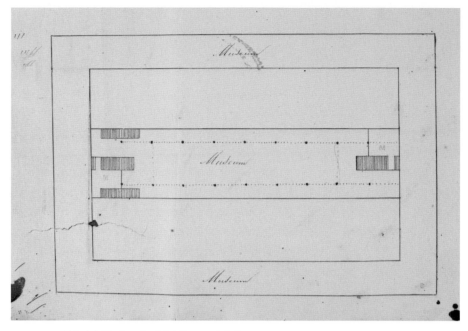

FIGURE 7.4. Philadelphia Arcade, third-floor rental plan.
(Edward Shippen Burd Papers, The Historical Society of Pennsylvania)

though they were restricted to a privileged few. For example, English ceramics manufacturer and marketing innovator Josiah Wedgwood often restricted sales of a new line to a few aristocratic customers, thus creating an appearance of exclusivity and obtaining a kind of endorsement before opening the line to mass sales. Others promoted their products as unique objects, offering manufactured goods as though they were custom-made. Eliza Ripley recalled how the New Orleans milliner Olympe used such a sales tactic in the 1840s. "She did not—ostensibly at least—make or even trim *chapeaux*. Olympe's ways were persuasive beyond resistance. She met her customer at the door with 'Ah, madame'—she had brought from Paris the very bonnet for you! No one had seen it; it was yours! And Mam'zelle Adèle was told to bring Mme. X's *chapeau*. It fit to a *merveille!* It was an inspiration! And so Mme. X had her special bonnet sent home in a fancy box by the hand of a dainty *grisette*."[4]

Before the end of the eighteenth century, most durable products were purchased in their makers' establishments, which normally combined residence, workshop, and sales room. In 1794, Mutual Assurance Company surveyors in Philadelphia found tallow chandler (soap maker) Andrew Kennedy living on the east side of Second Street between High and Chestnut streets, where the first-floor front room of his three-story house served as his ware room and the rear as his parlor. The three-story back building (rear ell) was "finished for a soap boiler's shop." A few blocks away, brass founder Samuel Parker's three-story house on Arch Street between Fourth and Fifth streets had a ground-floor front room that was "not plaistered and occupied for a workshop."[5]

Importing merchants and shopkeepers sold their wares from buildings that were equally likely to combine living and selling spaces. Shopkeeper-grocer Christian Gunkle's three-story house at the corner of Callowhill and Second streets housed a dry-goods business in its front room. Ironmonger-merchant Richard Blackham's "nearly new" dwelling house on Second Street contained a sales room, as did sea captain–shopkeeper John Woods's house, built in 1783 at Front and Lombard streets.[6]

All of these shops were rough-and-ready affairs designed to do little more than protect merchandise from the elements. The commercial portion of Michael Gunckel's High Street house-shop had "rough floor, Walls rough plaistered, and [was] occupied as a Grocery Store." William Tharp's front room at Walnut and Front streets was "plain for a Store with Shelves and Counter."[7]

These late-eighteenth-century traders tended to be general merchants. Luxury goods were one category among many that they carried. According to early Philadelphia historian John Fanning Watson, this state of affairs began to change in Philadelphia just before the Revolution, when John Wallace opened a "store for the sale of worsted, satin and brocade shoes for ladies only; most or all of which were imported." The new-style shops initiated movement toward specialization in all branches of trade. As the volume and variety of goods increased, it was easier to control a single line or related lines of merchandise, despite customary expectations that merchants would carry whatever their established customers wanted.[8]

These new retail stores were as rationally organized as gridded cities. Earlier merchants often heaped goods on tables and counters, piled them in chests, and sometimes did not even bother to separate them from their own personal possessions, but the wider variety of goods that American merchandisers handled after the middle of the eighteenth century were often categorized in walls of shelves and cubbyholes. The late-eighteenth-century White's Store, Isle of Wight County, Virginia, with its wall of shelves divided into compartments of varied sizes centered on thirty-six square cubbyholes for storing small items, embodied the new impulse to separate and classify in the shop (fig. 7.5).[9] A single wall was enough for that rural Virginia merchant, but by the mid-nineteenth century a gridded organization for the storage of goods was standard in retail stores (fig. 7.6). New York wholesale importers Phelps and Peck organized their entire store on the same principles (fig. 7.7).

A common spatial imagination united the store to the "multiplication table" urban grid and its offshoots and, as we will see in the next chapter, the desk

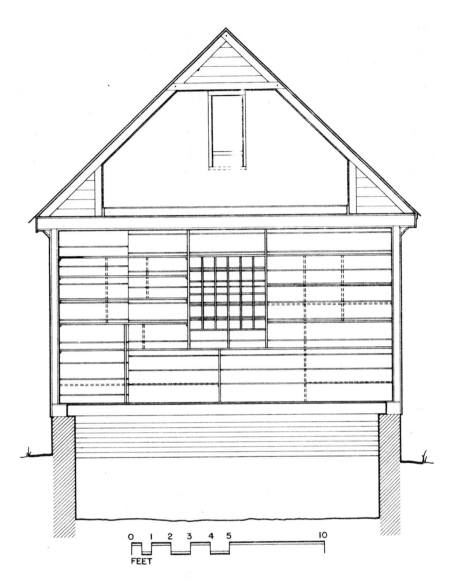

FIGURE 7.5. White's Store (late eighteenth century), Isle of Wight County, Virginia. The end wall of this plantation store was fitted with shelves and cubbyholes to allow the sorting of a variety of goods. (Colonial Williamsburg Foundation)

with its pigeonholes and the celled office building. It is easy to recognize the elements of the systematic city in all of these spaces. Yet changes in selling and buying challenged the premises of these separated and classified retail land-scapes, as specialization allowed for a kind of aggressive merchandising impossible in the older generalized shop.

Shopkeepers began to arrange their shops to display goods appealingly. The most conspicuous were the flat display windows and projecting "bulk," or bay, windows that began to appear on the streets of London in the mid-eighteenth

FIGURE 7.6. B. T. Walshe Men's Furnishings store (mid-nineteenth century), New Orleans. (Courtesy Historic New Orleans Collection, Museum/Research Center, acc. no. 1974.25.3.478)

FIGURE 7.7. Edward W. Clay, *The Ruins of Phelp's & Peck's Store, Fulton St., New York, as they appeared in the morning after the Accident of 4th May 1832.* (Collection of The New-York Historical Society, neg. no. 76193)

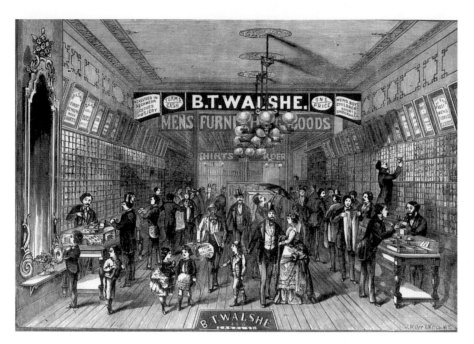

THE RUINS OF PHELP'S & PECK'S STORE,

Fulton St. New York, as they appeared on the morning after the Accident of 4th May 1832.

Lith of Pendleton N. Y.

century and in America very soon after. There were enough bulks in Philadelphia before the Revolution for the city council to include "jut-windows, bulks, and other incumbrances" in an ordinance forbidding obstruction of the streets, but they were not really common until the 1790s. Ordinary domestic windows still served most shops, with a few having old-fashioned shutters hinged at the bottom so that they could be fastened horizontally to act as sales counters.[10]

Show windows represented a radical departure in merchandising (fig. 7.8). The new retail merchants aimed to stimulate demand rather than merely to

FIGURE 7.8. William S. Mason, *John McAllister's Store*, Philadelphia, 1843. One of the earliest photographs of Philadelphia. McAllister's store has early-nineteenth-century bulk windows. (Print and Picture Collection, The Free Library of Philadelphia)

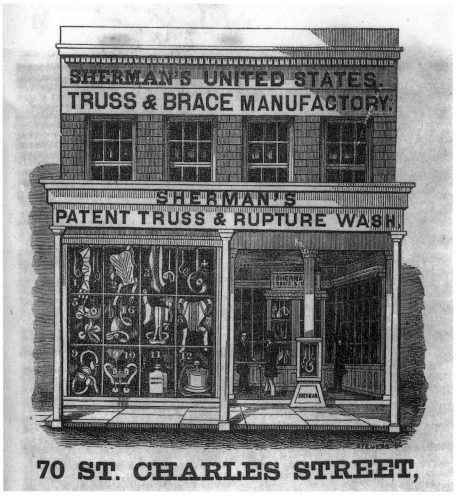

FIGURE 7.9. Sherman's United States Truss & Brace Manufactory, New Orleans, 1854.
(Courtesy Historic New Orleans Collection, Museum/Research Center, acc. no. 98-173-RL)

fulfill a need. They overwhelmed the consumer with insistent, profuse displays of merchandise set out in ways that would catch the eye and that would suggest purchases rather than simply providing goods the consumer had come to buy. Fabrics cascaded in dry-goods merchants' windows, and druggists filled their bulks with translucent colored bottles. Bulks were lighted at night as an additional form of advertising. Such extravagant displays of goods, which prefigured those in late-nineteenth-century department stores, seemed to some foreign visitors to be characteristically American (fig. 7.9).[11]

Inside such shops one might find "gilt and plated buttons, and the scissors, curiously arranged on circular cards, (a new idea)," according to Watson. More important, the interiors of luxury-goods shops presented late-eighteenth-century consumers with a strikingly novel urban space. The new architecture for sales was already evident in Joseph Anthony, Jr.'s goldsmith's and jeweler's shop on the south side of High Street between Third and Fourth streets in Philadelphia, when an insurance surveyor described it in 1793. As usual, the first-floor front room of Anthony's three-story house was his show room, and his workshop and forge were in his back yard, but "Two Circular Bulks . . . and [a] Frontispiece [doorway] with Fluted pilasters" enticed customers into the elegantly appointed shop, which was fitted with carefully made counters embellished with flat panels and mahogany tops. The display cases were also made of mahogany, like the furniture in elite households, with glass sash above and solid doors below. A decorative cornice encircled the room, and the back wall was decorated with "compass work," or arched niches, that may have held the display cases. Anthony's elite customers could patronize a shop whose elaboration rivaled or exceeded that of their own parlors and that was unmistakably different from that of ordinary stores.[12]

The forty-five other places of business described by Mutual Assurance Company surveyors in the decade after 1784 demonstrate how unusual Anthony's shop was. None approached it in elegance. In subsequent years, however, more elaborate commercial buildings began to appear in Philadelphia's busiest streets. The shops in the Shakespeare Building at Third and High streets, with their "carved work and images, . . . presented a scene of magnificence not surpassed by any place of business on the globe, at that day," claimed James Mease (see plate 2). Bailey and Kitchen's jewelry shop at 134 (now 428) Chestnut Street was even finer, according to a Franklin Fire Insurance Company surveyor. It included a "Groind Arch Cieling, form'd with wood & plaister'd, Stucco cornice & mouldings on the ceiling," bulk windows, folding shutters, hanging pilasters, and glazed front door.[13]

The first of these luxury establishments were staffed by shop assistants whose demeanor resembled that of an aristocrat's servants. "The shopman, behind the counter, powdered, bowing and smiling, caused [Thomas Natt's Market Street store] to be 'all the stare' for a time," John Fanning Watson noted. "There being too much of the 'pouncet-box' in the display, however, and the 'vile Jersey half-pence, with a horsehead thereon' being wrapped up, when given in change in whitey brown paper, with a counter bow to the ladies, seeming rather too civil by half for the (as yet) primitive notions of our city folks," he added.[14]

Watson's account of Thomas Natt's store emphasizes the importance of presentation in the new retail shops, as well as the need to flatter the lofty and the aspiring in a setting from which the mundane and the rough-hewn were excluded. Despite Watson's sardonic dismissal, clerks whose obsequious demeanor acknowledged the elevated social standing their customers claimed became an expected feature of fine shops (fig. 7.10).

FIGURE 7.10. C.B.G., *Life in Philadelphia: Silk Stockings*, ca. 1825. The clerk's costume, hair style, and use of French words ("Oui Madame! here is a pair of de first qualité!") exemplify the "pouncet-box" style that astonished J. F. Watson even as the cartoonist ridiculed the black woman's gentility. (The Library Company of Philadelphia)

The psychological process of consumption turns on the possibility of the transformation of self through acquisition and possession. This implied promise played on Euro-Americans' deep-seated materialism: from the time of the earliest colonial settlements Europeans believed that physical surroundings shaped their inhabitants for good or ill. It resonated as well with the early-nineteenth-century American emphasis on self-improvement and self-making, on the conscious actualization of one's inherent potential at its highest possible level.[15]

As we have seen, the boundaries of self are porous. Self extends beyond the body, strictly defined, into its environment, colonizing its surroundings. Because identity can be elaborated through psychological appropriation of one's material surroundings, goods hold out the possibility that selfhood can be purchased, that the tangible can supply some missing intangible. This is particularly true of clothing and other sorts of bodily paraphernalia that move with the body and are incorporated into our egocentric space. Thus, possessions can make us better. Through extravagant displays of merchandise—of more textiles or jewelry or other objects than one could perceive individually—the luxury shop redirected attention from the mundane qualities or purposes of individual items to their textures, colors, and other attributes valorized in the codes of gentility and refinement. The abundance of the luxury retail shop implied unlimited possibilities for self-transformation. But since the qualities we seek are diffuse and abstract while things are specific and limited, desire is never satisfied in the owning, so further purchases are necessary. In that liminal state between desire and purchase—in shopping—we come closest to achieving a new self.[16]

The obsequious clerk and domestic-style architectural refinement cued a culturally defined master-servant relationship that placed the customer in a position of social authority. That this might or might not be true outside the shop was irrelevant. The luxury shop overruled external social relationships by virtue of its physical environment and exclusivity. It created an environment directed to a select few—this hat was made just for *you*, madame. Although eighteenth- and early-nineteenth-century moral theory assumed the existence of a stable, authentic self, the commercial transaction in the shop promoted a situational definition of roles at the intersection of person and setting: one acted as the cues suggested.

The luxury shop succeeded spectacularly as a selling machine. As an institution of social exclusion, an alternative to the social heterogeneity of the traditional market, it failed equally spectacularly. Nevertheless, the early luxury shops provided the urban and social underpinnings for one short-lived but spectacular episode of republican city building—the construction of shopping arcades in the 1820s and 1830s.

Refinement was as essential to an arcade as to a luxury shop. The developer of London's Burlington Arcade (1815) advertised for "persons of respectability" as tenants of the structure, which would have a "uniform and handsome appearance," shops "on an elegant and commodious plan," and sell only articles "not offensive in appearances or smell." Conversely, observers of the Lowther Arcade (1831) in the same city believed that it grew seedy because its managers allowed freestanding stalls (which had been included in the early designs for the Burlington Arcade and later omitted), which "br[ought] it down to the level of a penny shooting gallery." The New York Arcade's rules required individual shopkeepers to maintain their stores "free of every nuisance or thing whatsoever, that would be unsightly, and . . . not [to] place or hang up any goods outside of said store or counter at any time during business hours." Smoking was forbidden and ushers "watch[ed] all suspicious looking persons" and reported them to the police.[17]

Like the operators of the New York Arcade, Haviland, Browne, and their associates intended their enterprise to have a genteel tone. As a Mr. McCauley learned, their plans left no room for the raucous commercialism of the streets around them. McCauley, an oilcloth carpet manufacturer, offered the Arcade Company a handsome sum, £200, for the northern store in the center block of the arcade, "provided he is at Liberty to put up his name on the N. End of the Building in large letters." The north end was the rear (Carpenter Street) facade, which was similar in appearance to the Chestnut Street front, but it is unlikely that McCauley's request was granted, judging from his absence from an 1829 tenant list. Once the arcade had been converted to a bathhouse and cheap hotel, signs appeared on its facade (fig. 7.11).[18]

The arcade offered nothing that could not be purchased elsewhere. Individually, its elegant, specialized shops were matched by any number of similar stores in other parts of the city. It was the number and types of shops, as well as the arcade's status as a genteel haven, that the managers believed would be the keys to its success. The Arcade Company vigorously controlled the mix of tenants to exclude undesirable ones, establishing a whole urban shopping zone free of the lower orders (or of lower orders in other than subservient roles). In 1829, most of the retail stores sold luxury consumer goods, while the offices housed such unobjectionable tenants as attorneys, including Peter A. Browne himself, teachers of drawing and bookkeeping, and the editorial offices of two magazines (table 4).

Not only was the Arcade Company careful in selecting tenants, but its managers understood the need to draw customers into the building, as bulk windows did for freestanding businesses and for the arcade's individual shops. They were pleased to attract the Philadelphia Museum as a tenant, for "by rendering

FIGURE 7.11. F. D. Richards, *Arcade Hotel*, Philadelphia, January 1858. The Philadelphia city seal remains affixed to the facade, but a cast-iron balcony has been added to the second floor, and bulk windows cover the statue niches. (The Library Company of Philadelphia)

Table 4 Tenants of the Philadelphia Arcade, 1829

	Basement	1st floor	2d floor	3d floor
Merchandise and artisanry				
Books and prints		1		
Boots and shoes		1		
Chacer shop			1	
Confectionery		1		
Dry goods		2		
Gilder of hat leathers			1	
Ladies' shoes		1		
Lamps and oil		1		
Minerals			1	
Tailors		3		
Fancy tobacconists		2		
Services				
Attorneys		1	4	
Dentist		1		
Editors			2	
Engraver			1	
Intelligence offices			2	
Lottery offices		2		
Museum				1
Restaurants	2			
Teacher of bookkeeping			1	
Teacher of drawing				1

Source: An Act to Incorporate the Stockholders of the Philadelphia Arcade
(Philadelphia, 1829), pp. 7–8.

the upper part of the Arcade an object of curiosity and attraction, as well to Citizens and Strangers," it would lure potential customers into the building. The museum, with its professed aim of elevating the understanding of the population at large, added an explicit promise of self-improvement to the implicit promise embodied in the consumer goods sold on the lower floors. Anticipating the mutual reinforcement of international exposition and department store in the late nineteenth century, the museum's claim to classify the entire human and natural world in a single system of display also lent the shops a borrowed inclusivity: their arrangement in a celled space beneath the museum suggested that they spanned the universe of what one could, or should, want. Finally, the

Arcade Company expected the museum to have a more specific and longer-term effect on its enterprise: "By increasing the publicity of the whole establishment, the Shops Stores & offices will become more desirable more eagerly sought after and command a better revenue."[19]

In adding a third story to accommodate the museum, the developers may have been seeking as well to solve another potential problem.[20] As they originally planned the arcade, only the ground floor would contain shops while the upper level would be given over to offices, which depended less on casual traffic. This was the standard arrangement of European arcades, which rarely exceeded two stories and whose upper stories were usually used for offices or residences. But how to get passersby to discover the shops? Arcades customarily based their rental values on their position as mid-block connectors of two major streets. In this way, they made land on the interior of a block as valuable as that on the street front because the passageway was potentially a busy street, and shopkeepers could count on casual custom. The Philadelphia Arcade fronted on Chestnut Street, but it ran back to Carpenter Street, a minor alley not used by shoppers (fig. 7.12). Although it was visible down an axial street (Decatur), that, too, was a service way. It was unlikely that the kinds of people the arcade sought to attract would use the building as a casual shortcut to these back streets. By adding the museum, a well-established Philadelphia institution, and advertising it on the facade, potential customers could be drawn to the building as a primary destination. To provide enticements to spend along their whole route to the museum, shops were introduced onto the second floor as well, although it was dominated by offices (see table 4). The provision of an upper level of shops accessible by galleries was a novelty that this arcade introduced to the building type.[21]

As specialized shops became more common at the end of the eighteenth century, they tended to cluster together. In Boston "as you receded from the waterside, the business of the town assumes more of a retail character," with retail trade centered just inland of Faneuil Hall Market. In New Orleans, Chartres and Royale streets, one and two blocks, respectively, from the levee, were the center of fancy goods and dry-goods retailing, although by the 1850s Canal Street was taking over this role. New York's Broadway was the fashionable shopping district, while the Bowery served artisans and the working classes and Chatham Square and Chatham Street, near the notorious Five Points, housed pawnbrokers, as well as shoemakers and dealers in second-hand and ready-made clothes and old furniture. Even Broadway was famously separated into its "fashionable" (west) and "unfashionable" (east) sides. Its most glamorous stretches migrated uptown block by block and eventually leaped over to Fifth Avenue.

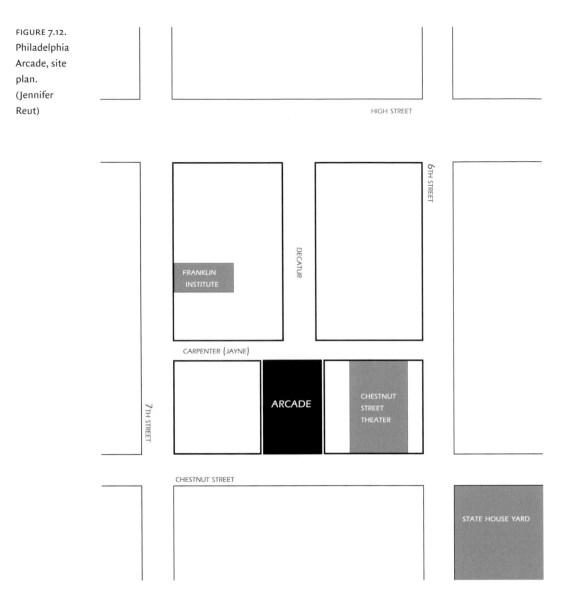

FIGURE 7.12.
Philadelphia
Arcade, site
plan.
(Jennifer
Reut)

HIGH STREET

6TH STREET

DECATUR

FRANKLIN
INSTITUTE

7TH STREET

CARPENTER (JAYNE)

ARCADE

CHESTNUT
STREET
THEATER

CHESTNUT STREET

STATE HOUSE YARD

Philadelphia's Third Street was the "dividing line between the wholesale and retail business of the town; partaking itself largely of both. Milliners and sellers of women's shoes could be found along Second Street between Dock and Spruce streets in the Quaker City, while men's shoe stores clustered on High Street.[22]

The Philadelphia Arcade's developers hoped to profit from the changing retail geography of the Quaker City, as genteel commerce and residences moved westward. Until after the Revolution, the site lay at the western edge of the built-up area of Philadelphia. Writing in 1830, John Fanning Watson recalled that as recently as thirty or thirty-five years earlier, neither Chestnut nor Arch streets, the parallel streets closest to High Street, had even been surveyed west of Tenth Street. Only in the preceding quarter century had "anyone" (meaning any significant person) built as far west as Eighth Street or had shops appeared west of Fourth Street. Once expansion began, however, it gained momentum yearly, with retail business following close behind prosperous residences. Watson painted a picture of frenetic construction and reconstruction, with "Houses . . . of grand dimensions . . . running up for dwellings above Fifth and Sixth streets even while stores were following close after from Fourth street. In a little while the reputation for stands [business sites] in High street became so great and rapid, that the chief of the large dwellings were purchased, and their rich and beautiful walls were torn to pieces to mould them into stores." Eventually the scepter of fashion pointed away from High Street, encumbered as it was by wagon traffic and market sheds, to Chestnut Street, which had "within a few years become the chief street in Philadelphia, as a fashionable walk," Watson wrote in 1830.[23]

The Tilghman property was fortuitously located to take advantage of the new real estate boom, and the family lost no time in doing so. They subdivided their land repeatedly after 1791, when they sold a lot for the construction of the first Chestnut Street Theater. Nevertheless, Tilghmans continued to occupy the Carpenter house until they sold it to the Arcade Company, which demolished it in April 1826.[24]

As real estate developers, the Arcade Company sought to create a shopping district with a single flourish of the architect's pencil. The use of shop fronts resembling those found on the street and even the reference to the passageways as "avenues" suggest the extent to which Haviland and Browne and their associates conceived of the arcade as a miniature, exquisitely regulated, separated, and classified city. Contemporaries understood the connection. One early historian of Philadelphia interpreted the building as an urban-beautification scheme that was superfluous: the Philadelphia Arcade "has languished, since its erection, probably owing to the general beauty of this city, and its great uniformity, the want of which, in many other cities, has rendered Arcades, more cherished objects. Philadelphia has almost all the conveniences of an extensive Arcade, so beautiful are the arrangement of its streets, for shade, and side-walks, etc."[25]

The instant creation of urban districts to compete with established retail centers was a common goal of early American arcade builders. Providence's arcade, for example, was a speculative venture of Rhode Island capitalist Cyrus Butler, who wanted to challenge the city's Brown-family-dominated Cheapside shopping district. Similarly, banker, financier, and developer Thomas Banks constructed an arcade on Gravier Street in New Orleans's Faubourg Sainte-Marie in 1833, in part to compete with Maspero's Exchange in the Vieux Carré, where French-speaking merchants gathered (figs. 7.13, 7.14).[26]

FIGURE 7.13. Banks's Arcade, New Orleans, in 1838. (Courtesy Historic
New Orleans Collection, Museum/Research Center, acc. no. 1950-10-4)

The New Orleans and Philadelphia arcades had revealingly different purposes. Banks's building was a straight real estate venture that provided space
for a mixture of services complementing those already existing in a district
dominated by banks and wholesale merchants. It made no claim to monumen-
tality but appeared from the streets as two parallel rows of three-story commercial buildings with the space between them glazed. The ground floor contained stores, John Hewlett's restaurant, and the offices of notaries, newspapers,
architects, commodity brokers, auctioneers, attorneys, and slave dealers. On the
second floor were offices, billiard rooms, and the Washington Guards armory,
while the third floor provided "sleeping rooms for gentlemen." One portion of
the arcade was used as a more conventional hotel, drawing customers eager to
stay in "the most flourishing business part of the 2d Municipality, where most
of the public sales of real estate and slaves are held." In fact, Banks himself lived
in the building.[27]

A "grand coffee room," 100 by 65 feet, 35 feet high, decorated with prints
and paintings and surrounded by a gallery, served as a gathering place for day-
to-day commercial transactions and for auctions of slaves and merchandise. Its
size—reputedly it held five thousand people—made it a popular venue for American political meetings. The *New Orleans Picayune* reported in 1844 on a "Calhoun and Re-Annexation meeting" that "drew one of the largest assemblages
we have ever seen congregated within the walls of that building." The meeting
promoted the annexation of Texas, a cause so dear to Banks that he bankrupted
himself in 1842 supporting it and was forced to sell his holdings and retire from
business.[28]

It is impossible to say how long Banks's Arcade might have prospered, but
it was a center of American New Orleans's business life for eighteen years, un-

til it burned in 1851. It succeeded in part by closely following the early European arcades' model in providing housing and a variety of services. Retailing was confined to the ground floor, with the upper stories let to tenants less dependent on fashionable or transient traffic. In the absence of a purpose-built exchange or other gathering place it provided an important service to the American mercantile community in the Faubourg Sainte-Marie. As *Gibson's Guide* declared, "A person may very well pass the whole twenty-four hours under the roof of

FIGURE 7.14. Surviving portion of Banks's Arcade

this edifice, nor desire other means, either of repose, excitement, pleasure, or food either for mind or body, than can there be obtained." Banks created a niche for his building within a business district that he helped build.[29]

The Philadelphia Arcade, on the other hand, was built at the edge of the existing business district by men who were more interested in enlarging the city than in developing its commercial core. Both Edward Shippen Burd and Peter A. Browne owned extensive property on the urban fringes. Burd, for example, lived off real estate holdings that may have been worth $600,000 when he died in 1848. In 1847, he paid taxes on approximately sixty parcels in the city, mostly rental housing and vacant land and mostly west of Sixth Street. His business ventures, such as Vauxhall Gardens, a public (amusement) garden built on his land at Broad and Walnut streets, were also sited outside the downtown. Thus his involvement in the arcade fit comfortably with his practice of investing in projects to develop land he had inherited around the perimeter of the colonial city.[30]

Peter A. Browne, too, was most interested in the urban fringe. His rental properties were found primarily in the urbanizing "districts" north and south of Philadelphia proper. In 1829–30, again in conjunction with Haviland, he built the Pagoda or Labyrinth Gardens, a public garden on Coates Street (now Fairmount Avenue) adjacent to the Fairmount Waterworks on the western edge of the city. By the mid-1830s it had been replaced by rental housing.[31]

Browne and Haviland described the Philadelphia Arcade as an "improvement." In words as well as in brick and stone, they offered it as a landmark of the systematic city, designed not merely to house the diverse functions of a developing business district as Banks's Arcade did, but to redefine the city's social and commercial landscape. The Philadelphia Arcade Company wished to show a monumental, highly symbolic public facade that would stand in striking contrast to the sign-covered exteriors of ordinary commercial buildings.

The term "improvement" was used by John Gwynn in 1766 in advocating coordinated planning for London and was eventually applied to the many sporadic public and private projects to rebuild and embellish the city's urban fabric in the late eighteenth century. John Summerson characterized the "spirit of improvement" as an attitude of builders who "took a much wider view of their obligations [to the city] than was necessitated by strict social or economic expediency."[32]

For Philadelphians in the late 1820s "improvement" would have evoked London's Metropolitan Improvements. These development and redevelopment projects in the fashionable West End were initiated by the Prince Regent and directed by the architect John Nash, with whom Haviland had studied in the latter part of his training. They were celebrated in the lavishly illustrated *Metropolitan Improvements,* published in 1827 by Haviland's principal teacher, James Elmes, in collaboration with Thomas Hosmer Shepherd. The royal Metropolitan Improvements enlarged upon the eighteenth-century London practice of private-estate development, in which determined landlords could enforce social homogeneity and coordinated land use in relatively large sections of the city. Regent's Park and Regent Street leading to it were the centerpiece of the royal efforts. Here the Prince Regent went the private landlords one better, carving an enormous swath through London that was intended to create a nearly self-contained genteel district of shops, amusements, and elite residences, all in a coordinated architectural style.[33]

The improvement ethos was strong in both arcade developers. Browne was involved in many forms of Philadelphia improvement in the 1820s. He supported the demolition of Latrobe's pump house to integrate the eastern and western portions of the city, advocated the introduction of gas light, and served as corresponding secretary of the Franklin Institute, whose mission was to promote technological innovations that might stimulate economic development. Haviland's American career was built on his renown as architect of Philadelphia's Eastern State Penitentiary, a major monument of early-nineteenth-century Euro-American social reform. The reputation he earned there sustained a career of prison, jail, hospital, and asylum building and consulting, even as it paid him a decade of lucrative fees as Philadelphia building boomed in the 1820s. During the decade that the arcade was built and the penitentiary begun, he designed houses, offices, meeting halls, and churches for the city's prosperous residents, carceral institutions for its dregs, theaters for its entertainment, and banks and offices in the satellite towns that grew up along the canal and railroad lines financed by Philadelphians.[34]

Nevertheless, Haviland and Browne's power to transform the city was not equal even to an eighteenth-century London landlord's, much less to the Prince Regent's. Instead, they sought to create a refined but more limited district by bricolage, through juxtaposing their building to nearby monumental structures and alluding to them visually. The arcade stood a few yards from the State House (Independence Hall), by then Philadelphia's city hall and the seat of federal and state courts. It was a block away from Washington Square, which, with State House Yard, had become a fashionable promenading site. Several elite cultural institutions, such as the Library Company, the University of Pennsylvania, and the American Philosophical Society, were close by, and Haviland's own Franklin Institute building was going up around the corner on Seventh Street at the same time as the arcade (see fig. 7.12).[35]

Most of all, the arcade's design acknowledged the Chestnut Street Theater, newly reconstructed from designs by architect William Strickland after an 1820 fire (fig. 7.15).[36] Here was another similarity to Nash's projects. In reworking the Haymarket portion of his Regent Street development, Nash built a new Royal

FIGURE 7.15. F. D. Richards, *Chestnut Street Theater* (William Strickland, 1822), Philadelphia, 1854. (The Library Company of Philadelphia)

Theater and completed the exterior of the unfinished Royal Opera House with an encircling colonnade that included a shopping arcade. Although Haviland had left England in 1815, before the Royal Opera project got under way, he and Browne evidently knew the project as well as the urban role of European arcades generally. Like Nash, Haviland connected a theater and an arcade, but he did so by allying his building visually with the existing theater, which stood only a few doors down the block.[37]

The arcade's visual obeisance to the theater is obvious. Strickland had placed "basso-relievos representing the tragic and comic muses" on the theater's facade. Above them he installed local sculptor William Rush's statues *Comedy* and *Tragedy* (1808), which had been salvaged from the ruins of the earlier theater. Haviland's reliefs of the city and state seals on the arcade's facade answered Strickland's reliefs. Had the decorations been completed, the figures of *Commerce* and *Navigation* that Haviland intended for the niches on the arcade's facade would have responded even more strikingly to Rush's *Comedy* and *Tragedy* down the block. By acknowledging Strickland's design, Haviland gave the 600 block of Chestnut Street a second monumental facade and contributed to a complex layering of Philadelphian and European references, defining the block as a principal site of genteel culture in antebellum Philadelphia. In addition, the arcade's facade connected the gay world of theater and the sober world of commerce, transforming the latter into the gay world of shopping.[38]

If the arcade offered self improvement and metropolitan improvement, it also explicitly alluded to the contemporary American political doctrine of "internal improvements," or the public promotion of a "perfect system of roads and canals" that would link the Northeast with the developing regions of the country, creating a systematic "domestic market," based on the articulation of the "difference of climate and interests" among the regions, in James Monroe's words. Internal improvements were first proposed in the 1780s by members of Philadelphia's American Philosophical Society as a way to promote national unity and economic development, and they were a continuing theme in the politics of the early republic. The arcade was begun the year after Congress had passed the General Survey Act, which authorized planning for a national system of canals and roads, an important element in the program.[39]

In that spirit, the company stressed in words as well as in architecture the arcade's siting west of the traditional business district, linking the city's westward movement with the nation's. To augment the city and state seals and the unexecuted statues, Haviland hired an "Italian Artist" to embellish the necking of each of the facade piers with masks of Mercury. These images of the messenger god were rich in overtones relevant to the arcade project. Mercury—Hermes to the Greeks—was a complex figure known for his brilliance and cunning. He was the god of roads, doors, and boundaries, the god of the stone-heap, or *hermaion*, that marked paths, the god who guided travelers and protected people dealing with strangers, the god of lucky finds. As the god of boundaries, Mercury was by extension the god of trade, an attribute acquired when markets were held at city boundaries and merchants were, in Homer's words, "professional boundary crossers." In a memorable speech to his mother, recounted in a Homeric hymn, Hermes celebrated profit taking and the comfortable life it afforded. Thus the iconography of Mercury meshed nicely with the Arcade Company's conception of its role in providing a marketplace on the edge of urbanized Philadelphia.[40]

The arcade's decorations celebrated the role of private enterprise in public life and demonstrated that, nearly forty years after the reorganization of the Philadelphia city council, republican imagery could still persuade. The seals, the heads of Mercury, and the projected statues mapped the arcade in the systematic space of the city grid and linked it to national and international systems of trade. They also underlined the project's republican capitalist context, symbolized by the seals of the state, whose constitution had been rewritten in 1790 as the culminating act of the republican counterrevolution, and of the city, which included the iconic Penn plan.

The Philadelphia Arcade Company offered itself to the public and to the legislature as a distinctively republican enterprise. As the company noted in its request for a state charter, the $162,000 cost of the land and building was a sum that few individuals in early nineteenth-century Philadelphia could comfortably have invested, so the arcade was necessarily a joint venture. Joint enterprises were familiar to Philadelphians accustomed to "subscribing" to costly undertakings. Colonial- and early-national-period merchants commonly engaged in "ventures" or "purchases in company," short-term partnerships to undertake voyages or quantity purchases too costly or risky for a single investor. Similarly, Philadelphians, particularly Quakers, were regularly solicited to subscribe both to short-term charitable initiatives and to the support of new institutions, ranging from asylums to libraries and historical societies, with civic or philanthropic missions. Those who subscribed became stockholders entitled to a voice in the selection of officers and the management of the institution.[41]

Neither of these earlier forms of financial association was quite like the arcade's. They involved smaller individual investments, so the risk was limited, in the former case by the short-term nature of the venture and in the latter by its charitable purposes. Not only was the arcade a costly project, it was a real estate speculation involving the construction of a monumental building. This implied that the Arcade Company was meant to be a long-lasting firm, while traditional enterprises rarely outlasted the death or resignation of a principal. Thus, the Arcade Company required a more formal structure and the limitation of liability. As the stockholders' petition emphasized, the "building [of] an Arcade of this magnitude was far beyond individual enterprize, and never would have been undertaken, much less carried on to a successful conclusion, except for a reasonable hope that the stockholders entertained, that a charter would eventually be granted to them."[42]

The investors' hope was grounded in the "enlightened and judicious" policies of republican America, particularly the "greater facility allowed by its legislatures to enterprising associations." They had in mind the new legal standing granted to private corporations. Incorporation was traditionally viewed as a concession of extraordinary powers for public benefit and consequently was most commonly reserved for public bodies, such as city governments and for some nonprofit institutions. The exigencies of developing the new nation led early-nineteenth-century courts to stretch the concept of the public good radically and consequently to expand the privilege of incorporation to include private profit-making bodies. In doing so, they overturned longstanding practice by privatizing the powers of public improvement and the decision-making processes that attended them. Willing legislatures responded by handing out corporate charters like business cards.[43]

The Arcade Company appealed to the legislature in this spirit, noting that "while little else but private gain is kept in view, every step of an operation has led to the most magnificent results of public utility." They repeatedly reminded legislators and the public that they had constructed a "very useful building, forming in the centre of the city a depot of various valuable articles of merchandize" that was at the same time a "stately, commodious, and beautiful edifice," a "splendid ornament to the city of Philadelphia, which excites the admiration of not only all our own citizens but of strangers and foreigners." According to the Company, the arcade typified the kinds of projects that Americans acting privately could undertake but that many foreign governments could not, or could accomplish only despotically. "Great works which in former times were sure indications of slavery, being executed in this manner, are so many proofs of perfect freedom." Such an exemplary republican enterprise ought to be rewarded with a charter, they insisted.[44]

The Arcade Company's republican capitalist arguments convinced Pennsylvania's Senate, which approved the charter, but they met resistance in the lower house, where egalitarian, anti-capitalist sentiments remained strong. Browne, in Harrisburg to lobby for incorporation, found it necessary to call on investor Edward Shippen Burd to assist in winning over Representative George Emlen, whose "objection is to corporations in general, not to this particular institution, and therefore any arguments which tend to shew that the arcade company are distinguished by no hostile feature towards the rights of the citizens generally will be useful."[45]

Despite the Arcade Company's vigorous promotion, their building never attracted a consistently genteel tenantry or clientele. Even in the earliest years the proprietors admitted two intelligence offices, which were slightly disreputable employment services for domestic servants that were "generally conducted at first by blacks." These offices attracted crowds of would-be servants whose presence undermined the arcade's air of exclusivity. The two resident lottery offices, "a new race, luxuriating on the imaginative schemings of some, and the aversion to honest labour in others," were even more worrisome.[46]

The intelligence offices and lottery brokers were admitted after bitter debate among the proprietors, occasioned by the Company's inability to make the building pay. Browne reported to Burd that "the tenants of the Arcade are very anxious that the Vacant stores should be filled up, as we have already a handsome income & it is better that it should be filled *at all events*. I propose to advertize and sell the other stores *at auction*." At the same time, however, he was anxious that no lottery offices be admitted, given the moral taint of gambling and the kinds of customers the shops attracted: "Every respectable person I have spoken to says that if there are more than two at most the ladies will not visit the Arcade." Browne was dismayed to learn that twelve spaces had been let to ten lottery brokers in his absence and pleaded with the managers to cancel the leases. He argued that "two respectable dry goods store keepers" and James Brown, a ladies' shoemaker, would take three of the shops let to lottery offices (they did) if the leases were rejected, and that R. McGregor, tenant of shops 28 and 29, would pull out if any were admitted (he did). He suggested that if two slots were auctioned among the ten lottery offices, the result would be a great profit and the retention of genteel trade. He concluded, however, by reiterating that "I hear but one opinion and that is that the admission of Lottery Offices will *ruin the Arcade*." The tenant list shows that Browne's compromise proposal won the day, but at the expense, apparently, of admitting intelligence offices.[47]

Within a few years the proprietors had begun to accept even more marginal and suspect businesses. Surrounded by shooting galleries, billiard parlors, and other popular amusements, the arcade became a bathhouse and billiard parlor in 1844 and then a cheap hotel in 1855 (see fig. 7.11) Its brief career came to an abrupt end in 1863, less than forty years after its construction. David Jayne, a drug manufacturer and real estate speculator who redeveloped most of the 600 block of Chestnut Street in the 1850s and 1860s, demolished the arcade and put up "three fine white marble-front stores" on its site.[48]

In part, the arcade failed through simple miscalculation. Although Philadelphia's urban edge moved rapidly westward, its commercial center of gravity lay considerably east of the arcade in 1825. As late as 1850 Third Street remained the dividing line between the city's wholesale and retail districts. Browne and Haviland decided to challenge this state of affairs. By purchasing the Tilghman tract they sought to place their arcade in the path of the "proper march of city improvement." But if late-nineteenth-century Philadelphia historian Willis Hazard was correct, these speculators in the city's expansion may not have been bold enough in their Chestnut Street venture. While some fashionable shops remained in the Second and Third street areas, others quickly leapfrogged the arcade farther out Chestnut Street. Because, Hazard wrote, "after a time [the arcade] became out of the walks of fashion and convenience," it "degenerated into shops of very petty tradesmen."[49]

Yet there was a moment when the arcade *was* in the walks of fashion and convenience, but it did not succeed even then. The arcade's brand of exclusivity never took hold in the expanding commercial world of the nineteenth-century city. Again, it is instructive to refer to Banks's Arcade of New Orleans. Banks, who had come to the Crescent City from England in 1810, opened a boarding house for sailors, built a fortune through investments in ships and real estate, and became one of the principal improvers of the new "American Sector," along with the Canadian-born, New England–educated Samuel J. Peters, James H. Caldwell, and Philadelphia native Benjamin Morgan. Among them they built stores, hotels, and theaters, installed gas service, and began to pave the streets of the faubourg. Banks had constructed the City Hotel in 1832, to a design of Prussian émigré architect Charles F. Zimpel. It served as an informal American merchants' exchange in the absence of a building formally dedicated to that purpose. When Banks undertook his arcade, also designed by Zimpel, he intended it to assume the role of an exchange and to contribute to the growing economic power and political influence of the Faubourg Sainte-Marie.[50]

Banks strove for an ethnic rather than a class constituency. His arcade played on the intense and bitter rivalry between the Crescent City's Francophones and Anglophones. Americans felt shut out of the French Quarter and clustered just outside its bounds. Yet they also maintained an arrogant sense of superiority to the longer-established Creole elite and, as the principal shipping merchants of the city, they had the capital to back up their arrogance. Thus the Faubourg Sainte-Marie was aggressively developed by the Americans as a challenge to the French merchants of the Vieux Carré. Banks's Arcade competed with a district owned by merchants whose economic and political power was declining, and it was one of a number of improvements in its neighborhood. It did not challenge the older business district singlehandedly.

The Philadelphia Arcade, on the other hand, was a lone venture in direct conflict with still-powerful merchants along Second and Third streets. In a pamphlet published to explain the arcade's problems to its stockholders and to rally public support, the Arcade Company claimed that the "proprietors of the old buildings in Second street and its vicinity, had been so long accustomed to receive exorbitant rents, that they regarded every attempt to carry the business to the westward as an encroachment upon their prerogative. The movement of a single store was looked upon with jealousy; but when a proposition was made to build an arcade to the west—to locate 100 shops out of the privileged bounds—the tocsin was sounded, the interested took alarm, and every artifice human ingenuity could devise was put into requisition," and "an effort was made to smother the whole plan, but this failed of success."[51]

The arcade's opponents rented shops but never opened businesses, hoping to thwart the formation of a new, self-contained business district. One man who did so "acknowledged that his *object was to injure the Arcade*." Some refused arcade tenants the professional courtesies that wholesale merchants traditionally extended to shopkeepers. This happened to a tailor who "called at a store where he was in the habit of dealing, and selected some goods, which the merchant was willing to sell him upon a credit; when he ordered them to be sent to the Arcade, *they were returned to the shelves again*." Similarly, a woman who opened a drawing school in the new building found that her students "*declined attending there*." In addition, the Company confessed that it had mistakenly rented some stores to "adventurers, who offered at the public sale very high rents, and of course expected to realize rapid fortunes. Being disappointed, they moved away, and attributed losses to the Arcade, which were occasioned by their own folly—one man brought *his all* upon a wheel-barrow, and decamped in about a month."[52]

The attacks on the arcade spoke of more than mere "jealousy" and imprudence. The expanding capitalist economy of the early nineteenth century left even its most active participants ambivalent about its incompatibility with traditional business ethics, which emphasized straightforward dealing, customary pricing, cautious trading, and the mutual loyalty of buyers and sellers. In an economy based as thoroughly as that of eighteenth- and early-nineteenth-century American cities on memory and personal reputation, no other ethos was practical. Many clung to these rules as moral imperatives even as their economic utility evaporated. A group of self-described merchants and manufacturers of Baltimore lamented the "great irregularity and artificial excitements" in the market that led traders, especially younger ones, "whose soundness of principle it would appear to be the true policy to foster, from the sober calculations of integrity . . . into rash adventure and habits of chance, which bear a greater affinity to gambling than to commerce or trade. The most artful generally overcome the more honest." Such practices could lead only to ruin, which affected not only the failed merchant but all of his associates.[53]

Bankruptcy might overtake anyone in a volatile economy, but businesspeople expected bankrupts to move quickly and frankly to settle their affairs. Even then, to fail seemed to some a humiliating sign of personal laxness or duplicity. Watson reported that in the case of one bankruptcy, "the whole house was closely shut up for one week, as an emblem of the deepest family-mourning; and all who passed the house instinctively stopt and mingled the expressions of their lively regret." Failed merchants' children disappeared from schools as their families withdrew from social life. Even though he remained a wealthy man, Philadelphia merchant Thomas Pym Cope was so aggrieved by the misdeeds of his trading partners that he contemplated suicide one evening in 1803. Only the sight of his infant daughter changed his mind.[54]

Of course, these commercial ethics were regularly violated, including, apparently, at the arcade. During the venture's travails John Haviland embezzled funds from the account of the U.S. Naval Hospital in Norfolk, Virginia, of which he had been appointed architect in 1826. In a draft letter to Navy Department official John Branch, Haviland acknowledged that "my enterprise in speculative Building called the Phi. Arcade was [illeg] unsuccesful [?]." A later draft charged Peter A. Browne with impropriety and explained Haviland's crime as a consequence of Browne's: "not satisfied with working on commission I entered into a very large contract and took a joint interest in its speculation[;] it promised a large profit which would have been realized but for the failure of my partner who misused the funds and [left] me responsable for all the debts[;] threatened with imprisonment I applied a part of the U.S.H. fund to remove the disgrace and save my credit with the firm intention of replacing it by a sale of my Arcade stock; but every intention to make a sale was unsuccessful until my creditors would wait no further delay."[55]

A further brake on unrestrained accumulation, implied in Haviland's confession, was the widespread allegiance to what was called a competency, whose premise was that people needed only so much to live. It was not an egalitarian idea, for some people deserved more than others by virtue of their social standing, but it did imply that to strive for more than one's portion was unseemly and perhaps immoral. Elite, middling, and poor Philadelphians all espoused the ideal of competency. Cope complained that but for a badly chosen partner, "I should long since have retired or at least have had a sufficiency to warrant my retiring from the thorny path of business," peopled as it was with "sordid lovers of gain." The idea of a competency also encompassed artisans' and small tradesmen's hope to attract a custom lively enough to allow them to live modestly during their active years and to have something for their declining years. As Watson wrote, "If they did not aspire to much, they were more sure of the end—a decent competency in old age, and a tranquil and certain livelihood while engaged in the acquisition of its reward."[56]

The concept of competency encompassed both the necessity of personal discipline and the mutual interdependence of the urban community. Each worker, many artisans believed, earned a niche in society by providing a service to the community as a whole, and each person consequently had a right to a life of reasonable comfort and access to necessities, however modest his or her circumstances. Service and self-respect demanded economic independence as a sign of public regard and gratitude. In this mood, a group of Baltimore merchants and manufacturers declared that when the benefits of commerce accrued to "resident merchants," they "contribute . . . in a very considerable degree, to support the artists and labouring classes of towns, and to furnish the agriculturists of our country, with the means of supplying themselves with such articles of foreign and domestic manufactured goods as are essential to their convenience; each deriving some benefit from the services and the expenditure of the other, and thus a general improvement results from the labor of all."[57]

Collectively, these ideas engendered distrust of unrestrained competition. If one acted ethically, if one occupied an appropriate pigeonhole in the communal store, it was unfair for others to undermine one's livelihood by circumventing the rules. Traditional merchants and artisans retained their clientele by personal service and decent treatment, as defined by customary relationships and pricing. The merchant's custom and the small tradesman's competency were threatened by others' acquisitiveness, which created "monopolies," a very broad category in the early republic.

Monopoly encompassed any attempt to "engross" or gain an unfair share of business. For John Fanning Watson, monopolistic practices included advertising, wholesale selling, auctions, and attempts to increase one's business by vastly enlarging one's stock or by shops "sought out at much expense, and display of signs and decorated windows, to allure custom," such as those in the Philadelphia Arcade. *Atkinson's Casket* condemned the practice as "drumming," a means through which new businesses in New York

> get custom by hook or by crook. . . . The new firms must stir themselves, and draw off the business from the old ones if possible. . . . A little impudence, well employed, will sometimes do wonders in the way of making money. To ask a man to buy of you, instead of your neighbours, is but asking him in other words to benefit himself—inasmuch as you will sell cheaper, of course, and give him better bargains than your neighbours. At least, it is your interest to

make him believe so; for as to telling the precise truth, that would not by any means serve your turn.

The passage might have been written by Philadelphia metals importer Nathan Trotter, who resisted advertising and salesmanship and even refused to install racks to display copper products as his rivals had. Instead, he believed that if he treated his customers honorably they would remain with him. He was shocked when they deserted him for competitors offering lower prices or better terms. To steal customers that way was unethical.[58]

Monopoly was sometimes described as an upper-class vice not found among modest artisans or merchants: "As none got suddenly rich by monopolies, they went through lives, gradually but surely augmenting their estates, without the least fear or the misfortune of bankruptcy." At its extreme, monopoly was an oligarchic practice; in response, the people rebelled. Writing in a year of New York food riots, Asa Greene compared the "two evils of mobs and monopolies." There was a "pretty close connection between them—namely, that of cause and effect—the oppression of the monopoly leading to the outrage of the mob," and indeed the New York protests denounced the "monopolies" responsible for high food prices. Nevertheless, accusations of monopoly could fall on anyone. The defense of traditional prerogatives and efforts to thwart monopoly often cloaked other kinds of competition, for they were intended to drive rivals from the field by ruling them out of bounds.[59]

The arcade proprietors' acknowledged violation of customary ethics cast their project into an antisocial light. The arcade failed because it violated traditional sanctions against competition by threatening the livelihoods of established businesspeople. Its owners aroused the anger of other property owners, just as tenants such as Joseph L. Moore, a New York dealer in "fancy dry goods," who opened an arcade store in which he offered goods purchased at New York auctions to be "sold at very reduced prices at Whole Sale and Retail," aroused that of established shopkeepers and merchants. Arcade merchants substituted consumerist imagery for the personalism of traditional business and inspired bitter opposition from competitors. But the arcade failed as well because it ran afoul of other forces transforming the commercial landscape.[60]

If the arcade was too impersonally competitive from the point of view of older business ethics, from the perspective of new mass-selling techniques it was not aggressive enough. The Arcade Company meekly accepted the premises of the systematic model of urban life. The building remained politely within its cell in the grid, insulated by the public circulation space around it. Inside, individual shops were ranged in careful ranks along the interior streets. In its acquiescence to the ethos of the separated and classified grid, the arcade was too genteel, too exclusively private, and too diffident at a time when retail selling increasingly depended on active contact with the street through shop windows and bold signs. Architecturally, the new stores were both more lavishly staged and less exclusive. By the third decade of the nineteenth century, urban dry-goods merchants such as New York's Alexander T. Stewart, an Irish immigrant who set up in business in 1824 and who built a strikingly monumental store on the unfashionable side of Broadway in 1845, radically expanded their businesses by employing the environmental and sales techniques of the luxury shopkeeper and the arcade merchant without restricting their clientele to the self-nominated elite (fig. 7.16). These merchants were even more extravagant in their architectural references than were the first luxury-goods sellers. They borrowed their imagery from European aristocrats' palaces and gathering places rather than from American elite residences, as the luxury shops and arcade tenants did. Stewart's "marble palace" "resembles somewhat the Palladian, and makes a nearer approach to some of the facades of the London Club houses than that of any building in the city," reported the *Broadway Journal*. In Stewart's, jokingly referred to as the Ladies Exchange (in contrast to the men's, or merchants,' exchange a few blocks south), shoppers encountered "urbanity, fairness of dealing, and [an] immense stock of goods."

They were tempted by "gorgeous brocades, suspended in the rotunda . . . , enticing cloaks and mantles . . . fleecy blankets, . . . and, above all, the snowy damask piled endwise, as children do their cob houses." Furthermore, the *Home Journal* added, "You meet with attention and courtesy from the clerks, but are not annoyed by undue solicitations to purchase." Like Thomas Natt, Stewart and his competitors preferred obsequious male clerks, despite occasional claims that clerking was too effeminate for men and deprived women of respectable and appropriate employment. The difference from the first generation of luxury shops was that dry-goods and allied merchants sold at fixed prices to anyone. At a sale at Bowen and McNamee's silk store in New York, the

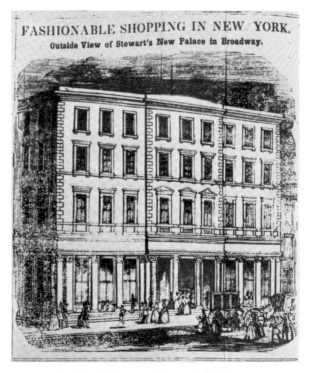

FIGURE 7.16. *Fashionable Shopping in New York*, ca. 1850. (Collection of The New-York Historical Society, neg. no. 70513)

"stately dames of Fifth Avenue were elbowed by their own Bridgets. . . . The luxuries of dress were to be had at a bargain, and thousands on thousands were availing themselves of the opportunity or the temptation." It may be a sign of popular regard for Stewart's that none of New York's "heterogeneous mass of population" threw a stone or a snowball through any of the store's inviting six-by-eleven-foot plate-glass show windows, as diarist Philip Hone expected them to do. Yet dry-goods stores and department stores did not kill the arcades: they never got off the ground in the first place.[61]

At a time of rapid transformation of urban space, urban society, and commercial practices, the Philadelphia Arcade occupied an awkward position at the juncture of the older merchant/artisan ethos, the systematic republican spatial ideal, and a third, less totalizing way of imagining and organizing urban space. The arcade exemplified the systematic spatial imagination. In its abstraction and impersonality, it violated the personalist commercial/artisan ethos, while its genteel restraint and its respect for the separation and classification of the grid, were swamped in the frenzied streets surrounding it.

This frenetic street scene, embodied in the commercial landscape of small retail shops, bill-posters, and of "*towering* business houses and hotels, &c." appeared to John Fanning Watson, as to many of his contemporaries, as a chaotic anti-landscape (plate 8). On closer examination it warrants labeling as a second variety of spatial imagination, one that might be called the competitive landscape, a product of an individualized understanding of the commercial world. Less often articulated or explicated in the early nineteenth century than the systematic point of view, the competitive spatial imagination nevertheless played an equally important role in shaping the city. Where the systematic ideal suggested a unitary, large-scale urban order, competitive practice encouraged multiple, small-scale urban orders. Individually they might resemble those the systematic paradigm proposed for the whole city, as in the interior gridding of stores and warehouses or the ways ballooning new business buildings filled out without eradicating their cells in the urban grid (fig. 7.17). Collectively, however, they were discontinuous, decentralized, and in some respects mutually exclusive. The enlarged size and new forms of commercial establishments, domestic and commercial land-use practices, and the density of development infused such energy and complexity into the urban landscape that it sometimes seemed to constitute a city beyond rational control.[62]

Both the systematic and the competitive landscapes incorporated many common landscape elements of earlier cities, but in extending, intensifying, and reinterpreting these features, antebellum city builders created a new city that was notably different from earlier ones. More important, Watson's "anti-

FIGURE 7.17. *Chestnut Street, from Seventh to Sixth (North Side.)*, Philadelphia, 1859.
The Arcade in its last years. (The Library Company of Philadelphia)

social" tendencies permeated both the systematic and competitive landscapes, because both promoted individual action in commercial and commercialized settings. Public life and public space were subsumed to a collective private; that is, the concept of the public was redefined as the sum of many private goods and actions. Proponents of the systematic landscape assumed that a public order would emerge from this collective private. Builders of the competitive landscape did not address the issue.

While the traditional commercial/artisan ethos was older than the other systematic or competitive landscapes, it is important to see all three approaches to the commercial city as simultaneous rather than sequential modes of thought. City people were quite capable of shifting their allegiance from one model to another as their interests demanded. As it happened, proponents of the systematic landscape were more successful in transforming the landscape of large public institutions, while the competitive builders succeeded most fully in shaping the private landscape of business. From this perspective, the arcade was probably doomed from its inception. But the outcome was less clear on the street, where the two landscape paradigms clashed most strenuously and least conclusively.

CHAPTER 8

{ **PERMUTATIONS OF THE PIGEONHOLE**
Architecture as Memory

In the early republic merchants lived by their memories, for trade was a thoroughly personal activity. They took intense pride in their involvement in their businesses, and they tended to limit their scope to that of which they could maintain an intimate grasp. As R. Campbell observed of London merchants, they needed to understand the "Character and Humour of their Traders, their Coins, Weights, and Measures, their particular Manner of keeping Accompts, the Course of their Exchange, &c . . . [and] the common Arts, Tricks, and Frauds, put into practice by the Dealers." For these reasons, they restricted their dealings to people of whom they had direct knowledge through personal contact, recommendation by trustworthy sources, kinship and, often, common ties of religion or ethnicity. In addition, Campbell wrote, "a Merchant ought to be a Man of an extensive Genius . . . ; he must understand not only Goods and Merchandize in general, and be a Judge of every particular Commodity he deals in, but must know Mankind and be acquainted with the different Manners and Customs of all the Trading Nations; he must know their different Products, the Properties of their Staple Commodities, their Taste in the several Sorts of Goods they want, their principal Marts and Markets, [and] the Seasons proper for buying and selling." Because he often dealt in real estate and finance as well as in hard goods, he must keep up with many aspects of the economy. Merchants were necessarily men (and sometimes women) of "Memory and Acuteness . . . Sagacity and Oeconomy, refraining to launch out of the Depth of their Stock and Knowledge."[1]

These merchants understood commerce in two very different ways. When making public pronouncements about economics or politics, or when attempting to structure the legal or physical environment of business, they took the long view of the economy as a system and grounded their arguments in abstract concepts of human nature. However, they conducted their own businesses as individual relationships governed by their personal knowledge and experience of their trading partners. Merchants treated individual transactions, in other words, as one-on-one encounters rather than as parts of a dynamic system of relationships centered on the ebb and flow of products and funds through the countinghouse. While instruction books on commercial practice advocated double-entry bookkeeping for the picture it revealed of the systematic shape of an economy, most merchants used account books and letter books as aide-mémoire, clues to business data that were impressionistic, unquantifiable, volatile, and hence impossible to formulate outside the merchant's memory. As late as 1910 an English commentator described the merchant's knowledge as a "great 'tradition'; it is a large mass of most valuable knowledge which has never been described," but one that required close, unceasing attention to "what is called 'the standing of parties'" and to the "inevitable changes which from hour to hour impair the truth of that tradition."[2]

Philadelphia lawyer and real estate speculator Peter A. Browne's 1837 rent book, compiled for the use of an agent while Browne was out of the country, reveals the everyday operation of this "great tradition." Browne was one of the principal systematizers of Philadelphia in the 1820s and 1830s, as an organizer of the Philadelphia Arcade and a developer of pleasure gardens and housing estates. In his dealings with his tenants, however, Browne chose to act according to his assessment of their characters rather than to apply a uniform, impersonal management policy. The rent book characterized each according to his or her creditworthiness: "This is a punctual tenant." "This man has to be sued every half year." "Pretty good pay; requires looking after." "Poor but honest." "This man is *poor*." His personalized strategy was not necessarily motivated by charity or humanity. Rather, it reveals the extent to which traditional businessmen preferred to rely on beliefs about individual human character rather than on ideas about economics, or rather the extent to which economic practice was based on the merchant's experience of individuals' character.[3]

The personalism of business practice applied both to the scale of individual enterprises and to their architectural settings. Incorporated businesses were rare and specialized phenomena. Even the largest commercial firms were organized as partnerships of two or three merchants connected by blood, marriage, religion, or long association. Their offices, or countinghouses, were located behind retail display rooms, at the rear or on upper floors of wholesale warehouses, on the ground floors of the combined residences and stores common on eighteenth-century waterfronts, or freestanding in the yards of merchants' mansions. A countinghouse was typically a single room organized around the proprietor, who sat at a desk toward

FIGURE 8.1. *Merchant*, 1837. (Edward Hazen, *Panorama of Professions and Trades* [Philadelphia, 1837])

the rear, often raised on a platform like a preacher, a judge, or a schoolmaster. The remainder of the room was occupied by clerks who worked standing at tall desks pushed against the wall. A small business might have a single clerk, while larger ones employed several, ranging from errand boys up through copyists or scriveners who transcribed letters and other documents into ledgers, to more specialized clerks, a bookkeeper, and possibly a confidential clerk who supervised the business in the absence of the proprietor(s) (fig. 8.1). A late-eighteenth-century view published by Alexander Lawson in Philadelphia shows such an establishment (fig. 8.2). Four clerks work at desks enclosed behind a railing and lit by a tall arched window. They confer with senior clerks or customers outside the enclosure, where more casually disposed desks and tables are available for their use. On either side of the window, ranges of vertical slots accommodate ledgers while banks of small drawers under them probably held filed letters. These represent a larger-scale version of a common kind of desk or "secretary" that contained ledger slots and pigeonholes within an elaborately architectural case and that could be found in both commercial and domestic settings (fig. 8.3).[4]

FIGURE 8.2. *A Merchant's Counting House*, Philadelphia, ca. 1795–1805.
(The Library Company of Philadelphia)

FIGURE 8.3. Desk and bookcase, Williamsburg, Virginia, ca. 1760, attributed to Peter Scott. Interior. (Courtesy of the Mount Vernon Ladies' Association)

As Campbell suggested, all the activity in this sort of enterprise was marshaled in aid of the merchant's memory, the indispensable foundation of the business. Clerks produced the documents on which the merchant relied, rather than taking an active part in the conduct of affairs. Contemporary accounting textbooks described as many as twelve different kinds of books that might go into a firm's bookkeeping system. These were distinguished by the type of transactions that they recorded and the principle of their organization. Waste books, for instance, were used to record transactions in absolute chronological order, while journals separated creditors and debtors, and ledgers contained "all the transactions of a Man's Affairs, in such order, as that those belonging to every different subject lie together in one place; making so many distinct or several Accompts," according to Thomas Dilworth, the author of a treatise on bookkeeping. Other books recorded debts, cash received, goods shipped, commission sales, receipts, prices, and incidental expenses. A final type of record book was "The Remembrancer or Note-Book, which, for the Help of the Memory, contains such business as the Merchant is to go about." Yet, as Dilworth noted, only the waste book or journal and ledger were essential. A merchant might choose to use one of the others "according to the Nature and Circumstances of his Way of Dealing in the World." Surviving account books suggest that most were satisfied with a journal organized and indexed by name of debtor or creditor.[5]

Rapid economic expansion in the late eighteenth century strained the capacity of the merchant's memory and he or she became more dependent on paper than ever before. The number of clerks increased to keep pace with newer, more copious, and more precise aids to memory that were now necessary. New devices helped create more paper more efficiently. For example, merchants traditionally kept letterbooks into which clerks copied outgoing correspondence for future reference. Pantographs that created two letters at once, and copying presses that made a second impression of letters using a special ink, allowed duplicates to be made automatically.[6]

The creation of more documents entailed the storage of more documents, a problem to which merchants had turned their attention even before the Revolution. Whereas images of businesses from premodern times to well into the nineteenth century often depict countinghouse interiors with a few shelves on which account books are casually placed, the busiest merchants turned to the flexible but precise spatial order intimated in the shelves and drawers of the "Merchant's Counting House" (see figs. 8.1, 8.2). The pigeonhole became the fundamental unit of organization for the antebellum merchant. "Pigeonholes are everywhere, and not a place to keep a secret," one writer recalled. As late as the mid-nineteenth century, merchants as wealthy and active as New Orleans's John McDonogh preferred this system of filing. The annotations on McDonogh's meticulously folded and labeled papers distinguished business correspondence, filed by name, from correspondence unrelated to mercantile transactions, including personal letters, pleas for charity, and solicitations of employment, which were simply endorsed "unimportant" and presumably filed together out of the way.[7]

In short, the increased scale of business after 1790 at first necessitated little change in the personal approach to business. Although the expansion forced merchants to reinforce and extend their memories by using more clerks, more paper, and newer technologies, most merchants clung to this mode of operation until the post–Civil War era, when the rationalized, multiunit organization that historian Alfred D. Chandler has labeled the "modern business enterprise" took shape. Until then, most continued to organize their desks, their countinghouse pigeonholes, their account books, and their business papers according to the names of their trading partners. In adopting a kind of spatial organization that allowed articulated access to the new variety of goods and records, merchants systematized their memories, not their operations. However, the pigeonhole contained the possibility of other, more abstract orders.[8]

Governmental agencies also used the merchant-and-clerk model. They produced documents that might be said to constitute the nation's memory, as the merchant's records constituted his own. During the antebellum era, the four major executive agencies—State, War, Navy, and Treasury—were organized like business firms, with the secretary of each corresponding to a commercial proprietor, assisted by a chief or principal clerk equivalent to the confidential clerk of a private business. As in a countinghouse, a handful of ordinary clerks did the paperwork, and one or two messengers performed incidental tasks. As in private enterprises, these steps constituted (except for the appointed secretary's position) a hierarchy of experience and seniority, and in the agency rosters published biannually after 1816 it is possible to trace the rise of individuals from messenger to messenger "acting as a clerk" to clerk and sometimes to chief clerk. But the expansion of federal agencies in the first half of the nineteenth century seriously strained this organizational structure. The tensions were most clearly revealed in the struggle over a new headquarters for the Department of the Treasury, constructed in the late 1830s. An attempt by the architect, Robert Mills, to reimagine bureaucratic work and its spatial order met fierce and lasting opposition from the building's intended occupants.

The federal agencies were initially very small, and domestic-sized spaces, even adapted houses, served them well. When the national government was located at New York and Philadelphia, government bureaus rented private houses for their accommodation. In 1781, for example, Congress decided to give day-to-day supervision of foreign affairs, previously handled by ad hoc congressional committees, to a new Department of Foreign Affairs, to be headed by a secretary "authorized to employ one or if necessary more clerks to assist him in his office." The enabling legislation of 1782 shows that the secretary was conceived as a kind of confidential clerk to Congress, which kept a close watch on international relations in those days. His duties were "to keep and preserve all the books and papers belonging to the department of foreign affairs, to receive and report the applications of all foreigners; to correspond with the ministers of the United States at foreign courts, and with the ministers of foreign powers and other persons, for the purpose of obtaining the most extensive and useful information relative to foreign affairs."[9]

The first secretary, Robert R. Livingston, rented a twelve-foot-wide house on Sixth Street in Philadelphia from Undersecretary Peter S. DuPonceau (fig. 8.4).

FIGURE 8.4. First State Department office, 13 South Sixth Street, Philadelphia, 1781–83. (Watson II)

Livingston used the front room on the second floor (traditionally the best parlor of a Philadelphia house) as his office, with his two major assistants occupying the rear room. The single ground-floor room, possibly built as a store, was used by two clerks and an interpreter. During the transition from Confederation to Constitution in 1788, the State Department occupied two rooms in a house in New York, one room for the secretary and one for his deputy and clerks. Records were kept very much as merchants kept them. Daily transactions were entered in a minute book as they occurred, then transcribed into a journal. Three sets of letter books separated foreign from American from congressional letters. Original papers were indexed and filed in boxes stored in cases provided for the purpose. A congressional committee commended the "neatness, method and perspicacity" of this operation.[10]

After the move to Washington in 1800, makeshift quarters remained the rule. The State, War, and Navy departments all rented space in speculative row houses on Pennsylvania Avenue, a practice that was still feasible, considering that the four executive agencies and the post office employed a total of 137 clerks in 1800. Indeed, some branches of these agencies were still accommodated in rented private houses as late as the 1840s. Treasury was the exception to this pattern. More dependent than any of the others on the meticulous creation, storage, and protection of paper records, it arrived in Washington to find waiting its permanent offices, designed by English émigré George Hadfield and constructed in 1797–98 (fig. 8.5).[11]

Along with much of the rest of the city, this first Treasury Building was destroyed when the British burned Washington on August 24 and 25, 1814. The conflagration presented an opportunity to reorganize the executive end of Pennsylvania Avenue on a more formal scale and to house the departments permanently. Four large Executive Offices, built of brick, two stories high, painted a "sort of diluted sky-blue color" (later a "plain drab color") and embellished on their north sides with monumental porticoes resembling that on the executive mansion, formed a square around the White House (plate 9, fig. 8.6). One was assigned to each of the four departments: State occupied the northeast building and Treasury the southeast, with War on the northwest and Navy on the southwest. Private paths from the White House to each of the buildings left

the "chief magistrate sitting, as it were, like a spider, in the centre of his web, from which he constantly overlooks the occurrences at its extremities."[12]

All four buildings were alike (fig. 8.7). A broad passageway running the length of the building bisected each floor. The structure was divided into three parts by a recess behind the portico and a corresponding projecting pavilion at the rear. The end blocks contained three equal rooms on each side of the corridor. In the central section, the rear projection created an alcove of the passage to accommodate the double stairway and its flanking closets. The central space on each facade served as an entrance hall on the ground floor and as an additional office on the upper floor.

These were among the earliest American public buildings to use double-loaded corridors (corridors with rooms along both sides) serving ranks of similar rooms. All of the rooms opened both into the corridor and into their neighbors, allowing for flexibility of circulation and use. At the same time, the varied sizes of the offices allowed for a clear differentiation of occupants or functions. No particular use was specified, however, and each department could organize its operations as it wished.

In fact, the Executive Offices did not suit any of the four agencies particularly well. The parity among the departments implied by the architecture was a fiction, for each department had a distinctive administrative history during the first half of the nineteenth century, as some stagnated and others ballooned in size (table 5). Thus, no building was ever small enough or large enough for its designated tenant. When the Executive Offices were first occupied in 1820, some departments filled only a portion of their buildings, while others required additional space in other Executive Offices or in rented quarters.

Dec. 1ᵗ 57.

The number of employees at State, for example, remained relatively stable, while War and Navy, as might be expected, fluctuated according to the aggressive moods of the government (see table 5). Only Treasury, always the largest of the departments by far, grew nearly continuously, officially by act of Congress, but also unofficially as managers found odd bits of cash to hire clerks to assist with the rising tide of paperwork. Congress complained during the period of the Treasury's most rapid expansion that "some extraordinary duty is imposed upon a certain legally constituted officer, and he appoints an agent under him to perform the duty. This latter officer is paid out of some contingent fund, or out of the money appropriated for the specified object. This practice goes on for years, when the salary is by design or accident incorporated into an appropriation bill; and thus a sort of half legal existence is given to the office, and the officer continues to hold the office after the object for which he was appointed has ceased." A period of stagnation in the 1820s did not significantly deter its 350 percent growth over the thirty years after 1816.[13]

State Department, 2nd Floor Use Plan

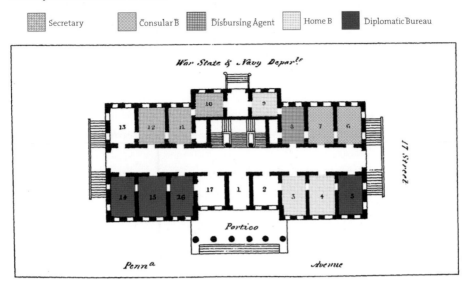

FIGURE 8.7. State Department (Executive Office) Building, second-floor use plan. (Jennifer Reut after Mills Papers)

Table 5 Growth of Major Government Departments in Washington, 1816–47: Number of Employees and Administrative Subdivisions

	1816	1821	1827	1831	1835	1841	1847
Treasury							
Employees	98	182	177	171	189	286	343
Pct. growth		95.9%	−2.7%	−3.3%	10.5%	51.3%	19.9%
Administrative divs.	7	11	11	12	12	13	12
War							
Employees	71	65	33	31	65	85	105
Pct. growth		−8.4%	−49.2%	−6%	109.6%	30.8%	23.5%
Administrative divs.	3	7	5	5	11	10	12
Navy							
Employees	29	[9]	20	21	22	24	[]
Pct. growth		[]	[]	5%	4.7%	9%	[]
Administrative divs.	3	[1]	2	2	2	2	[]
State							
Employees	9	13	16	17	17	40	23
Pct. growth		44.9%	23%	6%	0%	17.6%[a]	15%
Administrative divs.	1	1	1	3	3	4	3

Sources: U.S. Department of State, *A Register of Officers and Agents, Civil, Military, and Naval, in the Service of the United States . . . Prepared at the Department of State* (Washington: various publishers, various dates).

[a] Excludes special Census Bureau employees.

In every agency, the absolute number of employees was only part of the story. As their tasks became more complex, they were reorganized into a number of administrative subdivisions. In 1816, for example, the entire Washington staff of the State Department consisted of nine men: the Secretary of State, the chief clerk, five other clerks, and two messengers (see table 5). In 1841, the department still had only twenty regular employees, plus twenty more hired to work on the 1840 census. Besides the secretary's office, there were three bureaus—Diplomatic, Consular, and Home—established by executive actions of 1833 and 1836, and a special office to tabulate the Sixth Census. Yet while hierarchies and duties were clarified, the conception of bureaucratic work continued to follow mercantile precedent, with each subdivision reproducing the countinghouse model that had organized the entire agency before 1833.[14]

Thanks to the guides to the federal offices published by Robert Mills in the 1840s and 1850s, it is possible to understand, in general if not in detail, these structures' use. In 1841, the Secretary of State occupied Room 11 (in Mills's designation) on the second floor of the State Department building, with his chief clerk in room 12 next to him (see fig. 8.7). The small room 10 was unlabeled, and may have been the secretary's inner office. The three subsidiary bureaus were scattered throughout the second floor. The Diplomatic Bureau occupied rooms 14 and 15 at the east end of the building and room 5 at the west end, while the Consular Bureau occupied rooms 6 and 7 in the southwest corner of the building. The Home Bureau occupied rooms 3 and 4 on the north side of the west end and the small room 9 in the southwest corner of the west projection, the latter separated from the public corridor by the office of disbursing agent and building superintendent Edward Stubbs. Several rooms on this floor held the departmental library and an archive that contained a copy of the Declaration of Independence as well as the state gifts presented by foreign governments. In short, except for the secretary's suite, departmental clerks seem to have been distributed haphazardly, with little concern for establishing compact zones devoted to their subdivisions. Many had rooms to themselves; none shared his office with more than three other people. Because the department was so small, the east end of the ground floor was available for use by the fifth auditor of the Treasury, who oversaw State Department expenditures along with those of the Post Office and others arising from Indian affairs.[15]

The Treasury and War departments faced similar predicaments. Although the Treasury Department built a large new office building in the 1830s (discussed below), it continued to house its fifth auditor's office in the State Department building's ground floor at the site of its duties, and by 1845 the second comptroller's office had replaced the Census Bureau at the west end of the same floor. The War Department building, which also housed the second auditor of the Treasury (who oversaw the department), was supplemented by an annex. Its specialized bureaus were housed in rented quarters on Seventeenth Street and Pennsylvania Avenue diagonally opposite to its building. Despite the addition of a third story to the structure during the Civil War, increasing numbers of rented annexes scattered the War Department throughout Washington until the construction of the State, War, and Navy Building in the 1870s.[16]

Of the four federal executive departments, the Treasury Department felt the most intense pressure to alter its operations. In 1816, its ninety-eight employees were already organized into seven divisions: the offices of the secretary, treasurer, register, comptroller, and auditor (the offices of the Treasury under the originating legislation of 1789), the General Land Office (established 1812), and commissioner of the revenue (authorized in 1813 and replaced by the fifth auditor in 1817). A year later, the department was reorganized under two comptrollers and five auditors. A solicitor, added in 1820, and a sixth auditor appointed to oversee the Post Office Department in the late 1830s swelled departmental ranks still further. As at State and War, these subdivisions retained the mercantile model of organization: each had a principal, a chief clerk, several clerks, and a messenger or two.[17]

The Treasury's Executive Office Building burned before Mills's *Guides* appeared, but his manuscript plans of the 1833 state of the building survive. On the ground floor, the first auditor, his chief clerk and other clerks occupied the three rooms in the southeast corner and two of the rooms in the central block, while across the hall Treasurer John Campbell, his chief clerk Peter G. Washington, and subsidiary clerk Henry Jackson were accommodated in the three northeastern offices. All six rooms at the west end of the building were given over to the register (archivist) and his staff, as were the three rooms of the fireproof wing attached to that end of the building. The other rooms in the central block contained the auditor's records and the register's fireproof office.

The secretary's office was in the northwest corner of the second floor of the old Treasury Building, with his library housed in the upper floor of the fireproof wing. On the other side was his chief clerk's office, and beyond it that of the building superintendent, Andrew M. Laub. Across the hall, two rooms were occupied by clerks, with the third used as an audience room. At the east end, the south side was occupied by the first comptroller, his chief clerk, and clerk Lund Washington, from east to west. The northeast rooms housed three other clerks in the First Comptroller's bureau. A long narrow space on the south side of the center block was the Warrant room, staffed by clerk James Anthony, while across the hall the stairway was flanked by "fireproofs," walk-in vaults. In the attic, except for two clerks stationed above the Warrant room, "all the rooms on this floor were occupied by old records," according to Mills's annotation.[18]

More than any other agency the Treasury Department existed to process paper, so its repeated fires were potentially disastrous for governmental operations. When the first Treasury Building was burned by the British in 1814 it had already suffered a serious fire in 1801. On March 31, 1833, the second (Executive Office) building was destroyed in a fire set by government employees eager to conceal evidence of pension fraud. Chastened by the experience, Secretary of the Treasury Roger B. Taney reported to Congress in December of that year that while no records were destroyed "that can materially affect the public interest," a new building was required and "the loss already sustained in the documents and records of this office shows the propriety of erecting it upon a different plan from the former one, and of placing the archives of the Government in a situation less exposed to danger."[19]

Fire threatened the documentary foundations of the new economy. Most commercial assets were paper assets—artifacts of the merchant's memory—existing in the realm of account books, letters, invoices, bills of exchange, letters of credit, bills of lading. Their destruction could mean bankruptcy. It is no surprise that banks were among the first institutions to experiment with fireproof (more correctly, fire-resistant) construction, but other businesses and government agencies followed closely. For large-scale public buildings, masonry vaulting was the preferred method. Benjamin Henry Latrobe used masonry vaults in his Bank of Pennsylvania (1799–1801) in Philadelphia, setting a standard for its successors, including the fireproof wing he added to the first Treasury Building in 1805 following the 1801 fire.[20]

When Mills, an architect employed as a draftsman in the General Land Office, began to rethink the Treasury Building as a place for the work and preservation of the national memory, it was inevitable that he assumed the use of masonry vaults. He had already used them in the conversion of Philadelphia's old State House (Independence Hall) to municipal use in 1812 and a decade later at the state Record Office

FIGURE 8.8. South Carolina Record Office ("Fireproof Building") (Robert Mills, 1822) Charleston, S.C., plan. (Courtesy Oxford University Press)

(known colloquially as the Fireproof Building) in Charleston, South Carolina (fig. 8.8).[21]

After several years of Mills's reports, proposals, and lobbying, Andrew Jackson appointed him Architect of Public Buildings in 1836 and gave him the Treasury Building commission. The structure that began to rise in August 1836 and was substantially complete by the end of 1840 was T-shaped and three stories high, with a usable attic and a tall basement story (fig. 8.9). The head of the T lay along Fifteenth Street, stretching from the site of the burned building up to (and nearly abutting) the State Department's offices. A perpendicular east-west wing adjoined it at the rear. The plan was deceptively simple. Each wing contained a barrel-vaulted, double-loaded corridor flanked by groin-vaulted offices on each side, a pattern that Mills had used in the Fireproof Building. Where the wings met a large entrance vestibule housed a pair of curving staircases, and smaller staircases were placed in the middle of each of the Fifteenth-Street wings. A full-height colonnade ran the length of the principal facade while a six-column portico provided entrance from the White House side (fig. 8.10).

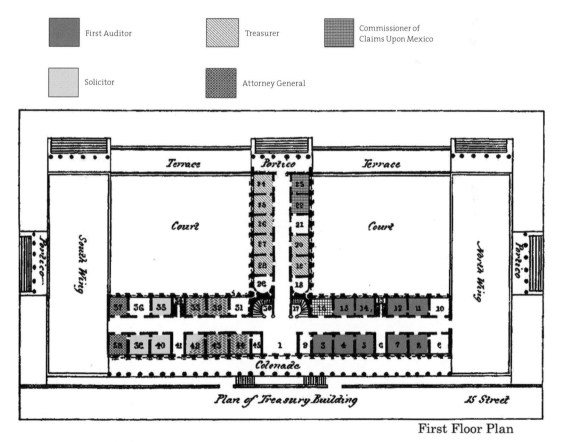

FIGURE 8.9. New Treasury Building (Robert Mills, 1836–42), first-floor use plan. (Jennifer Reut after Mills's *Guide*)

This, the first large office building in the United States, looked back to London's New Somerset House, designed by William Chambers and built between 1776 and 1801, and through it to early modern palaces grouped around courtyards (fig. 8.11). It is no surprise that Mills should turn to Somerset House, for governments were the first bureaucratic institutions large enough to be confronted with the problem of the large office building, and Somerset House was the first large office building in Europe. Mills began with Chambers's conception of a building organized around a courtyard that would house a disparate group of government agencies. The equivalents of England's Revenue Office and Surveyor General of Crown Lands, for example, were both parts of the Department of Treasury.

Mills's T-shaped building was intended as the central portion of a building that would eventually be grouped around two open courtyards when north and south wings were added and would house many of the agencies of the execu-

FIGURE 8.10. New Treasury Building. The pedimented ends belong to the additions of the 1850s–1860s, while the original Aquia stone colonnade was replaced with granite in 1909

tive branch (fig. 8.12).[22] In an undated letter to Secretary of the Treasury Thomas Corwin, he argued that the projected north wing could house the State Department (whose building it would replace), while the south wing would provide additional accommodations for the Treasury. By 1841 he claimed that "the plan of the Treasury building, as approved by the President of the United States, included in its design a building for the State Department, and also, if not in future required for the Treasury Department, for a General Post Office building, so as to constitute one entire range of facade, on 15th street, 457 feet, with a return of two wings, 100 feet each, and a centre building of equal projection with the wings."[23]

As constructed, Mills's building accommodated a department organized

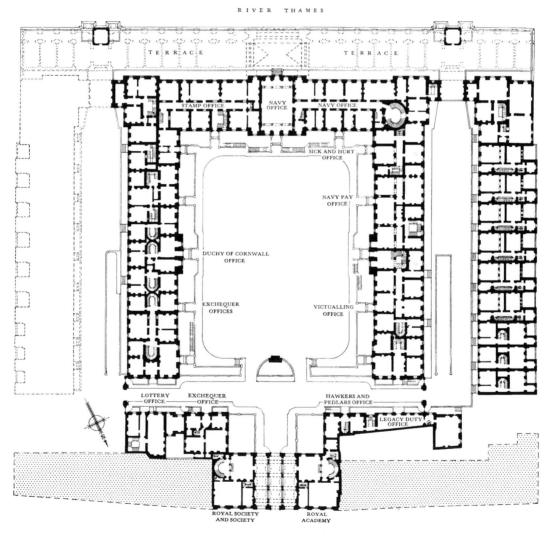

FIGURE 8.11. New Somerset House (William Chambers, 1775–ca. 1801), London. (Her Majesty's Stationery Office)

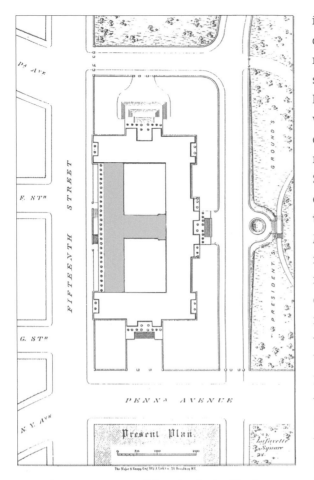

FIGURE 8.12. New Treasury Building, site plan in 1869 after the figure-eight plan was completed. The original portion is hatched. (Jennifer Reut, after *Treasurer's Reports*)

into several branches, each acting as a quasi-independent agency. The most significant difference between Mills's Treasury Building and Chambers's Somerset House was the conception of work and work spaces that each embodied. Mills drew on the republican spatial imagination to transform the basic concept of Somerset House in ways that promised— or threatened—to revolutionize the relationship of space and bureaucratic labor. Most of New Somerset House was arranged in suites with various plans and multiple entries. These often included elaborate public halls and "board rooms" more reminiscent of royal government with its audience and meeting chambers than of mercantile countinghouses. Each agency insisted on a separate entrance and staircase in keeping with its dignity. Mills, on the other hand, chose to construct a building of nearly identical vaulted modules (fig. 8.13). This was not required by the structural system: earlier vaulted buildings such as Benjamin Henry Latrobe's Bank of Pennsylvania (1799–1801) or William Strickland's Second Bank of the United States (1818–24), both in Philadelphia, vaulted every room, but the rooms varied in size, shape, and vault type.[24]

On the face of it the Treasury Building, with its repetitive vaulted spaces, echoed in the repetitive rhythms of the famous colonnade, seems quite close to the ideas of an architectural theorist such as Mills's French contemporary J. N. L. Durand, whose theory of architecture design was based on the additive combination of spatial and structural modules. Yet it is unlikely that Mills was influenced by such formal theories. The Treasury Building was a rationalized structure based on a very different module—the human user.[25]

Mills wrote little about the sources and intellectual basis of his design, but his thinking can be glimpsed in the fierce infighting that enveloped the Treasury Building during its construction and that surrounded it for over forty years afterward. His initial scheme was conceived during one of the recurring ef-

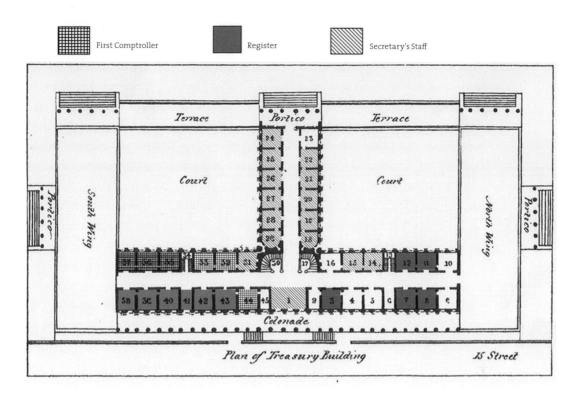

FIGURE 8.13. New Treasury Building, second-floor use plan. The third floor was given over to the General Land Office. (Jennifer Reut)

forts to reorganize the Treasury Department. The U.S. Senate asked the president in 1832 to make a proposal for restructuring the department "with a view to simplify the forms and keeping the accounts, and of rendering them more intelligible; of a more equal distribution of the labor and duties, and abolishing some of the subordinate branches, and reducing the number of clerks in the Executive Department."[26]

Divergent interpretations of Congress's instructions underlay the controversy that erupted even before the new building was complete, as it came under attack from members of Congress, abetted by department staff and by other architects and builders.[27] The committee hired Thomas U. Walter, a Philadelphia architect remarkable throughout his career for his intellectual and ethical malleability, to make a report on the structure that was expected to be unfavorable. In addition, they obtained a briefer report to the same effect from Boston architect Alexander Parris. Retired architect of the Capitol Charles Bulfinch also weighed in with critical opinions in a letter to Treasury official D. A. Hall.[28]

Much of the criticism was opportunistic: congressmen leaped at the chance to attack the administration, particularly after Democratic president Martin Van Buren was replaced by a Whig in 1841. At the same time, Treasury Department officials hoped to obtain more or better space, while rival architects sought to capture the lucrative commission for themselves. The critics attacked the building's siting, structural soundness, appearance, and suitability to its purpose. The latter is the most important to our discussion. In common with all the other congressional and architectural critics, Walter denounced the plan: the basement was too dark and damp for offices and record storage, the third story was too dark and ill-ventilated for that purpose, and the barrel-vaulted passage, 456 feet long but only a little more than 9 feet wide, was too narrow and badly lighted for so important a thoroughfare.[29]

Mills's formal response was brief and predictable: the rooms were *not* too dark, and they *were* dry enough. True, the light was low in the passages, but it was enough for "passing to & fro." These claims were disingenuous. While Mills told Congress that the foundations had been designed so as to keep the basement rooms dry, he informed commissioner of public buildings, William Noland, that the basement rooms would require a "system of warming" to keep the papers dry, although that would make them too warm for clerks to use in the summer. After occupying the third floor of the structure for nearly two years, the commissioner of the General Land Office claimed that "the entire tier of rooms are formed to be so very defective as to light that candles are frequently used at Noonday to enable the Clerks to conduct their business." He requested space for his bookkeepers on a lower floor.[30]

The architect's thinking must be inferred by comparing his building with the more detailed, and more considered, criticisms offered by Treasury Department officials. Mills's design was based on two considerations: occupancy and access. He had been instructed to consult the Secretary of the Treasury "on the number, size, &c., of the rooms required by his Department, which resulted in the arrangement, size, &c., of the plan executed." Each room would hold two clerks, based on the capacity of existing rooms in the "State Department, &c." which "were ample for the purpose" and "served as data to regulate the size of those in the new building."[31]

In other words, taking off from Congress's desire to simplify and equalize work, Mills assumed that each clerk represented an equal unit of work and assigned each one the same-size space. He then considered access. Like the urban grid or the pigeonhole system of a desk or an office, the Treasury Building was an articulated space in which equal, undifferentiated spaces were randomly accessible. The plan specified no architectural or management hierarchy. Instead, the identical cells could be grouped in any way desired, by means of the passageways and the doors connecting individual rooms.

The new Treasury Building was planned with public as well as staff accessibility in mind. Mills believed that all public officials should be available to their constituents. While the structure was under construction, he published the first of several editions of his *Guide to the National Executive Offices and the Capitol of the United States* to "afford to all the means of identifying both the building and the room occupied by every officer" of the federal government. The Treasury Building was designed to open the building to constituents not only through the corridors, but also through the colonnade, which Mills described as a "great public high way equally with the corridor, from which access is to be had to the interior of the building at several points, opposite to stair ways," although the windows of individual offices were large enough to enter as well. Charles Bulfinch was probably correct in declaring that the "walk which it affords cannot be intended for the recreation & amusement of the clerks, nor can the business of the offices be promoted by making it a promenade for the public," who might simply walk into any first-floor office whose window opened onto the portico.[32]

Treasury officials' vehement objections to Mills's design were more detailed. Three themes emerged in their incidental comments and in a series of letters to Secretary of the Treasury Walter Forward written in response to his predecessor's request for an assessment of the needs of the department's bureaus. First, the building was simply too small. Government officials rarely believe that their agencies are adequately accommodated. Treasury Department managers campaigned for more space even before they moved in, sometimes with good reason. The acting controller notified Forward that owing to a shortage of rooms he had been forced to assign four clerks to some rather than the two for which the spaces were intended, and he asked for at least one more room. Four to five clerks were also assigned to several of the rooms used by the General Land Office, while Charles B. Penrose, solicitor of the Treasury, told the secretary that "at present four rooms are *permanently* occupied by the Solicitor of the Treasury and his Clerks, and one temporarily. The room temporarily occupied, is that assigned to the Attorney General and Solicitor in common as a library and consultation room, and is occupied by one of the Clerks of this office from necessity for the want of another room. . . . At present the Clerk located in the Common Library and consultation room is often interrupted and *driven out* by persons calling to Consult with the Attorney General and Solicitor, and his duties must be unperformed for want of a room to perform them in, or he must remove his papers into another room to the annoyance and interruption of the Clerks there employed."[33]

Two other defects were even more pressing. First, the notion of random access and identical spaces was foreign to the way that Treasury officials preferred to conduct their business. They wanted larger and more formal spaces set aside for dignitaries. Both the solicitor and the attorney general were assigned private offices, but they demanded separate audience chambers as well. The notion of an undifferentiated river of paper equally distributed among interchangeable functionaries that underpinned Mills's design did not fit the hierarchical, personalistic mercantile mode of operation that Treasury officials continued to prefer.

Moreover, the articulated but unspecialized building prevented the proper supervision of clerks. Comptroller James William McCulloh requested an additional room "on the same floor with that I occupy—and, if practicable, contiguous to these nearest to it." Although they were able to establish departmental zones in most of the building, space was tight enough that some dispersal of offices was unavoidable (see figs. 8.9, 8.13). "Under the present arrangement," the register pointed out, "the business is conducted in five detached parts; some on the first and others on the second floor of the building, and the practical effect is, to separate the Clerks by inconvenient distances, whose operations should be through a continuous chain of direct communication." When Thomas U. Walter gained control of the project after 1851, he included in his designs additional rooms that were "much larger" than those in Mills's building, "which will bring the clerks under a more easy supervision."[34]

Treasury officials complained most loudly about the building's inadequate storage space. The register noted the "constant accumulation of public papers," a theme that echoed through everyone's remonstrances. The commissioner of the General Land Office described the "continually accumulating masses of its documents, books, papers &c [that] are every year demanding increased accommodation,—and the duties are such as to require a very great amount of cases and other office furniture of more than ordinary dimensions." In Penrose's office "the books and papers of the office are daily rapidly increasing and must continue to do so," while First Comptroller McCulloh noted that he had a basement room "in which many of the Records papers and books of this office are piled en mass." Additional space and new shelves, filing cases, and desks were needed to make the records available for reference. Although the accumulation of papers and the necessity of easy access to them weighed heavily on the minds of departmental officials, Mills had clearly given little thought to these issues, noting offhandedly that the rooms in the basement were never intended for clerks (thereby contradicting his other statements about the number of rooms in the building available to departmental personnel), but "for the deposit of boxes, lumber & when dry for Old papers &c."[35]

The mercantile tradition informed both Mills's design and the Treasury officials' objection to it. In a sense, both conceived of the building as a giant system of pigeonholes, but each pulled the metaphor in a different direction. Treasury officials were as concerned as Mills to reform their way of working. Those who studied the problem in the early 1830s concluded that the original organization of the department in 1789 had been efficient and effective, but that the ad hoc addition of auditors and other officers over the years undermined "unity and simplicity." Little was done, and at the end of the decade Secretary Woodbury continued to describe the agency as one in need of a "new organization . . . in such respects as to insure a more appropriate division of labor, a stricter accountability, and a closer supervision over the collection of the revenue by officers exclusively devoted to it." Yet another attempt was made in 1846. Nevertheless, while the Treasury officials were concerned with streamlining, they continued to imagine their work in the old way. For them the building was, like an old-fashioned secretary desk or a countinghouse's shelves and holes, a cabinet for keeping the nation's memory. The primary function of the Treasury was to create, store, and consult records efficiently. This was implied in the officials' letters and made explicit in an apparently unsolicited letter that architect-builder William Archer wrote to President Franklin Pierce in 1855, when the extension of the Treasury Department was being contemplated. Archer proposed to demolish Mills's building and replace it with a four-story building whose top story would be arranged "for the reception and preservation of all the archives of the nation," including the manuscript acts of Congress, the unpublished diplomatic archives, and copyright registrations (all under the purview of the State Department at that time), in addition to Treasury Department documents.[36]

Mills's conception emphasized the merchant's active life over the merchant's memory and in response he designed a building that was not only structurally dynamic, as William H. Pierson noted, but socially dynamic. Mills pigeonholed work and workers rather than papers, so paper storage really was incidental in his mind. His was a highly abstract and intellectualized conception of bureaucratic work, one based on human process rather than document storage.[37]

Thomas U. Walter, among others, had criticized Mills's long, unbroken colonnade, but it was the visual emblem of its architect's spatial imagination. In arguing for breaking up the colonnade with a pediment, Walter analyzed the exterior as an independent pictorial image. To Mills the uninterrupted colonnade with its walkway revealed the long, narrow passageway and its file of vaulted rooms. In choosing to make this link, he combined a didactic desire for legibility, a preoccupation of Euro-American architects for nearly a century, with a modular design method, but one in which the human being—the worker and client—rather than the structural vault or the grid module was the fundamental unit.

Thus, while the architect and the clients shared similar modes of thought, an unbridgeable chasm separated them. William Archer's was only one of the chorus of voices demanding the Treasury Building's demolition. Walter had recommended in January 1838 that "the course dictated alike by prudence and economy, is, to take down the whole building," a recommendation that congressional opponents probably expected and quickly endorsed. William Parker Elliot, Washington agent for New York architects Town and Davis and a professional enemy of Mills's, wrote to Davis that "the new Treasury Building has turned out to be a complete failure & is ordered to be taken down. The Architect, Mills, must go down also." This turned out to be a premature judgment, for the building was completed to Mills's design, but it was never safe from destruction. Isaiah Rogers recommended rebuilding the Fifteenth Street wing to conform to the newer portions of the building in 1863. Seven years later, the then-secretary denounced Mills's Treasury Building as "an unworthy sham, ... badly arranged, unsuitable for the wants of the building," and demanded its reconstruction. Somehow, Mills's building survived nearly intact as the core of the current Treasury Building, although its "long and discolored colonnade" was rebuilt in 1909, its "worthless sandstone" replaced by the granite that both the architect and his critics had preferred.[38]

CHAPTER 9

{ **GRIDDING THE GRAVEYARD**

At noon every November first—All Saints' Day—the Roman Catholics of antebellum New Orleans paraded to their cemeteries. The holiday brought out people "of every age, color and condition" in crowds ranging from a thousand to as many as three thousand on a pleasant day. Relatives of the dead lit candles, laid wreaths and garlands of flowers, and often renewed the whitewash and relettered inscriptions on tombs and grave markers. By these actions they "rekindled their affection for the dead" at the "shrine of friendship." The parish priest prayed for the deceased and sometimes blessed individual graves, as the beloved cleric Père Antoine did. Acknowledging the communal bonds uniting the living and the dead, the priest asked rest for the souls of the departed and forgiveness for their sins as well as those of the living.[1]

J. G. Dunlap "saw persons kneeling at the grave offering prayers for the repose of the dead. . . . The whole scene is quite imposing and caused feelings of the most solemn character." Others in attendance, especially those Protestants for whom the customs of Catholic New Orleans were exotic curiosities, found the occasion a pleasant outing but strolled among the tombs respectfully, devotedly, and without disturbance, according to the French-born immigrant Jean Boze. For some the spectacle was entertainment. Future New York mayor A. Oakey Hall complained that "the largest numbers were mere idle spectators—many, the butterflies of New Orleans, who gaped, wondered, chatted, and talked as though it were a gala day, and they invited or privileged guests at some great fête. But the humble kneelers heeded them not."[2]

These annual gatherings lasted until nightfall. Then the police came, people filed out quietly, and All Saints' Day ended for another year. Within a few days only the smoke stains of candles on the whitewashed tombs and a few withered garlands remained as reminders of the occasion.[3]

All Saints' Day celebrations in New Orleans call to mind rites of communion with dead ancestors that stretch back to neolithic times and that cross cultural, national, and religious boundaries. On All Saints' Day, wrote the Protestant editors of the *New Orleans Daily Picayune,* "the dead that are gone are not gone so far but that some thing of the mysteries of love and of life may be felt of them." The "mansions" of the "cities of the dead" were part of a network of holy sites that included "the places which give us birth—the homes where our fathers lived—the graves in which they lie." The bonds of community—the mutual obligations of living and dead—were further tightened by the presence in the cemeteries of the Cazadores and the Voluntarius Calatanes, charitable organizations who collected alms for orphans from those in attendance. But the antique, seemingly universal nature of this holy day and the ingrained touristic need to see New Orleans as an exotic, not-quite-American place obscure the degree to which the city's All Saints' Day partook of a new Euro-American reorientation of the relationship between the living community—the city extended in space—and the ancestral community—the city extended through time—bound equally by love and by dread.[4]

If All Saints' Day was an ancient rite, its settings gave it a modern tenor. Joseph Holt Ingraham, a northern traveler in New Orleans in the early 1830s, visited what was then the city's newest and most active Roman Catholic cemetery, St. Louis No. 2, opened in 1822. It was a treeless landscape with many mausoleums that suggested to Ingraham

> the idea of a Lilliputian city. . . . The tombs in their various and fantastic styles of architecture—if I may apply the term to these tiny edifices—resembled cathedrals with towers, Moorish dwellings, temples, chapels, palaces, mosques—substituting the cross for the crescent—and structures of almost every kind. The idea was ludicrous enough; but as I passed down the avenue, I could not but indulge the fancy that I was striding down the Broadway of the capital of the Lilliputians. . . . All were perfectly white, arranged with the most perfect regularity, and distant little more than a foot from each other. At the distance of every ten rods the main avenue was intersected by others of less width, crossing it at right angles, down which tombs were arranged in the same novel and regular manner. The whole cemetery was divided into squares, formed by these narrow streets intersecting the principal avenue (fig. 9.1).

Like most visitors and residents in New Orleans, Ingraham was fascinated by the resemblance of the cemetery to a city "composed of miniature palaces, and still more diminutive villas." For resident Madaline Selima Edwards, St. Louis No. 2 was a "neat and beautiful . . . dead City." Swedish visitor Fredrika Bremer and New Yorker A. Oakey Hall agreed that it was "really a 'city of the dead.'"[5]

Yet the cemetery that Ingraham described was a very new kind of landscape in New Orleans, one informed by a sentimentalized regard for the remains of the dead, a desire to believe that selfhood persisted after death, the newly assertive presence of ordinary families in urban society, and the appropriation of many legally public and communally used spaces by private use or ownership common in late-eighteenth- and early-nineteenth-century Euro-America.

FIGURE 9.1. *Sketches in Louisiana: The French Cemetery* [St. Louis No. 2], New Orleans, La.
(Courtesy Historic New Orleans Collection, Museum/Research Center, acc. no. 1974.25.6.408)

These impulses produced two major new kinds of privately incorporated urban cemeteries in the United States: the reformed cemetery and the picturesque "rural" cemetery. The inventors of both types of burial grounds chose the grid to articulate selfhood and personhood; individual, family, and community; public space and private property; the dead and the living; the community and family in historical time and present space.

In St. Louis Cemetery No. 1, adjacent to St. Louis No. 2, Ingraham might have seen the kind of burial ground that preceded the gridded order of No. 2. In 1801, St. Louis No. 1, which had been created only eleven years earlier, was surrounded by a "broken palisade . . . not a single grave stone marked the remains of either the noble or ignoble dead—Over some few, brick arches were turned—at the head of every grave was planted an Iron or wooden cross some of the Iron ones were indented with the names of the lifeless tenants below." When John H. B. Latrobe visited the same scene over thirty years later, the graveyard seemed to have changed little, but it was rapidly filling with unmarked graves (plate 10). Interments were haphazardly arranged, marked according to families' taste and finances. As early as 1802, James Pitot criticized "burials of strangers made without supervision, and those of Roman Catholics too close together for the nature of the soil." Private tombs and markers, set at various angles in an open field crossed by a meandering foot path, were "uniformly either of white mar-

FIGURE 9.2. St. Louis Cemetery No. 1, New Orleans. The pyramidal monument is the same one shown in Latrobe's view

ble, or plaister, or painted white." By the twentieth century, St. Louis No. 1 was completely filled with private tombs and mausoleums, crammed in as space permitted (fig. 9.2).[6]

St. Louis No. 1 was a traditional burying ground of the sort found in cities and towns wherever Europeans and their descendants settled. The earliest New Orleans graveyards were administered by the Roman Catholic Church, the state church in French and Spanish Louisiana, but were owned by the city. They were available to anyone "who died in the bosom of the catholic, apostolic, Roman church, and whose body is accompanied by clerics or only by someone carrying a certificate from the curate of the Parish or of the Conventual Church, attesting that the dead person was a Roman Catholic." In response to an incident in which a funeral procession accompanied by priests from the Ursuline convent was turned away by rival priests from the parish church, the city council warned that the cemeteries were "neither . . . private property nor that of any particular church, but intended to receive the bodies of all who live within the care of the faithful Catholic community" and imposed a ninety-nine piastre fine and corporal punishment on anyone who attempted to prevent a legitimate burial there. As consecrated spaces, however, they were officially closed to "heretics" and others whom the clergy deemed unworthy of burial there. Protestants (and later blacks) were assigned separate spaces outside the consecrated boundaries.[7]

Burying grounds were commons in the traditional sense. Anyone could use them but no one could own them or appropriate them for their exclusive use. They were places to return the dead to dust, not to preserve and celebrate them. By law and custom, public burying grounds were a kind of consecrated waste-disposal plant, processing the abandoned cadaver after the soul of the deceased had gone on to another realm. As an English judge noted, in deciding a case in which a family sought to bury one of its members in an iron coffin that would slow or prevent decomposition, a graveyard was "not the exclusive property of one set of persons, but was the property of ages yet unborn. . . . All contrivance, therefore, to prolong the duration of the body, was an act of injustice, unless compensation was made for such encroachment."[8]

In such a cemetery, bodies were buried willy-nilly, one grave overlapping another (fig. 9.3). "When a new tomb is dug, an old one is laid open; and one body that has been slumbering a few years in peace, is removed from its resting place to make room for another," wrote a horrified nineteenth-century reformer. Once the earth had done its work, graves were reopened to provide space for subsequent users. In European cemeteries and some American ones the skeletal remains were removed to charnel houses. In the light of its grisly function and high religious purpose, the cemetery was, in theory, a "garden of equality," a place of "modest simplicity." The original occupants' identities might have

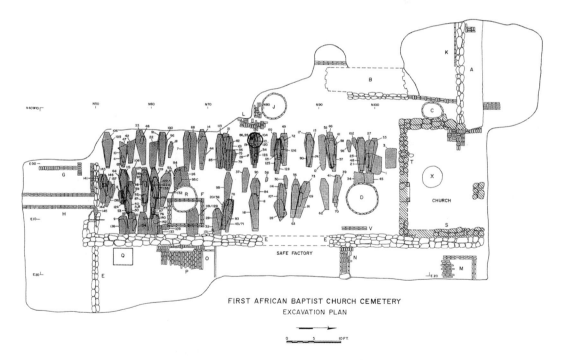

FIGURE 9.3. First African Baptist Church burying ground, Philadelphia, archaeological plan showing superimposed graves. (Courtesy John Milner Associates, the University of Pennsylvania, and the Redevelopment Authority of the City of Philadelphia)

been unrecorded, memorialized on perishable wooden markers, or occasionally inscribed on stone markers that were moved aside or discarded when the grave was reused.[9]

At the same time, longstanding popular traditions undermined both the "equality" of the graveyard and official Christian assurances of the unimportance of earthly remains. Many of the European-American elite insisted on discrete tombs and conspicuous markers so that, as one seventeenth-century English student of grave markers observed, "by the Tombe every one might bee discerned of what rank he was living: for monuments answerable to men's worth, state and places, have always been allowed, and stately sepulchres for base fellowes have always lien open to bitter jests."[10]

After the late middle ages, powerful laypeople might be buried under the floor of the church or in elaborate tombs inside the building, a privilege occasionally granted in American churches as well. In the eighteenth century (and well into the nineteenth century, despite severe criticism of the practice by reformers), new urban churches were often built with rows of subterranean vaults along an outside wall for the interment of paying parishioners (fig. 9.4). Other church members were permitted to wall in family plots in the churchyard. This appropriation of common space for private benefit was an extraordinary privilege granted to the elite.[11]

Honorific burial places effectively prevented graves' being disturbed by subsequent burials. This protection contradicted official Christian doctrines that downplayed the importance of the body, but accorded with traditional ideas shared among people of all classes and many cultural backgrounds. Early Christians believed that the body would be physically resurrected at the last judgment and preferred burial to the common Roman practice of cremation. A Roman Catholic priest in New Orleans who was of this mind explained "that the position of the coffin with the feet to the East and the head to the West, was of the first importance: because, that at the Resurrection, Christ would appear in the East, and if they were placed otherwise they would rise with their backs towards him."[12]

African traditions that survived in the United States venerated the undisturbed grave for other reasons. Africans and some of their descendants believed that the dead continued to exist as spirits with the power to influence the living for good or ill. Proper interment, often including a "second burial" or funeral held weeks, months, or a year afterward, and continuing respect for the holiness and integrity of the grave, were necessary to prevent the spirit's restless roaming. African Americans provided their dead with food and household goods and sometimes built shelters over their graves. The properly tended grave was a place of power, an emblem of the reunion of living and dead in the

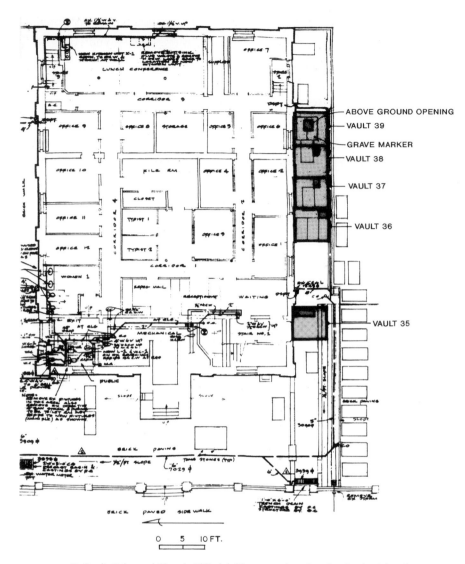

ABOVE GROUND OPENING
VAULT 39
GRAVE MARKER
VAULT 38
VAULT 37
VAULT 36
VAULT 35

0   5   10 FT.

FIGURE 9.4. St. Paul's Episcopal Church, Philadelphia, excavation plan showing burial vaults. (Courtesy John Milner Associates, the University of Pennsylvania, and St. Paul's Church)

spirit world and a place where the living could seek the assistance of spirits in redressing grievances.[13]

Among educated whites, and Protestants in general, traditional beliefs about the dead body were less explicitly articulated but no less strong. Respect for the corpse was manifested in elaborate funerals, elegant grave goods, and devices such as churchyard vaults, brick arches over individual graves, and strong coffins to prevent the earth's crushing the body. In the decades following the Revolution these traditional beliefs were complicated by newer ideas that emphasized affectionate or "companionate" family relationships and the political, religious, and ethical affirmation of the inherent worth of the individual self.

Long-held religious concepts of the separation of soul and body at death were still widely voiced, and heaven was discussed more openly and confidently than in earlier centuries. Yet the importance of bodily coherence to selfhood, exemplified in genteel bodily practice, meant that the lifeless body acquired new importance as a vessel that still sheltered some essential part of the deceased, rather than being the abandoned husk of the all-important soul. Benjamin Latrobe expressed it in strikingly psychosexual terms: "Those who have lost friends, especially of a different sex from themselves, and have hearts to feel, need not be told, that whatever philosophical indifference may have existed respecting the fate of their own bodies after death, those of their friends become infinitely dear to them, and that no display of their affection is considered too extravagant or too expensive to be indulged and executed." Yet he personally believed that the "delightful sentiment of posthumous affection" would be better served by cremation, with the cinerary urn kept at home rather than among the "deaths heads and cross bones of our Church Yards." Latrobe's views presaged those of many nineteenth-century cemetery founders, particularly those who were physicians. They dismissed the sentimentalization of dead bodies, arguing that decomposition was natural, inevitable, and unobjectionable if it happened in a peaceful setting.[14]

In short, American urban burial grounds at the end of the eighteenth century were heterogeneous places shaped by their status as public spaces, by contradictory ideas about disposal of the dead, and by the socioeconomic stratification of burial practices. As the corpse was increasingly cherished and as a growing segment of the urban population demanded the same kinds of privileges of protection and display that were accorded to the elite in previous centuries, these traditional graveyards were ill equipped to allay fears or to satisfy the new desires for commemoration of the dead. By 1800 small colonial churchyards and public burying grounds had been filled beyond capacity and engulfed by commercial development. Tiny Trinity churchyard in New York was believed to contain 120,000 burials in 1822, while the equally small Granary burying ground in Boston contains about 3,000, and New York's somewhat larger African Burial Ground and eighteenth-century potter's field about 10,000 people, buried three to four deep.[15]

Not only were graveyards overcrowded, but as cities grew, burying grounds that had been located, like other space-extensive institutions, at or beyond the edges of settlement were engulfed by urbanization (fig. 9.5). They became valuable center-city real estate whose continued existence depended on the power of the institution that owned the tract or of the friends of the deceased to stave off redevelopment. Potter's fields, the burial places of the indigent poor, were readily abandoned when the land was wanted for more lucrative uses. The

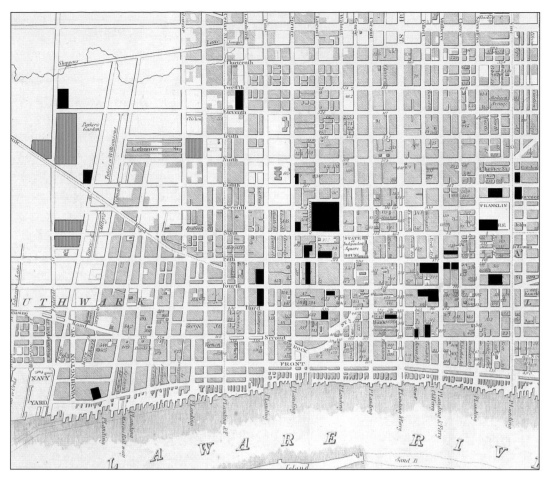

FIGURE 9.5. First- and second-generation Philadelphia cemeteries. (Jennifer Reut)

burial places of politically weak groups were, not surprisingly, subject to the same fate. Like potter's fields, they were located on the worst land and were eradicated nearly at will. Philadelphia's First African Baptist Church moved its church and cemetery several times owing to internal divisions and foreclosures. Its last cemetery was closed under pressure from the Board of Health for overcrowding, although the multiple burials in a single grave there were in keeping with standard urban practice. Soon after the closure, houses and a factory were built on the site, which was entirely erased in the 1980s by the construction of a commuter-rail tunnel.[16]

Even the wealthiest citizens were not always able to protect their ancestral burying places. In the late 1790s Philadelphia's Quakers disturbed "that part of [their own] Grave Yard where Rhoadses and many other families lays" to build the present Arch Street Meeting House. The meeting's leaders were adamant that their course was the right one: "To build a House in ye burial ground, H[enry] D[rinker]. says has been long concluded on," wrote Elizabeth Drinker.

Yet it took several years to accomplish the project for, as she noted five years earlier, "many are much opposed to it—It is not a pleasing thought to have the bones of our Ancestors disturbed." Drinker and her husband, a member of the building committee, were "of opposite oppinions relative to the propriety of such a step."[17]

When graves were moved the remains were not always treated respectfully. John Fanning Watson witnessed the removal of one Philadelphia burial ground for development in 1830, where the "skulls and bones of the dead were kicked about the street during the process of digging cellars for a row of houses afterward built upon the lot." The treatment might be just as offhanded in active cemeteries. In New Orleans's relatively new St. Louis Cemetery No. 2 Joseph Holt Ingraham discovered a "desolate area, without a tomb to relieve its dank and muddy surface, dotted with countless mounds, where the bones of the moneyless, friendless stranger lay buried.... Fragments of coffins were scattered around, and new-made graves, half filled with water, yawned on every side awaiting their unknown occupants." In many potter's fields, paupers and victims of epidemic disease were piled in deep holes. These were left open for weeks or months until enough people had died to fill them. Such accounts were particularly troubling in the context of rapidly shifting attitudes toward the remains of the dead.[18]

The theft of recently buried bodies to supply cadavers for medical study was even more disturbing. Citizens in several American cities, most notably in New York in April 1788, rioted against the practice. In 1780, a Philadelphia newspaper complained that "the theater for dissecting dead bodies has become . . . a terror to the citizens." A half century later, Boston's health commissioners offered five hundred dollars' reward for the capture of the "resurrection men" who regularly stole cadavers from the city's South Burying Ground, while a mob in New Haven rioted against grave robbing to supply Yale University's medical students. The architect Ithiel Town, a practical man who usually stood on the side of science and learning, wrote of the Yale corpse-snatching that "if this unprincipalled business is continued you will undoubtedly have the [medical school] building demolished and I should not be among those who would be sorry, [as] there is no necessity for such means being taken to procure bodies."[19]

For all these reasons, cemeteries began to change in the early republican years as a result both of individual practices, with more and more families erecting permanent, conspicuous monuments to their dead relatives, and of systematic changes in the institutions themselves, as cemetery founders and managers devised new legal and landscape techniques to meet the popular demand for individual recognition and burial security. St. Louis No. 2 in New Orleans is an example of the new type of cemetery. The peculiar topography of the Crescent City tested the new sensibilities even more than grave robbing and cemetery removals did elsewhere. Since the city lay below the level of the Mississippi River, the water table was near grade. Observing a pauper's burial, Ingraham saw "some of the assistants . . . stand upon [the coffin], and keep it down until the grave is re-filled with the mud which was originally thrown from it, or it would float." A British visitor wrote indignantly that the process "may more properly be termed *inundation* than *interment*." Genteel New Orleanians, particularly those from the north, were increasingly discomfited by the notion of a soggy burial. Madaline Edwards, an immigrant from Tennessee, watched a gravedigger work in Lafayette Cemetery and told him that "it was my desire to be buried elsewhere than in the holes of water he was making." Mortuary statistician Bennett Dowler had "watched the bailing out of the grave, the floating of the coffin, and [had] heard the friends of the deceased deplore this mode of interment."[20]

"The citizens . . . having a very natural repugnance to being drowned, after having died a natural death upon their beds," Ingraham observed, "choose to have their last resting-place a dry one," and in the early years of the nineteenth century New Orleanians began to construct tombs and mausoleums to challenge the city's sodden topography by raising the bodies above the water. Appropriate as they may have been in the local context, these ground-level enclosures, or "above-ground burials" as they are commonly called, were not unique to New Orleans, nor were they local inventions. They had their counterparts all along the Gulf Coast and the southern Atlantic Coast of North America and, less commonly, in early graveyards elsewhere on the East Coast (fig. 9.6). Those tombs were first built in the decades before the Revolution, and thus antedated the New Orleans examples. By the 1830s, wealthy New Orleanians, like their

FIGURE 9.6. Burial vault (ca. 1840), Colonial Park Cemetery, Savannah, Georgia

FIGURE 9.7. Mausoleums ("family tombs") (mid-nineteenth century),
Lafayette Cemetery No. 1, New Orleans

counterparts in other parts of the nation, were erecting elaborate family mausoleums to house their dead (fig. 9.7).[21]

So John H. B. Latrobe's watercolor rendering of St. Louis No. 1 recorded a cemetery in transition from the older model to a newer one. The ground is dotted with tombs, some with gabled roofs, but most with flat or stepped roofs. They are larger than most single graves but smaller than mausoleums. They appear to be recessed into the ground, while a few have upper stages. Latrobe's father had visited the cemetery in 1819 and described the tombs as structures "of bricks, much larger than necessary to enclose a single coffin, and plaistered over, so as to have a very solid permanent appearance. They are of these and many other Shapes of similar character covering an area of 7 or 8 feet long and being from 5 to 7 feet high (fig. 9.8). They are crouded close together, without any particular attention to aspect." He was even more impressed by the wall tombs, which locals called *fours* (ovens) because their brick vaults resembled domestic bake ovens. At the time of his visit, there were only two three-story blocks of these "Catacombs" in St. Louis No. 1 (figs. 9.9, 9.10). They stand at the right rear of John Latrobe's watercolor, where they probably formed part of the cemetery's enclosure (see plate 10).[22]

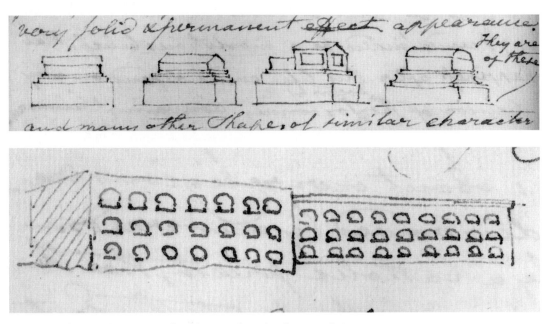

top FIGURE 9.8. Benjamin Henry Latrobe, private tombs and vaults, St. Louis Cemetery No. 1, New Orleans, 1819. (The Maryland Historical Society)

above FIGURE 9.9. Benjamin Henry Latrobe, "catacombs" (fours), St. Louis No. 1, 1819. (The Maryland Historical Society)

FIGURE 9.10. Fours, St. Louis No. 1

FIGURE 9.11. *Scene at a Cemetery* (mid-nineteenth century), New Orleans. Placing a coffin in a fours. (Courtesy Historic New Orleans Collection, Museum/Research Center, acc. no. 1957.124.24)

FIGURE 9.12. Fours, Lafayette No. 1, New Orleans

Like the cemetery itself, fours were public facilities. They were temporary accommodations as an earthen grave theoretically was, but they were rented for a fixed period rather than sold or offered for use for an undefined period. In the 1830s, the term was one to ten years, while by the middle of the century fours rented for fifty dollars for twenty-five years. Unless the lease was renewed, at the expiration of the time "the tenant was removed . . . and the premises were then ready for a new comer." The construction of fours permitted the commemoration of the dead through inscriptions and graveside rituals even among people who could not afford a tomb or vault or who were not allowed to appropriate space for one (fig. 9.11). Moreover, the fours protected the body as long as possible from New Orleans's peculiar environment.[23]

In democratizing access to individualized burial (for a fee), the fours epito-mized a new attitude that affected cemeteries throughout the United States and Europe, one that extended the privilege of individual commemoration and undisturbed interment from the elite to a larger public. New political, religious, and ethical ideas stressed the value of each person and encouraged the assump-tion that everyone (or at least, a growing number of white everyones) had a right to visibility and security in death as in life. In the late eighteenth century more people felt entitled to demand these privileges, particularly in republican America. To protect the bodies of their loved ones, urbanites began to seek fixed burial places. To organize these places, officials in charge of burial grounds re-sorted to the grid as a way of sorting the dead. The undifferentiated common space of the cemetery was articulated, with each body mapped in space and time. The structure of fours was inherently gridded, so that each locus had an address of sorts within the grid of fours, which in turn fit into the grid of the cemetery, and the cemetery in turn into the urban grid (fig. 9.12). For example, Charles W. Bradbury was interred in 1880 in St. Louis No. 2 in square number 2 (of the cemetery), in fours number 2, of the fourth range along Claiborne Street as one moved from Conti to St. Louis Street. The gridded fours were new-style graveyards stood on edge.[24]

New Orleans's rapid growth after 1803 and the new demand for individualized burial led the city to establish several new cemeteries in the early 1820s. At the same time that the city council authorized the establishment of St. Louis No. 2 for Roman Catholics, it gave Christ Episcopal Church a large parcel at the end of Girod Street, at the rear of the American-dominated Faubourg Sainte-Marie, for a new Protestant burying ground (fig. 9.13). Unlike St. Louis No. 1, both of these long, narrow graveyards were platted as grids organized around a center aisle and parallel side aisles (fig. 9.14). Within the plan, individual tombs were strictly aligned, following the 1822 orders of the city council that the city sur-veyor visit the new St. Louis No. 2 and Girod Street cemeteries weekly "to give a line for the graves and tombs." At the same time they specified building stan-dards for tombs and ordered earth graves to be dug at least four feet deep and three feet apart. A year earlier they had established a price of two dollars per foot of ground as the price for those wishing to build tombs.[25]

The new Crescent City cemeteries, gridded to facilitate separation and clas-sification and the orderly sale of lots to be held in perpetuity as individual prop-erty, followed a model created in 1796 when James Hillhouse, a prominent Con-necticut politician and urban systematizer, took the lead in purchasing and preparing a ten-acre field behind the original town of New Haven. This New Burying Ground (now Grove Street Cemetery), would provide sanitary, secure,

FIGURE 9.13. Map of New
Orleans cemeteries.
(Jennifer Reut)

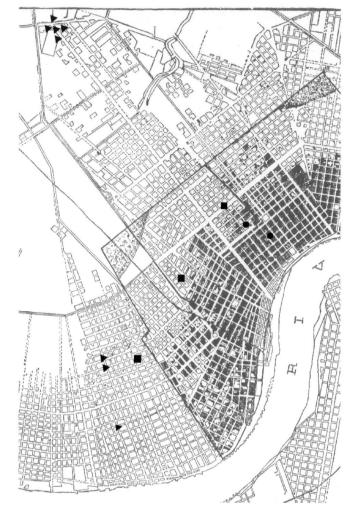

respectful burial for Hillhouse's own and his fellow lot holders' families (fig. 9.15). The town's central common was its original graveyard. Diversion of burials to the urban edge was part of a plan to gentrify the New Haven Green. The redesign also included the erection of fences to prevent one from driving across the Green, and ultimately the construction of three new churches, some covering or displacing old graves. The last of the old grave markers were removed in 1821, "thus freeing one of the most beautiful squares in the world from so improper an appendage."[26]

Hillhouse's concern for the fate of his family's graves on the town green first led him to consider establishing a private family graveyard, but he decided that since land easily changed hands, the long-term security of such a plot could not be guaranteed. It occurred to him that a larger, legally incorporated cemetery privately held among many owners could be a secure burial place if plot ownership were granted in perpetuity. So he chartered the New Burying Ground as

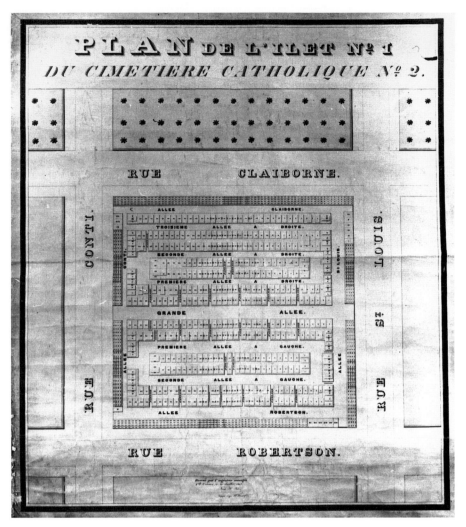

FIGURE 9.14. Plan of square 1, St. Louis Cemetery No. 2, New Orleans. Fours line the outside walls. (Courtesy Historic New Orleans Collection, Museum/Research Center, acc. no. 1975.25.6.407)

a "sacred and inviolable" site, a place of eternal rest because it would also be a place of eternal property.[27]

The choice to create a private corporation to sell burial plots to individuals, rather than a public facility that anyone could use, was novel, but the rationale rested in Hillhouse's emphasis on the affectionate or "companionate" family as the social-spatial building block of the New Burying Ground. He made the lots large enough for family burials and resisted selling plots to individuals. The new cemetery was platted into sixty-four-by-thirty-five-foot rectangles or "parallelograms," as Timothy Dwight called them, separated by alleys wide enough for carriages. Each parallelogram was divided into four numbered family lots of thirty-two by eighteen feet (Dwight apparently did not check his arithmetic),

FIGURE 9.15.
New Burying
Ground
(Grove Street
Cemetery),
New Haven
(Josiah Meigs,
1797), copy
of original
plan. (The
New Haven
Museum &
Historical
Society)

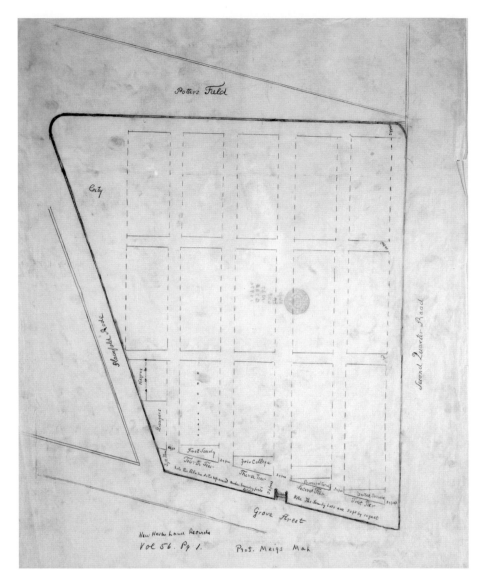

"and against each an opening is made to admit a funeral procession. At the divisions between the lots trees are set out in the alleys."[28]

Family units organized space visually as well as legally. Dwight observed that it was common to place an obelisk at the center of each family lot, "and thus [they] stand in a line successively through the parallelograms. The top of each post and the railing [that surround the plots] are painted white; the remainder of the post black," creating a visible, floating grid. "The squares, or half squares, are so many freeholds; and the names of the several freeholders are painted on the railings," added Edward Kendall. "Hence, the names, both of the living and the dead, are to be seen together." In short, the primacy of family in the new-model cemetery was defined in terms of property and celebrated by monuments and other embellishments that called attention to the familial articulation of the grid. Family names, family plots, and the resemblance to urban lots emphasized that the living and dead citizens of New Haven formed a single community united in space and through time.[29]

This mutual mirroring of city and cemetery is critical for understanding the space of the New Burying Ground and its many imitators of the first third of the nineteenth century. The state of Connecticut chartered the Proprietors of the New Burying Ground as a private corporation in 1797. Four lots were given to the town's three churches and to Yale College, three were "destined for the reception of the poor," and one was for African Americans. In addition, lots were given to each of the clergymen then serving in New Haven. Most of the remaining lots were sold to private citizens, although there were few sales in the first decades.[30]

As Dwight's and Kendall's comments suggested, the New Haven cemetery was an urban grid in which each address, or family plot, was individually accessible from the alley-street. As on the streets of the living city, these family lots in the New Burying Ground were articulated within a framework of spaces for common and public use. No longer was the graveyard a single common space. It was now a series of individual locations like the New Orleans fours or like the domestic and commercial lots in the city of the living.

As in living cities, the new cemeteries permitted the assertion of social difference within a common order. A visitor to the New Burying Ground thirty-five years after its establishment found the floating grid still in place, "but the first glance impresses the stranger with the very unequal distribution of monuments; some of which are clustered together so closely as almost to touch, while large intermediate vacancies yet wait for their destined tenants." Both the markers themselves and their materials varied widely, from the dominant obelisks to urns, pyramids, broken columns, and "countless" table tombs and gravestones, and from white marble to green marble, red sandstone, brownstone, and gray granite (fig. 9.16). Just as the grid of the city of the living was gradually differentiated by uneven development, so was that of the city of the dead.[31]

FIGURE 9.16. New Burying Ground, 1998

The New Burying Ground showed visitors an idealized image of the systematically ordered city. Its formal connection with New Haven was reinforced by a suburb that Hillhouse laid out adjacent to the cemetery. According to Edward Kendall, Hillhouse had undertaken "the building of a new and entire city, in the immediate rear of the old one. He builds his houses of stone, in a very solid and costly manner, and has marked out the area of a spacious square, in which are to be ornamental plantings." In the midst of his subdivision, on a hill overlooking his cemetery, Hillhouse set his own residence.[32]

Plantings further unified the cities of the living and the dead. Hillhouse and his fellow beautifiers planted elm trees along the main streets of New Haven, a "great multitude of shade trees" that Dwight celebrated as a "species of ornament in which the town is unrivaled." Visitor Algernon Sydney Roberts found the town a "delightful place . . . truly a classic spot—an elysium! . . . each house has a small yard or lawn in front ornamented with trees and shrubbery," while fellow Philadelphian Sidney George Fisher also commented on the gardens "adorned by shrubbery, and the wide streets lined & shaded by magnificent old elms." When Hillhouse gave the land of his subdivision to the city, he retained control over its plantings during his lifetime. And in the New Burying Ground he planted the "alleys" or streets with Lombardy poplars, a species then being introduced as street trees in many American cities.[33]

These trees connoted refinement rather than nature in the romantic sense. As a group of Philadelphia residents pointed out in a petition to the city council, the planting of trees would show the world "the Character of Philadelphia as to taste and magnificence." Landscaping lay a veneer of gentility over the articulated space of the commercial city, its cemetery, and, by extension, its inhabitants. Rather than positing culture-nature, city-suburb, or living-dead dichotomies, Hillhouse and his systematizing colleagues imagined the city and its cemetery as complementary aspects of urban life unified by the cultivated, artificial refinement of landscape plantings. The cemetery, separated and classified within itself, was in turn incorporated into the articulated landscape of the town, holding present and past generations in proper relationship, allowing appropriate commemoration while at the same time preventing the living and the dead from intruding on one another.[34]

New Haven's New Burying Ground defined the reformed cemetery, but the grid and privatization did not come to most American cemeteries until the 1820s, as the oldest cities outgrew their colonial graveyards and required new ones. Like the New Burying Ground these reformed cemeteries were usually founded as one of a number of projects of urban reordering by men who articulated a systematic understanding of the city, men such as Philadelphia's James Ronaldson (1768–1841), who established the Philadelphia, or Ronaldson's, Cemetery just outside the city's limits at Tenth and Shippen (now Bainbridge) streets in 1826–27.

Ronaldson was as deeply engaged in the political and economic life of Philadelphia as Hillhouse was in New Haven's. A Scottish immigrant who began his American career as a biscuit baker, Ronaldson and fellow Scot Andrew Binny later established a type foundry that for a time also produced Queensware ceramics. By the 1820s he owned a cotton spinning and weaving mill as well. His wealth and his lack of a family allowed him to be one of Philadelphia's most energetic systematizers. He was a founder and first president of the Franklin Institute, contributed to the Pennsylvania Hospital, served as president of the Louisville Canal Company, helped promote the Columbia Railroad, organized Philadelphia's first soup kitchen, and took an interest in the city's public school system.[35]

Through these activities Ronaldson was able to indulge an obsessive and occasionally overbearing passion for rationalizing and organizing urban life at every level. He published pamphlets about the effects of paper currency on the economy, the kinds of goods merchants ought to import, and the disposition of Stephen Girard's legacy. No subject was beneath his attention or foreign to the expertise he assumed. During the War of 1812 Ronaldson offered "hints" to General Thomas Cadwalader about the best way to lay out and administer his military encampment and reminded him to make sure his men used the proper-sized ammunition in their guns, to keep them as healthy as possible, and to serve them well-cooked food.[36]

In the fall of 1826, Ronaldson began to prepare several adjacent parcels of land, including a vacant lot that had been used as a skating rink, as a graveyard. The first burial took place in June 1827. It was Ronaldson's proudest achievement, and he reputedly sited his row of houses to be near it, as Hillhouse had his mansion. Ronaldson occupied the end building, from which he could look out on his burial ground (see fig. 4.2).[37]

Ronaldson's Philadelphia Cemetery was one of six private cemeteries established south of the city in the years 1825–27, following a city ordinance forbidding inner-city burials. Yet Ronaldson introduced several innovations that were absent from the others—the Mutual Association, Machpelah, Philanthropic, Union, and La Fayette cemeteries. Ronaldson's Cemetery was famous for accepting people with any or no religious affiliations and people, notably actors, who were excluded from most churchyards on moral grounds. As a result, Ronaldson was opposed by people who believed that his burying ground infringed the vested rights of the church or who were offended that it was unconsecrated. Some clergymen refused to officiate there.[38]

Like the New Burying Ground or New Orleans's St. Louis cemeteries, the Philadelphia Cemetery fostered ties between the living and dead generations. Ronaldson "hope[d] that [the cemetery] will contribute to cherish those tender feelings that connect the living with their deceased friends." His intended clients

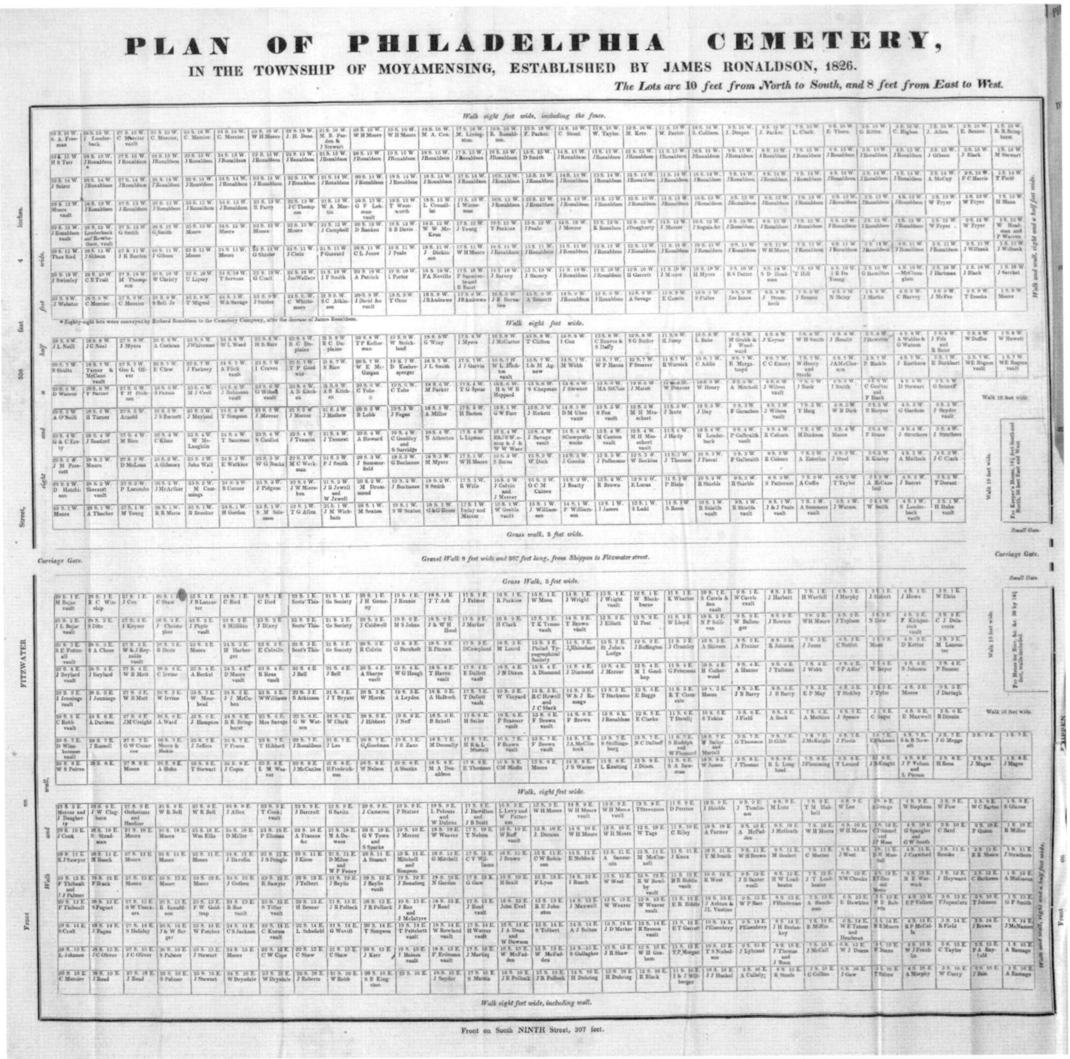
PLAN OF PHILADELPHIA CEMETERY,
IN THE TOWNSHIP OF MOYAMENSING, ESTABLISHED BY JAMES RONALDSON, 1826.
The Lots are 10 feet from North to South, and 8 feet from East to West.
Front on South NINTH Street, 307 feet.

FIGURE 9.17. Philadelphia (Ronaldson's) Cemetery, 1827, plot plan. (The Library Company of Philadelphia)

were the kinds of people who rented fours in New Orleans: respectable citizens of middling means who were unable to construct a tomb or to obtain space in a churchyard vault, but who wished to bury their loved ones in permanent graves. The dead were to be rescued from the anonymity of a trench in the potter's field or an unmarked and crowded grave in a churchyard by interment in a precisely platted, privately owned plot. Ronaldson protected the respectability of his cemetery by forbidding African Americans or the coroner (who would bury paupers) from owning lots there, although he donated several lots to the cemetery association for the burial of strangers, as well as two for the use of the Scots' Thistle Society, an ethnic fraternity that he had helped organize.[39]

As Hillhouse did, in other words, Ronaldson built an improved city at the edge of the old one. He enclosed the property (which was 306 by 307 feet after the addition of a small triangular parcel in 1831) with a wall and an iron railing. An eight-foot walk encircled the grounds, which were bisected by a gravel carriageway running from Fitzwater to Shippen streets (fig. 9.17). Grass walks flanked the carriageway, and two other eight-foot walks paralleled it, creating four rectangular superblocks eight lots wide. Unlike Hillhouse's cemetery, Ronaldson's offered no large family plots. Each lot was eight by ten feet, enough for a small vault or a couple of graves, and cost only twenty-six to thirty dollars.[40]

In Ronaldson's Cemetery, as in other gridded cemeteries, security was defined in terms of property. Every lot was held in fee simple (a proviso that delayed the ultimate demolition of the cemetery until 1950, since it took thirty years to clear all the titles individually), and every lot had a specific address, determined by its position south and east or west of the main gate. For example, the lot nearest the entry on the east was 3S.1E, since lots 1 and 2S were occupied by the gatehouse. Property lines were strictly maintained: no grave could be dug within four and one-half inches of the line and no monument could restrict access to other lots. Lot enclosures were permitted on the two central ranges of lots in each large block, and on the south half of all odd-numbered lots and the north half of all even numbered lots, which would create de facto cross alleys between enclosures. They might be stone or brick walls two feet high or iron railings of any height. The former might follow the "party wall rule" (the law governing the placement of shared walls) and project four and one-half inches onto the adjacent lot, with each owner paying half the cost.[41]

At Ronaldson's Cemetery, the gatehouse was a double-faced structure that policed the border between the living and the dead. On one side was the gatekeeper's house, protecting the dead from the living. On the other was the cemetery's bier house, which protected the living from the dead. The corpse was laid out there for three days before burial with a string tied around its finger and connected to a bell in a cupola to warn the attendant that a living person was in danger of being buried alive.[42]

Ronaldson's gatehouse stood as a reminder that the sentimentalization of the dead and feelings of communal bonds with deceased family and neighbors was tempered by an equally powerful fear of death and of the dead. While William Cullen Bryant advised his early-nineteenth-century readers to "approach thy grave,/Like one who wraps the drapery of his couch/About him, and lies down to pleasant dreams," New Orleanian Madaline Edwards observed that "we see those who have looked upon human suffering agony and pain in every shape, and these scenes they can underg[o] with scarce a change of countenance, but say to them let us walk in the grave yard and pass an hour and they are terrified at the idea of sitting with, or walking among the cold forms that possess no power to touch or speak to them."[43]

The two attitudes shared the same psychological roots. If an embodied idea of self led many to see the corpse as an essential component and remnant of the deceased rather than the abandoned shell of an unchanging self/soul gone on to other realms, the dead body then intimated the extinction of self. In the face of physicians' and clerics' acceptance of death's inevitable physiological and spiritual transformations, Americans (and others) in the early nineteenth century were increasingly committed to the integrity of self as fixed, bounded, and inviolable, as the codes of gentility suggested. Dead bodies, particularly recently dead bodies or bodies not quite dead, were uncomfortable reminders of the permeability and uncertainty of the boundaries between life and death, existence and nonexistence, that urbanites found increasingly difficult to accept.

Edgar Allan Poe's stories and poems exposed the deep fears that lay beneath the dryly scientific and euphemistically sentimental arguments for burial reform. The living and the dead clash in many of Poe's stories, which often revolve around premature burial. The epileptic heroine of "Berenice" (1835) and Fortunato in "The Cask of Amontillado" (1846) suffer that fate, while the living and the dead betray each other in "The Black Cat" (1843) and "The Tell-Tale Heart" (1843). In "The Fall of the House of Usher" (1839), Madeline Usher is entombed in "one of the numerous vaults" located in the family mansion, a pathological version of the community unified in space and time promoted by the reformed cemeteries. Like many of Poe's contemporaries, the story's narrator is uneasy with the idea of burying the young woman in the house, but her brother Roderick fears that in the family graveyard her body would be exposed to theft by physicians curious about her exotic illness. Just before Madeline is sealed in her coffin, the narrator notes a suspicious "faint blush upon the bosom and the face" and a "lingering smile," but dismisses them as the "mockery" of her "cataleptical" disease. Of course she is not dead, but claws her way out of her coffin and makes her way to her brother's room, where he dies of fear as she expires: the betrayal of the dead by the living is avenged. As the narrator escapes the house that had been used prematurely as a burial vault, it collapses and becomes the siblings' tomb.[44]

Poe knew his audience well. Suspicion of the dead and the not-quite-dead was an omnipresent theme in antebellum popular culture. The sense of betrayal could be read in A. Oakey Hall's warning against visiting New Orleans's cemeteries: "To many a tender frame," he wrote, "has issued upon such occasions from the damp alleys and causeways, a death warrant which was sealed, delivered, and executed before the expiration of another month." As Madeline

Usher's tale demonstrated, premature burial, the most horrifying betrayal, was a distinct possibility in the antebellum era, given the state of medical knowledge, so the necessity of policing the line between death and life was real. Philadelphian diarist Thomas P. Cope recorded an "interesting, thrilling statement of premature interments—or, rather, of their fortuitous prevention" in a newspaper he had read. The article spoke of ninety-four such escapes in one decade in France.

> Of these, 35 persons awoke of themselves from their lethargy at the moment their interment was commencing, 13 recovered from the affectionate care of their families, 7 in consequence of the falling of their coffins, 8 or 9 were recovered by the providential infliction of wounds made in sewing up their winding sheets, 5 from the sensation of suffocation on closing their coffins, 19 from their interments being delayed by accidental circumstances & 6 from doubts having been entertained of their actual death. These cases present very serious subjects for caution & reflection.[45]

The grisly sights and sounds of the cemetery confronted urbanites in a less melodramatic manner every day. Madaline Edwards reported a conversation with the gravedigger at New Orleans's Lafayette Cemetery No. 1 that touched on the "stench that arose from the water in the grave arising from the next graves in which lay the decomposed flesh of what had once been the object at least of a Mothers love."[46]

Irrational fear of corpses took on a scientific coloring when physicians and their associates confronted the dead en masse. The odors of putrefaction in the cemetery marked it as a prime generator of miasmas. If anything that smelled bad was dangerous, urban cemeteries, with their constant turnover of earth and poorly maintained tombs, smelled very bad, and they were consequently very dangerous. New Orleans's medical experts harped on this theme relentlessly. To yellow-fever specialist J. M. Picornell, the inhabitants of New Orleans were endangered by their own ignorance and carelessness. They built tombs in the St. Louis cemeteries so badly that the walls began to deteriorate before decomposition was complete, allowing dangerous miasmas to escape into the atmosphere. Thirty years later, yellow-fever epidemiologist Edward H. Barton still felt compelled to warn that "there is probably no climate in America where the vicinage of *cemeteries* would and does do, so much damage to public health as here. . . . Burying, almost universally above ground, . . . the mortar connecting the brick work soon splits, giving exit to injurious exhalations from the within decompositions [and] . . . contaminating the atmosphere for a great distance around it."[47]

Picornell's and Barton's arguments, although tailored to a New Orleans audience, presented the orthodox medical view of urban cemeteries. Spurred on by physicians, public authorities and educated advocates had denounced inner-city or "intramural" cemeteries since the eighteenth century. As low-density land users, cemeteries, like other large-scale public institutions, tended to be sited at the urban edge. But as the city embraced them, Timothy Dwight argued, "the proximity of these sepulchral fields to human habitations is injurious to health." The yellow-fever epidemics that ravaged most North American cities between the 1790s and the 1820s aggravated the anxiety. Abolition of intramural cemeteries was the measure that seemed most likely to avert future epidemics. Following an 1822 outbreak of yellow fever, New York City prohibited in-town burials, and other cities did their best to discourage them in subsequent years. Even churchyard vaults, although less subject to disturbance by subsequent burials, came under attack for bringing the dead too close to the living.[48]

From the time of the Revolution, then, criticism of urban cemeteries depended both on a rising secular sentimentality in individuals' views of the dear departed and on an equally powerful fear of the dead. A party line view emerged among reformers that depicted intramural cemeteries as inappropriately located theaters of disease, disgust, and desecration, created by callousness, venality, and benighted religious views. It was routine to dismiss older cemeteries as "unwholesome-looking" or "low, flat, gloomy," even though astute observers sometimes noted the meticulous care given to individual graves. Despite the complex nature of early cemeteries, this campaign set the tone for several decades of efforts to conceive a new kind of cemetery.[49]

As older cemeteries filled or were abandoned, new ones were platted farther from urban settlement. The reformed cemeteries created a ring of burying grounds just beyond the city limits in the first quarter of the nineteenth century (see fig. 9.13). By the 1830s, a second round of cemetery building moved cities of the dead not blocks or yards, but miles beyond the cities of the living.

The encroachment of tombs on scarce common space in New Orleans's St. Louis No. 1 and the rapid filling of St. Louis No. 2 and Girod Street cemeteries in the decade after their founding prompted some citizens to advocate the creation of spacious, gridded cemeteries farther from town. Alarmed by the devastating cholera epidemic of 1832, an anonymous correspondent of the wardens of the Catholic parish proposed that they establish one as part of their new *Système d'améliorations,* but the proposed location proved too distant for New Orleanians to reach conveniently, and the idea was abandoned. The city planned a never-realized nondenominational cemetery on the Bayou Road in 1835. Private organizations and other religious groups leaped into the breach left by the failure of these two schemes, and new gridded cemeteries were founded along the dry Metairie Ridge four miles northwest of town. Cypress Grove, or the Fireman's Cemetery, begun in 1840, was followed by the Irish Catholic St. Patrick's Cemetery in 1841, the Charity Hospital Cemetery (potter's field) in 1847, Odd Fellows' Rest in 1849, and Greenwood Cemetery in 1852. By 1849 there were eight cemeteries in New Orleans other than the St. Louis and Girod Street burial grounds. Seven of these lay on Metairie Ridge.[50]

A new cemetery was dedicated at Cambridge, Massachusetts, in 1831. Mount Auburn, as it was called, was the product of a six-year campaign led by Jacob Bigelow, a horticulturist, physician, and Harvard professor with wide contacts among Boston's ruling elite. Bigelow orchestrated the project as a cooperative venture of a newly organized cemetery association (incorporated as the Proprietors of the Cemetery of Mount Auburn in 1835) and the Massachusetts Horticultural Society, of which he had also been a founder.[51]

Mount Auburn introduced a new aesthetic to cemetery landscaping. Burying grounds such as New Haven's or Ronaldson's or those in New Orleans were carefully planted with trees and shrubs, but these were relatively sparse, relatively formal, and ornamented a landscape that maintained the grid's ideal plane. Edward Augustus Kendall observed sardonically that in deference to the New Burying Ground's grid the Lombardy poplars planted there "promised to grow with the least irregularity possible," although some lot holders had also planted weeping willows "from which quite so much cannot be hoped."[52]

Mount Auburn Cemetery, on the other hand, was shaped "in conformity to the modern style of laying out grounds," according to its principal designer, H. A. S. Dearborn. This meant that it consciously incorporated elements of the landscape architecture tradition that had originated on English country estates in the eighteenth century: it was "richly picturesque," in Andrew Jackson Downing's words. The site was rolling farm and woodland that made it impossible to see the entire cemetery at one time. Dearborn laid out winding roads and paths that followed the topography (fig. 9.18).[53]

Graveyards of this kind, which were called "rural cemeteries," were planned by intellectuals and members of the gentry whose independent interest in horticulture and landscape gardening often antedated their cemetery projects. George W. Brimmer, the owner of the wooded Mount Auburn tract, wanted it to be preserved in its natural form "for some parklike use" even before he donated it to the cemetery. The new cemeteries were highly artificial spaces that incorporated aesthetic principles their makers had learned from a century-old landscape tradition. Topography was necessarily and without regret "improved

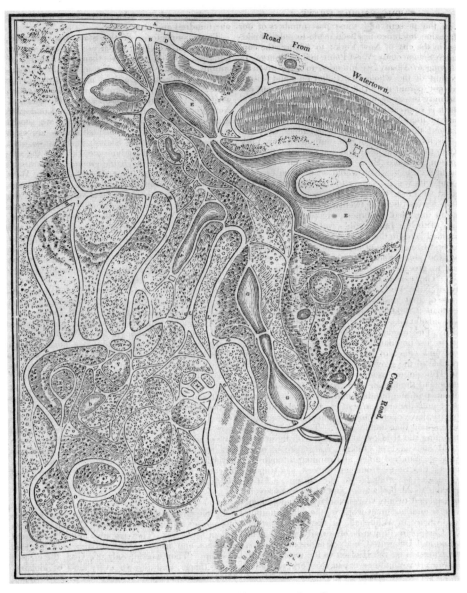

FIGURE 9.18. Mount Auburn Cemetery (1829), Cambridge, Mass., plan, 1834.
(Courtesy of the Dartmouth College Library)

by human care," as one contemporary writer noted. "It is unnatural," he went on, "to leave it to itself; and the traces of art are never unwelcome, except when it defeats the purpose, and refused to follow the suggestions of nature."[54]

Proponents of rural cemeteries seized on the diffuse critiques and varied impulses that animated the reformed cemeteries of the previous thirty years. Their claims that older burial places were dangerous to public health, impediments to development, and insufficiently respectful of the dead had all been heard many times before. The romantic attraction-repulsion to death and the dead was equally familiar, as was the desire to create secure, orderly, healthy, meditative settings for interment. Promoters of rural cemeteries fashioned these ideas into a comprehensive argument for the new burying grounds and encouraged the belief that their movement was something radically new both by downplaying the similarities between their own projects and the reformed cemeteries of the preceding decades and by promoting a change in terminology, from the traditional *graveyard* or *burying ground* to the less stark *cemetery*, but even that word had already been adopted by the proprietors of reform cemeteries such as Ronaldson's before the advent of the rural cemetery. Nevertheless, the influential landscape architecture writer Andrew Jackson Downing brushed off the prehistory of the rural cemetery by noting that twenty years before 1849, when he published his essay "Public Cemeteries and Public Gardens," "nothing better than a common grave-yard, filled with high grass, and a chance sprinkling of weeds and thistles, was to be found in the Union. If there were one or two exceptions, like the burial ground at New Haven, where a few willow trees broke the monotony of the scene, they existed only to prove the rule more completely."[55]

At first glance, nothing could be farther from the reform cemetery's imagery of the city of the dead than that attributed to the rural cemetery by its proponents. In the artificially pastoral landscape of a rural cemetery, the mourner and the visitor would encounter death as a natural phenomenon. It was a place, as William Cullen Bryant had written, where the dead would "mix forever with the elements,/To be a brother to the insensible rock/And to the sluggish clod." Mount Auburn was to be a "garden of graves": the dead would be the seeds from which the landscape would grow. For these reasons, the picturesque landscape of the rural cemetery has been heralded as a rejection of the gridded urban landscape, an anti-city or at best a counterpoint or complement to the city, a place that ameliorated some of the worst aspects of the city and allowed it to exist. Like the idealized Victorian household, the cemetery in this view was a haven rather than a heterotopia, a safety valve rather than a competing model, a complement rather than an antithesis of the living city.[56]

On closer examination, though, it is evident that the rural cemetery was a fully urban place, not only in the obvious sense of its urban origins and connections but in the spatial imagination that shaped it. Presentation renderings of cemetery plans, pamphlets issued when a cemetery was first projected, speeches delivered when it was finally dedicated, guides to casual visitors, and the comments of travelers and others seeking atmospheric literary effects all glossed over the foundation of the rural cemetery on a grid of private property. The by-laws of cemeteries and the literature issued to prospective buyers, on the other hand, rushed through the natural advantages with a few stock phrases to get to the heart of the matter for lot holders: the security of interment and the permanent visibility of family mementos through the institution of private property.

The contrast between the visual unity and underlying fragmentation was apparent at Philadelphia's Laurel Hill Cemetery (plate 11, fig. 9.19). Its chief organizer was John Jay Smith, librarian of the Library Company of Philadelphia, who was distressed at being unable to locate his daughter's grave at the Quak-

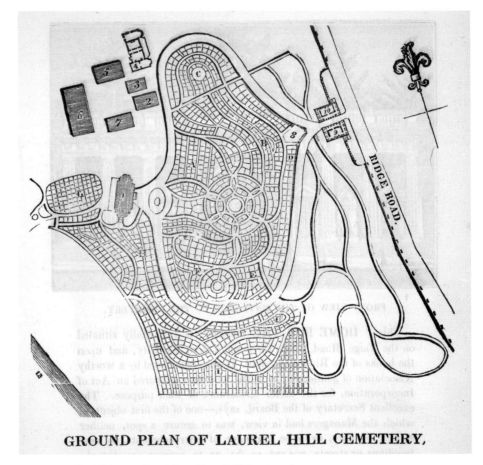

GROUND PLAN OF LAUREL HILL CEMETERY,

FIGURE 9.19. Daniel Bowen, *Ground Plan of Laurel Hill Cemetery*, 1839.
(The Library Company of Philadelphia)

ers' Western burying ground in the city. Like Joseph Bigelow before him, Smith assembled a group of interested men in November 1835 to discuss the creation of a rural cemetery. They purchased Joseph Sims's former estate, Laurel Hill, which had been used briefly as a Roman Catholic boys' school and which was already landscaped. William Strickland (one of the original committee), Thomas U. Walter, and John Notman were asked to submit designs for a cemetery on the site. Notman's design was chosen, although in many ways the design was a collaboration among Notman, the unsuccessful competitors, the surveyor Philip M. Price, and Smith.[57]

Laurel Hill was organized around a pair of irregularly looping drives ascending a hill from the entrance on Ridge Road. One rose to the right (north), passing the original Laurel Hill mansion and outbuildings, while the larger loop to the left (south) enclosed a formal central roundabout and narrower curving paths. Outside the area defined by the main roads, other curving paths gave access to grave sites on the south and central portion of the tract, while north of the house and its outbuildings the site was laid out as three rectilinear tracts intersecting at irregular angles.

Contemporary descriptions and views for general consumption celebrated the "rural and romantic beauties" of the site. For example, the map Notman drew for Smith's guidebook to Laurel Hill emphasized the plantings over the roadways and the geometry of the site (see plate 11). The "General View of Laurel Hill Cemetery" in the same guide is an oblique aerial panorama that stresses the Gothic-detailed wall and classical gate in the foreground (fig. 9.20). The sparse, irregular clumps of plantings open to reveal the presence of grave monuments, while the topography is made to seem much more rugged than it is. The wild character of the terrain resembles those in which Renaissance painters often set portraits of holy recluses. The difference from the flat, gridded regularity of Philadelphia was evident.

Smith's guidebook text took a much different tack from those of the map- and viewmakers, however. He addressed the aesthetic qualities of the cemetery, but more of his comments were intended to guide the decisions of prospective monument buyers than to praise the works of nature or of Notman. The cemetery's managers were "anxious to unite in carrying out the intention of creating at Laurel Hill a *toute ensemble,* which shall evince that, with superior facilities, there is growing up an improved taste in monumental sculpture."[58]

Smith's primary concerns were the same as those of the burial-ground reformers of earlier decades. In fact, he acknowledged Ronaldson's Philadelphia Cemetery as Laurel Hill's direct Philadelphia progenitor, for it "undoubtedly prepared the public mind for the innovation on established uses." Smith argued that Laurel Hill represented a significant advance over Ronaldson's work, but

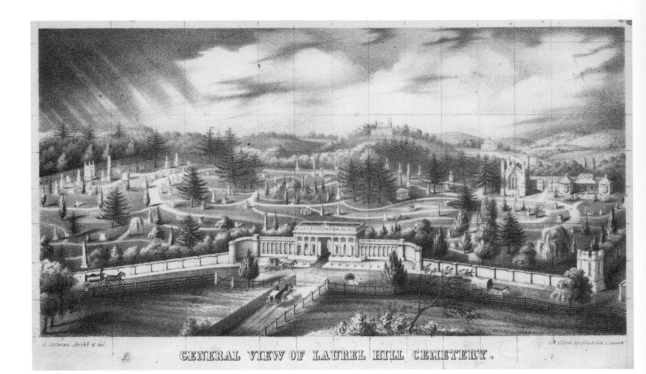

GENERAL VIEW OF LAUREL HILL CEMETERY.

FIGURE 9.20.
*General view
of Laurel Hill
Cemetery, 1844.*
(The Library
Company of
Philadelphia)

the nature of the advance is striking. He made no reference to the difference in sizes of the two burial places (Philadelphia Cemetery was slightly over 2.1 acres whereas the original Laurel Hill tract was 32 acres, of which 20 were devoted to the cemetery proper) or to the differing landscape styles of the two cemeteries. Instead, the decisive advance for him was the greater security of Laurel Hill with respect to the earlier cemetery, which had been surrounded by the city and was nearly full: "The proprietors of Laurel Hill were first to emulate the risk and expenditure, incidental to the establishment of a Cemetery, on a scale commensurate with the wants of so large a population, and removed beyond the probable approach of active business, or private dwellings." In addition to being distant from any possible urban encroachment (in fact, Laurel Hill was surrounded by industrial development within two decades), individual property in the cemetery was carefully delineated and protected.[59]

The cemetery's by-laws detailed the managers' strategies for guaranteeing the security of property. "To protect the interests of each separate purchaser," the managers reserved the right "to prevent the erection of large improvements which might interfere with the general effect, or obstruct any principal view." Certain other practices, such as raising the level of the plot above the surrounding and planting or removing trees without permission, were forbidden in the interests of the overall aesthetic effect of the landscape. To maintain the social

cachet of Laurel Hill, family domains were protected by prohibiting land speculation, shunting individual graves away from family plots and, not least, by restricting burial to white people. African Americans were banned from purchasing burial plots, and white proprietors were forbidden to bury black relatives,
friends, or servants in their own lots.[60]

Within these limits private property and individual expression were para-
mount. Boundary walls must be confined to the lot lines and must not rise
higher than two feet, with railings allowed to rise four more feet above the
walls. Vaults were permitted, but the managers frowned on them. Vaults were
expensive and inconvenient to neighbors, "defacing the beauty of the contiguous enclosures, grass, flowers, and other ornaments." Although the custom was
an old one, in Laurel Hill they were unnecessary since "the boundaries are defined," so property lines protected the integrity of the grave without resort to
vaults or other demarcations.[61]

The boundaries were "mathematically surveyed." Early maps of Laurel Hill
demonstrate how indelibly the gridded skeleton was inscribed even on the picturesque surface (see fig. 9.19). A site plan owned by the cemetery company
shows that ranks of contiguous rectilinear lots covered most of the surface. At
the very center of the cemetery some of the lot lines and individual borders
were deformed to follow the curving paths, but the closer one moved to the
edges of the cemetery, the more regular the grid. Along the southern third
of the tract, the plot grid overlay the curvilinear paths. On the northern third of
the site, paths made the grid visible.[62]

Far from denying the grid, then, rural cemeteries depended upon it. The nineteenth-century insistence on individualized commemoration and the security
of bodies and property required the kind of articulated sorting that the grid
provided. The picturesque landscape inflected the urban spatial order rather
than repudiating it. Cemetery directors admitted the grid but were reluctant
to acknowledge its privatist and urban implications. These were quickly driven
home to them by the actions of lot holders. Despite pleas from directors not to
diminish the unity of the vista, lot holders quickly filled Laurel Hill with tombs,
mausoleums, and monuments that turned it into a sculptural suburb more than
a landscape garden (fig. 9.21). Visitors devoted more attention to these than to
the landscape they were meant to embellish. Even the official guides eventually began to emphasize notable monuments.

As in the earlier generation of reformed cemeteries, social presence was
equated with property, displayed by fences and walls that interrupted the
unity of the landscape design and that angered and frustrated committed
aesthetes. Andrew Jackson Downing denounced the "violent bad taste" of the
"hideous *ironmongery*, which [rural cemeteries] all more or less display," par-

FIGURE 9.21. Laurel Hill
Cemetery, 2006

ticularly "several lots in one of these cemeteries, not only inclosed with a most barbarous piece of *irony,* but the gate of which was positively ornamented with the coat of arms of the owner, accompanied by a brass doorplate, on which was engraved the owner's name, and city residence!"[63]

In such an urban context the deep transformations that rural-cemetery promoters argued, quite sincerely, would be wrought by contact with nature and the religious sensibilities that would be stirred were still other manifestations of the ideal of refinement as an urban public virtue. The monuments and embellished burial plots were intended as permanent witnesses to good taste and delicate feeling and provided stages for public performances of grief whose contents and mannerisms were taught in an extensive sentimental literature. As with the orthogonal cemeteries that followed the New Burying Ground, the picturesque landscaping at rural cemeteries, although more elaborate, more extensive, and more varied, remained an ornament, a sign of gentility. The founders of Philadelphia's Monument Cemetery noted that they had planted "200 ornamental trees . . . indicative of the refinement of the age."[64]

As refined landscapes, rural cemeteries—held forth by cemetery promoters as places of solitary commune with the dead, sites of "the lone grave in nature"—became popular promenading grounds. The founders of rural cemeteries were surprised and somewhat disconcerted by their immediate popularity for this purpose, but they should not have been. Promenading in newly landscaped urban squares and in dramatic natural settings at the city's edge was a genteel European custom that took firm root in American cities in the early nineteenth century, and from one perspective the habit of visiting cemeteries simply transferred the promenade to a spacious new setting. Still, the numbers of visitors could be staggering. In 1848 the managers of Laurel Hill counted 30,000 visitors between April and December. In 1860 they estimated 140,000.[65]

The rural cemetery incorporated many of the elements of urban space and society that had characterized the gridded reformed cemetery. In fact, reformed cemeteries continued to be created throughout the antebellum period. More important, the label "rural cemetery" was qualitative rather than descriptive. It was adopted by the great middle ground of graveyards that were called rural cemeteries but whose allegiance to the picturesque aesthetic embodied at Mount Auburn was often limited to some plantings and the use of the names of trees and flowers for paths. Even Laurel Hill and its near contemporary, Philadelphia's Woodlands Cemetery, both established in existing villa gardens, owed more allegiance to Philadelphia's local landscape tradition than to the dramatic picturesque aesthetic espoused at Mount Auburn. Moreover, as business entrepreneurs eager to attract investors and customers, the managers of the new rural cemeteries were often willing to allow large-scale lot holders and stockholders considerable latitude in designing their own sections of the cemetery. Thus the Mount Auburn example was honored as often in the breach as in faithful imitations. And in every kind of cemetery—reform, rural, and hybrid— the urban spatial imagination ruled.[66]

Philadelphia's Monument Cemetery (1837), on the site of an estate called Sydney Place, is a noteworthy example (fig. 9.22). Although its founder, Dr. John A. Elkinton, had "visited and carefully investigated the beneficial results" of Mount Auburn, and described Monument Cemetery as a rural cemetery, it was a square, flat, twenty-acre tract turned diamond-wise. Four major east-west avenues set at right angles to one another were intersected by a grid of narrower paths. At the center was a circle called Monument Square, which contained an artificial mound.[67]

Monument Cemetery synthesized the landscape forms and rhetoric of the reformed- and rural-cemetery movements. Like Smith and his colleagues at Laurel Hill, Elkinton stressed the superior security of the Monument Cemetery arising from its remoteness from the center of the city. The "distress and excitement which encroachments upon grave-yards have frequently occasioned in our city," he wrote, have "proved a strong incentive to the establishment of public rural Cemeteries." A cemetery's first job was "to furnish a place for the bodies of the dead, where they may repose free from the insults of the living—where they may not offend the senses in their progress of corruption, and where they may return quietly to their mother earth." The cemetery's rules, like those of its contemporary Laurel Hill, were designed to defend the integrity of property lines, to promote a uniform appearance, and to reinforce the social distinctions

Design for an Entrance to Monument Cemetery, on Broad Street.

J. D. Jones, Archt.   R. S. Gilbert, Eng.

Ground Plot of MONUMENT CEMETERY.

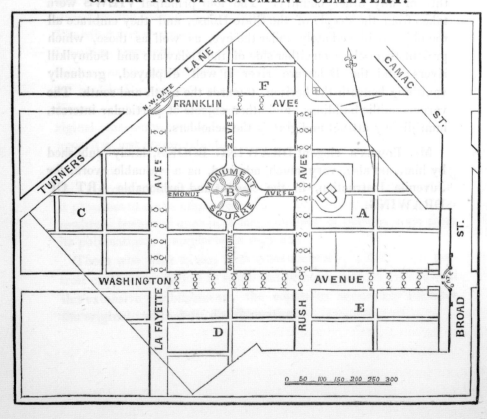

FIGURE 9.22. Dr. John Elkinton, Monument Cemetery (1837; demolished 1956), Philadelphia, plan
(Dr. John Elkinton) and gatehouse (J. D. Jones). (The Library Company of Philadelphia)

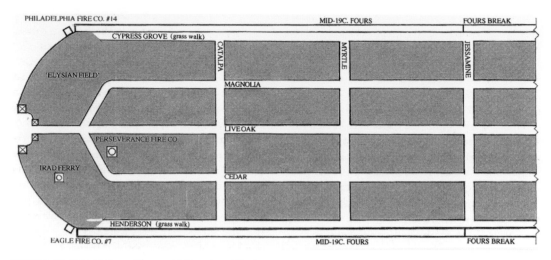

FIGURE 9.23. Cypress Grove (Firemen's) Cemetery (1840),
New Orleans, sketch plan as of 1995. (Zeynep Kezer)

maintained among the living. As usual, paupers and African Americans were
excluded. Unlike other rural-cemetery founders, however, Elkinton pointed
out the ease with which private vaults could be excavated at his site, and he
encouraged visitation rather than viewing it as an unavoidable evil. The plan
was arranged so that one could drive a carriage into the east entrance on Broad
Street, pass by the chapel on the main avenue, ride around the monument, and
depart through the west gate on Turner's Lane without interrupting the medi-
tations of pedestrians. Elkinton's promotional tract thus acknowledged the natural but emphasized the cultural. Monument Cemetery was "a place in which
natural beauties, and conveniences may be combined with the labors of art." It
embraced the urban, sociable character of the rural cemetery assumed by lot
holders and visitors but disguised by the rhetoric of nature that some cemetery
planners and literary expositors preferred.[68]

Cypress Grove, or Firemen's, Cemetery, opened in 1840, was typical of New
Orleans's third generation of cemeteries. A flat, gridded plot, it nevertheless enjoyed a reputation as the city's premier rural cemetery until the equally flat
Metairie Cemetery was opened on a former horse-racing track after the Civil
War (figs. 9.23, 9.24). After passing through a gate modeled on an Egyptian pro-
pylaeon as reinterpreted in Jacob Bigelow's gates for Mount Auburn Cemetery,
visitors to Cypress Grove entered a wide lawn. In the center was the tomb of
Irad Ferry, a fireman killed in action in 1837 (fig. 9.25). Ferry had first been buried in the Girod Street Cemetery but was brought to Cypress Grove and interred
under a monument—a broken column standing on a sarcophagus—designed
by the French émigré architect Jacques Nicolas Bussière de Pouilly. Near Ferry's
grave was the freestanding society tomb of the Perseverance Fire Company

FIGURE 9.24. Cypress Grove Cemetery, view of Live Oak Avenue looking toward Egyptian-style gate

No. 8, and built into the cemetery walls on each side of this lawn were the classically styled tombs of two other fire companies, the Philadelphia Fire Engine Company No. 14 on the left, and the Eagle Fire Company No. 7 on the right. In the latter lie the remains of two of New Orleans's most renowned early clergy, Sylvester Larned of the First Presbyterian Church and his successor Theodore Clapp.[69]

This Elysian Field, commemorating local heroes such as the firemen who protected the city (and founded the cemetery) and two ministers famous for their courage in the face of epidemics, reflected the new emphasis in rural cemeteries on graves and cenotaphs of renowned or historic figures as symbols of the temporal dimensions of the urban community celebrated in New Orleans's All Saints' Day festivals. History in rural cemeteries was dynamic, locating individual decedents in past society as the spatial arrangement mapped them in contemporary society.

Rural cemeteries reenacted human, and particularly American, development, returning to the primeval forest to construct a revised social landscape. A keen sense of this progressive vision for the cemetery is evident in Madeline Edwards's musings in New Orleans's Lafayette Cemetery No. 1 (see fig. 9.7). As a young woman who had endured a failed marriage and a tormented relationship with a married man and who had taken another married lover, Edwards saw herself as a lonely pariah unsuited for most human society. She read the cemetery as an emblem of her alienation and spun out a long fantasy of her own and her lover's future gravesites. She wished to be buried in a solitary, secret grave on a lonely hillside (in flat south Louisiana!) where her lover and her unborn child would mourn her, and where her oaken headboard would soon decay. She would bury him in a similar fashion, but with a marble slab that would eventually be engulfed by the city. The grave, its natural setting lost, would be transformed from a private shrine to a public monument, embedded in a new urban setting where those who were wronged or overlooked in the old city would be deservedly celebrated. A secluded grave was appropriate for herself, but she accepted that most people viewed the urban cemetery as an appropriate instrument of sociability and archive of human memory.[70]

FIGURE 9.25. Irad Ferry monument (J. N. B. de Pouilly, 1841), Cypress Grove Cemetery

In looking over what she had written, Edwards was "astonished to find I have gone to such lengths into the imaginary," and acknowledged that in reality "that day may come and very soon when [her lover] will lay my last remains in a less romantic spot." She confided to her diary that if she died in New Orleans "I hope to rest in the firemans"—Cypress Grove Cemetery. In 1854 she was buried in an unmarked grave in San Francisco's potter's field.[71]

CHAPTER 10

{ **GRIDDED UTOPIAS**

Philadelphia boasts one of the most significant architectural monuments of the early republic, one that embodied all that its builders thought was best about their society, as well as their fondest hopes for its future. That monument is not Independence Hall or any of the other landmarks associated with the Revolution, but the Eastern State Penitentiary (fig. 10.1). Although we think of modern prisons as symptoms of society's failures, early republicans saw penitentiaries as emblems of social progress. Behind Eastern State's forbidding gray stone walls, their height exaggerated by the narrow streets over which they now loom, the most depraved and luckless of the nation's residents could be transformed into republican citizens, men and occasionally women worthy to travel the streets of the new nation and equipped to prosper honestly there. Eastern State Penitentiary and a host of similar prisons founded in other states in the half century after the Revolution presented a utopian vision—albeit a grim one to modern eyes—of a republic of introspective, self-regulating, productive men and women.

At the same time, early republican penitentiaries were desperate responses to urban chaos, born out of elite impatience with social disorder and longing for a decisive solution to it. Penitentiary builders answered the noises, the smells, the filth, and the epidemics of the growing cities, the frenetic construction and demolition of the urban fabric, the muddy, traffic-clogged streets, the masses of goods and people crowding the sidewalks, the crude egalitarianism of public spaces, and the anxieties over authentic identities with stolid stone fortresses fitted with heating, ventilation, and sewage systems meant to purge the space of odors and eliminate the threat of disease. These were places where a simple, easily legible spatial order matched one person to one space, where virtue supplanted vice, where false criminal identities were exchanged for authentic new ones, where social disorder was replaced by a simple hierarchy of keeper and convict, and where silence reigned over all. Penitentiary founders, theorists, and architects made explicit the assumption implicit in other aspects of city building: that an environment carefully designed to control bodies could mold the kinds of citizens best suited for republican society.

The penitentiary was the brightest star in a constellation of "therapeutic" institutions that also included jails, bridewells, houses of industry, and houses

FIGURE 10.1. Eastern State Penitentiary (John Haviland, 1823–36), Philadelphia

of refuge; hospitals; a panoply of asylums for housing everyone from orphans and the insane to inebriates and repentant prostitutes; and Lancasterian schools. The isomorphic language of system linked politics, science, society, and space in ways that made penitentiaries, asylums, and schools appear to be effective solutions to the political and social questions that American republicans asked themselves. A rhetoric of iron-fisted benevolence runs through the voluminous prospecti, polemics, managers' reports, and visitors' comments that documented these institutions. The elite promoters of penitentiaries and the many other new social institutions were motivated more by a desire to make a new political system work than by any abstract fondness for power or oppression. But while their therapeutic vision was undeniably repressive, it was an *optimistic* repression, a misguided attempt to recruit republican citizens from among the downtrodden. Their new institutions defined and defended the boundaries of republican citizenship, but they were also meant to teach their value.[1]

To their founders, the therapeutic institutions formed a coordinated system of social development. Although the details varied among institutional types, all were designed to construct or reconstruct behavior and personalities through regimes based on silence and choreography. Despite the attention given then and recently to the gaze—to social control based on disciplinary surveillance—the spoken and unspoken word, the precisely coordinated bodily movement, and physical coercion were the defining elements of order and reconstruction in antebellum institutions.[2]

The buildings that housed the new institutions were as much metropolitan improvements as the commercial and civic structures of the central city. For a small fee, urban residents and visitors could tour them (except the insane asylums, usually), they could buy books that described them glowingly, and they could embellish their homes with prints and even ceramics decorated with their images. So although these new establishments usually lay at or outside the urban edge, they were essential parts of the city, embedded in the urban spatial imagination.[3]

The theory and practice of early-republican therapeutic institutions were created by small groups of local activists who also belonged to a national and international intelligentsia. Mathew Carey revealed in 1829 that most of the charities and asylums in Philadelphia could boast fewer than one hundred annual donors. Some were supported by only one or two people, others relied on as few as thirty-five, and even the House of Refuge, one of the city's most visible institutions, attracted only three hundred subscribers. In most cities a core of reformers—men such as Thomas Eddy (1758–1827) of New York and Roberts Vaux (1787–1836) of Philadelphia—turn up on the lists of directors of institution after institution. Often their financial support was all that kept the establishments going.[4]

Eddy, a Philadelphia-born Quaker, made his money in insurance and financial speculation. He was a supporter of the New-York Hospital; a key player in the hospital's decision to spin off the Bloomingdale Asylum, a mental hospital; a central figure in the Free School Society and the instigator of its adoption of Lancasterian pedagogy; a driving force in the Society for the Reformation of Juvenile Delinquents and its establishment of a house of refuge for New York; and a notable actor in the New York Manumission Society and many other charities, in addition to being the prime mover of the first and second New York state penitentiaries at New York and Auburn. He was also a director of the Western Inland Lock Navigation Company and a state-appointed commissioner of the Erie Canal. Eddy saw his political support for internal improvements, or government-subsidized economic infrastructure, and his promotion of social-reform institutions as complementary exercises of the same "improving spirit."[5]

Roberts Vaux, Eddy's counterpart, was equally active. Vaux, another Quaker, inherited a fortune and retired at twenty-six to pursue his charities. He was involved in the same range of penal, therapeutic, medical, psychiatric, and educational institutions as Eddy, as well as in temperance and other moral-reform societies and in the antislavery movement. Vaux worked for agricultural reform and helped organize and run Philadelphia's Lancasterian public schools. He was among the founders of the Historical Society of Pennsylvania, the Philadelphia Athenaeum, and the Academy of Natural Sciences, and he served as an officer of the Pennsylvania Temperance Society, the Friends' Bible Association, and the Pennsylvania Abolition Society. Most of all Vaux supervised the construction of the Eastern State Penitentiary, and he enthusiastically supported the institution and its principles publicly and privately.[6]

These civic activists corresponded with each other and with European, particularly English, reformers such as William Roscoe and Jeremy Bentham. Reformers on both sides of the Atlantic read and responded to one another's works and visited the institutions their colleagues had established. In 1803, for example, Patrick Colquhoun sent Eddy Bentham's panopticon writings "by the desire of the author," along with reports on several British penitentiaries and various tracts on the education of young and poor people. Bentham sent another packet of his writings on social theory directly to Eddy, noting that "Mr. Eddy will see that Mr. Bentham has read his work on the New York state prison." Eddy also cited Montesquieu, Cesare Beccaria, and John Howard as influences.[7]

Men such as Vaux and Eddy were linked not only in their purposes—the imposition of moral discipline and social order in the new republic—but in the techniques they employed to do so. They created thoroughly materialist institutions in which architecture was assigned a central role in shaping good citizens at the intersection of embodied selfhood and republican space. An equally committed corps of architects such as John McComb, Jr., in New York, Charles Bulfinch in Boston and Washington, and John Haviland, William Strickland, and later Samuel Sloan in Philadelphia, assisted them. These designers organized each of the new prisons, asylums, and hospitals as a variation of the same spatial type—a grid of identical cells opening off a single- or double-loaded corridor. The defining institution, the epitome of the founders' and architects' spatial and behavioral strategies, was the penitentiary.

On October 25, 1829, Philadelphia's not-yet-completed Eastern State Penitentiary received its first inmate, Charles Williams. From the moment the cornerstone was laid six years earlier, the Commonwealth of Pennsylvania's visually striking new prison had been the object of intense national and international curiosity as the harbinger of a new kind of "prison discipline," or penal regimen. By the time Eastern State's gates opened to swallow up Williams, it was the subject of ferocious debate among proponents of its "separate" or "silent" system and those of its rival, the "congregate" system made famous at New York's Auburn State Prison. Vaux strenuously advocated the former and Eddy the latter.[8]

Pennsylvania's legislature authorized construction of the penitentiary in 1821 in response to public panic following a riot in Philadelphia's Walnut Street Jail, then the state's principal prison. Yet penal reform had been on the public agenda for years, and Pennsylvania had already begun work on a Western State Penitentiary at Pittsburgh three years before the riot. The inauguration of Eastern State, however, presented an opportunity for some energetic Philadelphians to advocate a novel theory of prison discipline that stressed not only punishment but the awakening of inmates to their religious and moral obligations and to the personal happiness that would arise from meeting them, enabling criminals "to estimate justly the enobling privileges of virtue and independence."[9]

Eastern State Penitentiary stood on Cherry Hill northwest of the urbanized district of Philadelphia. It was encircled by gray gneiss walls 30 feet high and 650 feet on a side, with a castellated Gothic (or, in Haviland's term, Anglo-Norman) gatehouse and corner towers—the "only edifice in this country," wrote critic Thomas B. McElwee, "which is calculated to convey to our citizens the external appearance of those magnificent and picturesque castles of the middle age, which contribute so eminently to embellish the scenery of Europe." Contemporary prints commonly depicted it in a setting that, despite a few traces of its former agricultural use, along with hint or two of encroaching urbanism, was reminiscent of a remote British moor (plate 12). The picturesque exterior was meant to inspire cautionary dread, a strategy derived from eighteenth-century European prison designers, who thought that a forbidding appearance, often embellished by chains, keys, sundials, and other ominous emblems of lost liberty, was an effective warning to those who might be tempted to break the law. Turning McElwee's phrase tellingly, novelist George Lippard, a bitter critic of Eastern State, described it as "an imposing image of the feudal castle of the dark ages."[10]

The desolate image eloquently conveyed Philadelphians' ambivalence toward the new penitentiary. It was both an object of civic pride and an emblem of civic pain. As Vaux observed at the cornerstone-laying ceremony on May 22, 1823, the construction of the new penitentiary was "*Painful,* because such was the erring character of man . . . that it was necessary society should provide means for the punishment of offenders against its laws. *Gratifying,* because a correct view of human nature, coupled with the indispensable exercise of Christian benevolence, had led to the mitigation of punishments. *Justice* was now mixed with *Mercy.*"[11]

In contrast to the prison's romantic exterior, those who toured it found a much less familiar scene inside. After passing through the double gates of the front building visitors entered a two-story octagonal hub, the "observatory" from which prison officers supervised the inmates (fig. 10.2). An early plan showed the gridlike regularity that Haviland intended. Seven equal arms, each containing eighteen cells on each side of a double-loaded corridor, sprouted from the hub. During thirteen years of construction, however, the state's needs changed and Haviland's design evolved with them. After the completion of the first three one-story cell blocks (those on the right side of the plan), the architect was ordered to redesign the other four as two-story blocks and to extend the diagonal arms all the way to the exterior walls (figs. 10.3, 10.4). The

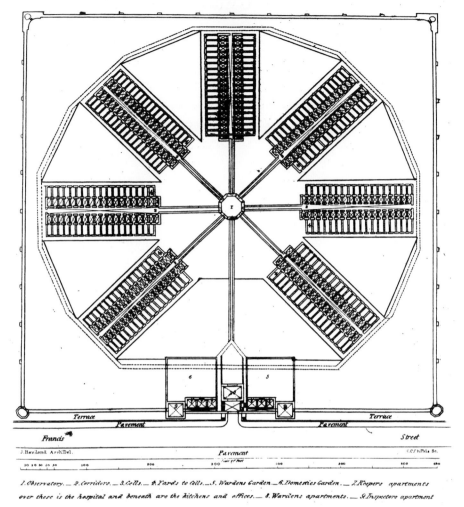

PLAN OF THE EASTERN PENITENTIARY.

J. Haviland Arch. Del.

Francis

Terrace Pavement Terrace

Street

Pavement

Scale of Feet

1. *Observatory.* _ 2. *Corridors.* _ 3. *Cells.* _ 4. *Yards to Cells.* _ 5. *Wardens Garden.* _ 6. *Domestics Garden.* _ 7. *Keepers apartments over these is the hospital and beneath are the kitchens and offices.* _ 8. *Wardens apartments.* _ 9. *Inspectors apartment over which are two hospital rooms.* _ 10. *Base of the great tower over which is the apothecarys office above which is the belfry.*

FIGURE 10.2. John Haviland, *Eastern State Penitentiary*, original plan with seven equal one-story cell blocks, ca. 1830. (The Library Company of Philadelphia)

FIGURE 10.3. James Queen, *The State Penitentiary for the Eastern District of Pennsylvania*, ca. 1855. (The Library Company of Philadelphia)

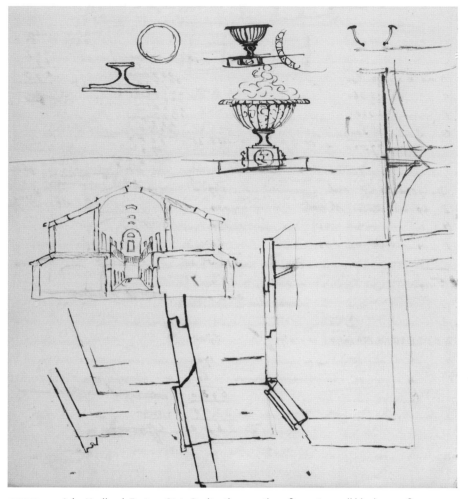

FIGURE 10.4. John Haviland, Eastern State Penitentiary, section of two-story cell blocks, ca. 1830. The larger drawings around the edges are studies for this section. (University of Pennsylvania Library)

result was a more capacious, less regular plan that could confine 550 prisoners rather than the 252 originally expected, but one whose initial spatial conception remained intact.

Eastern State Penitentiary differed radically from traditional prisons in which large groups of prisoners—convicted criminals, debtors, untried suspects, and some insane people with nowhere else to go—were held in common rooms. It was also different from the first, late-eighteenth-century generation of reformed prisons such as the Walnut Street Jail, where convicts were "separated and classified," then housed in 18-by-20-foot group cells (fig. 10.5). The first cells at Cherry Hill, in contrast, were 8 feet by 12 feet, with angled barrel vaults rising to 10 feet at their highest points. An individual exercise yard the same width as the cells but a little longer was attached to each ground-floor cell. Each cell-and-yard was built to hold a single convict.[12]

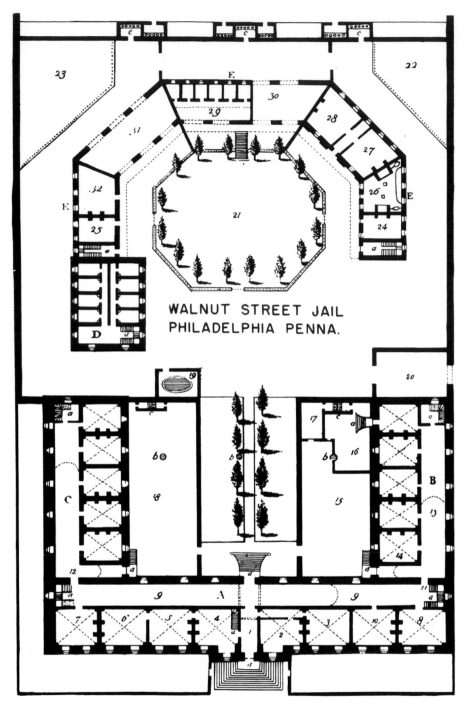

WALNUT STREET JAIL
PHILADELPHIA PENNA.

FIGURE 10.5. Walnut Street Jail, Philadelphia (1773–74; dem. ca. 1835). Plan in 1798.
(Pennsylvania Prison Society)

The move from the mass accommodation of traditional jails to the separated and classified common rooms of the Walnut Street Jail then to the individual cells at Eastern State Penitentiary represented two shifts in European and American thinking about detention, crime, and punishment. According to the standard histories, premodern jails were holding facilities where suspected criminals could be detained until they were tried or punished, where debtors could be held to keep them from fleeing their obligations, and where such troublesome people as lunatics or political opponents could be kept out of sight. Punishment was imposed primarily by public shame or through the infliction of bodily pain. In the eighteenth century, refined sentiment shifted away from such "sanguinary" penalties toward incarceration and private correction of the soul rather than punishment of the body.[13]

This is the history that antebellum prison reformers learned from eighteenth-century predecessors such as John Howard. There *is* truth in it, but it is oversimplified. As early as the sixteenth century, some European authorities began to experiment with incarceration and hard labor in houses of correction to punish and correct all varieties of social deviance, as part of an initial centralization of state power. By the eighteenth century, these had become institutions for criminals, with other kinds of disciplinary institutions provided for vagrants and other lesser offenders. At the Vatican's House of Correction at San Michele in the early eighteenth century some offenders were even held in solitary confinement to promote the same sort of introspection that monastic isolates practiced.[14]

In the second half of the eighteenth century European legal scholars and philanthropists such as John Howard, Cesare Beccaria, and Jeremy Bentham, inspired by religious piety, Enlightenment humanism, or theories of political economy, began to demand the replacement of corporal and even capital punishment with incarceration and hard labor. They also called for the reform and reconstruction of existing prisons to facilitate corrective detention and to alleviate the dangers to life and health posed by the older buildings. In the United States, these ideas made important inroads in the years after the Revolution. Spurred by the European example and by the obvious contradiction between penal practices and republican ideals of human dignity and potential, American reformers argued for the twin goals of abolishing or drastically restricting capital punishment and of replacing corporal punishment with corrective incarceration.[15]

Pennsylvania was the first to respond. Following a revision of the legal code, the state took over the city of Philadelphia's Walnut Street Jail (1773–74; dem. 1835) in 1790 (see fig. 10.5). The jail's U-shaped plan with its groin-vaulted cells opening off a single-loaded corridor followed a standard Anglo-American in-

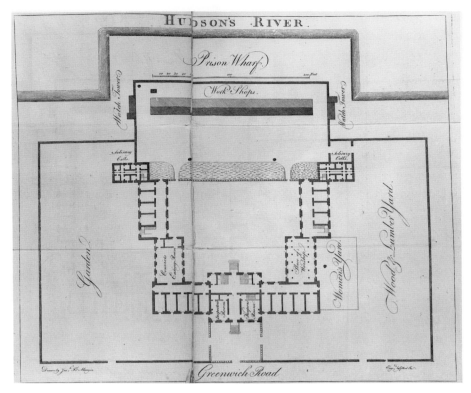

FIGURE 10.6. Joseph F. Mangin, *New-York State (Newgate) Prison* (John McComb, Jr., 1797), Greenwich Village, New York. (Collection of the New-York Historical Society)

stitutional formula. So did the pedimented three-bay pavilion that projected from a rusticated facade regularly pierced with barred windows (plate 13). The jail might have been mistaken for a hospital, a college, an academy, an almshouse, an insane asylum, a factory, or any of a number of large Anglo-American institutional structures. At about the same time the Walnut Street Jail was constructed, for example, very similar buildings were erected to house the schools that are now Princeton and Brown universities and Dartmouth College. In a sense that was the point. A single building type was used for all the institutions in which British and American subjects were trained or retrained in social norms. The jail's barred windows and its weather vane, whose arms represented keys, offered the only clue to its specific purpose.[16]

The state authorities used this building to sort prisoners by sex and race, and again into four classes that ranged from the most serious offenders to vagrants to the untried. The walled yard behind contained workshops in which the inmates engaged in a variety of tasks, including nail manufacture, blacksmithing, and stone cutting, as well as carpentry, joinery, and wood turning, with vagrants and runaway servants assigned the traditional mind-numbingly menial tasks of beating hemp and picking moss, hair, wood, and oakum. There was a 90-by-32-foot courtyard for women prisoners' exercise and one of the same size for debtors, with the remainder used for exercise and gardening by the other male inmates.[17]

Although the Walnut Street Jail had not been built with prison reform in mind, it was the first of the initial wave of American reformed penitentiaries. The most important was the purpose-built New York State (or Newgate) Prison on the Hudson River at Greenwich Village, a refined version of the Walnut Street Jail opened in 1797 (fig. 10.6). Its central block contained living rooms for the head keeper and an elaborate meeting room for the inspectors (board of directors), after the fashion of contemporary hospitals and asylums. Aside from a small women's yard against the north wall of the prison, the remainder of the site was given over to gardens and a wood and lumber yard, with workshops along the prison wharf. Similar prisons, such as the Massachusetts State Prison designed by the Boston architect Charles Bulfinch and built at Charlestown, Massachusetts, in 1804–5, were constructed in other states and similar regimes were enforced in them.[18]

The shops and large work yards of the first-generation postrevolutionary prisons manifested the prevailing Euro-American belief that dull, onerous labor was the most effective way to reform criminals. In the late eighteenth century some theorists began to tout the reformative qualities of solitude, silence, and introspection. The English merchant Jonas Hanway's *Solitude in Imprisonment* (1776) was particularly influential in introducing this idea. As the French investigators Gustave de Beaumont and Alexis de Tocqueville summarized the argument for solitary confinement, "Thrown into solitude [the criminal] reflects. Placed alone, in view of his crime, he learns to hate it; and if his soul be not yet surfeited with crime, and thus have lost all taste for anything better, it is in solitude, where remorse will come to assail him." Silence and introspection must have appealed powerfully to Quakers, whose worship service was built around those practices as paths to spiritual enlightenment. Since Friends were among the most vocal proponents of legal and penal reform on both sides of the Atlantic, solitude, or solitary confinement, was quickly placed on the reform agenda. Pennsylvania ordered the solitary confinement of certain offenders in its postrevolutionary penal reforms. When it took over Walnut Street Jail in 1790 the state added a Penitentiary House containing six-by-eight-foot solitary cells to house the "more hardened and atrocious offenders who . . . have been sentenced to hard labor for a term of years" (see fig. 10.5, D). Solitary cells were also provided in the Newgate prison (see fig. 10.6, ends of each rear wing).[19]

Solitary confinement gained new adherents in the second decade of the nineteenth century when Thomas Eddy, a leading proponent of the Newgate prison, turned his attention to a penitentiary that New York State began to build in 1817 at Auburn in the Finger Lakes district. Auburn's original plan enlarged and modified Newgate's, with a projecting central building housing keepers and inspectors, flanked by L-shaped wings containing two-person cells, all surrounded by workshops and gardens (fig. 10.7). Even before the new prison was completed it was evident that the two-prisoner cells were "essentially erroneous. . . . It would have been better to throw together fifty criminals in the same room, than to separate them two by two," Beaumont and Tocqueville reported. Eddy persuaded the state to build another wing comprised of tiny seven-foot-by-three-and-one-half-foot cells that would house a single prisoner in each (fig. 10.8; see fig. 10.7, Z). After a brief experiment with complete solitary confinement, the state initiated the controversial Auburn system at the prison. In the early years, convicts slept and ate dinner in their cells but took breakfast in a common hall where they were "seated, *in single file,* at narrow tables, with their

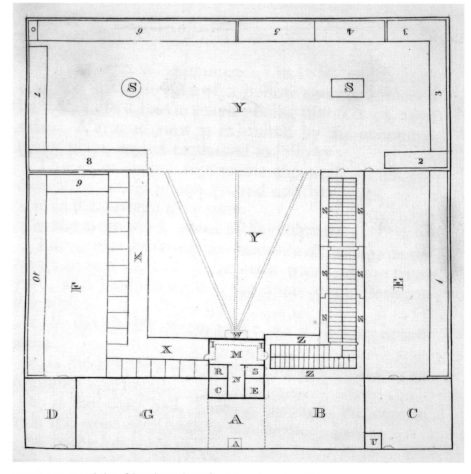

FIGURE 10.7. *Ground View of the Auburn Prison* (1817–21), Auburn, New York. Schematic plan, ca. 1828. (The Library Company of Philadelphia)

backs toward the centre, so that there can be no interchange of sign" (fig. 10.9). Absolute silence was required at all times. Infractions of this and many other rules were answered with the lash.[20]

Solitary contemplation leading to moral and spiritual regeneration was a secondary element of the disciplinary systems at the first generation of reformed American prisons as well as at Auburn, the inaugural landmark of the second generation, but it was promoted as the centerpiece of the Eastern State Penitentiary's method. The proponents of the Pennsylvania or "separate" and "silent" system and those of the Auburn or "congregate" system became fierce rivals. They published countless polemical tracts and articles and enlisted allies wherever they could find them. Roberts Vaux wrote a series of pamphlets in response to letters published by the English reformer William Roscoe criticizing the separate system. Vaux was ecstatic when Beaumont and Tocqueville, who studied American penitentiaries on behalf of the French government, appeared to favor the Pennsylvania system over its rivals. Thomas Eddy wrote equally passionately on behalf of the congregate system, while the Boston Prison Dis-

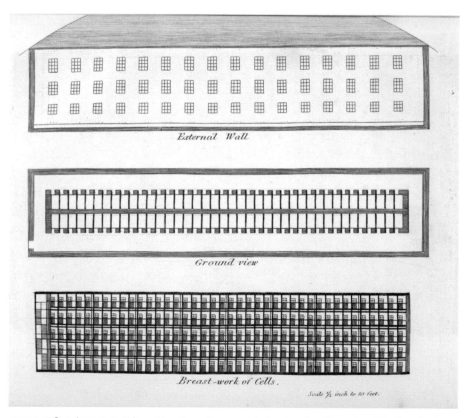

External Wall

Ground view

Breast-work of Cells.

Scale ½ inch to 10 feet.

FIGURE 10.8. Auburn State Prison. Elevation, plan, and interior elevation ("breastwork") of north wing in 1828. The array of back-to-back cells in a block enclosed by an outer building became a standard feature in Auburn-system penitentiaries. (The Library Company of Philadelphia)

CONVICTS AT DINNER.

FIGURE 10.9. *Convicts at dinner*, Ohio State Penitentiary, Columbus, 1850. All convicts face in one direction to prevent conversation and visual signaling. They dine under the surveillance of two keepers seated on a platform. (James B. Finley, *Memorials of Prison Life* [Cincinnati: L. Swormstedt and A. Poe, 1850, 1853])

cipline Society, which favored the Auburn system, refused to publish Samuel Gridley Howe's report to it praising the Pennsylvania system. These debates were closely followed by prison builders in other states and nations. While the Pennsylvania system enjoyed a greater international reputation and inspired prison reformers abroad, the Auburn system attracted prison officials in most of the American states for its apparent economy, humanity, and relative ease of implementation compared to the Pennsylvania system.[21]

Nevertheless, it is more important to understand the principles the warring camps shared than the differences that separated them. Both congregate- and separate-system proponents shared assumptions about human psychology, the origins of crime, and the techniques for eradicating it. The chains of analogy and metaphor that organized the republican spatial imagination convinced American social thinkers and reformers of the European argument that criminality was a kind of communicable social-behavioral disease passed from one offender to the other by precept and example. They spoke of "moral contagion," of crime as a "cancer." Just as victims of epidemic diseases were quarantined from healthy people, so offenders should be quarantined from innocent society. According to Louisiana legal reformer Edward Livingston, "Vice is more infectious than disease; many maladies of the body are not communicated even by contact, but there is no vice that affects the mind, which is not imparted by constant association; and it would be more reasonable to put a man in a pesthouse, to cure him of a headach [*sic*], than to confine a young offender in a penitentiary, organized on the ordinary plan, in order to effect his reformation."[22]

While the second-generation reformers of the 1810s and 1820s accepted their predecessors' diagnosis of crime, the prognosis seemed more dire to them, so the treatment needed to be proportionately more severe. Those who became ill during epidemics avoided fever hospitals for fear that contact with the sicker and the dead would prove fatal, the second generation of reformers reasoned, and any contact among criminals, even those of a similar degree of "depravity," would have a similar multiplier effect. If "a class could be formed of individuals who had advanced exactly to the same point, not only of offence, but of moral depravity, still their association would produce a further progress in both, just as sparks produce a flame when brought together, which separated, would be extinguished and die," Livingston wrote. "It is not in human nature for the mind to be stationary," he added. "It must progress in virtue or in vice." No system of classification, however finely tuned, could be adequate. Even if one could assess another person's moral condition adequately, "no two would be found contaminated in the same degree." Rather than separating and classifying prisoners as groups, they should be housed and punished individually.[23]

Criminality was social and discursive. Antebellum understanding of the role of language in social formation shaped nineteenth-century prison reformers' remarkably phenomenological analysis of criminality. They imagined that society was permeated by an invisible criminal empire united by a secret criminal tongue—the "flash" language—known to every wrongdoer in the world but impenetrable to all but a few initiates from the honest world. The innocent were converted to wrongdoers by criminal "conversation," which meant both communication and sociability. One became a criminal by acting like a criminal and participating in criminal discourse, which lent meaning to one's actions and formed a criminalized self. So every theorist of both camps agreed that the first goal was to dissipate the "contagion of evil associations." Separation and silence destroyed the connective tissue of criminal society.[24]

Nevertheless, one should not overemphasize the role of solitary confinement at Eastern State. The Pennsylvania system's proponents emphasized uninterrupted contemplative solitude to distinguish their method from Auburn's. Yet after briefly considering the technique as its only reformative strategy, Pennsylvania prison authorities decided even before the Eastern State Penitentiary opened to include labor as part of its program, although architect Haviland had made no provision for work spaces in the convicts' cells. Convicts were left idle only during the two weeks immediately after they were imprisoned. When their spirits had been sufficiently softened they were given work. Indeed, prison authorities noted with satisfaction, they usually begged for it. In Beaumont and Tocqueville's words, it was a "favor" rather than a requirement. Enforced idleness was one mode of punishing the unruly. "Good design is to produce, by means of sufferings principally acting on the mind and accompanied with moral and religious instruction, a disposition to virtuous conduct, the only sure preventive of crime; and where this beneficial effect does not follow, to impress so great a dread and terror, as to deter the offender from the commission of crime in the state where the system of solitary confinement exists," wrote the committee that superintended the construction of the prison.[25]

The major differences between the Auburn and Pennsylvania systems turned on the degree of isolation from human society needed to destroy guilty association. Pennsylvania-system advocates demanded complete and unrelenting separation from other inmates. Their opponents believed that health and even sanity required some contact with other human beings. A brief experiment with total separation at Auburn convinced the authorities there that the practice "does not reform, it kills." Auburn-friendly reformers, former inmates, and journalists united in declaring long-term solitary confinement a "murder of Body and Soul." The popular press was full of stories of "Insanity, idiocy, and great physical injury" in Pennsylvania-system penitentiaries. To John Reynolds, a critic of all prevailing penological doctrines, the "solitary confinement plan is an unwise, unfeeling, and ruinous innovation upon penitentiary discipline" that "evinces a cruel recklessness of the feelings and personal comfort of the prisoner." Solitude, not human society, bred resentment and a criminal disposition, he argued. "The genius of crime dwells in the dark places of retirement, and always communes with its followers *alone*" while "Social life . . . is the garden of every virtue." Auburn-system supporters believed that their amended regimen of separation at night and silent group work during the day provided the proper degree of human contact while still destroying criminal association.[26]

Silence during incarceration to purge the felonious self and to destroy criminal society was only a first step. Old selves had to die and new ones to be reborn. At Auburn, Howe observed, each convict lay in "a bed as narrow as his coffin; and though all around him, as close as the dead in a well-filled graveyard." Authorities at both Auburn and Eastern State boasted of their jails' all-encompassing "stillness of death" or "of the tomb" that pervaded them. Charles Dickens heard the same deathly silence but found it "awful." The convict "is truly a man buried alive, to be dug out in the slow round of years; and in the meantime dead to everything but torturing anxieties and horrible despair."[27]

The penitentiary was a stage for carefully calculated rituals of death and rebirth. Elaborate initiation—or perhaps mortuary—rites preceded entombment in both systems. In upstate New York a felon was taken in irons from his local jail to Auburn soon after his trial. Upon arrival the new convict "generally appears serious, and evinces pretty strong apprehensions in regard to his reception and treatment," noted Auburn's renowned keeper Gershom Powers. Prison authorities took advantage of this liminal moment. After removing his irons they cut his hair, shaved his face, and "thoroughly purified" his body of the dirt and vermin endemic to a county jail. He was then "decently clad in the clean striped dress of the prison." This moment, when "he is obliged to take of[f] his citizen dress and to put on the convict's jacket," Auburn proponent Louis Dwight believed, "was the one great moment in every convicts life, which might almost always be turned to good account."[28]

After a clerk carefully described the new man in the prison register the keeper took over, eliciting from the convict (and the sheriff who accompanied him) "his habits of life, temper, prevailing passions, and extent of his intelligence." This narrative was a confession, a datum point from which to measure reform, and a final summing up and articulation of the criminal self, on whom the keeper then passed judgment. Powers addressed the dazed man, "a sad picture of human degradation," at length, showing that by his transgressions the man had offended God, wounded his family, forfeited his liberty, and lost the privileges of human association. The keeper warned the new inmate not to blame society for his incarceration but to be grateful that he had not been required to pay with his life as in other times and places. Imprisonment was an opportunity for the convict wise enough to profit from the moral and religious instruction offered. "You are to be literally buried from the world: but when you again return to it, the fault will be entirely your own, if you do not acquire for yourself a new reputation, become a blessing to your friends and to society, and exemplify the power of deep repentance and thorough reform."[29]

Most new-model American penitentiaries of the 1820s, as well as European prisons that were inspired by American models, practiced some form of this initiation ritual. Often verbal refinements reinforced the allusions to Christian baptism evident in Powers's language of death and rebirth, confession and forgiveness, repentance and renewal. Thomas Eddy's biographer Samuel Knapp, as well as Beaumont and Tocqueville, explicitly compared the process of reform in the penitentiary to religious conversion. Like the revivalist's sermon, the words read to the convict upon commitment to his cell made his guilt and the promise of reform clear. Then, alone in his cell, "nothing can reach him but the voice which must come to him, as it were, from another world."[30]

Not only were criminals purified by water, but at Eastern State Penitentiary, where they would theoretically never see another inmate, they surrendered their names and acquired a number by which even the guards would know them. Hooded on entry to the penitentiary, the new convict was hooded again when he was taken to his cell. This "dark shroud, an emblem of the curtain dropped between him and the living world," as Charles Dickens called it, prevented his accidentally recognizing or being recognized by another. More important, it was intended to disguise the location of his cell within the prison. In his cell, severed from all human associations and spatial orientation, unaware of where he was or with whom, he heard a speech similar to Powers's at Auburn. "The consequences of his crime are portrayed, the design to be effected by his punishment manifested, and the rules of the prison, as regards the convicts, amply delineated."[31]

Despite the allusions to baptism, penitentiary initiation rituals more closely resembled those of non-Christian societies or that portrayed in Mozart's *Magic Flute*, for the ceremony was only a prelude to a years-long purifying ordeal. Prisoners' every moment was ostensibly closely monitored. The word "inspection"—surveillance—permeated the contemporary literature. At Auburn, a passageway at the rear of the shops allowed the keeper (warden) to observe the convicts *and* the turnkeys without their being aware of it. In the cell blocks, the jailers moved about at night "having socks on their feet, and walking so noiselessly, that each convict does not know but that he is at the very door of his cell, ready to discover and report . . . the slightest breach of silence or order." Haviland claimed that the radial plan of the Eastern State Penitentiary allowed the jailers to police the cells aurally from the central rotunda or "observatory" and to look down from its second floor into all of the yards. In fact, everyone other than Haviland agreed that it was impossible to see into the yards at Eastern State or to supervise the inmates adequately from the center point.[32]

This would have been a problem had the Philadelphia penitentiary been conceived as one of Jeremy Bentham's infamous panopticons, in which prisoners were intended to be physically visible at all times. For Bentham, the "essence of it consists . . . in the *centrality* of the inspector's situation, combined with the well-known and most effectual contrivances for *seeing without being seen*. As for the *general form* of the building, the most commodious for most purposes seems to be the circular: but this is not an absolutely essential circumstance." Although several visitors identified Haviland's design as a panopticon, as have some modern historians, the architect himself never made the connection. A British visitor accurately recognized that Eastern State was not a panopticon but thought that the "Panopticon principle is on the whole preferable." American reformers, who were aware of Bentham's theories by the beginning of the nineteenth century, when Irish reformer Patrick Colquhoun sent Thomas Eddy two volumes of Bentham's writings "explaining the construction and general currency of his Ponoplicon," disagreed. The anonymous author of a tract urging the construction of a new Massachusetts state prison discussed Bentham's idea but dismissed panopticons as "imaginary buildings" that could succeed only on a small scale. By the time Haviland designed Eastern State most prison reformers had concluded that the panopticon, which was never widely popular, was impractical. They preferred some version of a radial plan such as that at Eastern State, which Haviland and his partisans claimed should be known as "the Haviland plan," although radial-plan prisons could be found in England by the late eighteenth century.[33]

Nevertheless, architecture was intended to carry the brunt of supervision in every new-model penitentiary—in Haviland's most of all. Even more than the first-generation reformed prisons, all the new penitentiaries relied on a precisely calibrated architecture to accomplish their goals. For Haviland, "the success of the [Pennsylvania] System more than half depends on the construction of the prison in which it is attempted to be introduced; the leading feature of the System, (that of the total separation of the prisoner from his companions in crime,) depends almost entirely, on the construction of the cell." Auburn- and Pennsylvania-system authorities agreed that the key was to house prisoners individually in small cells organized in such a way that the prisoner was readily accessible to the oversight of keepers and to other prison facilities, but not to each other. Long lines of identical cells ranged on one or both sides of a corridor met both requirements. In other words, the penitentiary was another grid (see fig. 10.8).[34]

The penal grid had several advantages: First, it definitively atomized criminal society, breaking the "power of combination." Second, just as the urban grid articulated individually developed properties within a common network, so the penal grid articulated prisoners within a system in a way that "every prisoner forms a class by himself," even if he did not know it. The prison's grid formed the basis of a system with "A place for every man and every man in his place," according to the Boston Prison Discipline Society. "A convict should have the same cell at night, the same place in the shops, and the same relative position in the column while marching to and from the shops." When he left his place, it should be marked by a token.[35]

In such spaces every convict received the same *kind* of treatment, but it could be individually calibrated. Just as prisoners served different terms, so they could be subjected to varying degrees of privilege or deprivation. Sameness and individualization were equally important to penal theorists. The rules must be uniform and uniformly, inevitably applied. Paroles and pardons undermined the "certainty of punishment" and should be abolished. Yet William Roscoe reminded his American readers not to let the individual be "sacrificed to system." The degree of each criminal's depravity varied as much as the seriousness of crimes. Within the system, separation allowed a "specific graduation of punishment."[36]

The architecture of prison discipline at all the new-model prisons was firmly grounded in the embodied nature of morality. As we have seen, for late-eighteenth-century thinkers such as the Philadelphia physician Benjamin Rush, the corporeality of the moral faculty made it susceptible to the same kinds of environmental influences that undermined physiological health. Those who lived degraded lives in degraded surroundings were most likely to commit crimes, just as they were most likely to contract diseases. Robert Turnbull reminded his readers in 1796 that "from the connection of the body with the mental and moral faculties, or rather from the influence which the disposition of the former must have on that of the latter, it is certain, that a man's morals must, in some measure, depend on the proportion of ease and comfort the body enjoys." This old belief in the physiological nature of morality survived as a less explicit but no less influential substratum of penological theory among the second generation of prison reformers.[37]

The reformers understood that selfhood is encoded in bodily memory, shaped by repeated, often unconscious gestures, postures, and actions. Criminality was a mode of being and acting as well as a discursive practice. Criminals were absorbed in criminal environments, saw criminal things, thought criminal ideas, spoke criminal words, and committed criminal acts. Like the preceding generation of reformers, that is, both Auburn- and Pennsylvania-system theorists believed that convicts' ethics were matters of habit and could be reformed by restraining bad actions and instilling good ones through repetition of word and deed. So architecture first restrained then retrained. According to Samuel Gridley Howe, the Pennsylvania-system penitentiary's architecture made it impossible to do wrong, which defused conflict. "These walls and bars restrain, but do not irritate by seeming to watch and suspect [the convict]. He does not personify them, and make them objects of ill-will and hatred. His keepers, having little to fear of his escape, need not appear to watch him, and not seeming to be the immediate obstacle in the way of his escape, are less liable to be regarded with ill-will on that account."[38]

Restrained from wrongdoing, the convict lost his grip on his criminal self. At Eastern State Penitentiary, inmates were meant to undergo a kind of total sensory deprivation, as architect and keepers scrupulously sought to isolate convicts aurally and visually, as well as physically. The penitentiary's fabric—eighteen-inch-thick walls, floors, and vaulted ceilings—was made entirely of stone to discourage attempts to escape or to communicate from cell to cell (fig. 10.10). The cell-block eaves were carried down to the height of the exercise yard walls to make it impossible for convicts to stand on the steps of their cells and converse over the walls. Passage doors could be fixed partially open to prevent seeing into the hallway while allowing inmates to hear Sunday sermons that were preached from a post in the passageway.[39]

The only light admitted into each cell came from an oculus or "dead eye" eight inches in diameter set into the barrel-vaulted ceiling. The oculus, too small to use as an escape hatch and too high to facilitate communication from cell to cell, was also a distorting lens that prevented the occupant from recognizing any animal or object that might pass overhead. The passage wall of each cell was pierced by a quarter-inch cast-iron viewing cone, widest on the interior and stoppered on the exterior, so that the jailer could see the convict but the convict could not look back (fig. 10.11). Food was served through a slot in the cell wall fitted with a six-by-sixteen-inch sliding drawer that also served as a dining table. Vertical metal screens fastened to each end of the draw-

FIGURE 10.10. Eastern State Penitentiary, cell in cellblock 1. The vertical rod at the center hangs from the oculus. The low door at the rear once led to the exercise yard

ers prevented sight or conversation through the slot. The meticulous attention to detail extended even to the toilets, for which Haviland carefully calculated the water level that would prevent foul air from entering the cells while thwarting efforts to use the pipes as speaking tubes (fig. 10.12). We begin to understand Howe's claim that the separate-system cell enforced good behavior without the aggravating intervention of a human hand.[40]

The spatial constriction and sensory deprivation that Haviland sought to achieve through the architecture of his penitentiary found their congregate-system counterparts in silence, restricted vision, and the lockstep. The lockstep or lock march was a close-order march, cued by the "ringing of a little bell, of the softest sound," in which the prisoners were so tightly arrayed that they were compelled to move as the men before and after them did. "At a signal, the men step out [of their cells] upon the platform, all facing one way. At a second signal, they close up and form a line, the breast of each in close contact with the back of the person before him." (fig. 10.13). Although the lockstep was described as a measure to prevent prisoners' communicating, "flocking confusedly into

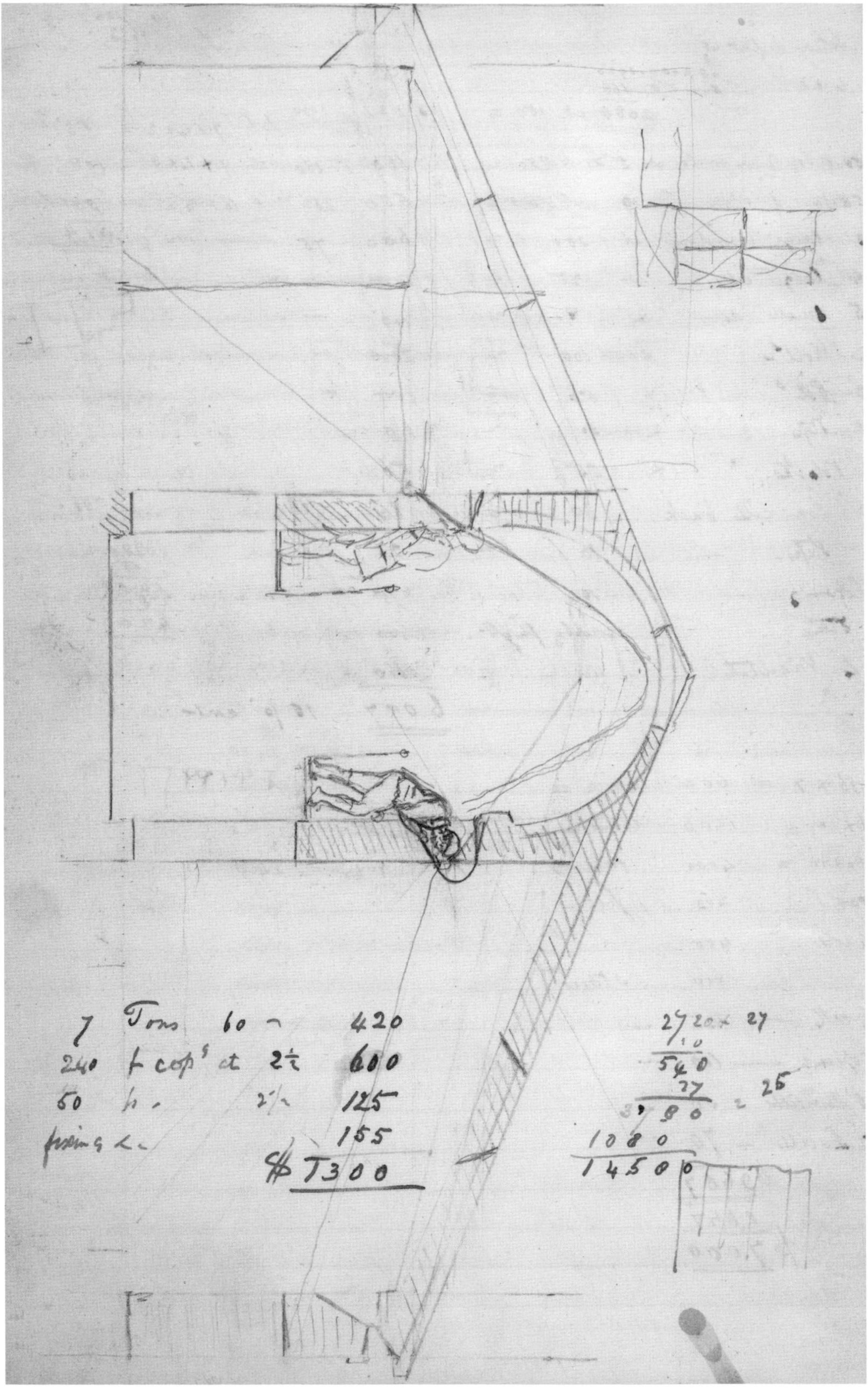

$$
\begin{array}{llll}
1 & \text{Tons} & 60 & 420 \\
240 & f \ cop^s \ at \ 2\frac{1}{2} & & 600 \\
50 & h. & 2\frac{1}{2} & 125 \\
\text{fixing} \ \&c & & & 155 \\
\hline
& & \$ & 1300
\end{array}
$$

$$
\begin{array}{r}
27 \ 20 \times 27 \\
1 \ 0 \\
\hline
5 \ 4 \ 0 \\
27 \qquad = 25 \\
\hline
3 \ 8 \ 0 \\
1 \ 0 \ 8 \ 0 \\
\hline
1 \ 4 \ 5 \ 0 \ 0
\end{array}
$$

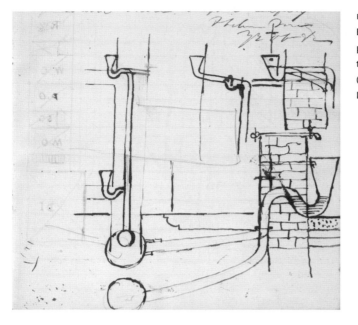

FIGURE 10.12. John Haviland, Eastern State Penitentiary, plumbing scheme for one- and two-story cell blocks, ca. 1830. (University of Pennsylvania Library)

the yard," or "moving like an undisciplined mob to the mess-room," it offered reformers and keepers a vision of system and order in which convicts, often arranged in order of height, were precisely mapped in time and space (fig. 10.14). It was a choreographed pantomime of the independent yet coordinated social ideal at the core of the republican spatial imagination. "So close and compact did they march," wrote one observer, "that one would imagine that the movement of their legs is controlled by one will." "The convicts silently marching to and from their rest, meals and labor, at precise times, moving in separate corps, in single file, with slow lock-step, erect posture, keeping exact time, with their faces inclined toward their Keepers (that they may detect conversation,) give to the spectator somewhat similar feelings to those excited by a military funeral," wrote Gershom Powers.[41]

Powers admitted that "to the convicts, [the lockstep creates] impressions not entirely dissimilar to those of culprits when marching to the gallows." Ohio inmates found it "hateful and degrading," and they were grateful when military-style drill was substituted for it. They understood that like other penitentiary rituals its purpose was to break down the independent sense of "opposition and boldness" that prison reformers attributed to the criminal personality and to substitute "subordination and *subdued feeling among the convicts*." The lockstep violated both the circumscribed but inviolable bodily envelope of gentility and the expansive and assertive bodily boundaries of counter-gentility. Harriet Martineau noted that lock-marching white prisoners at Auburn felt an "agony of shame" to be seen by visitors. African American convicts, though, turned the display on its head, which Martineau saw as a sign of their "social degradation"

opposite
FIGURE 10.11.
John Haviland,
Eastern State
Penitentiary,
studies for
surveillance
of inmate,
ca. 1830.
(University of
Pennsylvania
Library)

FIGURE 10.13. *Prisoners at the State Prison at Auburn, 1842. Lockstep.*
(Library of Congress, Prints and Photographs Division)

and inability to feel shame. These men, "who are remarkable for exaggeration in all they do, figured away ridiculously in the march, stamping and gesticulating as if they were engaged in a game of romps." Their performance was the penitentiaries' counterpart of the provocative faux-genteel street behavior of black "dandies and dandizettes" that so offended whites.[42]

Voicing the common goals of prison reformers of every stripe, Howe argued that after shattering the criminal personality, penitentiary discipline should teach "habits of sober industry" and provide the "companionship of good men whom he can learn to love and imitate." In this way, the convict could "exercise his good resolutions and strengthen his conscience by the greatest freedom of action, and the most perfect self-control that is consistent with his safe keeping."[43]

This vision of the convict's ascent to freedom was deeply colored by prevailing notions of social hierarchy and self-control. The republican conception of virtue as the free exercise of independent but identical or nearly identical wills and values defined reformed behavior. In republican society, essential sameness was nevertheless marked by differences of degree, so the convict's freedom was to be characterized by "subordination, regularity, and industry." Since prison reformers assumed that criminals were overwhelmingly lower-class white men—the "unfortunate or degenerate citizens of the State," as Charles Dickens put it—both congregate- and separate-system penitentiaries enforced the kinds of spatial separation and hierarchical deference that genteel authorities imagined for the civilian world. This utopian aspect of penitentiaries masked a significant difference from the civilian world: behavior that signaled refinement and mutual respect outside the penitentiary acknowledged authority and abjection inside. Convicts were not allowed to look at each other, or at visitors "idly" or "impudently." The restricted genteel gaze became a gesture of subordination demanded of prisoners. "Looking at a petty Keeper, *as he thinks,* impudently," occasioned severe punishment in most prisons.[44]

Convicts' "whole duty" was "to obey orders, labor diligently in silence, and whenever it is necessary for him to speak to a Keeper, to do it with a humble sense of his degraded situation." When they were allowed to speak, they "must approach the officers of the Institution with deference, and bestow on them, when addressing them, all the civic titles which politeness demands in the respectable circles

FIGURE 10.14. *Convicts retiring to their cells,* Ohio State Penitentiary, 1850. (James B. Finley, *Memorials of Prison Life* [Cincinnati: L. Swormstedt and A. Poe, 1850, 1853])

of life, and when speaking of or to each other, they must omit those distinctions." To reinforce the convict's sense of debasement, prison officers at Auburn were to maintain a "uniform gravity and dignity of deportment" and "to treat each other with that mutual respect and kindness that become gentlemen and friends."[45]

Inmates' words could not be used against an officer or even another convict. Their speech was assumed, like that of women and African Americans in the civilian world, to lack truth, honor, and authority—to be noise. Inmates at Auburn, like African Americans in New Orleans, were not to "laugh, dance, whistle, sing, run, jump, or do anything that will have the *least tendency* to disturb or alarm the Prison" or to use profane or obscene language.[46]

Abjection was emphasized by uniforms carefully devised to differ as much as possible from civilian dress to aid in identifying escaped convicts but more importantly to enforce a sense of isolation and disgrace in the wearer. In this era the familiar black and white stripes made their appearance at Auburn and elsewhere, but that was only one of many distinctive schemes (see figs. 10.13, 10.14). Inmates at the Massachusetts State Prison wore clothes that were half red and half blue and so constructed that they could be put on and removed even while the prisoner was in chains. Vermont uniforms were half green and half scarlet. Kentucky convicts first wore country uniforms of yellow-checked linen shirts ("with the diamonds one inch square"), overalls, and hunting shirts, and in the winter country linsey suits of the same style and pattern, with a flat-crowned leather hat.[47]

In light of the current canons of dress, which emphasized a unified body image, the intended effect of the prison uniform was clear: to destroy this unity, dissipating any sense of coherent, bounded selfhood or self-respect. Jeremy Bentham thought costume offered intriguing possibilities for augmenting punishment "by holding up the wearer in an ignominious light." Edward Livingston, who was constantly alert for ways to refine the common practices of the northeastern states, proposed that standard prison uniforms carry marks indicating the number of recidivists' convictions, that life-term inmates be specially costumed to indicate their offenses, and that murderers wear black outer garments spotted and streaked with red, a horrifying emblem of their crimes.[48]

Dress was also a vehicle for encouraging and rewarding reform. Massachusetts and New Jersey both provided better-quality, more conventional outfits for Sunday worship services, even though the New Jersey institution operated on the separate system. Nevertheless, the authorities thought, the change of clothes was appropriate "to distinguish [the Sabbath] from the other days of the week, and help [convicts] to mark the time." An 1818 Massachusetts act provided for abating the outlandishness of the uniform for well-behaved prisoners. "The first class . . . shall be dressed in cloth of the quality now used, but of one colour only." Second-class convicts were forced only to wear multicolored trousers, while the third, or worst, class of prisoners wore the established particolored uniform.[49]

By mid-century some reformers began to worry that prison uniforms were *too* humiliating. Samuel Gridley Howe described them as "purposely contrived to be so grotesque as to be an unmistakable badge of degradation" that was "unkind, unjust, and pernicious." The Massachusetts authorities abandoned such uniforms in 1865 because they were "calculated to drive [the prisoner's] manhood from [him]."[50]

After subordination, prison disciplinarians sought to instill mental and corporal habits of virtuous behavior through the verbal, sensory, and kinetic monotony of penitentiary routine. Because they assumed that most of their charges would be working-class men, prison reformers also assumed that prison labor should be manual labor. In congregate-system prisons, lesser jails, and almshouses, treadmills or "stepping wheels," an idea introduced from English bridewells and jails, were briefly popular in the 1820s (fig. 10.15). Twenty to forty convicts at a time passed whole days endlessly climbing a wheel, with only brief

FIGURE 10.15. *Tread, or Stepping Mill, 1823.* (Library of Congress, Prints and Photographs Division)

hourly breaks. Sometimes the wheel was connected to a grist mill or other machine in pursuit of the always seductive dream of making the institution pay for itself. In other prisons the wheel was purposely not connected to any useful device, since the futility of the arduous labor was part of the punishment.[51]

Stepping wheels seemed ideal for prisoners of all abilities and ages and of both sexes. They required no training and little supervision to operate them, and they were difficult to sabotage. Advocates believed that like solitary cells treadmills allowed all prisoners to undergo the same punishment while individuating its severity. Everyone worked at the same time and took the same number of steps, but the labor was also individualized, since "all must work equally, *in proportion to their weight.*" In any event, whether convicts engaged in the pointless turning of a treadmill, the quarrying and shaping of stone to build one's own prison as at Sing Sing, or the practice of a skilled craft such as chairmaking or weaving, they learned habits of industry manually.[52]

Of course, correctional systems that required absolute obedience and perfect uniformity of behavior inevitably disappointed. It was clear to some observers from the first that not everyone was receptive to the new methods. The British traveler Basil Hall dismissed the idea that "all, or any great number of the convicts, are to be reformed," but in his eyes the Auburn system "affords the best chance for success" of any so far tried. More important, the racial and gender assumptions that marginalized blacks and women in civil society also raised doubts about their liability to penal discipline.[53]

By the beginning of the nineteenth century public authorities were already bemoaning the high proportion of African American convicts in prisons and jails. Inevitably, they formed a "very unfavourable estimate of the moral character of the coloured inhabitants" rather than questioning the administration of the law (see plate 13). Reformers assumed that blacks were both more prone to the moral weaknesses leading to criminal behavior and less amenable to reformative measures. While criminality was a disease to which the white population was susceptible, the "character of the colored population" made it an inherent attribute of African Americans. It was said that black people were unable to adjust to the salubrious physical environment of prisons; indeed, they seemed to fare badly in prisons generally. "It is a well known fact, that the colored race endure confinement in prisons with much more suffering than the whites. They are supposed to have less vitality and are more susceptible, or predisposed to certain diseases, such as scrofula and consumption. Eight out of the above thirteen deaths [of black inmates] occurred from chronic affections of the lungs, and from the first named disease," explained the directors of the Philadelphia County (Moyamensing) Prison. Nevertheless, African Americans were usually assigned to the worst cells.[54]

Assumptions about the differing capacities and natures of men and women often allowed women to escape conviction for crimes in which they were equal participants with men who *were* punished, the Pennsylvania legislator Thomas B. McElwee noted with disgust. "I have no faith in the ethereal qualities of the female gender, and believe much evil has occurred to society, by stuffing their heads with the idea, that they are angels, goddesses, &c. &c. . . . when their faults, their follies, and their vices drive men mad, and produce fatal disruptions in families. . . . If there is in their composition, an admixture of heavenly qualities, it is sprinkled so sparsely that much research is necessary to enable us to detect its existence."[55]

It is true that women formed a tiny portion of penitentiary inmates relative to their representation in the population at large, or even to the numbers of women arrested. As an example, in 1830, 2,630 men and 1,376 women passed through Philadelphia's Arch Street Jail as short-term detainees. In the same year there were 416 men and only 66 women in the state's old-system Walnut Street Jail. There were 54 men and no women in the newly opened Eastern State Penitentiary, while the Western State Penitentiary in Pittsburgh held 56 men and only 6 women. The total for all three state penitentiaries was 526 men and 72 women.[56]

When they were convicted, women received different treatment. At New York's Sing Sing prison, noted for its brutal treatment of male prisoners, women were not subjected to the whippings administered freely to men, although they were subjected to the equally brutal gag (see below). In fact, inspector J. W. Edmonds told Dorothea Dix that "it has been only among females that it is has been rendered *absolutely* necessary!" At Auburn, where men lived in individual cells, women were housed together in the attic story of the prison's south wing. They picked wool desultorily or sewed, all without supervision. "The attempt to enforce silence was soon given up as hopeless," Harriet Martineau observed, "and the gabble of tongues among the few who were there was enough to paralyze any matron." The treadmill appealed to authorities in large part as a harsh physical punishment that did seem appropriate for women.[57]

Both separate and congregate systems were undermined by the weaknesses of their architecture and disciplinary routines. Despite their claims, they failed to isolate a convict completely from others or to subordinate his will. At Auburn, wrote Samuel Gridley Howe, the industrial shops were so noisy and required so much movement by the prisoners that they "may whisper almost without chance of detection." They could also speak "behind their teeth, without moving the lips, while at work in the day," Harriet Martineau noticed, and from cell to cell through ventilation ducts at night.[58]

The Auburn-partial Boston Prison Discipline Society questioned whether Eastern State's ventilation system, then under construction, could be used by prisoners to communicate. The answer was yes. Haviland had originally placed iron plates in the flues that conveyed heat to the cells to prevent sound transmission. Unfortunately, they also obstructed the hot air. When the plates were removed the flues became communication devices. These passages were blocked by masonry and replaced by Perkins' high-temperature heating system, which supplied heat through hot-water pipes. These passed in a straight line through the cells carrying "sonorous vibrations" that were "used by the convicts for the purpose of conveying signals, and as a means of annoyance." The inmates also enlarged the holes through which they passed, offering another way to communicate between cells. They also found it possible to converse over the walls of the exercise yard, despite Haviland's precautions.[59]

Penal silence and solitude, then, were corporeal concepts intended to transform criminals by manipulating their relationships to their environments. Late-eighteenth-century revulsion against "sanguinary" punishment can mislead one into thinking that it disappeared or survived only as an aberration and anachronism in the new systems. Corporal punishment was widespread and generally accepted as a response to the failure of architecture and prison discipline to make wrongdoing impossible. The new theories differed from the old in aiming at rehabilitation of convicts rather than mere revenge, but they were just as fixated on the guilty body as premodern forms of punishment were.[60]

The most common instrument of corporal punishment was the rawhide whip used at Auburn-style penitentiaries. New York's Sing Sing Prison, which

FIGURE 10.16. *John Cool Whipping Coker with the Cat*, Ohio State Penitentiary, 1854. (Ohio Historical Society)

housed the most desperate criminals, was notorious for the frequency and savagery with which beatings were administered (fig. 10.16). Pennsylvania-system advocates denounced whipping as a cruel punishment that could only degrade the victim and harden him against reform, but as the humanitarian Dorothea Dix put it, the lash is "sometimes the only mode, under the Auburn, or congregated system, by which an insurrectionary spirit can be conquered." Gershom Powers acknowledged that it was useful only to maintain elementary discipline, not as an instrument of reform, and by the 1840s even Sing Sing was trying to get away from the practice.[61]

Nevertheless, every penitentiary system inflicted physical pain as supplementary punishment. At the very least offenders were confined in dark solitary cells, fed bread-and-water rations for weeks, or chained to wooden blocks or to cell floors. More and more, penalties increased restricted movement to the point of torture. At New York's Newgate prison, the "Sunday cell" was used. This was an unventilated box, three-and-a-half feet square and five feet high, too small to stand or lie in. According to W. A. Coffey as many as six men at a time were placed in the box, "snugly handcuffed, without bread or water, for two or three days together, during the heat of summer, in the brutal caprice of the Principal Keeper. Instances have not unfrequently been known, of convicts being kept here, for more than ten days together, without the visitation, or, perhaps, even the *knowledge* of the Inspectors."[62]

By the 1830s many prison authorities preferred the gag, a device consisting of a bridle-like metal tongue inserted into the victim's mouth (fig. 10.17). Chains passing around the head connected the mouthpiece to another chain attached to the wrists, which were cuffed behind the back. If the recalcitrant victim continued to resist, the rear chain could be tightened, drawing the head backward

FIGURE 10.17. James Akin, *Implements of Torture*, 1835. The gag used on Matthias Maccumsey at the Eastern State Penitentiary. (Library of Congress, Prints and Photographs Division)

THE IRON GAG.

FIGURE 10.18. *The Iron Gag.* Matthias Maccumsey gagged, Eastern State Penitentiary, 1835. (The Library Company of Philadelphia)

STRAIGHT JACKET.

FIGURE 10.19. *Straight Jacket,* Eastern State Penitentiary, 1835. (The Library Company of Philadelphia)

MAD, OR TRANQUILLIZING CHAIR.

FIGURE 10.20. *Mad, or Tranquillizing Chair,* Eastern State Penitentiary, 1835. (The Library Company of Philadelphia)

toward the wrists (fig. 10.18). This device—"shocking and extremely objectionable," said Dix—was used on both men and women.[63]

The authorities at Eastern State Penitentiary also used a variety of other tortures common in American penitentiaries. They placed convicts in sackcloth straitjackets (other prisons used iron ones) and in "mad" or "tranquilizing" chairs, which restricted a prisoner's movement equally closely and which were also favored punishments for women (figs. 10.19, 10.20).

> The Mad-Chair, was a large box chair, constructed of plank, having some of the peculiarities of a close stool. The prisoner was placed in this chair, his arms above his elbows were fastened by straps to the back of the chair. A strap was passed round his body, through holes in the chair, and fastened there. His hands were linked together by hand cuffs. Straps were passed round the ankles and firmly fastened to the lower part of the chair. He had no resting place for his feet, there being no foot board. It was impossible for an individual so manacled to move any part of his body or limbs. The pain must have been intense; and yet prisoners have been beaten while in this painful and helpless posture.

Jailers also hung naked prisoners from the exercise walls by their wrists, pouring water over them from the wall above, a torment used even in the winter. This was Eastern State's version of a practice called showering that gained currency throughout the antebellum years. A restrained prisoner was drenched, sometimes by a high-pressure water stream (fig. 10.21). This punishment was "considered the most mild" at the Ohio penitentiary, but some prisoners preferred stripes. At Auburn the shower bath, which replaced whipping in the early 1840s, targeted the head of an inmate locked in a box and restrained at the neck (fig. 10.22). The sensation must have been that of drowning. According to some reports inmates who readily withstood the lash were unable to tolerate the shower for very long.[64]

We know about Eastern State's punishments only because so many convicts had already been injured by them within a few years of the prison's opening that the state legislature investigated. A convict named Matthias Maccumsey strangled when the gag was applied too tightly as punishment for speaking to another prisoner through the grated door of his cell. Another inmate, Seneca Plimly, reputedly lost his mind after being drenched with thirteen buckets of icy water on a frigid day. Others lost the use of their limbs when too-tight straitjackets constricted circulation.[65]

Not surprisingly, the state investigators cleared the jailers and particularly the warden, Samuel R. Wood, who had ordered the gag placed on Maccumsey, of any wrongdoing. The gag, they wrote, was "not naturally calculated to produce

MODE OF SHOWERING PRISONERS.

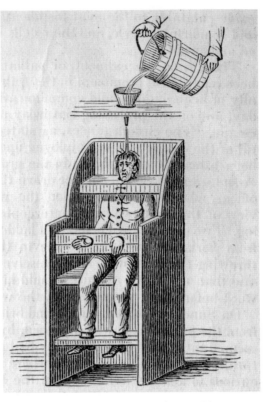

left FIGURE 10.21. *Mode of Showering Prisoners,* Ohio State Penitentiary, 1856. The man's head is bound into a position that prevents his turning away from the stream of water. (Ohio Historical Society)

above FIGURE 10.22. *Cold Head-Bath,* Auburn State Prison, 1842. (The Library Company of Philadelphia)

death," so it was not objectionable. The straitjacket and the mad chair "served a good purpose in bringing to tranquility and subjection the refractory and the violent." Key testimony was provided by Benjamin Coates, a physician at the Pennsylvania Hospital, who testified that the straitjacket and the shower bath were harmless techniques used at the hospital as "medical agent[s]." James Gillaspy, cell keeper at the county almshouse, confirmed that both devices were used on insane men there "as a medical treatment principally." Dr. Charles Lukens gave the same testimony about the Friends' Asylum. These techniques, described by some of their victims as tortures, were not punishments but physical techniques for controlling the moral faculty, according to the expert witnesses. Like the penitentiary routine itself, corporal punishment used the body as the path through which the mind could be reached. By restraining the body the will was brought under control. Throttling speech quelled the misplaced voice. In short, the expert testimony at the Eastern State inquiry normalized corporal discipline in the prison, transferring it from the realm of sanguinary punishment to the realm of therapy.[66]

Despite having described the lash as punishment, not therapy, Gershom Powers thought it, too, accorded with the norms of civilian life. The administration of stripes "with humanity and discretion, and without passion [was] . . . based upon the principle, that the officers legally stand in the same relation to the convicts, as the master to his apprentice, and the schoolmaster to his scholar; and that the officer, having the immediate charge of the conduct and labor of convicts, may lawfully exercise the same means of coercing the observance of any of the known duties of the convicts, and for preventing their mischievous and riotous practices, as the master or schoolmaster may exercise in coercing the observance of duty in the apprentice or scholar."[67]

If criminals' faults resembled the errors of the physically and mentally ill or the rambunctiousness of apprentices and schoolchildren, and if all were equally susceptible to correction through the interaction of architecture and the body, then the prison and civil society were complementary, and the same kinds of spatial and environmental thinking were appropriate to both. Criminals were not merely deviant, they were deviant in ways that reflected on and affected civil society. Again, a bodily metaphor served to express the link. "A Penitentiary," wrote the English reformer William Roscoe, is "in the community, what the lungs are in the human body, an organ for purifying the circulation, and returning it, in a healthy state, to perform its office in the general mass."[68]

Thus, the equation could be reversed: what was appropriate to criminals was also appropriate in other institutions that might be used to preempt crime. Eighteenth-century British reformers envisioned the penitentiary as one of a range of institutions that defended society from deviancy. Americans made the same connection, envisioning the penitentiary as an institution of last resort when other means had failed. "One of the first duties, as well as the true policy, of every government, is to adopt measures *for the prevention of crime*," wrote Roberts Vaux. The "most powerful instrument" was *"universal education."* Edward Livingston agreed that the penitentiary should be seen less as a reformatory institution than as part of a larger system of formative institutions organized to teach citizens their duties to one another, to the state, and to religion.[69]

Americans advanced these commonly articulated assumptions by elaborating the idea of an institutional system and fine-tuning their methods to each of its forms. Architecture was the foundation on which all else was based. In 1829, after only four years of operation, the directors of the Boston-based Prison Discipline Society looked back on the group's accomplishments. They were pleased with changes that they had effected in the management of the Massachusetts

State Prison in Charlestown and at the House of Reformation for Juvenile Delinquents in Boston, but the officers were even prouder of their organization's "indirect influence." Chief among them, they noted in a memorable passage, was to have demonstrated "the connexion between architecture and morals": "there is such a thing as an architecture adapted to morals; [and] other things being equal, the prospect of improvement, in morals, depends, in some degree, upon the construction of buildings."

> If there are principles in architecture, by the observance of which great moral changes can be more easily produced among the most abandoned of our race [criminals], are not these principles, with certain modifications, applicable to those persons who are not yet lost to virtue, but prone to evil? If it is found most salutary, to place very vicious men alone, at night, and give them opportunities for thought, without interruption, is not the principle applicable to others subject to like passions?

Those who might benefit from such moral architecture included the "vicious poor" in their almshouses, as well as those residing in institutions where "large numbers of youth of both sexes are assembled and exposed to youthful lusts," such as colleges, boarding schools, and "large families."[70]

The celled form, separation and classification, sensory reorientation, narrated selfhood, individualized attention within a uniform context of treatment, coordinated actions that dramatized both commonality of values and hierarchies of achievement or status also characterized the regime of asylums, Lancasterian schools (public schools for poor children), and hospitals in their own distinct ways. Convicts stood at a central point on a scale of deviance that pointed in one direction toward "innocent" physical and mental disability and in another toward "culpable" physical and moral disability. The first direction pointed toward the hospital and the insane asylum, the second to the house of refuge and the almshouse, with the penitentiary as the institution around which the others orbited. As Jeremy Bentham observed, communities provided a range of institutions suited to the "different modes of treatment that may be due to what are looked upon as the inferior degrees of dishonesty, to idleness as yet untainted with dishonesty, and to blameless indigence. The law herself has scarcely eyes for these microscopic differences."[71]

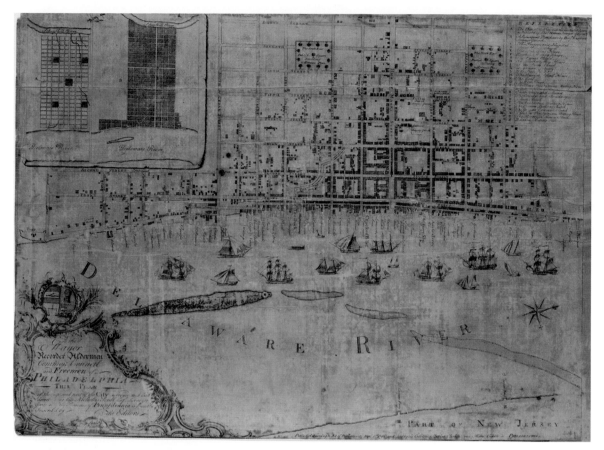

PLATE 1. Matthew Clarkson and Mary Biddle,
Plan of the Improved Part of the City of Philadelphia, 1762.
(The Library Company of Philadelphia)

PLATE 2. William Birch, *South East Corner of Third, and Market Streets*, Philadelphia, 1799. Note the vendors in the foreground. (The Library Company of Philadelphia)

PLATE 3. J. C. Wild, *The Girard College* (Thomas U. Walter, 1833–48), Philadelphia, 1838; reissued by J. T. Bowen, 1840. The building complex was only half finished when this lithograph was made. (The Library Company of Philadelphia)

PLATE 4. Creole cottages, St. Peter and Orleans streets, New Orleans, 1844.
The images were made in conjunction with a land sale. (Courtesy New Orleans
Notarial Archives)

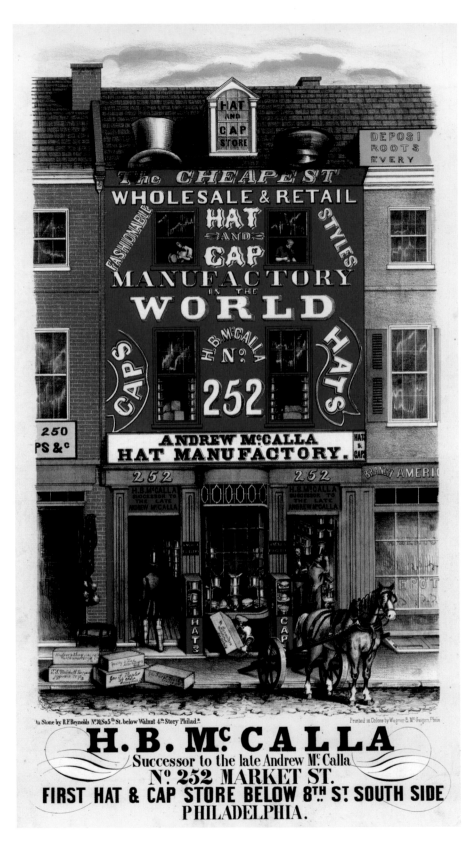

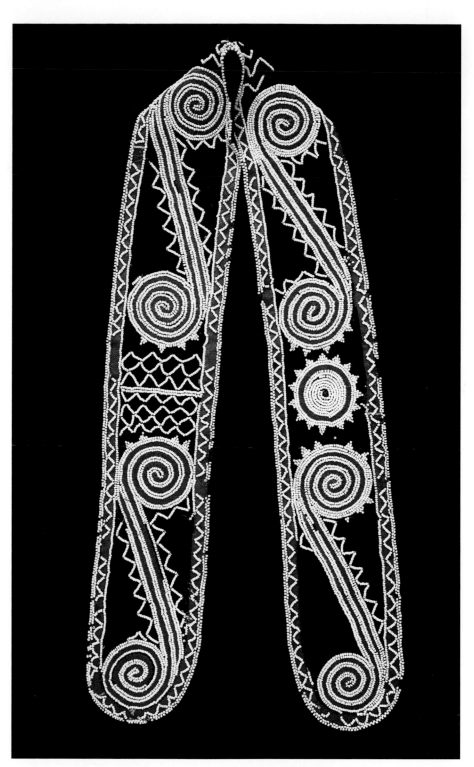

PLATE 6.
Sash,
probably
Choctaw,
ca. 1820s.
(Peabody
Essex Museum)

PLATE 7.
Charles Willson Peale,
*The Long Room, Interior of Front
Room in Peale's Museum*, 1822.
(Founders Society Purchase,
Director's Discretionary Fund.
Photograph © 1990 Detroit
Institute of Arts)

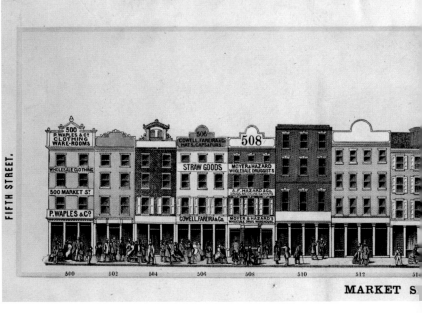

PLATE 8.
*Market Street, from Fifth to Sixth,
(South side.)*, Philadelphia, 1860.
Tower Hall was a clothier's
palace built in the 1850s.
(The Library Company of
Philadelphia)

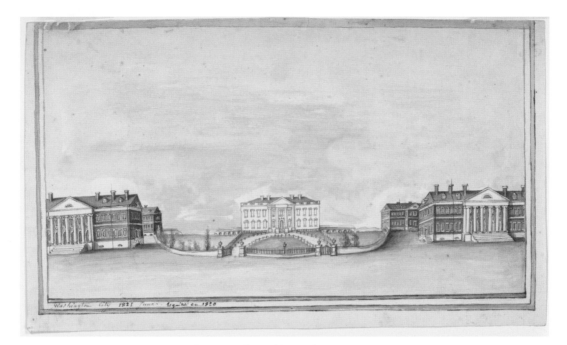

PLATE 9. Anne Marguerite Henriette Hyde de Neuville, *Washington City.*
White House and Executive Office Buildings, 1821. (New York Public Library)

PLATE 10. John H. B. Latrobe, *Catholic grave yard N.O.*, ca. 1834. Latrobe's watercolor shows St. Louis No. 1, a cemetery that his father had carefully inspected twenty years earlier. It is considerably more open than the current state of the cemetery would suggest. (Courtesy Historic New Orleans Collection, Museum/Research Center, acc. no. 1973.37)

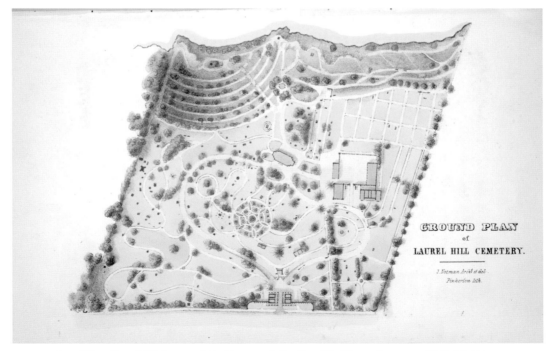

PLATE 11. *Ground Plan of Laurel Hill Cemetery* (John Notman, 1836), 1844. (The Library Company of Philadelphia)

PLATE 12. George Lehman, *Eastern Penitentiary of Pennsylvania. Near Philadelphia*, 1833. (The Library Company of Philadelphia)

PLATE 13. William Birch, *Goal, in Walnut Street Philadelphia*, 1799. The foreground shows men moving a blacksmith shop in 1794 to be used as Philadelphia's first independent African American church. Birch seems to imply that black independence leads to crime and imprisonment. (The Library Company of Philadelphia)

PLATE 14. John Lewis Krimmel, *Night Life in Philadelphia—Oyster Barrow in front of the Chestnut Street Theatre*, 1811–c. 1813. Oysters were customarily sold by black men. (Metropolitan Museum of Art, New York, Rogers Fund, 1942 42.95.18)

PLATE 15. William Birch, *State-House Garden*, Philadelphia, 1798. (The Library Company of Philadelphia)

PLATE 16. J. L. Bousquet de Woiseri, *View from the Plantation of Marigny*, New Orleans, 1803.
At the center of the image are the oft-mentioned lines of "Pride of China" (Chinaberry) trees
that travelers often mentioned. (Chicago History Museum)

PLATE 17. Louis Pessou & Benedict Simm after J. Dürler, *Jackson Square*, New Orleans, ca. 1855.
The gentrification of the newly renamed place d'armes is complete, with the remodeling of the
cathedral, the construction of the Pontalba buildings, the installation of Clark Mills's equestrian
Andrew Jackson at the center, and the enclosure of the redesigned and relandscaped square by
a new iron fence. In the foreground, piles of bales and rows of casks reveal the proximity of the
working waterfront, and a couple sets off between them, apparently continuing the traditional
practice of promenading on the levee despite the availability of the new park. (Courtesy Historic
New Orleans Collection, Museum/Research Center, acc. no. 1948.3)

PLATE 19. *Front Street at Market Street*, Philadelphia, ca. 1848. (The Library Company of Philadelphia)

PLATE 20. Independence Hall, February 2006

PART THREE

Public Spaces and
Private Citizens

CHAPTER 11

{ **ON THE WATERFRONT**

Urban elites fired by the republican spatial imagination built a systematic urban landscape to articulate and, when necessary, enforce social solidarity and political unity. Each new building type tested this project, straining materialist assumptions about the relationship between the physical environment and human conduct. When the men who founded asylums and prisons and cemeteries turned their attention to the workaday landscape, they discovered strong political differences in their assumptions about the way that the systematic city should be realized and governed. This was particularly apparent as early-nineteenth-century urban leaders turned their attention to their waterfronts, where the health of their cities' population and their economies seemed to demand a systematic solution.

No city was more aware of its precarious relationship to its waterfront than New Orleans. The Mississippi River levee's appearance and function changed noticeably in the half century after 1803, as it was pushed farther into the river's channel, although these changes were constrained by the Crescent City's precarious site. In light of the riverfront's inordinate significance even for a commercial port, the city vigilantly maintained its levee and guarded it against encroachment, which shaped development of the levee along a distinctive trajectory.

New Orleans's levee was an expanded and reinforced version of the existing natural levee, a low, tilted, fragile ridge of earth deposited on the bank by the river's annual inundations. The natural levee was a small, dry, or more accurately damp, perch, the highest point between the river's edge and the back swamp a quarter mile away. The city grid occupied most of the available natural levee, but especially at high-water periods the city was lower than the river, and frequent landfill was required to keep the urbanized area habitable. First and foremost, then, the levee held back the river, guaranteeing the city's existence. If Orleanians needed to be reminded of their precarious position, periodic levee breaches such as the Macarty Crevasse of May 6, 1816, a break (crevasse) a few miles upriver that left much of the city underwater for several months, or Sauvé's Crevasse of May 3, 1849, which flooded the city for forty-eight days, helped them to remember. To stave off such disasters, the natural levee was continually reinforced with an ever-expanding human-made levee constructed of earth-filled timber pilings, so that by the antebellum decades it was a broad, four-mile-long quay.[1]

The Mississippi had some of the threatening qualities customarily associated with a wilderness. It claimed the unwary by accident as well as by flood. On the levee, "if a man falls in, he is lost beyond all doubt, the undercurrent is so strong," wrote Caroline Hale to her sisters in Massachusetts. "When our Stevadoor fell in, no one moved to save him, he never rose again." As a wilderness, the Mississippi was also a waste in the traditional sense of an unimproved common available to anyone to use for any purpose. Pervasive, ominous, and unorganized, the Mississippi demanded that a human realm be won from it, as the levee "conquer[ed] the solid earth from the inundations" of the Mississippi.[2]

To the extent that the river threatened the city, New Orleans was a "Wet Grave," but in equally important ways it was New Orleans's life. Given the vast human disadvantages of the site, only the prospect of riches could justify building a city in that location. The levee at New Orleans was the strategic and immensely profitable point of contact between the vast Mississippi basin and hinterland and the Caribbean basin. By 1820, it was the second-busiest port in the United States, even though it was far from being the second-largest city in the nation (see table 1). As New Orleans grew, so did its levee. While only sixty feet separated the water's edge from Levee Street in 1822, by 1849 the distance was one hundred to two hundred yards of intensely used open space (fig. 11.1).[3]

The annual rise and fall of the river left an alluvial deposit between the levee and the river bank. This deposit—the incipient natural levee if undisturbed—was called the batture. The batture could be defined as "that portion between the high, and low water mark, which we call the Beach." Unlike most beaches the batture came and went very quickly. As one contemporary explained the process, the Mississippi "carries down sand and slime in great quantity and forms Batures not indeed in an imperceptible manner as the term alluvion implies, but very visibly, and so quickly that a single swell of its waters deposit[s] usually about one foot of slime on the whole surface of a Bature, in so much that the course of the river is constantly changing." The batture was an essential natural resource to the inhabitants of New Orleans, who mined it for earth for filling their building lots as well as streets and cemeteries. Periodically the batture provided the soil necessary to move the levee itself to increase the area of the city.[4]

In light of the levee's significance to New Orleans's environmental, economic, moral, and medical well-being, French, Spanish, and early American-period city officials vigorously defended its integrity and that of the batture, treating them as public space in the broadest sense: no alteration for private purposes was allowed. They routinely refused permission to men applying "on various pretexts

FIGURE 11.1. New Orleans levee, 1860. (Courtesy Historic New Orleans Collection, Museum/Research Center, acc. no. 1974.25.17.13)

of public utility" to build brick kilns on the batture to help rebuild the city after the fires of 1788 and 1794. When one man built an enclosure on the batture to contain some lumber, the city allowed it to remain but declared that everyone else had an equal right to use it. Under the Spanish, the Cabildo (city council) routinely ordered structures built on the batture and the levee demolished, declaring that the "batture was to serve for the public in general, and in no manner for a private person to make profit thereof."[5]

After the Louisiana Purchase, the Creole-dominated city council continued to defend the waterfront against private appropriation. They ordered the removal of all private structures and all goods from the levee (except certain categories allowed to remain for a brief time during loading and unloading) because they were prejudicial to the public welfare and obstructed air and movement. They even demanded that the U.S. Navy remove its signal station, which had been turned over to a tenant who was "encroaching more and more every day on said property by building huts and enclosures all around this building." The Corporation could "no longer tolerate" such intrusions. Throughout the antebellum period the levee was a sacrosanct public space—a common in the most basic sense. The first ranks of private buildings stood well back from the waterfront on the far side of Levee (now Decatur) Street. Only with the arrival of the railroad after the Civil War did private interests capture it.[6]

The Americans who flooded into New Orleans after 1790 brought a different conception of the waterfront. Traditionally, American urban governments had left waterfront development to private initiative, using strategic grants of water lots to encourage individual entrepreneurs to fill and improve the shoreline, so in most northern ports the waterfront was quickly engrossed by private owners. The difference between American and Creole attitudes was thrown into high relief by a lengthy legal battle that arose immediately after the Louisiana Purchase, precipitated by Edward Livingston, a recent immigrant to New Orleans.[7]

Livingston became entangled in a financial scandal while serving both as mayor of New York City and U.S. Attorney for New York State. He fled to New Orleans in 1804 hoping to repair his fortune as well as to evade the federal government, to which he owed $44,000. In a complicated transaction whose motives and potential consequences were matters of intense public dispute, he acquired from the heirs of Bertrand Gravier the right to the batture "in front of" the Faubourg Sainte-Marie, the suburb immediately upriver from the Vieux Carré that was later known as the American Sector, subject to the courts' recognizing his title. This was an enormous tract of land, estimated to be between 122 and 247 yards wide in 1806 and, in Thomas Jefferson's opinion, worth about half a million dollars. Livingston's workmen began to dig a 64-foot-wide, 276-foot-long canal through the batture and to prepare to move the levee out to allow him to convert the batture to building lots (fig. 11.2).[8]

Jean Gravier began to develop the batture shortly after the Louisiana Purchase, but neighbors protested. Livingston brought suit on Gravier's behalf in the territorial Superior Court, and on May 23, 1807, the court unanimously decided the case of *John Gravier v. the Mayor, Alderman, and Inhabitants of the city of New Orleans* in Gravier's favor. Livingston then stepped into the limelight as the true owner of the tract and began to rework it on his own account. The matter came to a head in the fall of 1807 when President Thomas Jefferson, acting on information relayed by Louisiana Governor William C. C. Claiborne, ordered the U.S. marshal to evict Livingston from the batture as a trespasser on public lands. Lawsuits and countersuits arising from Gravier and Livingston's seizure of the batture and the government's eviction lasted for decades.[9]

These legal proceedings raised complex, never clearly resolved questions

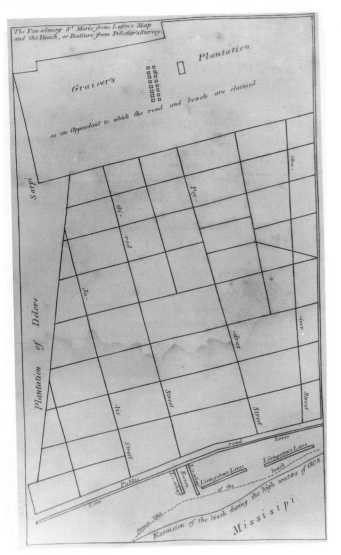

FIGURE 11.2. Thomas Jefferson, Faubourg Sainte-Marie batture, 1812. (Tulane University— Louisiana Collection)

about the ownership of the batture and ultimately about the *possibility* of owning it. Was the batture the property of Bertrand Gravier and his heir Jean Gravier as a perquisite of their ownership of the former Jesuit plantation that comprised the Faubourg Sainte-Marie? Or, since the Graviers had developed that portion of the growing suburb between their own residence and the levee, did the batture belong to the purchasers of the lots adjacent to the levee? To the city, as urban waterfronts usually did (fig. 11.3)? Perhaps it was public land belonging to the U.S. government as successor to the Spanish and French crowns. The answers to these questions turned on whether the batture was categorized as an alluvium, a river bed, a beach, or terra firma, and on the implications of each of those categories in Spanish, French, and even Roman law. Other contestants

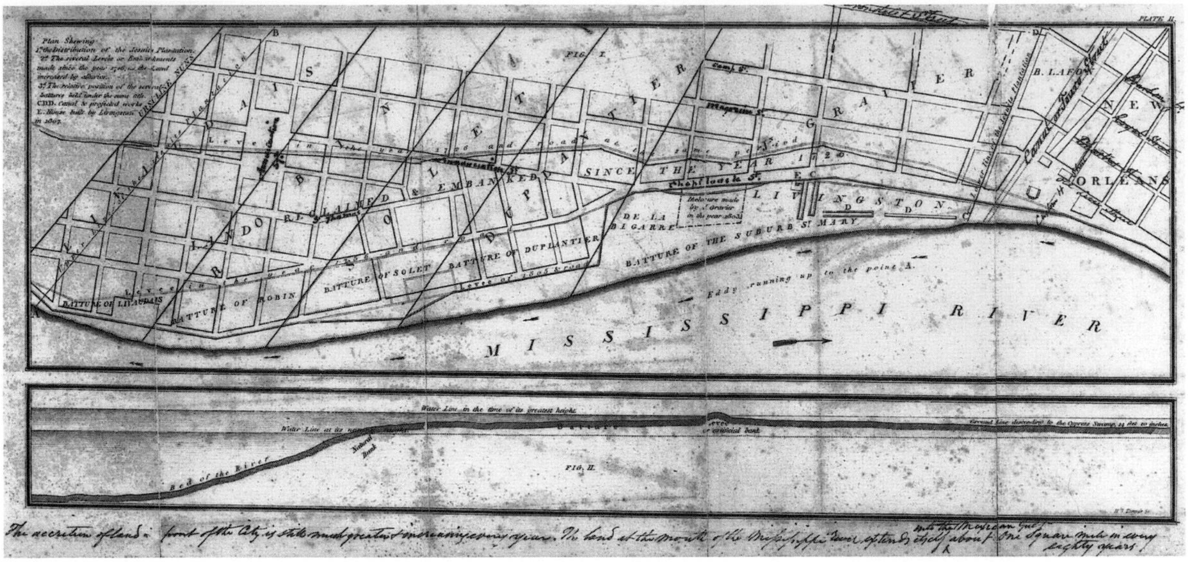

FIGURE 11.3. Edward Livingston, Faubourg Sainte-Marie batture, 1813. (Courtesy Historic New Orleans Collection, Museum/Research Center, acc. no. 1981.226.i, ii)

debated whether the Graviers had ever given any indication that they believed they owned the batture until a buyer presented himself.

With one exception—the suit of *Morgan v. Livingston et al.* of 1819—the courts decided repeatedly and unequivocally for Livingston and his successors, but these were only legal victories whose justice was vigorously and publicly challenged. Claiborne and Livingston both described a series of dramatic confrontations on the site beginning on August 24, 1807, when a mob of angry townspeople gathered and drove away Livingston's black workmen. The next day another confrontation at the site pitted the townspeople against Livingston himself. Each day for several days running a crowd assembled at the building site, summoned by the beating of a drum, the customary New Orleans notice of official public announcements. These events were repeated until August 31, when Livingston's men were able to work for several hours before being driven off again. Another attempt on September 14 was met by two town constables who took down the names of those obstructing the project. This time the mob not only drove off the workers but also seized and destroyed the constables' list. According to Livingston these demonstrations were "encouraged by the presence of the commanders of the militia, and carried on under the eye of the mayor of the city, and the judge of the county court, who never made the smallest visible attempt to restore the order of the city."[10]

On September 15, Livingston tried again after having notified the governor that he would do so and that "he shall not be surprised to see the people change the insolence of riot into the crime of murder." This time Livingston brought white laborers rather than black ones, thinking that the townspeople would be less willing to harm whites (or perhaps that white laborers would be more willing to fight than black ones had been). The governor himself (or, according to other accounts, U.S. marshal Le Breton Dorgenois) addressed a crowd of "several hundreds" of Livingston's opponents at the site, urging them to obey the law but also telling them, according to Livingston, that in his opinion the Superior Court's decision in Livingston's favor was not the final word. The demonstrators conveyed their response through a spokesman who described

> the serious uneasiness which the decision of the court had excited, the long and undisturbed possession of the batture by the city, as well under the French as the Spanish government, and the great injury which would result to the inhabitants if the land should be built upon and improved. And another declaring that they wished the decision of Congress, and in the mean time, no work to be done on the batture, there was a general exclamation from the crowd, "that is the general wish," followed by a request that they might nominate an agent to bear to the President of the United States, a statement of their grievances.

Jean-Baptiste Macarty (later mayor of New Orleans) was chosen to collect affidavits from townspeople about the historic use of the property, and the crowd dispersed. Livingston waited until later in the year, then resumed the work. On January 25, 1808, Jefferson sent a federal marshal to seize the property. Livingston obtained an injunction suspending the warrant and returned to the site accompanied by three militia regiments. Nevertheless, a mob estimated at one hundred people once again drove off the workers, destroyed their tools and materials, and allowed the rising river waters to demolish the unfinished works, in which Livingston claimed to have invested $12,000. Livingston once more regained possession of the batture and decided to allow people to load water carts or to beach boats on it, but he prosecuted those who attempted to remove earth from it.[11]

Eventually, confronted with his first serious legal defeat in the state Supreme Court in *Morgan v. Livingston,* Livingston engineered what became known as the "Donation" or "Compromise of 1820." He and his co-claimants agreed to cede title to the levee and batture to the city in return for title to the new lands formed behind it. The transaction was a legal fiction that provided a way out for the litigants, giving Livingston a concrete title to the newly created terrain in return for the "gift" to the city of a title that was never Livingston's to give. The new state of affairs created more ambiguities that required a second act of legal sleight of hand in 1851 and that even complicated a redevelopment scheme in the 1990s.[12]

Historians have tried unsuccessfully to clarify the batture case by over-simplifying it. Some have seen it as a purely legal problem in which right and wrong could be determined by a close reading of the pertinent texts and a careful parsing of the facts. To others it was a political controversy created by opportunists such as Jefferson or Livingston, by players still smarting from the fallout of the Burr Conspiracy of 1805–7, which deeply affected local politics in the Louisiana Territory, or by the citizens of New Orleans as a consequence of their inadequate understanding of legal principles and procedures. Still others treat it as an ethnic conflict between "French" and "American" parties. All of these were intertwined and inseparable aspects of an issue that was first of all one about competing conceptions of the urban community and its spatial domain.

The combatants advanced incompatible assumptions about public space and the rights of citizens and communities that roughly (but only roughly) divided along ethnic lines and that were roughly (but only roughly) grounded in differing civil- and common-law concepts of property, but that ultimately had to do with broader popular concepts of property and equity. In the continental civil-law tradition that prevailed in French Louisiana, resources such as the batture had obvious "uses for which nature intended them" that, like the sky and the air, were available to everyone. Most important, civil law distinguished public from private law. Public goods always took precedence over private ones. So while it was possible to own land as private property—in fact, as George Dargo has observed, the concept of ownership was more clearly articulated in the civil law than in the Anglo-American common-law tradition, where it remained encumbered with feudal notions of tenure and dependency—private property must always yield to public need. There was no balancing of the two as equal or nearly equal contestants, as in the common law.[13]

To those who took what might be termed the Creole position, the public good encompassed the physical security of the city, its salubrity, and its ability to conduct trade. These included the city council and its representatives, and anti-Livingston pamphleteers such as Pierre Derbigny, Louis Moreau Lislet, and J. B. S. Thierry, but also Governor Claiborne and Thomas Jefferson, who adopted it in defense of his official actions in the case. Livingston's project appeared to them to threaten the health of the city in the usual ways—through disturbing the earth and impeding the free passage of the air—and it threatened New Orleans's trade even more severely by removing the customary landing place of flatboats and, some believed, by forcing the river out of its natural channel, which would ruin the port and the city's economy. In addition, Livingston's claim deprived individual citizens of customary rights held in common, including the right to take earth from the batture to fill their lots, the right to a place of an "evening walk, so necessary in that hot country," and even the right to "enjoy the freshness of the river air, and the agreeable view of the water, and of the country on the opposite shore." The waterfront was, as the civil-law tradition put it, a *locus publicus,* defined by the principal seventeenth-century expositor of French civil law as a place "the use of which is common to all particular persons. . . . And these kinds of things do not appertain to any particular persons, nor do they enter into commerce." In his never-adopted proposal for systematizing Louisiana's entire legal code, Edward Livingston parsed this passage as meaning: "Things which are common are those 'of which the,' property belongs to nobody 'in particular,' and which all men may freely use, conformably to the use for which nature has intended them, such as air, [running water,] the sea and its shores." These included rivers and their banks, streets, squares, and other places that provide for the common good. They were not the property of the government, although the sovereign's name was often attached to them. Instead, they were unowned assets of the community as a whole. If property might be defined, in Hendrik Hartog's words, as "not simply as material possessions but as all the attributes of personality that created individuality," then the levee and its batture were attributes of the people of New Orleans. To be a New Orleanian was to have a right to use the waterfront, and, conversely, the peculiar status and qualities of the New Orleans waterfront were among the distinctive attributes that defined the community.[14]

This sense of communal identity and undivided possession also surfaced in the charge that Livingston's works would damage the urban image. "The delightful aspect of the harbor and city, which extends itself along the river in a regular semi-circular form, with elegant houses in front, would have been destroyed. It would have intercepted the view which the city now enjoys of the river and opposite country, and the view from the river and country of the city and harbor; while the loathsome appearance of irregular and filthy store houses and stinking canals would have made it look like the doleful abode of death and desolation; and, in truth, it would soon have become so." Indeed, Livingston's "unnatural contrivance" would "take from the view of the inhabitants every object fitted to cheer their spirits and gratify their senses."[15]

Thus Livingston's opponents argued that there was a public good separate from and transcending all private ones and that the New Orleans waterfront must serve that good above all. Any attempt to preempt the public right was an "offence against the laws of nature . . . perverting her most valuable gifts." It was "speculation," a moral offense akin to "forestalling" (attempting to manipulate the prices of food in the public market) or to using auctions to undercut wholesale merchants' customary prices. So Livingston's actions were "criminal speculations," undertaken by a "Hercules of chicane," that were intended to commandeer "a public property so useful, so indispensably necessary to all the inhabitants of this territory" that its loss would be economically fatal. Claiborne told Jefferson that Livingston, an "unprincipled man," was "alike feared and hated by most of the antient inhabitants. They dread his talents as a lawyer, and hate his views on speculation." More than public health or economic vitality was at issue: the Creoles saw the customary use of the batture as a defining quality of their own citizenship and urbanity, of what it meant to live together as something called New Orleans.[16]

The Livingston party acknowledged no such no common land or common existence. All land was available to be owned privately. Government's role was to protect individual property, not collective rights. If the people had enjoyed the privilege of taking earth or of promenading on the waterfront, it was because its legal owners had not chosen to exclude them before. Now, however, if New Orleanians needed the earth, let them buy it from Livingston. If they wanted to promenade, let them find somewhere else to stroll. While the Creoles complained of private greed's undermining the public good, Livingston believed himself to be the victim of the "exercise of arbitrary power . . . from persons high in office, whose influence may seduce, or whose power may overawe opposition." It was, quite simply, a case of "the destruction of personal liberty."[17]

The pro-Livingston argument rested on an English political-legal tradition, articulated by John Locke, that assumed a primal collectivity in the earth and its bounty: "God . . . has given the world to men in common," Locke wrote. People have a right to appropriate from the common whatever they need and can use, as long as they do not prevent others' satisfying their own needs. In this spirit, Livingston's party often pointed out that there was plenty of other batture available to serve the city's needs. But Locke went on to say that the invention of money represented a social agreement to accept and to defend the inequality of property, which made it natural and ethical for people to enter into commercial relations and to accumulate more than they needed. His argument reflected the deemphasis of communal responsibility by seventeenth-century English economists in favor of individual autonomy. By this light Livingston was confident that his appropriation of the batture was legal, and he expected the authorities to defend his property rights.[18]

In New Orleans the issue was framed as a clash between conceptions of equity and law in the civil- and common-law traditions. Civil law saw equity as the goal of law, and legal officials were obliged to seek remedies for inequities by whatever means they could. The common-law tradition separated the two, as George Dargo has observed. The officers of the court were charged with applying the correct laws using the correct procedure, let the chips fall where they may. Equity lay in the impartial functioning of process—hence Livingston's complaint—rather than in the outcome.

But the batture conflict overflowed simple legalities into conceptions of individuals' relationships to community and to property. The Creole party members envisioned themselves as a collective, hierarchically differentiated but undivided civic body, while the Livingstonians imagined the urban community as a collection of fictively identical but independent selves. Theirs was the republican idea that we have been exploring. In law this view matched places to individuals by "title" as commodities rather than matching them to communities as resources that transcended property. The property relationship was clearly simpler than the collective model, and it permitted the unambiguous, cellular mapping and distribution of gridded terrain.

Both Livingston's contemporary defender Peter S. Duponceau and the modern historian George Dargo thought that Livingston's title was procedurally sound under either civil or common law. Livingston's opponents and some of his defenders understood that the law, and particularly the common law, was not neutral. It was designed to protect property. In the world of Locke's social compact to establish private property, it favored those who had the means—the money, or in Livingston's case, skilled knowledge of the common law and a lot of nerve—to acquire property over the mass of those who did not. While anyone *might* have used the laws to acquire property as Livingston did, only a few were *able* to do so. So while a procedural view asserts equal opportunity in theory, the outcome-based conception of justice articulated by Livingston's critics countered that in practice only a few people were able to avail themselves of the opportunity. Consequently, there were legitimate public goods and ends that could never be achieved by procedural justice, however vehemently a Livingston might insist that his private actions promoted the public good.[19]

Conflicts over the private appropriation of public resources flared in other parts of the new nation undergoing capitalist transformation—for example, when new industries' waterpower needs impeded traditional fishing rights in the late eighteenth and early nineteenth centuries, or when urban residents challenged industrialists' right to foul the common air and water in the early to mid-nineteenth century. The batture controversy was distinguished by the undertone of colonial resentment that it tapped. While citizens of the East Coast colonies had chosen their new government by revolution and shaped it through a Constitution, Louisiana was simply purchased. As with the initial foundation by France and the earlier transfers from France to Spain and back (briefly) to France, the residents of New Orleans had no voice in choosing their new rulers. They were colonial subjects of the United States. Some Americans argued that they should never gain equal status with the original states. While changes of authority under the French and Spanish mostly meant changes of officeholders and minor political and legal differences, under American rule a new political regime and a very different legal system were imposed, and the region was inundated with new residents (see tables 1, 2). The newcomers were omnipresent, noisy, and arrogant, "assuming somewhat the manner of conquerors—and an intellectual superiority which they did not always merit," according to the son of one of New Orleans's early Anglo-American merchants. They refused to learn French and even attempted to invalidate French-language legal documents. They built separate, Protestant churches, separate cemeteries, and separate residential and commercial districts. And they pushed to replace the French-Spanish civil code of laws with English common law.[20]

Not surprisingly, the Creole residents of Louisiana saw these as concerted attacks on their everyday practices, their economic well-being, and, in the case of the elite, their political and social power. The Americans did not, could not, or would not understand their values and their traditions. Julien Poydras, a wealthy planter, member of the House of Representatives, and, at his death, benefactor of several charitable institutions in New Orleans, summed up the conflict as one in which the "rich and wealthy inhabitants of this country" had always respected "municipal property, which could not . . . belong to any one but the public," only to have "a stranger without fortune . . . come and pluck up the fruit that grew at their feet." J. B. S. Thierry, one of Livingston's most vocal opponents, put it more bluntly: "France did not cede this country to the United States, nor did the American government acquire it, in order that a gang of blood-suckers, of ravenous lawyers, of foreign capitalists, should, in contempt of all notions of justice and humanity, combine under the most criminal compact, for the purpose of chaining its inhabitants under the double yoke of wretchedness and chicane."[21]

Language—a facility with French, Spanish, and Latin, as well as English—was a key weapon. The anti-Livingstonians employed their linguistic expertise to parse volumes of French, Spanish, and Roman law. They disputed the ways that English lawyers translated Romance languages, and they complained that "the language in which the case was pleaded, is unknown to a great majority of the inhabitants of this country." They used the printed word very effectively to craft a common voice, a "supervising agency," in Michael Warner's terms, that would call the new rulers and their legal system to account. Their tracts and briefs "were exhibited on the Exchange, and read for the instruction of the bye standers."[22]

Livingston's enemies also applied more traditional forms of public pressure. According to Bernard Marigny, a Livingston opponent who later came to admire him, the leading Creole landowners who felt their own power threatened by the Americans "provoked all the popular tempests against M. Livingston."[23] "Mobs," historians have come to understand, are not spontaneous outbreaks of frustration. Someone organizes them, and that someone is often a powerful person who remains in the background while the crowd does his bidding. Nevertheless, the anti-Livingston demonstrators—"mobs" to Livingston, "friends of order" to his enemies—might not have responded to elite provocation had it not suited their own interests as artisans, householders, and propertyless people who depended on the waterfront for their livelihoods, if they had not shared the elite's resentment of the American invasion, and if they had not believed that the new legal system favored outsiders and property owners who understood it over longtime residents without their resources. As one newspaper correspondent put it, "A fair trial of the cause could not be expected from three judges speaking a different language . . . and bred under different laws, usages and religion."[24]

The colonial resentments, cultural conflicts, and legal ambiguities that permeated the batture controversy plagued the Crescent City until long after the Civil War. New Orleans's original grid was set tangent to a broad curve in the river, with the waterfront curving away from Levee Street at both ends, leaving broad triangular areas known as the quays (fig. 11.4). The city tried to use the quays in two different ways. It constructed a vegetable market adjacent to

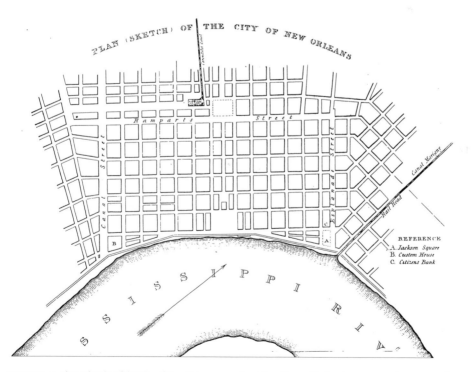

FIGURE 11.4. *Plan (Sketch) of the City of New Orleans*, ca. 1837. The city and federal governments contested ownership of the sites marked B and A, the former locations of colonial-era fortifications. (Library of Congress, Maps Division)

the meat (now French) market on the downriver quay in 1823, and a year later it advertised the land in the upriver quay for sale to private buyers.

After having declared the riverfront federal property as a tactic to thwart Livingston, the city now found the federal government claiming it, particularly the quays where its custom house and an old fortification stood, and the central part of the levee and batture where the Navy maintained workshops for repairing its vessels. The municipality prevailed in court in 1836, and the national government surrendered the quays to the city and moved its naval operations downriver. In opposing the federal government the city used two different arguments. It attacked the naval facilities on the same grounds that it had used in opposing Livingston, claiming that they deprived the people of their customary access to the waterfront. But the city also argued that it should own the quays because it needed to sell them to pay for street paving and other improvements elsewhere in the city. In using the waterfront land in this way, they were moving closer to the northern practice of selling off large municipal commons to raise cash.[25]

Although city policy drifted toward the newer American understanding of urban government as a facilitator of private enterprise, the older conception of the levee as an inviolable common never disappeared. It surfaced whenever specific alterations to the levee were proposed. Both proponents and opponents of new development often cast their arguments in the newer language of private-property rights *and* of the older one of the inviolability of the levee. Legally, however, the levee and batture remained locus publicus—a space for everyone that belonged to no one, and that status had an unexpected consequence. Louisiana state courts defined the city as an administrator of the waterfront on behalf of the public, rather than as its owners as a municipal corporation. This left an opening for privately owned railroads to persuade the legislature in 1868 to grant them the administration of the levee on behalf of the public after the legislature added railroads to the list of "natural" uses of the space. In this way the levee was finally privatized despite remaining "unowned."[26]

In Philadelphia the struggle to retain the waterfront as a common resource was lost in the earliest years of the city's history. William Penn had planned to give lots along Front Street, with their advantageous proximity to the Delaware River, to the First Purchasers to reward their heavy investments in his colony. However, he intended the land between Front Street and the water to be a vaguely defined commercial common. But the First Purchasers felt that they had been shortchanged of their bonuses. They had "with their own great costs & large expence within this Citie built upon their Front Lot[s]," but since the riverbank at that time was too high for traditional wharves, each builder ought to have the "priviledge to build vaults or store in the bank against his Lot, & enjoy them as his Right." Penn responded angrily that the riverbank was on "top common from end to end," while the waterfront "belongs to the [front] lott men no more then back lott men." They could build a public walk above and construct stairs down to public wharves, "but into the water & the sho[re] is no purchasors [property]." Penn was defeated and the waterfront was privatized, with no benefit to the city at large, as the Corporation of the City of New York obtained through its water-lot grants. Consequently, Philadelphia's waterfront transformation took place after many of the changes so hotly disputed in New Orleans had long been accepted. The waterfront was already parceled and would remain so. No Philadelphians who left a written opinion doubted that the waterfront needed to be reordered and systematized. They disagreed over the role of the city government in the project.[27]

When Philadelphians began to resurrect Penn's plan in the late eighteenth century they found the Delaware River fraught with almost as much danger as New Orleans's levee. After the first great yellow fever epidemic in the new United States broke out in Philadelphia in 1793, most experts located its cause in ships that had arrived from the West Indies. Yellow fever visited the Quaker City almost annually, and each time the explanation was the same. After a second major outbreak in 1798, the Philadelphia Academy of Medicine pointed its collective finger at the "noxious air emitted from the hold of the snow Navigation . . . which arrived . . . from the port of Marseilles on the 25th of July," and at similarly noxious air emitted by putrefied coffee in the hold of the Huldah, docked at Kensington. Attention eventually turned from specific vessels to the waterfront itself, to the miasma that its damp and filth generated.[28]

In 1798 the religious polemicist Thaddeus Brown called for all the waterside buildings to be replaced by "one or two ranges of low and wide stores" interspersed with rows of trees and paved or gravel walks. Brown's proposal anticipated a much more ambitious plan by Paul Beck, Jr., who offered his *Proposal for Altering the Eastern Front of the City of Philadelphia* as a response to urgent medical and economic needs that was "Conformable to the Original Design of William Penn." He acknowledged the "well known fact that the disease always commences in the neighborhood of the wharves," but he also promised his readers that his plan would "give employment to a great number of mechanics and laborers; it would put into circulation a large sum of money, and principally among that portion of our citizens who are the most in need of succor." It would also strike a blow at the shadow landscape by eradicating "many dram-shops and other immoral nuisances; it would materially lessen the risk from fire; and in fine, it would make Philadelphia the handsomest of cities."[29]

Beck was a merchant-reformer in the vein of Roberts Vaux, Thomas P. Cope, and John Fanning Watson, and like them he conceived public works, commercial enterprises, charitable organizations, and cultural institutions as aspects of a single project of metropolitan improvement. He served as Port Warden for eighteen years and helped promote the construction of the Chesapeake and Delaware Canal. As a devout Episcopalian he was also treasurer of Christ Church Hospital and president of the Deaf and Dumb Asylum, a founder and vice president of the American Sunday School Union, and a founder of the Pennsylvania Academy of Fine Arts, the Historical Society of Pennsylvania, and the Apprentices' and Mercantile libraries.[30]

Beck wanted the municipal government to buy all the land from the east side of Front Street to the Delaware River and from Vine Street to South Street (nearly the entire riverfront of the incorporated city). Every building between Vine and Spruce Streets, including all the structures on Water Street, the street closest to the river, and all of those on the eastern side of Front Street, would be demolished (fig. 11.5). A retaining wall and iron fence would be built along the east side of Front Street, where the grade dropped off one story to the level of Water Street, and 132 uniform, 2½-story, 40-by-80-foot double stores, built of roughcast (stuccoed) brick with slate roofs, would be erected along the river and "New Water Street" (fig. 11.6). The project could be carried out either on an ad hoc basis as individual tracts on the waterfront required repair or replacement or in a single extended campaign, with the city purchasing the entire tract then reconstructing one or two squares a year, leaving the remaining structures standing as income-producing properties to defray costs.

In collaboration with the architect William Strickland, who furnished a plan and elevation of the scheme for the *Proposal,* Beck calculated that the Vine to Spruce Street portion of the tract could be acquired for about $3 million, while the cost of the Spruce to South Street tract would be negligible and would be offset by rents, taxes, and fees. Another $650,000 would cover demolition of the older structures and construction of the new ones, as well as paving and regulation of the wharves and streets. The entire project could be funded by sale or rent of the stores and by wharfage fees.

Merchants in many other European and American cities were busy reorganizing their waterfronts at this time. The opening of London's West India Dock in 1802, for example, inaugurated fifty years of aggressive construction of port facilities east of the city. Three years later Boston's Broad Street Associates began to transform that city's Town Cove, erecting a series of piers and warehouses north and south of the colonial-era Long Wharf. One, India Wharf (1803–7), boasted a row of fifty-four stores, four stories high, designed by Charles Bulfinch. The London and Boston projects aimed to rationalize the logistics of commerce, to protect goods in secure, fire-resistant buildings that

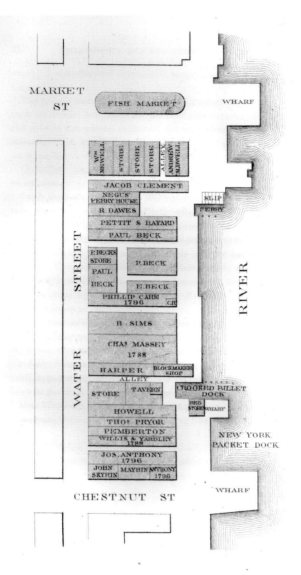

FIGURE 11.5. Philadelphia waterfront from Market Street to Chestnut Street in 1810. Paul Beck's buildings (labeled P. Beck and E. Beck) are located near the center of the map. (Author's collection)

below
FIGURE 11.6. William Strickland, Beck's proposal for redeveloping the Philadelphia waterfront, 1820. (The Library Company of Philadelphia)

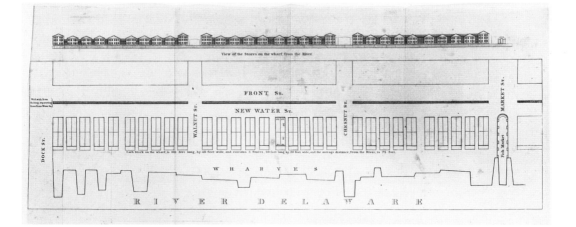

were sometimes walled in to prevent pilferage, and (in the case of the London Docklands) to break the city corporation's grip on port privileges and wharfage fees.[31]

Paul Beck knew about India Wharf, for which, he said, "about fifty gentlemen . . . subscribed half a million dollars . . . : must it be said that the city of Philadelphia cannot accomplish a highly important improvement that will cost but about seven times the amount of what was done by a few individuals in a sister city?" But the Philadelphia scheme was more ambitious in its aspirations, if not in architectural splendor, than the others. In embracing moral, hygienic, and sanitary goals along with commercial efficiency, Beck's *Proposal* foreshadowed the great urban clearances and landscape reforms of the second half of the nineteenth century such as the construction of London's Embankment in the 1860s and 1870s in response to the "Great Stink" of 1858.[32]

Most important, the Boston and London wharves were privately financed and privately owned, albeit with significant public subsidies. They might be thought of as grander and more systematic versions of infrastructural development through municipal water-lot grants. Beck's plan reversed that process. Just as the city and state of New York took the responsibility for master planning the island of Manhattan from the individual developers who had laid out early subdivisions (and who continued to do so in most American cities), so Beck wanted the city of Philadelphia to assume an active role in waterfront development. In some respects, his project anticipated the great publicly sponsored, often state-financed, late-nineteenth-century projects that rationalized the waterfronts of port cities worldwide, from Rio de Janeiro to Brussels, Izmir, Cape Town, and Calcutta, but his thinking remained close to eighteenth-century attitudes toward urban government and development. In that view, it was the responsibility of governments "to maintain the order of society by insisting that private individuals fulfill their public responsibilities." Critics of the Philadelphia waterfront all attributed its poor state to merchants' "bad taste and avidity for converting every piece of ground to the greatest possible revenue," contrary to the enlightened public-spiritedness evident in Penn's original plan. According to Thaddeus Brown, "covetousness, regardless of the beauty—the convenience—the natural order—and the health of the city" had led to a crowded and unsanitary waterfront and was one of the causes for God's wrathful infliction of yellow fever on Philadelphia in 1798. Robert Waln, Jr., agreed. The docks and warehouses along the Delaware River were "standing monuments of the folly and avarice of our fore-fathers," he said, as well as the economic, moral, and medical hazards that Brown and Beck described. Thus Beck envisioned a waterfront that would be sold or rented to private merchants after it had been reconstructed by the municipality, which would act less as a developer than as a referee or intercessor to defend the public welfare from the consequences of undisciplined private action.[33]

Nevertheless, Beck's project "failed of like spirits to carry out the idea," according to one early biographer, although another noted that it had been strongly supported in principle by the Select and Common Councils, the College of Physicians, the Board of Health, and some merchants. While such a project would have strained the financial resources of most municipalities, this proposal foundered on theoretical grounds before economic objections were raised. Like other spatial innovations of the first quarter of the nineteenth century, Beck's waterfront scheme demonstrated the still-fluid implications of the republican spatial imagination.

Beck's modular plan was designed to link the waterfront to the already-gridded interior streets of the city. It would be effected by the municipality acting to promote its corporate goals. But, as the batture controversy showed, early-nineteenth-century American judicial decisions, government policies, and political theories were moving toward a conception of government as a neutral intercessor, deferential to and protective of private goals but without vested interests of its own. Rather than treating public welfare and private goods as discrete entities, this interpretation defined the public welfare as nothing more than the sum of private goods, with government simply providing a legal and administrative medium within which to pursue them. In this role, the law was the procedural equivalent of the urban grid. Beck, though, remained more interested in the outcome—in an orderly and salubrious waterfront as a civic value—than in the process—in urban fabric as a neutral environment within which many disparate goals could be pursued. This left his plan open to critics who understood the city in the newer way.

Stephen Girard was such a man, and Beck's pamphlet goaded him into action. Girard, whose strong, if shifting, convictions matched his great wealth, fired off a letter to Beck and other Philadelphia leaders as soon as he learned of the pamphlet. In a brief statement he rejected Beck's factual premises. The merchants of Water Street were *not* derelict in their public responsibilities. As a resident of Water Street since 1779 (and, he might have added, as the principal organizer of Philadelphia's relief efforts in the 1793 yellow fever epidemic), he could say confidently that Water Street was "as healthy as any other part of the city." Therefore there was no need for public action. Nothing in Girard's cryptic note contradicted Beck's theoretical assumptions, but in other clashes with public officials and neighbors over the next decade, Girard articulated a different conception of public authority and public space from Beck's.[34]

Girard saved a copy of an undated Philadelphia "ORDINANCE to grant a Lot near the Drawbridge . . . for the purpose of erecting thereon a Place of Worship and Instruction for Mariners" in his business papers. This act would have given the congregation's organizers a city-owned lot at Front and Dock streets. Girard objected that the only audience for such an institution lived in the working-class districts of the Northern Liberties and Southwark, north and south of the city proper, not around the prime waterfront site that the council had designated. In any event, he said, the gift was unfair and probably illegal. "Have the Select and Common Councils of the City of Philadelphia the Power to legislate on Religious matter or to create a new Sect of Religion?" Had they the right to give away any city property to private persons or organizations? If city land were to be given to the Mariners' Church, shouldn't merchants or traders, or even mechanics belonging to other denominations, receive grants? "Surely those permanent Members of our Community have as much claim on the City as these Seamen, who pay no tax and are absent three fourths of the time." Girard noted that the city had rejected similar applications in the past and that the tract in question would be better used to create an opening to ventilate the surrounding neighborhood.[35]

Traditionally urban corporations had acted as persons in owning, protecting, and disposing of city property for their own benefits and as they saw fit. Girard argued against this practice: city land did not belong to the government but to the citizens as a kind of common property. It could not be disposed of for the benefit of any single group or person, however deserving or socially useful the city councilors might find them. Yet Girard was not making the same argument as Livingston's opponents had. The public common was not a resource to be appropriated by anyone, like the batture dirt, but a medium of individual action that could be used, like the levee's open plain, only in a manner that did not preclude or impair others' use of it.

The issue resurfaced in the last months of Girard's life. Although he was ill and housebound, he found the energy to oppose a request from the mercantile firm of Hollingshead, Platt, and Taylor to improve a public ten-foot alley between their newly acquired Front Street property and Girard's house and countinghouse, a space that was then "at all times offensive" (figs. 11.7, 11.8). Girard's neighbors offered to refurbish this passage at their own expense and to allow the public its continued use, framing their proposal in eighteenth-century terms: it was "in the interest of the city" to allow the firm to improve its own property and a bit of the city's since the work would "contribute to change the appearance of this now unsightly portion of the eastern front."[36]

Once again Girard vehemently objected. He did "not suppose, that Councils have a right to grant, to any private persons, for any term of time, the right, title, interest and property of this city in any part of any public street or alley."

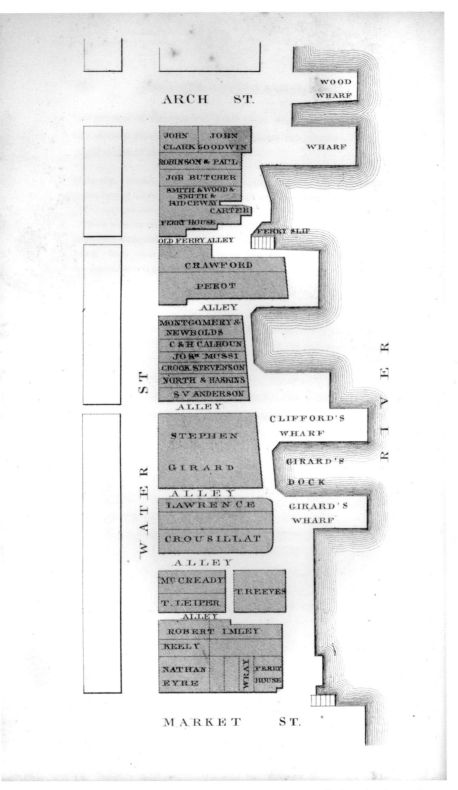

FIGURE 11.7. Philadelphia waterfront from Market Street to Chestnut Street in 1810. Showing Stephen Girard's property and the site of Hollingshead, Platt, and Taylor's store (labeled "S. V. Anderson"). (Author's collection)

FIGURE 11.8. Stephen Girard house and countinghouse, 23 Water Street, Philadelphia, ca. 1865, as it looked in 1831. (The Library Company of Philadelphia)

Then he switched tacks, alluding to older legal doctrines then being repudiated by American courts, to claim that prior occupation entitled him to the alley. "When his past improvements, his long residence on the spot, and his desire further to improve, are considered, a preference should be given to him: he does not, however, seek a favor; he merely objects to the grant of a favor to others, to his own injury." Girard countered Hollingshead, Platt by offering to pay for the privilege of taking over the alley, bidding $500 more than anyone else might tender in return for a grant for twenty-five years only, not one in perpetuity, as his neighbors asked.[37]

The Hollingshead firm responded that they had not asked for a grant "but merely wished to promote an investment, in which the public as well as ourselves are interested." Girard's wharf already extended into the river forty feet beyond their own, and they intended to extend theirs to match his, "wishing to enjoy our just rights, without prejudice to the rights of others." "To make the improvement perfect," they said, the alley must be included. Otherwise it would be impossible to align their new block of stores with Girard's existing buildings in a way that would beautify the "city front." They offered to pay either a use fee or a percentage of their wharfage in compensation, in addition to shouldering maintenance costs and taxes as the council had already demanded. The council decided that its proposal would benefit the public but, either from fear of Girard's wrath or for lack of an acceptable solution to the dilemma, tabled both Girard's and the Hollingshead, Platt petitions.[38]

Apparently Girard's dispute with Hollingshead, Platt, and Taylor remained unresolved at his death, three months after his initial protest, but he had the last word anyway. When his will was made public, it "absorbed nearly the whole attention of our population," Roberts Vaux told Governor George Wolf. It was a "splendid benefaction." In a document the length of a small book Girard laid out a vision of urban reform that he backed with his enormous fortune.[39]

Girard dispensed cash and land to New Orleans, "being the first port on the said Continent at which I first traded, in the first instance as first officer, and subsequently as master and part owner of a vessel and cargo"; to New York, where he first landed in the United States; and most of all to Philadelphia, where he made donations to the Deaf and Dumb Asylum, the Orphan Asylum, and the Society for the Relief of Poor and Distressed Masters of Ships, their Widows and Children. He gave $10,000 to the city to fund Lancasterian education in the city's schools and $6,000 for schools to the adjacent township of Passyunk, where he owned a farm. He left a sum to improve the Philadelphia police. The Pennsylvania Hospital received $30,000 to fund matrons and nurses and "to increase this last class of useful persons much wanted in our city." Girard set aside $2 million to create a school (now Girard College) for "white orphan boys" from Philadelphia, Pennsylvania, New York, and New Orleans, in that order of preference. The city of Philadelphia inherited the remainder of his real and personal estate "to improve the neighbourhood of the river Delaware, so that the health of the citizens may be promoted and preserved, and that the eastern part of the city may be made to correspond better with the interior," and for other public works.[40]

Never one to leave anything to others' judgment, Girard included a detailed description of the waterfront improvements he funded. He designated half a million dollars to "layout, regulate, curb, light and pave a passage or street" to be named Delaware Avenue. This was less than the $651,000 that Beck and Strickland budgeted for Beck's proposal, but Girard did not intend his gift to be used to reconstruct all the buildings on the waterfront as Beck wanted. Delaware Avenue would be at least twenty-one feet wide and run north from South Street, stretching from the eastern edge of the Water Street squares to the "west side of the logs, which form the heads of the docks, or thereabouts." The city must demolish every structure that might be in the way and forbid new construction of any buildings east of the new street. The heads of any docks that might impede the work were to be filled, and the city should "compel" the owners of wharves to "keep them clean and covered completely with hard materials, and to be so levelled that water will not remain thereon after a shower of rain; to completely clean and keep clean all the docks within the limits of the city, fronting on the Delaware, and to pull down all the platforms carried out, from the east part of the city over the river Delaware on piles or pillars." In ad-

FIGURE 11.9. Front Street steps, Philadelphia, after 1831. These are the last survivors of the steps from Front Street to Water Street built under the terms of Girard's will, and virtually the only remnants of any aspect of his waterfront improvement scheme that survived the construction of Interstate 95 in the 1970s

dition to building the new waterside street, Philadelphia was to improve Water Street for the entire distance from Vine Street in the north to South Street. Characteristically, his own premises were the model: Water Street would be regulated for its length "in like manner as it is from the front of my dwelling to the front of my stores on the west side of Water Street, and the regulation of the curbstones continued at the same distance from one another, as they are at present opposite the said dwelling and stores." The new Water Street would be at least thirty-nine feet wide, with a "large and convenient footway" that should be as unobstructed as possible by cellar entries.

Bit by bit, Girard directed, the city should acquire properties to complete Water Street's improvement "until there shall be a correct and permanent regulation of Water Street, on the principles above stated, so that it may run north and south as straight as possible." He wanted the "ten feet middle Alley[s] running through each block from Front Street to Water Street [to] be kept open and cleaned as city property." To connect the reconstructed waterfront to the interior of the city, each alley would be provided with a flight of "plain and permanent" stone steps that should "be washed and kept constantly clean" (fig. 11.9). To link the waterfront to the urban network even more effectively, Water Street would be connected to the city's Schuylkill water system by pipes as large as those elsewhere in the city and provided with fireplugs at the southwest corners of all major streets. These changes should transform the wharves into "a condition which will correspond better with the general cleanliness and appearance of the whole city, and be more consistent with the safety, health and comfort of the citizens." Girard assured his legatees that his plan was founded on "principles at once just in relation to individuals, and highly beneficial to the public."[41]

What Paul Beck could not accomplish through persuasion Girard effected with a mountain of cash. Within three months of his death, the state had passed legislation granting the city the authority to carry Girard's wishes, an act that adopted the text of the will nearly verbatim. Four months later, a city ordinance directed the work to begin. In 1835, with construction well underway, Philadelphians looked forward to the day when "one broad avenue shall supply the place of the disjointed front that has hitherto disfigured our city."[42]

Girard's will seemed so obviously to echo Paul Beck's proposal that some contemporaries thought it represented a capitulation to Beck's vision but "in a way much inferior, it must be admitted." Yet the physical similarities concealed very different assumptions about urban public space. Rather than undertaking to restrain the antisocial behavior of waterfront merchants, Girard wanted the city to provide the kind of neutral framework for private activities to which he had alluded in his response to Hollingshead, Platt, and Taylor. In fact, his will offered a kind of posthumous riposte to his neighbors. The alleys, one of which they wished to take over and which he proposed to improve with steps, "were in the first instance, and still are, considered public property, intended for the convenience of the inhabitants residing in Front Street to go down to the river for water and other purposes; but, owing to neglect or to some other cause, on the part of those who have had the care of the city property, several encroachments have been made on them by individuals, by wholly occupying, or building over them, or otherwise, and in that way the inhabitants, more particularly those who reside in the neighbourhood, are deprived of the benefit of that wholesome air, which their opening and cleansing throughout would afford." The difference was subtle but important. Beck would have had the city promote a certain definition of the public good, with public space as an instrument of collective purpose, while Girard wanted it to provide a matrix within which the only legitimate public good was the ability of every Philadelphian to go about his or her business unimpeded by private infringement on common space.[43]

Philadelphia and New Orleans confronted similar issues in modernizing and rationalizing their waterfronts in the first half of the nineteenth century. Paul Beck and Edward Livingston's antagonists had envisioned an urban landscape that embodied a collective interest and collective goals that transcended those of individual citizens. Stephen Girard and Edward Livingston both denied that public space had any public content: it was a void, a medium for accomplishing private ends. Despite differences in history, culture, and legal structure, both Philadelphia and New Orleans arrived at the same place in their quest to define legally and politically what was public about public space. At the same time they were doing so, other urbanites were asking similar questions about public social domain.

{

In the late 1780s a French visitor to New York was astonished by the ubiquity of cigars, objects unfamiliar enough to his European readers that he described them as "leaves of tobacco, rolled in the form of a tube, of six inches long, which are smoked without the aid of any instrument." Jacques-Pierre Brissot de Warville declared that cigar smoking was revolting to the French generally and rendered men disagreeable to women in particular "by destroying the purity of the breath." At the same time he acknowledged smoking's function in pacing and tempering conversation: "It accustoms to meditation and prevents loquacity. The smoker asks a question; the answer comes two minutes after, and it is well founded."[1]

Fresh off the boat, an English visitor was struck by the number of people who were smoking in the streets, while Philadelphia merchant Thomas Pym Cope noted that "lads many years younger [than eighteen] are constantly met in our streets with cigars in their mouths." In New Orleans "nearly every other man had a segar in his mouth" along the levee, and old mulatto women could be seen puffing on them on the balconies of the French Quarter, while at balls the smell of the pipe often overpowered women's perfume. Tobacco smoke filled the galleries at New York's Castle Garden as well as the ladies' parlor of the Brooklyn ferry. Fredrika Bremer observed prisoners in the Tombs, New York's House of Detention, "walking about, talking, smoking cigars."[2]

By the 1830s tobacco's antisocial qualities seemed more notable than its sociable ones. Urban Americans found themselves lost in a fog of tobacco smoke as they waded through puddles of tobacco-colored spittle. Spitting was universal in streets and public places, and spitters were equally active in confined spaces such as railway carriages. "The constant spitting which takes place from the moment the passengers take their seats, is carried on to so formidable an extent, that scarcely five minutes elapse before the floor is absolutely moist with it," Alexander Mackay reported. "I once ventured to walk from one end of the carriage to another, and got such a fright, from the many perils I encountered, that I never afterwards subjected myself to the risk." Those "loafers" who could be persuaded not to smoke in the ladies' lounge of the Brooklyn ferry "chew and expectorate as much as they please." On the Philadelphia-Baltimore railway, "the seats, the sides of the car, the window hangings, where there are any, and sometimes the windows themselves, are stained" with tobacco juice.[3]

Even the most solemn public settings did not deter nicotine addicts. A Philadelphia lawyer named Meredith made his courtroom arguments "chewing tobacco & spitting all the time he was speaking." In Washington, "the headquarters of tobacco-tinctured saliva," boxes were placed at the feet of monuments in the Capitol to redirect visitors' expectorate away from the artworks. For want of such protection, tobacco-juice libations ruined the base of George Washington's statue in the Massachusetts State House before it could be fenced in to keep spitters out of range. In New York's respectable Hotel Prescott, the guests "spit on the floor. . . . I am afraid if there were portraits on the walls they would squirt tobacco-juice at the eyes, simply to try their skill," wrote one newspaper editor.[4]

Spitters were as terrifying as they were annoying. In the Baptist meeting-house at Willington, Connecticut, Edward Augustus Kendall found himself seated in a pew below the gallery from which twenty "swains" were constantly spewing into the aisle directly next to him. Despite the young men's pinpoint accuracy, Kendall was unable to quell his "constant alarm."[5]

It is no exaggeration, then, to say that antebellum Americans and their visitors were obsessed with tobacco. Edward W. Clay's brilliant 1837 lithograph *The Smokers* rings changes on smoking and its meanings for antebellum Americans. Men and boys of many sorts—well-dressed businessmen, a dandy, an Irish hod carrier, a Scot in full ethnic regalia, a well-off boy, a newsboy, and a country bumpkin—as well as an African American or Native American woman carrying a basket on her head—smoke cigars and pipes on a crowded New York sidewalk (fig. 12.1). A verse beneath the image tells us that

Tobacco is a stinking weed,
It was the Devil sow'd the seed.
It drains the purse & fouls the clothes,
And makes a chimney of the nose.

In the center background two young women, one white and one black, hold their noses. The white woman complains that she is "half blinded and suffocated," while her black counterpart exclaims that the "nasty practice" is "enough to make a dog sick." Sure enough, a dog retches at curbside.

At the most obvious level, *The Smokers* is a Whig political satire. Andrew Jackson—the object of many of Clay's barbs in the 1830s—hovers over the scene at the upper right. Below him a seated Martin Van Buren mimics Jackson's pose, costume, and meerschaum pipe, explaining that "I follow in the footsteps of

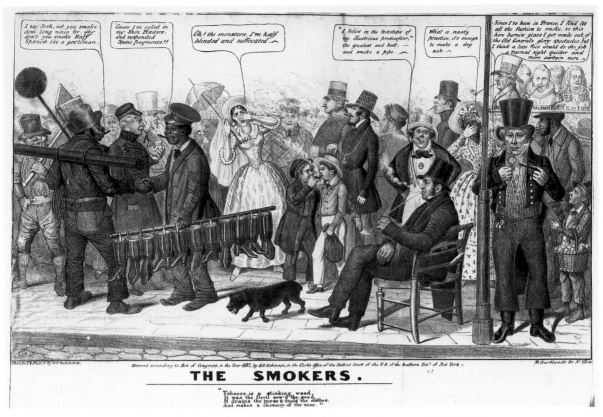

FIGURE 12.1. Edward W. Clay, *The Smokers*, 1837. (The Library Company of Philadelphia)

my illustrious predecessor." At the right an unidentified figure uses a "burnin'
glass" made out of "the Old General's glory spectacles" (a common symbol of
Jackson's grandiosity in Clay's cartoons), but decides that a loco foco (a kind of
match, but also the nickname of a faction of the Democratic party that promoted working-class political interests, supported hard money, and opposed
the chartered banks that issued paper money) would work better. His reference
to France alludes to conservative fears that the New York City bread riots of 1837
would lead to a French-type revolution for, as a sympathetic contemporary observer noted, the Loco Focos promoted the "realization of social equality, so that
the actual condition of men in society shall be in harmony with their acknowledged rights."[6]

At the left of the scene two black men discuss their cigars. One, a chimney sweep, asks the other, a shoe-shine man (who appears as a stock character in many of Clay's cartoons), why he does not smoke Half Spanish "like a
gen'leman." The reply—"I'se called in my Shin Plasters, and suspended Specie
Payments!!"—refers to the banks' self-protective policies during the 1837 panic
and by extension to Van Buren, whose policies were initially pro-bank. Since

it is a premise of all Clay's cartoons that blacks could never become gentlemen and only made themselves ridiculous by trying to do so, the man's comments associate smoking, banks, and Van Buren with buffoonery. Smoking becomes an emblem of crudity, of black inferiority, economic instability, and of the Jacksonians. In *The Smokers,* then, the crowded street, with its indiscriminate crush of people of all ages, conditions, nationalities, occupations, and ethnicities, and of both races and sexes, exemplified the disorder of Democratic rule.[7]

Clay published many partisan cartoons throughout his career, but this one essays a much more sweeping sociopolitical critique that uses tobacco smoke as its vehicle. Tobacco stank—it was another of the early republican city's assaults on the senses. It invaded the nasal cavities, offended the lungs and, as is the nature of smoke, permeated the clothes like the "fomites" blamed for epidemic disease, so that its memory lingered long after one had left the smokers' vicinity. In passing through the streets of New York, complained one editor, "it is awfully odious to have our nasals and our *gabardines* both infected with the fumes of these fiery dragons, preparatory to an *entree* into a drawing-room, or a *tete-a-tete* with a fair acquaintance." On hot days the entire city of New York smelled like the "stale cigar smoke of a country bar room."[8]

Thus tobacco smoke exacerbated the claustrophobic experience of the crowded urban street. Unlike others sorts of urban stenches, however, its sources were easily identified. Although people of all sorts used tobacco, it was conventionally assumed to be a plebeian indulgence. A Philadelphia newspaper declared that "street smokers" were of two sorts only: "puppies," meaning young men eager to appear sophisticated, and "blackguards."[9]

Yet tobacco's unifying cloud drew men and women of all ages, ethnicities, and conditions into atmospheric equality. Smokers forced their betters to join them in their indulgence. They exemplified the democracy, which "suffer[ed] the most stupid beggarly & criminal wretch, just escaped from the hands of justice, or vomited from the jails of Europe, with not a rag to cover his nakedness but what he has either stolen or received in charity, to possess the same political consequence at our elections with a native citizen of the first rate, probity & talents, the largest landholder & most wealthy of any in the commonwealth," according to Philadelphia diarist Thomas P. Cope. Another Philadelphia diarist agreed: republican politics put the "gentleman & boor on the same level." This was because ardent republicanism was "not . . . a respecter of persons."[10]

The Smokers is a window onto the struggles to balance liberty and order, citizenship and social hierarchy, public space and personal privacy in the early republic. As cities began to be sorted functionally and socially in the early nineteenth century the control of public space was contested in the heat of everyday life as well as in the council chamber and the courtroom. Who had a right to use which spaces? How? In finding a political message in this street scene, Clay offered his most significant insight: that politics encompassed every aspect of urban life, from political organization to personal habits. The difference between electoral politics and street behavior was only a matter of degree. The street was the primary political arena, and the struggle to control the street was one of the most pervasive and multifaceted political activities in the antebellum years.

Antebellum New Yorkers organized three great parades to celebrate the completion of colossal public works: the Erie Canal in 1825, the Croton Waterworks in 1842, and the Atlantic Cable in 1858. All three emphasized the projects' spatial nature by means of a ritual journey. In 1825 an Erie Canal boat descended the Hudson River to bring a vial of Lake Erie water, along with water from several of the world's great rivers, to be poured into New York Harbor, marrying the Atlantic world to the rapidly growing interior in the presence of a flotilla of witnesses.[11]

In 1842, four engineers in a specially built vessel, the *Croton Maid*, floated down the aqueduct on the first surge of water on June 23, 1842, "sometimes at a depth of 75 feet below, and then again 80 feet above the natural surface of the earth, at the rate of a mile in 40 minutes, the velocity of the current." This journey was "evidence that no insignificant stream was flowing into the city." The water completed its journey during the formal celebration on October 14, 1842, when it traveled several miles through Manhattan mains to be jetted forty to fifty feet into the air from fountains in The Park (now City Hall Park) and Union Square.[12]

Sixteen years later, on September 1, 1858, another procession celebrated the connection of New York to the world through an electrical network. In making its way up Broadway, the nocturnal parade knit the international network of commerce and information to the local network of the city streets. Businesses along the route vied to produce striking illuminations and thematic decorations. H. Sperry and Company's clock manufactory at 338 Broadway was illuminated with the legend "Time Works Wonders," while D. Devlin's wholesale and retail clothing outlet at Broadway and Warren Street was festooned with a banner that read "THUNDER and LIGHTNING!!/The Telegraphic Lightning is our Thunder!" Ball, Black and Company's illumination proclaimed "HONOR TO CYRUS W. FIELD" and depicted a handshake flanked by the words "England" and "America." Tiffany and Company, which had acquired over six miles of surplus cable to sell in four-inch lengths as souvenirs, simply festooned the front of its store with coils of it.[13]

Each parade celebrated the systematic conception of the city and a feat of human ingenuity, but they constructed their meanings in far older ways. Most human societies use some form of procession as a way of celebrating their most cherished values. Typically processions combine "walking, carrying, showing, viewing, praying, singing, and being seen," according to anthropologist Ronald L. Grimes, and all these were parts of the New York celebrations. Members of the community walked through the principal streets seeing and being seen, carrying banners symbolic of the accomplishment, along with "relics" of it—a "machine for tapping the Croton water pipes" or a large coil of the Atlantic cable, the "mystic wire," accompanied by the sailors of the steam frigate *Niagara* who had helped lay it. Bands played, and at the culminating ceremony the blessings of heaven were invoked and a specially composed ode was sung.[14]

Traditional processions suffuse their world with divinity and create or restore its divine order. They typically follow routes that call attention to fundamental social and spatial relationships, and "take possession . . . , thereby making visited space home space." The Croton Water Works parade moved from the Battery up Broadway past The Park to Union Square, then back down The Bowery, across East Broadway, and back to The Park by way of Chatham Street. It threaded its way through some of the most emblematic New York spaces, connecting elite and plebeian shopping streets (Broadway and The Bowery), and elite and plebeian residential neighborhoods (Union Square and Chatham Street, which passed by the Five Points), linking all to the center of the city's political universe, City Hall and The Park. The link was closed as the last marchers passed The Park for the first time just as the head of the procession was returning to it down Chatham Street.[15]

New Yorkers' march through the city's streets proclaimed a renewed civic order. In a New York watered from the Croton, "Pale Contagion flies affrighted / With the baffled demon Fire! / Safety dwells in her dominions, / Health and Beauty with her move," sang the members of the New York Sacred Music Society as they gathered around the The Park's fountain. Water meant a healthier city, and consequently a more moral one, in keeping with nineteenth-century hygienic doctrine that linked bad health with weakened moral fiber: "Filth and crime, cleanliness and virtue are near kinfolks," Water Commission president Samuel Stevens told the celebrants. "The more means and conveniences for cleanliness that are furnished our population the more industrious and virtuous they will be." Most immediately, it meant that drinking water no longer need be laced with alcohol on hygienic grounds, for Croton water was clean enough to drink straight. One temperance society's banner "represented a water hydrant in full chase of a rum-cask, literally driving him off the ground."[16]

According to those who wrote about them, these grand civic festivities bred democratic fellowship among New Yorkers of all classes. The Croton Waterworks inspired the "proud consciousness which every citizen of New-York felt that his or her own cherished and honored city had, in this mighty undertaking, accomplished a work with no superior," a "gratification such as it is not often the pleasant lot of a municipal people to enjoy," wrote the *New World*. The anthropologist Victor Turner called this effect of public rituals "communitas"—in this case, "*existential* or *spontaneous* communitas . . . what William Blake might have called 'the winged moment as it flies,' or, later, 'mutual forgiveness of each vice.'"[17]

Turner went on to distinguish this form of communitas from two others. One, ideological communitas, prescribed the social conditions or arrangements that might lead to the perpetuation of existential communitas. For the *New World* reporter, it was the republican spatial imagination, the idea of the city as a systematically articulated social space in which all moved freely but as if by common impulse. This is exactly what the writer believed happened in The Park on October 14, 1842. After a day of parades, speeches, and illuminations, he found that "There was much, . . . very much—indeed we may say everything—in this celebration—to excite strongly the most grateful feelings and reflections. . . . There was the sense of grandeur always called into being by the sight the presence of a great multitude, animated by one impulse, and moving or acting in the attainment of a common object. Nor was the proud reflection absent, that under the benign influence of political institutions which give and secure to every man his equal share in the general rights, powers, and duties of citizenship; amid this great convulsion, as it may be called—this mighty upheaving and commingling of society—where half-a-million of people were brought together into one mass as it were, there was not a guard, a patrol, a sentry, not even a solitary policeman, stationed any where to hold in check the ebullition of social or political excitement; that there was need of none. . . ."[18]

The grand vision of a unified democratic people conjured up by the *New World* contrasted in many respects with the visual evidence that the processions themselves presented. As historian Mary Ryan has noted, nineteenth-century American parades such as the Croton celebration or the Atlantic Cable parade presented a "detailed, descriptive portrait of the urban social structure." In the Croton Water parade, military and militia divisions "so stuffed up in their arms [that they] looked like the inverted antenae [*sic*] of strange insects" formed the matrix in which other citizens' groups were embedded. There were remnants of an older practice of parading in occupational groupings, in artisanal floats like those of the Typographical Society, the butchers, gold and silver artisans, a miller and his men, and ironworkers, but even here there was a hint of change. The ironworkers were employed by a single company, the Phoenix Foundry, while the typographers were accompanied by a float containing a new steam press. With it, W. L. Stone, Esq., printed and distributed to the crowd "The Croton Ode," a literary production the *Western World* thought "trashy" and "entirely unworthy of the occasion . . . a nauseating dose upon every one in whose hands it fell." There were also many "firemen & their red shirts," of course. The firemen were volunteers who performed a necessary civic service but, in the days before professionalization of fire departments, their companies also served as social organizations, and even gangs, and were often organized along ethnic lines. Other citizens marched as members of ethnic fraternities, of political action groups such as temperance societies, of "various benevolent societies . . . mostly made up of foreigners," and of other, less easily categorized, groups. At the rear were "citizens and strangers . . . in considerable numbers." These parades embodied Victor Turner's third kind of communitas, normative communitas, where "under the influence of time, the need to mobilize and organize resources, and the necessity for social control among the members of the group in pursuance of these goals, the existential communitas is organized into a perduring social system."[19]

Recently, scholars have emphasized the importance of such civic festivities in shaping political consciousness from the earliest years of the new nation's history. In parades, feasts, anniversary celebrations, dedications, statesmen's funerals, and other rituals, some officially sponsored but many more mounted by militias, voluntary organizations, and political parties, urbanites acted out the polity that they sought. The street was the primary arena of these activities, and the procession or parade perhaps its most important expression. Parades allowed participants to array themselves in an ideal order and to show themselves to a nearby audience. In contrast to a speech in a park or a dinner attended only by a segment of the population, everyone could see, and every vantage point was a good one.[20]

The street setting was critical to the interpretation of these rituals, for it supplied two fictions on which they were based. The first was that as a "public" place the street was a neutral space, which implied that any ritual that took place there was an image of a unified citizenry and its values, and that marchers and watchers were two parts of a single whole. The second fiction, following from this, was universality. Public and private accounts repeatedly stressed the near-perfect attendance of the population at parades. George Templeton Strong's belief that the "whole population of the City [was] in the street either as actors or participants" in William Henry Harrison's New York funeral was typical.[21]

By the time of the three New York parades, the composition of these processions had changed from their late-eighteenth-century form. Marchers increasingly organized themselves according to political, social, or ethnic identities rather than as members of trades, as they did in the first parades in the new nation. And, as we have seen in the New York celebrations, parade organizers became increasingly canny in their choice of parade routes. Yet the fiction of universal participation and public approbation was a constant.[22]

Parades were always political. Whatever the occasion, it was marked by and presented in relation to the body politic. While that body expanded over the years in certain ways, as more male urbanites were included, it also shrank in some ways. Elites withdrew from parades in the mid-nineteenth century, paralleling their withdrawal from local electoral politics: the increasingly working-class parade corps vividly figured the increasingly working-class electorate. But there were also constants, marked only by absence: women were rarely included in parades, and then only as the companions of men or as allegorical figures like the "24 young ladies, attired alike, representing the 24 STATES" who appeared in the Philadelphia parade that honored the Marquis de Lafayette's return to America in 1824. Blacks were almost always excluded, as were noncitizens and Native Americans. Natives appeared, like women, as embodied ideas. Unlike women, Indians were usually represented by non-Indians, a practice that dated back to prerevolutionary political agitation and that was revived in the Grand Federal Procession, held at Philadelphia on July 4, 1788, to celebrate the ratification of the Constitution. Spectators saw "*Peter Baynton, esq.* as a citizen, and Col. *Isaac Melchor,* as an Indian chief, in a carriage, smoking the calumet of peace together. The sachem magnificently dressed according to the Indian custom."[23]

Scrutinized more closely, however, parades lacked the sharp focus with which many historians credit them and the political or ideological unity that contemporary officials wished to project. Within any procession one might find marchers whose points of view modified, supplemented, or even contradicted the ostensible message of the parade. For example, a parade such as the Grand Federal Procession, which was organized around the hierarchical structure of Philadelphia's occupations and society, contained artisans whose own politics were considerably more egalitarian.[24]

In addition, parades were often the central elements of civic festivities whose edges were difficult to define. Formal public rituals were accompanied by private festivities and by amusements with little, if any, connection to civic purpose. Philadelphia diarist William B. Davidson complained of the ways July Fourth was observed in his city. The militia and the Society of Cincinnati organized ceremonies and parades, but "the mass of the people distinguish it by nothing except that such as are inclined to frolicking Spend the day in dissipation." Drunkenness, brawling, occasional riots and gang warfare, the detonation of private fireworks, and the private firing of guns ranging from pistols to small cannon on the Fourth provided the larger public context within which parades took place.[25]

Yet the fictions of public space were critical to large civic parades and even more so to smaller ones mounted by fragments of the population, particularly occupational groups and political parties. These criticized dominant political voices and equated their own cause with the general welfare. Some lower-class urbanites of many sorts staged parades that ridiculed the military tenor of civic processions and the exclusivity of the elite volunteer militias who formed the principal marching units in most civic processions. Political and occupational groups often adopted or parodied the paraphernalia of more general civic processions. On election day 1800 Elizabeth Drinker saw paraders draw a boat containing burning tar barrels through Philadelphia's streets, probably as an allusion to the ship of state included in the Grand Federal Procession of 1788 and as a comment on its plight under Federalist rule. Two decades later a self-promotional parade of the Philadelphia victuallers, recorded by the painter John Lewis Kimmel, also included a ship of state.[26]

If, as Ronald Grimes says, processions do "take possession . . . , thereby making visited space home space," they were also significant means of staking a claim to the public sphere. Ethnic and racial groups—the Irish, African Americans—political parties, trade associations, and religious bodies all held marches that played on the universalizing premise of the street parade. Black men in northern cities staged a variety of parades in the early nineteenth century, many celebrating emancipation in their states and implicitly claiming the full rights of citizenship that should accompany freedom. Paraders always dressed in their most elaborate and striking costumes, as if to make sure that no one overlooked them.[27]

In New Orleans, religious processions assured Roman Catholic visibility. Their parades on All Saints' Day moved from St. Louis Cathedral in the Vieux Carré to the cemeteries on the northern edge of town. On Mardi Gras, religious processions and maskers' parades similarly moved from the old city to the new. Observers always noted whether they crossed Canal Street into "American" territory and whether Protestant men violently drove them back into the Quarter. In 1847 Albert Pickett saw maskers on foot attacked by "scores of boys," who pelted them with sticks and mud and stripped one man of his female costume and mask.[28]

As the Mardi Gras maskers knew, paraders' legitimacy was likely to be challenged in ways that ranged at best from ridicule to mild resistance. During a New Orleans Catholic religious procession, the celebrants were "shoved and jostled by the crowd, who scarcely gave way to them." Often marchers met violent opposition from spectators. Paraders in any but the great civic processions could expect to fight their way through the streets. Thomas Cope saw the same "boat on fire" that Elizabeth Drinker did, as well as another parade of boys carrying lighted tapers in support of Israel Israel's candidacy for sheriff. "They were of the same party; neither being opposed, no disturbances ensued," he noted. The most widespread and varied abuse seems to have been directed toward blacks' processions. Genteel observers lampooned them in diaries, newspapers, and cartoons, while less restrained whites attacked marchers and often chased them for blocks through the city.[29]

Common threads ran through all these civic ceremonies, counter-ceremonies, and attacks that connect it with *The Smokers*. The first is that politics and the street were both male preserves. Marchers were men, and those who fought them were men, sometimes attended by flocks of boys. At issue in peaceable and violent contests was *which* men were to be admitted into the body politic. The second is that membership in the polity depended upon mustering the strength—the independence, antebellum Americans would say—to defend one's right to public space. Increasingly, as *The Smokers* claims, it was the hoi polloi who did that best.[30]

Clay's cartoon demonstrated that the political street mirrored the everyday street: the social relations enacted in the civic parade reified those that governed use of public space. The street was a white male space in which others struggled to claim a place. And it was increasingly a plebeian space.

The ideology of domesticity, which declared the home to be women's proper "sphere," became entrenched in respectable American society in the second quarter of the nineteenth century, but long before that men assumed that the street was their territory and felt free to comment to, or on, any women they saw there. In Philadelphia at the beginning of the nineteenth century, John Davis remarked on the group of young men who sat in front of the Indian Queen hotel, smoking and drinking punch, discussing their sexual exploits in Philadelphia brothels and in Charleston's Mulatto Alley, "unless some young lady (who, finding the pavement blockaded by their chairs, was compelled to walk in the carriage-road,) called forth the exclamation of 'That's a fine girl! So is that coming up the street now. There are no snakes if *Philadelphia* does not beat *Charleston* hollow!'" Thirty years later New York's city fathers felt compelled to appoint an inspector to prevent women's being "insulted or annoyed" by the language of Broadway stage drivers.[31]

Of course women were always present in public. Poor women had no choice: much of their livelihood depended on passing through or even working in the street. But they risked being judged and sometimes addressed as "public women," or prostitutes. As the domestic ideology took hold, however, a more aggressively articulated rationale for women's absence from public places attempted to drive "respectable" women home.[32]

Women, it was thought, did not have the physical or moral strength to defend themselves in public. Alone, they were subject to insults or simply to the approach of strangers. Male authorities claimed that women were out of place in public because their delicacy might be offended. Sidney George Fisher objected to charitable fairs as occasions where people "not in our society will take the opportunity to speak to these ladies & make their remarks upon them. There is something indelicate in the thing I think." A correspondent for *Niles' Weekly Register* seconded him: these fairs exposed women to "the coarse jokes and the vulgar gaze of those who ought never to approach her but with respect and deference."[33]

But domesticity was more than simple paternalism. It was not a feminine ideology but a *gendered* ideology: it grounded both women's and men's identities. True, women *were* the life of the home and the ceremonial centers of genteel family life. As the avatars of respectability's reticence, women were supposed to be the most cloistered members of the household. The girls in Mr. Picot's French School in Philadelphia, for example, were even forbidden to go near the windows, where they might be seen by passersby. However, through the designation of home as a feminine place, and through the identification of that place with personal identity, women were established as the ideal to which all genteel people, male and female, aspired. Women's fragility was exemplary of the easily wounded delicacy that genteel women and men both affected.[34]

As the foundation of respectability, the home's sanctity was closely guarded. British visitor Alexander Mackay compared the inclusivity of public life, the willingness of Americans to deal with others outside the home, with the exclusivity of home life. Using a spatial metaphor, Mackay observed that the American home was "fenced round by . . . lines. . . . The circle once drawn, it is not very easy for those without to transcend it." He thought Philadelphia the most exclusive of cities, the place where the "fashionables" were wariest of allowing strangers into their sanctuaries.[35]

As John Lewis Krimmel's *Sunday Morning*, with its Quaker family moving through the streets in familial array implies, genteel people effectively carried a bit of home with them into public, wrapping themselves in their privacy and wearing it through the neutral public channels of the urban grid until they reached another private node (see fig. 5.5). But by extension, to walk through the streets wrapped in the mantle of domestic privacy was to walk the streets as a woman. Men located themselves both inside and outside that feminized identity. As genteel men, they were as guarded in their public privacy as women were supposed to be. As gentle*men,* however, they also transcended and defended female gentility.

But this model is too simple to be left undisturbed. For one thing, the privacy of the street *was* public, and intentionally so. As historian Elizabeth Blackmar has noted, it was important to be seen being private, at least by one's peers. The performance of privacy was formalized in the promenade, a ritual in which the elite turned out in their finery at a specific time each day to stroll at a particular spot to see and be seen by each other. For another, this public privacy was matched by a private publicity in the home. Philadelphian Thomas Pym Cope made the point in an odd way, by comparing women to certain types of residences. Although they should be "guileless, dignified, modest," they should never pretend either "to a platonic purity which is void of all passions" or "make a display which may catch the libertine & invite aggression and insult." In other words, he said, a woman should neither resemble a cloister nor should she be "set open like apartments, to be occupied by any one who will pay the rent." The domestic equivalent of the promenade was the visit, particularly the New Year's Day visits that were an annual ritual in most large cities, including New York, Philadelphia, and New Orleans. Although "refreshments" were offered during these calls, the pace was too frenetic for much socializing. Women stayed home to receive visitors and men called at as many "temples of womankind" as possible, "scour[ing] the streets at a truly American pace, so as to lose as little time as possible on the way." In some cases, servants merely stood in the door and collected the cards of gentlemen as they raced past. The New Year's visitation was a processional marking of territory as much as any parade, one in which visitors assured themselves that all was as it should be domestically among their circle.[36]

The ideology of domesticity postulated that women were too delicate to venture into public, and they were judged for their failure to play that role, genteel women more harshly than ungenteel ones. Women who were "unwomanly" were particularly disturbing to male, and some female, observers. Actress Fanny Kemble's forcefulness repulsed Sidney George Fisher, who naturally described it in physical terms. Her "conversation and manner are too exaggerated & theatrical in company," her physique "powerful," and consequently "her whole appearance and bearing are the reverse of the feminine." Thomas Pym Cope happened upon Kemble one day when she was fishing in Chester County, Pennsylvania, dressed in a costume "having every outward appearance of a male . . . it seemed wonderful that she should thus outrage the accustomed laws of decorum among so plain a people," ostensibly meaning the country people, but referring equally to himself.[37]

Consequently, no concession was made to unescorted women's excursions into the public realm. Eliza Ripley recalled that during the 1850s there were "no restaurants, no lunch counters, no tea rooms and (bless their dear hearts, who started it!) no woman's exchange, no place in the city where a lady could drop in, after all this round of shopping, take a comfortable seat and order even a sandwich, or any kind of refreshment," even though there were many such facilities for men.[38]

Even conventionally respectable women chafed at the boundaries that enclosed them. As the nineteenth century wore on and retailers began to appeal to a female clientele, genteel women made more of a public show, although always singly or in very small groups. European visitors remarked on women's relative freedom of association and movement in the United States. One noted his surprise at the well-dressed women who frequented New York's Broadway shopping district unaccompanied by servants or chaperones. A North Carolinian visiting Philadelphia wrote home that "there is hardly a belle in the town who does not walk Chesnut [street] twice or three times during the day, and as soon as dark they begin with carriages which 'keep it up.'"[39]

Yet by intruding into public space, respectable women continued to risk being embarrassed by male stares and comments as they always had. "Are we to understand," asked *Godey's Magazine and Lady's Book* in 1853, "that no females traverse Chestnut Street [Philadelphia's most fashionable shopping street], day or night, morning or evening, but 'such as have thrown off the mask;' or who are willing to court the 'peril' of 'the most degrading vices, emboldened it would seem by the encouragement afforded to it by law?" And indeed Madaline Selima Edwards, a young woman living alone in New Orleans in the 1840s, was often the target of crude remarks and even sexual propositions from male passersby as she went about her daily round.[40]

The simple fact is that women were unwelcome in the male realm of the streets. Like other despised pedestrians, they were described as taking up too much space (fig. 12.2). In the 1850s, the decade of Eliza Ripley's young womanhood, the *New Orleans Bee* ridiculed women's presence in the commercial district with a set of satirical rules entitled "Advice to Ladies." They advised, "When you go out shopping, select a narrow street where it will be impossible for your charms to escape notice." Also, "If you discover your charms neglected, or if perchance you wish to display your fair proportions irresistably to some gentleman behind you, stop exactly in the middle of the banquette [sidewalk] to admire a picture or a gaudy dress in a shop window."[41]

A poem, "Old and New Times," published in a Philadelphia almanac of 1830, made it evident that women's boundaries were intended to protect men at least as much as women. Alluding to centuries-old ideas of women's brute, barely

FIGURE 12.2. James Baillie, *Inconvenience of Wearing Coffee Bag Skirts*, New York, 1848. (Library of Congress, Prints and Photographs Division)

INCONVENIENCE OF WEARING COFFEE BAG SKIRTS.

contained power that coexisted in the nineteenth century with notions of their putative frailty, the poet claimed that women's huge bonnets "fright / The beau that ventures nigh them," while their gowns were so large "They'll hold a dozen men; / And if you once get in their sleeves, / You'll ne'er get *out* again."[42]

The female public threat was even more extravagantly expressed in anti-prostitution crusader William W. Sanger's astonishing image of public females, used to illustrate the dimensions of prostitution in New York. Sanger imagined New York's six thousand prostitutes in a horrifying parody of a civic parade.

It requires a man who is in the habit of seeing large congregations of persons to comprehend at a single glance the aggregate implied in this statement. Place this number of women in line, side by side, and if each was allowed only twenty-four inches of room, they would extend two miles and four hundred and eighty yards. Let them march up Broadway in single file, and allow each woman thirty-six inches (and that is as little room as possible, considering the required space for locomotion), and they would reach from the City Hall to Fortieth Street. Or, let them ride in the ordinary city stages, which carry twelve passengers each, and it would be necessary to charter five hundred omnibuses for their convenience.

The images reveal more about the dimensions of Sanger's social paranoia than about the scope of prostitution in New York City. But most of all they confirm that a desire to preserve public space as a male domain lay behind the high-minded chivalric rhetoric.[43]

These were the terms on which the celebrated battle between General Benjamin Butler and certain upper-class women of New Orleans was fought in 1862. The women showed their resentment of Union occupation of the city by gathering up their skirts and turning away to prevent contact with passing soldiers. That is, they drew in their boundaries and refused to recognize the occupying soldiers as gentlemen. The northern press represented the women in just the opposite manner (fig. 12.3, left). Two women, their homely faces violently contorted, spit into the faces of nearby soldiers. Their body language, their postures, their boldly projecting Confederate flags, and of course their great arcs of spittle—the feminine analog of tobacco juice—all violate the boundaries of genteel self-presentation and of the soldiers themselves.[44]

On May 15, 1862, Butler issued his famous "Woman Order," technically General Order No. 28, which declared that his soldiers had "been subject to repeated insults from the women (calling themselves ladies) of New Orleans," and ordering that anyone proffering future insults would be "regarded and held liable to be treated as a woman of the town plying her avocation," that is, as a public

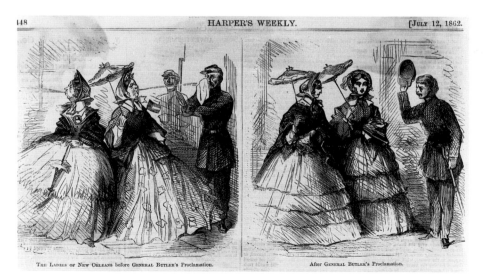

FIGURE 12.3. *The Ladies of New Orleans before General Butler's Proclamation./After General Butler's Proclamation,* 1862. (Courtesy Historic New Orleans Collection, Museum/Research Center, acc. no. 1974.25.9.35 i, ii)

woman—a prostitute. Butler later explained that he meant they would be ignored as beneath the notice of gentlemen. The women realized they had been beaten on their own terms, and although southern women and men made loud noises about avenging honor, they withdrew from the field. *Harper's Weekly*'s version of the post–Woman Order ladies of the city shows two comelier women, their postures and costumes more subdued, their faces more composed, as they accept the compliments of a Union soldier (fig. 12.3, right). The one hardcore Confederate who refused to back down, Eugenia Levy Phillips, already marked as a notorious spy and provocateur during an earlier residence in Washington, D.C., was the object of Butler's Special Order No. 150. Butler declined to treat her "as a common woman," but sentenced her to two years at the Ship Island prison camp in Mississippi as an "uncommon, bad, and dangerous woman," an affront whose force was exacerbated in her father's eyes by "Coming after the provoking notoreity [sic] of having her name a second time in the newspapers."[45]

In earlier decades, before New Orleans became heavily Americanized, women moved about somewhat more freely than did those in the North. Even in the 1830s Harriet Martineau observed that the ladies of New Orleans "walk more than their country-women of other cities" owing to the bad state of the streets, which made vehicular travel difficult.[46]

Travelers were particularly amazed by the mixed society of the levee. As early as 1801 New Yorker John Pintard complained about "noisey drunken labourers & sailors . . . Almost naked Indians—Negroes & Mulattoes . . . patrolling this walk & jostling against the ladies whose delicacy must often be offended at such disgusting sights—Custom however reconciles everything and the Creoles from early habitude do not discriminate with the nicety perhaps of my fair countrywomen. My own repugnance has diminished by becoming more familiar with what at first was very singular & shocking." This easy sociability among New Orleanians lay Crescent City women open to the same insinuations as their northern sisters, for it was a short step from thinking New Orleans's women hardened to the levee's social promiscuity to seeing them as willing participants in an undisguised "traffic de coeur," as Thomas Ashe called it, whose openness and ethnic profusion echoed the variety of the adjacent market. On the levee

> all the beauties assemble; and there all those who need the [quadroon] kind of companion joyfully repair; all walk up and down for a considerable time, or sit under orange-trees occasionally, with the objects of their separate choice. Such an expression of reserve, morals, and decency, reigns over the women of every sort, that a stranger passes and repasses, before he can as-

sume sufficiently to tell the one he admires the most *qu'elle est belle comme une ange,* and so forth. . . .

The mothers always regulate the terms and make the bargain. The terms allowed the parents are generally fifty dollars a month; during which time the lover has the exclusive right to the house, where fruit, coffee, and refreshments may at any time be had, or where he may entirely live with the utmost safety and tranquillity.

An Englishman required several visits to "surmount [his own] sense of virtue" enough to approach these women, Ashe claimed.[47]

Not all visitors accepted this often-repeated story or the implication of moral laxity that it conveyed. Both James Stuart and Harriet Martineau dismissed it, while William Darby argued that "divested of pre-conceived ideas on the subject [of morality], an observing man will find little to condemn in New Orleans." Nevertheless, Anglo-American readings of New Orleans's sociability epitomized a new American view of public space. The apparently free and easy common ground of the levee, unowned and unappropriated to individual use, deprived New Orleans of the careful spatial and functional sorting northerners had come to prize in a nineteenth-century city. Lacking clear boundaries, the levee was read as a scene of commercial and sexual expediency in a city without recognizable order. What at first seemed picturesque or merely annoying came to appear dangerous. Increasingly visitors stressed the sinister nature of promenaders, seeing the crowd as entirely male and hostile: "Every, or nearly every gentleman carried a sword cane, apparently, and occasionally the bright hilt of a Spanish knife, or dirk, would gleam for an instant in the moon-beams from the open bosom of its possessor, as, with the lowering brow, and active tread of wary suspicion, he moved rapidly by us. . . . In groups—promenading, lounging, and sleeping upon the seats along the Levée—we passed several hundred of this canaille of Orleans."[48]

Outsiders' uneasiness on the levee arose from their home experience as respectable men. The paradox of gentility, as we have seen, is that as men carried the values of domesticity into the street their own demeanor was, by the canons of nineteenth-century masculinity, feminized. Their respectability, like women's, was endangered by the crowds of the poor, the foreign-born, and the ungenteel who increasingly filled the streets, and who took possession of everyday spaces as they did political space.

To self-confined genteel people, the city seemed socially and physically claustrophobic. They complained bitterly about the ways that their neighbors infringed their newly drawn boundaries. They held at arm's length the "vulgar,

FIGURE 12.4. John Lewis Krimmel, *"Worldly Folk" Question Chimney Sweeps and Their Master*, 1811–ca. 1813. An uncomfortable meeting between a genteel white couple and a black chimney sweep and his young assistants on Second Street, Philadelphia, near Christ Church. (Metropolitan Museum of Art, New York, Rogers Fund, 1942 42.95.15)

nouveau riche people who are now crowding into society," and ordinary neighbors seemed even more distasteful, yet it was increasingly difficult to avoid them. The streets were filled not only with the catalogue of "types" that antebellum journalists and genre artists loved to catalogue, but with real people of many sorts, many shabbily dressed and barely surviving on the livelihoods they could win there (plate 14, fig. 12.4). They were not shy about accosting their betters when it served their purposes, and they often stationed themselves at places where they were most likely to be able to do so. Beggars clustered near the doorways of fashionable hotels and the stoops of elite houses. Vendors and hucksters planted themselves where they were likely to encounter the most traffic (see plate 2). Omnibus and cab drivers parked near genteel places of assembly such as Park Row, adjacent to The Park in New York and the fashionable

Park Theater, or outside the University of Pennsylvania and Peale's Museum in Philadelphia. A journalist complained of the "impertinent importunity, which every one must undergo who has the temerity to pass" the Park Row cabbies. "Their last persecutor is the fellow seated on the box of the foremost carriage, a compliance with the law which very few of them will imitate. His face is turned toward the exquisite, with a sardonic grin, which seems to say, 'You are no gentleman, bad luck to ye, or ye'd give the famale a sate in my carriage. No lady ever walks out in my country, unless she rides in a coach.'" That the driver was apparently an Irish immigrant exacerbated the offense.[49]

A draft petition to the Philadelphia city council offered more general objections. The presence of cabs in places "which have been the accustomed and favourite promenades of Strangers and of the female part of our population . . . are undoubtedly a *Very great nuisance*—even altho the Cab drivers may be a decent and orderly Set of people." The drivers stood on the sidewalk, thus "the *footway* is almost entirely occupied by a description of persons calculated by their [illegible] to deter ladies and respectable strangers who visit our City, from walking in such parts of the metropolis." The last passage replaced the crossed-out line "occupied and rendered filthy by the accumulation of Saliva and other offensive matter." "It is not pleasant," the author (probably Edward Shippen Burd) went on, "for every foot-passenger, whether Gentleman or Lady, promenading in Such a part of Philadelphia, either for exercise, or on a visit to a Building where the fine arts are being exhibited, to be perpetually Saluted by a Cab driver with the question 'Do You want a Cab?' or to Come in Contact with their horses and Vehicles." He wanted the cabbies moved away from the university and the museum.[50]

The eagerness for work that prompted these encounters was mixed with a less-articulated ethnic or class hostility that sometimes surfaced openly. It was not uncommon for lower-class urbanites, even those with much to lose, to challenge their social superiors in the streets. The *New York Tribune Semi-Weekly* reported that on New Year's Day in 1853, when gentlemen were out in great numbers visiting their peers, "certain gangs of short boys and other rowdies . . . banded together, in some instances in droves of thirty or forty, and took possession of the sidewalks, driving respectable people into the gutters. . . . Broadway was in full possession of these fellows and their kindred."[51]

It was a short step from being repelled by one's new neighbors to assuming that they were all criminals. One-time New York mayor George Templeton Strong described New York streets filled with "hordes of dock thieves—& of children who live in the streets & by them—no one can walk the length of Broadway without meeting some hideous troop of ragged girls, from 12 years old down—brutalized almost beyond redemption by premature vice—clad in the filthy refuse of the rag-pickers collections, obscene of speech, the stamp of child-hood gone from their faces, hurrying along with harsh laughter, & foulness on their lips that some of them have learned by wrote . . . with thief written in their cunning eyes—& whore on their degraded faces. . . . On a rainy day such crews may be seen by dozens." Fire alarms brought out crowds of equally ragged boys, "some packed away with old newspapers into their fathers' boots, others bare-foot and hatless, and others with the stumps of cigars in their mouths, which they have picked up about the purlieus of Frankfort-street." Strong's language is telling. Like many of his class and education, he saw streets filled not with poor people but with criminals.[52]

Demeanor that the genteel read as uninhibited, uncouth, or even criminal could be read equally easily as an expression of comfort with, and a sense of be-longing in, the mixed society of the antebellum street. If we view *The Smokers* from the view point *of* the smokers, rather than from that of the two women, we see something very different from the reading I offered in the first pages of this chapter: a varied group of people appear to enjoy their tobacco and to be confident of their rights to smoke and to foul as much air as they please. Nor is there any indication that any of the smokers feels imposed upon by any of the others, although each one partakes of a different form of tobacco. Each is self-possessed, many appear self-absorbed, all are self-confident. Only the women and the dog are offended.

So an English visitor to New York in the 1820s saw the ever-present tobacco smoking and spitting as a sign of a free country. Lady Emmeline Stuart Wort-ley was surprised that in the shadow of the "Cradle of Liberty," Faneuil Hall, Bostonians submitted so meekly to antismoking regulations. An engraving of the *Smokers' Circle, on Boston Common* depicts a circle of benches that accom-modates a crowd of socializing tobacco addicts, while in the foreground sev-eral more lounge on the grass (fig. 12.5). All are men and all emit great clouds of smoke. Although they appear to be well-dressed, their smoking and their pos-tures reveal these men as people unconstrained, at least for the moment, by the mutual deference that polite behavior demanded.[53]

Harriet Martineau, an English visitor to New Orleans who was at pains to dismiss travelers' most common stereotypes of the Crescent City's ordinary and non-English-speaking inhabitants, sensed something different in the ungen-teel urban masses that other observers of her class were unable or unwilling to see. Her account of a Sunday evening walk stressed the spatial expansiveness of that city's sociability: "In the market there is traffic in meat and vegetables, and the groups of foreigners make a Babel of the place with their loud talk in many tongues. The men are smoking outside their houses; the girls, with broad

FIGURE 12.5. *Smokers' Circle, on Boston Common*, 1851. (Library of Congress, Prints and Photographs Division)

coloured ribands streaming from the ends of their long braids of hair, are walking or flirting. . . . The river is crowded with shipping. . . . The quivering summer lightning plays over the heads of the merry multitude, who are conversing in all the tongues, and gay in the costumes of the world."[54]

Even in the Five Points, New York's most notorious antebellum slum, one journalist claimed, "The streets swarm with men, women and children sitting down. The negro girls with their bandanna turbans, the vicious with their gay-coloured allures, the sailors tired of pleasures ashore, the various 'minions of the moon' drowsing the day away—they are all out in the sun, idling, jesting, quarrelling, everything but weeping or sighing, or complaining. . . . A viler place than the Five Points by daylight you could not find, yet to the superficial eye, it is the merriest quarter of New-York. I am inclined to think that care is a gentleman, and frequents good society chiefly."[55]

South Carolinian William Bobo agreed. He compared the "pale and sickly beings who pace languidly" along New York's genteel shopping street, Broadway, with the heartier specimens, the men and women who inhabited its livelier "democratic rival," the Bowery. The "b'hoy" could be recognized by "the good big cigar placed in his mouth at the proper angle to express perfect content with himself and perfect indifference to all the rest of the world [which] put the last and finishing touch" on his appearance (see fig. 5.10). He was "a fair politician, a good judge of horse flesh . . . and renders himself essentially useful, as well as ornamental, at all the fires in his ward." Compared to this engaging specimen, the genteel milquetoast found on Broadway was "not only a fop but a ninny, knows about as much of what is going on out of the very limited circle of his lady friends, as a child ten years old." *His* cigar smoking was limited to a single cigar after dinner, after which this emasculated dandy visited a lady friend "if he should be lucky enough to have one."[56]

The b'hoy seemed at least as enviable as he was fearsome, then, but most of all he was at home in the city. The Broadway stroller knew few people except those in his immediate circle, but the b'hoy "speaks to every acquaintance he meets, and is hail-fellow-well-met with every body, from the mayor to the beggar."[57]

The sense of plebeian agency and entitlement is evident in the portrait of *Two of the Killers,* the Philadelphia street gang (see fig. 5.9). The young men appear relaxed and confident as they stand on the curb. Indeed, nineteenth-century viewers would recognize that the Killers were depicted in their native habitat, like the zoological specimens in Peale's Museum. Posters on the wall advertise grocery stores where one could drink hard liquor, disreputable amusements such as a circus and a minstrel show, and an auction, which many conservative people thought unethical. Even the fireplug was telling: until the professionalization of firefighting in the 1850s, Philadelphia's overabundant fire companies were often little more than ethnic gangs, excuses for young men to gather together and fight rival companies, whom they often lured into combat by setting fires at strategic places. The Killers were connected with the Irish Catholic Moyamensing Hose Company, whom they escorted to fires, and they were fond of battling native Protestant gangs and fire companies as well as African Americans, invading their rivals' territory when their rivals were afraid to enter theirs. In fact they were widely acknowledged to be the fiercest gang of all. Their field of operations encompassed the entire range of everyday and political uses of the street. They acted on the immigrant Catholic side of all the formal and informal, peaceful and violent clashes of the 1840s and 1850s. They fought for their religion, for their ethnicity, for their territory, and for the fun of it. In the peculiarly gendered world of the mid-nineteenth-century city, they epitomized politicized manhood.[58]

The genteel could do little to turn back the lower-class conquest of the streets. Tellingly, their first response was to legislate street behavior. Since public smoking was ostensibly a habit of the rough-hewn, antismoking laws were favorite tools to drive them out of public spaces where they were not wanted. A Philadelphia ordinance forbade "any person to smoke a segar or segars, pipe or pipes, in any of the public squares, or during market hours in any of the market houses." As a pastime that expanded the smoker's personal space into the passerby's, smoking was an aggressive act that violated the genteel code of getting along and giving no offense and created a connection among people who might otherwise have avoided one another. Its connotation of equality and social presence, evoked so vividly in *The Smokers*, helps to explain ordinances in cities such as Richmond and New Orleans that forbade African Americans to smoke in public. In the Crescent City, the reason given was that blacks were careless with their butts and likely to start fires, but one newspaper observed that no small part of the reason was "the offensiveness to some, of coming into contact with a negro's cigar puff."[59]

In effect these rules imposed the codes of polite domestic behavior on public space. Gentlemen refrained from using tobacco around women. Alexander Mackay thought that other travelers were guilty of exaggeration in claiming that tobacco use "is a habit indiscriminately practised under all circumstances." It had not, he claimed, invaded "the sanctuary of private society": "I never yet saw any one, in the presence of ladies, violate with the practice the decorum of the drawing-room." That men felt free to smoke and chew everywhere else, including the streets, public transportation, and government buildings, emphasized the masculinity of these spaces.[60]

Self-defined respectable urbanites eventually realized that it was futile to try to gentrify the street, and they withdrew from the field. The social satirist Francis Grund was amused to see the New York gentry abandon attractive promenading grounds such as the Battery to avoid the hoi polloi. "The people follow their inclinations and occupy what they like; while our exclusives are obliged to content themselves with what is abandoned by the crowd." Instead, the genteel turned their efforts to creating more exclusive, feminized public spaces where the rules of home could be enforced. Parks became the genteel alternative to the streets.[61]

Beginning in the 1810s and intensifying in the 1840s and 1850s, every city fitted up one or more of its public squares as a promenading ground for the genteel. In New York it was Bowling Green, although a private park, St. John's Square, served some of the same purposes (see fig. 5.4). In Philadelphia it was State House Yard (Independence Square), later supplemented by Washington Square, the southeast square of the original city plan. Washington Square had been a potter's field and a revolutionary burial ground, as well as a site for African American gatherings similar to the more famous ones in New Orleans's Congo Square. In 1802, some Philadelphians made a request to plant two rows of trees along the Walnut Street side of the square for "public walks." Efforts to adapt the square to genteel promenading were made again in 1805 and again in 1816. Finally in 1816–17 George Bridport laid out new paths and Andrew Gillespie planted trees in the square. It was renamed in honor of George Washington in 1825 and soon became a favorite promenading spot (see fig. 5.8). An iron palisade in the late 1830s emphasized the square's separation from the adjacent streets.[62]

At the center of the eight-acre tract, a 120-foot circle was connected by diagonals to the street. These walks were fitted with smaller circles where they intersected. Tree-lined walks paralleled the sides 25 feet from the street and screened the central circle from the street. The park was legally protected from the lower orders by ordinances forbidding putatively lower-class amusements such as smoking, walking or lying on the grass, climbing the trees, or bringing horses, cows, carts, or wheelbarrows (or carriages) into the park. Washington Square's plan was typical of the newly gentrified squares, and it was key to their success. The gentry preferred to move slowly and quietly in small, self-contained groups in a manner that became ritualized in the promenade (plate 15). The circular walk permitted promenaders to stroll away from the street and, equally important, to watch one another obliquely without violating the genteel prohibition against staring directly at another person.[63]

New Orleans followed a more torturous path to the same goal. As the European urban habit of promenading spread through the upper levels of urban society in many parts of the European-dominated world after the eighteenth century, New Orleans found itself with no gardens, squares, boulevards, or other traditional promenading grounds. The city's oldest public square, the place d'armes (renamed Jackson Square in 1851), abutted the levee, with St. Louis Cathedral, the Cabildo, and the Presbytère lined up facing it on the opposite side. However, it was unsuitable for genteel social purposes owing to its crude landscaping and workaday uses, while the city was hemmed in by earthenwork fortifications and surrounded by swamps and fields that left little space around the edges for informal socializing. For a brief time, "lanes formed of trees and serving as public walks" had been laid out inside the upriver ramparts, but this land was granted to private builders in 1797 and lost to public use. Thus the levee was the only place available for promenading, and orange trees (later Melia Azedarach or "Pride of China" trees) were planted along the downriver portion of the Vieux Carré to enhance the setting (plate 16). After the demolition of the fortifications, Canal, Rampart, and Esplanade streets were laid out on their sites as tree-lined "Promenade[s] Publique[s]," but the levee remained the favored place of resort.[64]

New Orleanians's eyes turned toward the place d'armes as a substitute, but it remained a rough-hewn parade ground used for public executions and mass spectacles, and as a kind of informal marketplace. Intermittent efforts to fence and improve it throughout the antebellum years usually failed, but a major

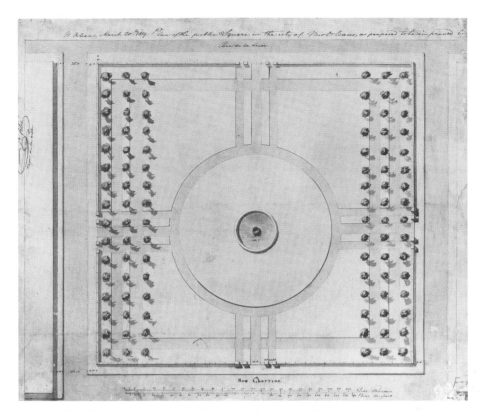

FIGURE 12.6. Benjamin Henry Latrobe, landscape plan for the place d'armes,
New Orleans, 1819. (City of New Orleans)

renovation in 1819–20 installed a stone-based iron fence and landscaping by city engineer Joseph Pilié, who was assisted by suggestions from Benjamin Henry Latrobe. Latrobe was also commissioned to design a fountain for the center and to redesign the cathedral's facade (fig. 12.6). At the same time, the vendors who had booths inside the place d'armes were warned to vacate.[65]

A quarter-century later the square had fallen back into the levee's orbit. In 1846 New Yorker A. Oakey Hall noted the remnants of the Pilié-Latrobe beautification: "a very neat railing, one or two respectable aged trees, a hundred or two blades of grass, a dilapidated fountain, a very naked flag-staff. . . . It has a water view, and with a judicious expenditure of a few thousand dollars might be made an inviting promenade; it is now but a species of cheap lodging-house for arriving emigrants, drunken sailors, and lazy stevedores; and occasionally the review ground of the most forlorn looking body of military . . . I have seen outside a New England village upon 'training day'" (fig. 12.7). In sum, Hall claimed, the name "Place des Armes may be freely translated 'the beggar's retreat.'"[66]

Four years after Hall's visit the square was improved a final time. The Bar-

FIGURE 12.7. X. Magny, *Ancienne Cathedrale*, New Orleans, ca. 1850. Magny's view shows the place d'armes at the beginning of its gentrification and transformation into Jackson Square. The 1849 remodeling of the Cabildo (left) and Presbytère (right), with mansard roofs and belfries, has taken place, but the eighteenth-century cathedral still shows the results of its remodeling in 1819 and 1824 by Latrobe and Antoine Leriche. In 1851, it was remodeled to assume its present form. The only visible remnant of Joseph Pilié's 1819 redesign of the place is the iron fence in the background. (Courtesy Historic New Orleans Collection, Museum/Research Center, acc. no. 1957.39)

oness Micaela Almonester de Pontalba, whose family had dominated New Orleans in the late Spanish regime, constructed two rows of houses with ground-floor shops along two sides of the place. To complement them, the city redesigned the square with the customary circular walks and replanted it, erected a new fence, and added a statue of Andrew Jackson. The Cabildo and the Presbytère were updated with new mansard roofs and the cathedral facade was modernized again, creating the genteel square we now know (plate 17). Nevertheless, the gentrification of the newly named Jackson Square was effected only a few feet from the levee, which intruded into the realm of gentility as much as the old place d'armes had remained within the realm of the working levee. To people convinced of the necessity of clear social and spatial order, of separation and classification in all things, this mixture of people and activities on New Orleans's riverfront still appeared morally suspect.[67]

The gentrification of small parks and squares in the first half of the nineteenth century culminated in the construction of New York's Central Park beginning in 1858, where long lists of rules posted at the park's entrances claimed the space for genteel behavior, if not for the gentry exclusively. By the mid-nineteenth century, city people had effectively created a dual, gendered urban landscape. The masculinized world of the streets, the docks, and the financial district was opposed to the feminized world of the respectable home and the gentrified public space. Both men and women inhabited both realms, but the gendered conceptions of behavior that distinguished the rough-hewn and the genteel shaped expectations and interpretations of what went on in each.[68]

{ **CONCLUSION**

Two favorite Philadelphia lithographs bring this work to a close. The first is a trade card for Charles Oakford's Hat and Cap Store at 104 Chestnut Street, drawn by James Queen and printed by P. S. Duval, two of the Quaker City's most prolific antebellum lithographers (plate 18). Oakford's store is an early-nineteenth-century commercial building with a pair of bulk windows flanking the door, but the muntins have been removed and replaced with large plates of glass, newly available at mid-century. They show us the full range of Oakford's wares, some of which are illustrated around the margin. The text emphasizes Oakford's stylish currency and the elite status of his wares: he supplies headgear for army and naval officers, as well as "gentlemen's fashionable hats & dress caps." In his newly refurbished store, stocked with the latest and finest goods, Oakford seems to stand squarely within mid-century consumer culture. Looking more closely at the storefront, we see a lonely-looking man, presumably the proprietor, peering out at an empty street. There could be no more eloquent image of the republican spatial and the genteel personal ideals: "There in their little cells, divided by partitions of brick and board, they sit strangers," as Thomas Carlyle said of London during this era. Yet the image is not as straightforward as that, for Oakford also advertises "Plain Hats for Friends wear" and assures potential customers that "This Branch of the Manufactures is conducted by an old and experienced Workman," invoking an earlier business ethos.[1]

The second view, published at about the same time, is very different (plate 19). The architectural setting is similar to that in Oakford's trade card. Brick houses of similar size and shape, mostly converted to commercial uses, line High (Market) and Front streets. The market, its merchants and customers gathered in small groups, is equally orderly. But the pig in the foreground is of a different mind. Pursued by a knife-waving Quaker butcher, the porker bowls over one after another of the genteel passersby. Two cats have climbed a hitching post at the left to clear the way, while a bemused match seller, liquor bottle in his pocket, looks on from the right. If Charles Oakford is a melancholy exemplar of republican and genteel ideals, this cartoon, in its good-humored way, reminds us of the ways that those ideals were constantly upended in the antebellum street.

The specific social and political conditions that gave these two pictures meaning were seriously eroded by 1850, along with many of the urban practices and forms that characterized it. This is not to say that systematization, rationalization, or classification vanished after the middle of the century. They gained importance as urban strategies in the second half of the nineteenth century and much of the twentieth. Vaster cities demanded even more complex systems of public works, public transportation, and public utilities to manage them, and they inspired ever more grandiose ways of thinking about them. Intellectually, the modernist notion of the functional city was an heir of the Enlightenment rationalism of the republican spatial imagination. But a significant change had occurred by the mid-nineteenth century. The elite who imagined a republican city of hierarchically organized but essentially similar citizens had begun to abandon their project of optimistic repression. Occasionally they questioned their right even to conduct it. In the 1830s, Philadelphia County built a prison in Moyamensing (the working-class district south of Philadelphia, home of the Killers) to hold minor criminals and debtors, as well as vagrants and other poor Philadelphians. In 1848, at the height of the city's lower-class turbulence, the inspectors of the prison asked the state legislature whether laws against vagrancy, disturbing the peace, disorderly conduct, and other urban annoyances were not "altogether indefinite, and of questionable legality; and it is submitted that great injustice might be done, and certainly often is practiced, against a miserable and destitute class of persons, whose condition renders them unable to vindicate their rights." Compare that to the words written thirty years earlier by John Ely, head of the Quaker-run Adelphi school for poor black boys: poor children were a "kind of vermin in society, which, if they cannot be reformed, should be removed from the streets, as the wheel-barrow-men [vendors] were."[2]

The inspectors of the Philadelphia County Prison were unusual, at least according to the written record. Most urban elites simply gave up. Therapeutic institutions such as asylums, schools, and orphanages—institutions that had their roots in medieval religious charity—became holding tanks for outcasts. Philanthropists turned their attention to libraries, museums, and colleges, institutions that ostensibly benefited everyone, but that were in fact carefully organized to discourage patronage by the lower orders. Entrance standards for colleges required the knowledge of arcane subjects not taught in public schools. New codes of etiquette like those instituted in promenading grounds were enforced in formerly raucous theaters, creating a division between those with a refined clientele and those that catered to the masses. Public art galleries, which were conceived by civic-minded philanthropists at the beginning of the nineteenth century to educate republican citizens, began to charge admissions, or raise admissions, to "preserv[e] the rooms from the intrusion of disreputable persons." A critic advised the opera conductor at New York's Academy of Music not to bother trying to please the patrons in the galleries, since those in the parquet and dress circles were much more capable of appreciating his work. He compared an "admiration for fine bearing on the street, for high-born features or noble-gifted" to "superior judgment, a vigorous intellect, and ambition with deep-moved feeling" and concluded that "the *elite* of society . . . are ever the patrons of genuine art."[3]

All of this seems very distant from our present circumstances, but it shouldn't. Although the republican urban landscape has been decimated by time, and the social and political ideas that built it have for the most part disappeared, eerie echoes of the world of two hundred years ago are often heard. We hear the ghost of John Haviland when the Eggers Group of architects proposes turning old-fashioned grain elevators into prisons because "grain elevators have several qualities that make them ideal for conversion to correction use." Their semicircular forms would permit the use of central control points "from which all cells could be viewed." "New Jails Breaking Down Old Habits" promised the *New York Times*, channeling Roberts Vaux. As contemporary Americans debate waterboarding, "stress positions," and other forms of torture, nineteenth-century showering, gags, and mad chairs remind them that such abuses are, to paraphrase H. Rap. Brown, as American as cherry pie.[4]

The ways we talk about urban public space are an even more obvious legacy of the antebellum years. Residents of a New York hotel echoed Stephen Girard when they complained about CBS's use of a public plaza to stage its shows: "They've simply annexed a public space for private profit, and that's wrong," says a Harvard planning professor. The streets continue to be battlegrounds between the refined and the rude, or "rowdy," as nineteenth-century Americans would have called them. Building owners in Center City Philadelphia installed curbside bollards to drive away vendors and claim the sidewalk as their own. Two years later the city entered the conflict with a proposed bill to regulate the number of vendors and their places of business. "The largely white business establishment" supported the proposed ordinance, the newspapers reported, but the Chamber of Commerce thought it too lenient. The bill was expected to be opposed by "lower- and middle-class voters," while an association of African American vendors denounced it as a racist attempt to drive them off the streets.[5]

As in the nineteenth century, then, Americans continue to experience the meaning of the civic through everyday encounters with others. Visually and materially based judgments about personal space, security, conflict, or simply comfort govern our decisions about where to visit, where to shop, where to play. "It seems to me that the right of free speech is counterbalanced by the right of

Americans not to be accosted unnecessarily on the streets," writes a New Yorker, echoing his early-nineteenth-century predecessors. "Panhandlers—whether for themselves or for charities—may legitimately be barred from intruding on the privacy of passers-by."[6]

These attitudes are more than anachronistic curiosities. The issues that they addressed in the early decades of the republic remain alive, but the implications or the now-vanished social practices and political theories that grounded them are no longer clearly understood. What the sociologist Henri Lefebvre called the "right to the city" is at stake. Who has the right to do what in public, and who decides? In recent years urban governments have worked to recapture the streets for the gentry under the rubric "quality of life." Businesses that offend middle-class sensibilities are outlawed. Benches, street furniture, and other amenities are removed or altered to make them useless for sleeping or skateboarding. New Orleans undertook such a program and at the same time, despite deriving much of its tourist income from its reputation as a hotbed of African American music, also began to ticket street musicians. It was a "quality of life" issue, said city council member Jacquelyn Clarkson. "I took my cue from [Rudolph] Giuliani," who, as mayor of New York, strove to turn the city into a fusion of Rodeo Drive and Devil's Island.[7]

Distaste for urban neighbors has long been a staple of American urban politics. Since 2001 it has morphed into a more generalized, easily manipulated fear. Restriction of the public rights of the homeless, vendors, teenagers, and other marginal members of the economy has laid the groundwork for a level of control over public buildings and spaces and private-public spaces (office lobbies, shopping malls) that few Americans would have accepted thirty years ago or, indeed, in the early nineteenth century.[8] Unaccountable authorities create unexamined and often unpublished regulations, expecting unquestioning obedience whenever they mutter the word "security" (plate 20). Optimistic repression and the battle for the street continue.

APH   Archives of Pennsylvania Hospital. Originals at the hospital; microfilm at APS.

APS   American Philosophical Society, Philadelphia

Cope   Thomas P. Cope, *Philadelphia Merchant: The Diary of Thomas P. Cope, 1800–1851,* ed. Eliza Cope Harrison. South Bend, Ind.: Gateway, 1978.

Drinker   Elizabeth Drinker, *The Diary of Elizabeth Drinker,* ed. Elaine Forman Crane. 3 vols. Boston: Northeastern University Press, 1991.

Fisher   Sidney George Fisher, *A Philadelphia Perspective: The Diary of Sidney George Fisher Covering the Years 1834–1871,* ed. Nicholas B. Wainwright. Philadelphia: Historical Society of Pennsylvania, 1967.

HC   Heartman Collection of Manuscripts of Slavery, XUL

HNOC   Historic New Orleans Collection

HP   John Haviland Papers, Van Pelt Library, University of Pennsylvania

HRP   *Hazard's Register of Pennsylvania* (later *Register of Pennsylvania*)

HSP   Historical Society of Pennsylvania

JSAH   *Journal of the Society of Architectural Historians*

Latrobe, *Corr.*   Benjamin Henry Latrobe, *The Correspondence and Miscellaneous Papers of Benjamin Henry Latrobe,* ed. John C. Van Horne and Lee W. Formwalt. 3 vols. New Haven: Yale University Press for the Maryland Historical Society, 1984–88.

Latrobe, *Jnls.*   Benjamin Henry Latrobe, *The Journals of Benjamin Henry Latrobe,* ed. Edward C. Carter II, John C. Van Horne, and Lee W. Formwalt. 3 vols. New Haven: Yale University Press, 1977–80.

LC   Library of Congress

LCP   The Library Company of Philadelphia

LH   *Louisiana Historical Quarterly / Louisiana History*

MAC   Anthony N. B. Garvan, Cynthia Koch, Donald Arbuckle, and Deborah Hart, eds., *The Mutual Assurance Company Papers,* vol. 1: *The Architectural Surveys 1784–1794.* Philadelphia: Mutual Assurance Company, 1976.

NOA   Friends of the Cabildo, *New Orleans Architecture,* various authors and eds. 8 vols. to date. Gretna: Pelican, 1971– .

NOCVa   New Orleans, Resolutions and ordinances of the Conseil de Ville (French version). Microfilm, Library of Congress photoduplication service, 1949.

NOCVb   New Orleans, Resolutions and ordinances of the Conseil de Ville (English translation). Microfilm, NOPL.

NOMP/T   New Orleans Municipal Papers, TUL Manuscripts Division

N.O. Ord.   *Ordinances Ordained and Established by the Mayor and Council of the City of New-Orleans.* New Orleans: J. C. de St. Romes, 1817.

NOPL	New Orleans Public Library
NYHS	New-York Historical Society
Penn, *Papers*	William Penn, *The Papers of William Penn,* ed. Richard S. Dunn and Mary Maples Dunn. 5 vols. Philadelphia: University of Pennsylvania Press, 1982.
PHC	Philadelphia Historical Commission
Phila. Ord.	Charles A. Poulson, John Trucks, and Saunders Lewis, comps., *Ordinances of the Corporation of, and Acts of Assembly Relating to the City of Philadelphia.* Philadelphia: Crissy & Markley, 1851.
PMHB	*Pennsylvania Magazine of History of Biography*
SGP	Henri de St.-Gême Papers, HNOC
SHC	Southern Historical Collection, University of North Carolina, Chapel Hill
TUL	Tulane University Library, New Orleans
VP	Roberts Vaux Papers, HSP
Watson I	John Fanning Watson, *Annals of Philadelphia.* Philadelphia: Uriah Hunt, 1830.
Watson II	John Fanning Watson, *Annals of Philadelphia and Pennsylvania, in the Olden Time.* 1860 ed. 2 vols. Philadelphia: J. B. Lippincott, 1868.
Watson III	John Fanning Watson, *Annals of Philadelphia, and Pennsylvania, in the Olden Time*, enlarged by Willis P. Hazard. 3 vols. Philadelphia: Edwin S. Stuart, 1905.
Watson MS	John Fanning Watson, *Annals of Philadelphia* ["Manuscript Annals"], MS, 1829, HSP
WMQ	*William and Mary Quarterly*
XUL	Xavier University Library, New Orleans

1. "Great Cities," *Putnam's Monthly Magazine* 5, no. 27 (Mar. 1855): 256–57.

2. Joyce Appleby, *Liberalism and Republicanism in the Historical Imagination* (Cambridge: Harvard University Press, 1992), p. 298; Daniel Walker Howe, *Making the American Self: Jonathan Edwards to Abraham Lincoln* (Cambridge: Harvard University Press, 1997), p. 12; Joyce Appleby, *Capitalism and a New Social Order: The Republican Vision of the 1790s* (New York: New York University Press, 1984), pp. 14–15. The term republicanism (with a lower-case r), used here to signify the widespread complex of political ideas discussed in the following paragraphs, should not be confused with uppercase Republicanism, signifying a specific political movement in 1770s and 1780s Pennsylvania, or with the Republican party, which was organized after my story ends.

3. Paul Boyer, *Urban Masses and Moral Order in America, 1820–1920* (Cambridge: Harvard University Press, 1978), pp. 1–5, 30–33, 54–55.

4. Anthony P. Cohen, *Self-Consciousness: An Alternative Anthropology of Identity* (London: Routledge, 1994), pp. 23–32, 56–57.

5. Edward T. Hall, *The Hidden Dimension* (Garden City, N.Y.: Anchor, 1966, 1969), p. 44.

6. [James Mease], "A Brief Sketch of the Origin and Present State of Philadelphia," *Port Folio* 5, no. 13 (Apr. 6, 1805): 98; Watson I, 312; Richard Webster, *Philadelphia Preserved: Catalog of the Historic American Buildings Survey*, 2d ed. (Philadelphia: Temple University Press, 1981), p. 97; *NOA* 2: 39.

7. William John Murtagh, "The Philadelphia Row House," *JSAH* 16, no. 4 (Dec. 1957): 8–13; Kenneth Ames, "Robert Mills and the Philadelphia Row House," *JSAH* 26, no. 2 (May 1968): 140–46; Donna J. Rilling, *Making Houses, Crafting Capitalism: Builders in Philadelphia, 1790–1850* (Philadelphia: University of Pennsylvania Press, 2001), pp. viii–ix.

8. "Proceedings of Councils," *HRP* 13, no. 6 (Feb. 8, 1834): 85; Thomas S. Stewart Ledger, 1829– , MS, n.p., Thomas S. Stewart Papers, Athenaeum of Philadelphia.

9. For example, the Franklin Institute (1825) rented one floor of its building for use as court rooms, the Mercantile Library (ca. 1845) let offices in its building, the Merchants' Exchange (1832–34) rented the ground floor to the post office and to individual merchants, and the Athenaeum (1845–47) rented the ground floor of its building to the Controllers of the Public Schools and to an attorney, and the third floor to the Historical Society of Pennsylvania, retaining the second floor for its own use (John Haviland, draft letter to Thomas P. Cope, ca. Dec. 1844, HP, 4: 192–93; Cope, pp. 500, 503; R. A. Smith, *Philadelphia as It Is, in 1852* [Philadelphia: Lindsey and Blakiston, 1852], p. 199).

10. "Monumental Structures," *New-York Mirror* 7 (Dec. 12, 1829): 183.

11. Demetri Porphyrios, "Notes on a Method," in *On the Methodology of Architectural History*, ed. Demetri Porphyrios (London: Architectural Design, 1981), p. 99.

12. Henry Glassie, *Vernacular Architecture* (Philadelphia: Material Culture; Bloomington: Indiana University Press, 2000), p. 17.

13. I prefer "intellectual history" to the vaguer anthropological term "culture," which too often takes on an abstract, extrasomatic role as a quality that explains everything while explaining nothing. Ideas are the property of individuals, who decide whether and how to adopt and employ them.

14. Cf. Porphyrios, "Notes on a Method," p. 101.

15. Thomas S. Kuhn, *The Structure of Scientific Revolutions* (Chicago: University of Chicago Press, 1962); Peter Galison, *Image and Logic: A Material Culture of Microphysics* (Chicago: University of Chicago Press, 1997), pp. 782, 844.

16. Galison, *Image and Logic,* p. 844.

17. Calvin O. Schrag, *The Self After Postmodernity* (New Haven: Yale University Press, 1997), pp. 35–36, 128, 129.

18. Gilles Deleuze and Felix Guattari, *A Thousand Plateaus: Capitalism and Schizophrenia,* trans. Brian Massumi (Minneapolis: University of Minnesota Press, 1987), pp. 10–11; David R. Olson, "Introduction" to *Modes of Thought: Explorations in Culture and Cognition,* ed. David R. Olson and Nancy Torrance (Cambridge: Cambridge University Press, 1996), pp. 2–3; Hayden White, *Tropics of Discourse: Essays in Cultural Criticism* (Baltimore: Johns Hopkins University Press, 1978), pp. 81–100, 121–34.

19. Henri Lefebvre, *Critique of Everyday Life,* trans. John Moore (London: Verso, 1991), p. 72.

20. Schrag, *Self After Postmodernity,* p. 79; James Deetz, *In Small Things Forgotten: The Archaeology of Early American Life,* rev. ed. (New York: Anchor, 1996), pp. 24–25.

CHAPTER 1. **CITIES OF PERPETUAL RUIN AND REPAIR**

1. *The Biographical Encyclopedia of Pennsylvania of the Nineteenth Century* (Philadelphia: Galaxy, 1874), pp. 462–63; Deborah Dependahl Waters, "Philadelphia's Boswell: John Fanning Watson," *PMHB* 98, no. 1 (Jan. 1974): 3–52; Watson II, 2: 588–91 (emphasis in the original).

2. Timothy Dwight, *Travels in New York and New England* [1821–22], ed. Barbara Miller Solomon (Cambridge: Harvard University Press, 1969), 3: 329–30; Carole Shammas, "The Space Problem in the Early United States," *WMQ* 57, 3d ser., no. 3 (July 2000): 506–7; Jean Boze, New Orleans, "Nouvelles diverses," to Henri de St.-Gême, St.-Gaudens, France, SGP, fol. 167, Feb. 13, 1831.

3. "The City of Modern Ruins," *New-York Mirror* 17 (June 13, 1840): 407.

4. "The World in Little," *New-York Ledger* 12 (Sept. 27, 1856): 4.

5. I borrow the term "armature" from the architectural historian William L. McDonald, who applied it to Roman colonial cities. For McDonald, an "armature" is a dynamic array of streets, squares, and public buildings that ties a town together through their "directional and spatial unity." Armatures are produced by the application of contextual rules that establish relative positions rather than by a predetermined or static overall design (William L. MacDonald, *The Architecture of the Roman Empire* [New Haven: Yale University Press, 1982–86], 2: 3, 17–18, 25).

6. Mary M. Schweitzer, "The Spatial Organization of Federalist Philadelphia, 1790," *Journal of Interdisciplinary History* 24, no. 1 (summer 1993): 35.

7. Campbell Gibson, *Population of the 100 Largest Cities and Other Urban Places in the United States: 1790 to 1990,* Population Division Working Paper No. 27 (Washington, D.C.: Population Division, United States Census Bureau, 1998), tab. 2, 3; online at www.census.gov/

population/www/documentation/twps0027.html; "Comparative Views of the Population of the City and County of Philadelphia," *HRP* 8, no. 5 (July 30, 1831): 65; Billy G. Smith, *The "Lower Sort": Philadelphia's Laboring People, 1750–1800* (Ithaca: Cornell University Press, 1990), p. 42.

8. John K. Alexander, "The Philadelphia Numbers Game: An Analysis of Philadelphia's Eighteenth-Century Population," *PMHB* 98, no. 3 (July 1974): 324; Clement Biddle, *The Philadelphia Directory* (Philadelphia: James and Johnson, 1791), p. ix; R. A. Smith, *Philadelphia as It Is, in 1852* (Philadelphia: Lindsey and Blackston, 1852), pp. 18–19; Martin P. Snyder, *City of Independence: Views of Philadelphia Before 1800* (New York: Praeger, 1975), pp. 182–85.

9. Elizabeth Blackmar, "Re-Walking the 'Walking City': Housing and Property Relations in New York City, 1780–1840," *Radical History Review,* no. 21 (1979): 131–48; Gary B. Nash, *The Urban Crucible: Social Change, Political Consciousness, and the Origins of the American Revolution* (Cambridge: Harvard University Press, 1979), pp. 4–5; Stuart M. Blumin, *The Emergence of the Middle Class: Social Experience in the American City, 1760–1900* (Cambridge: Cambridge University Press, 1989), pp. 20–26; Smith, *"Lower Sort,"* p. 195; Sharon V. Salinger, "Spaces, Inside and Out, in Eighteenth-Century Philadelphia," *Journal of Interdisciplinary History* 26, no. 1 (summer 1995): 8, 22, 26; Thomas M. Doerflinger, *A Vigorous Spirit of Enterprise: Merchants and Economic Development in Revolutionary Philadelphia* (Chapel Hill: University of North Carolina Press, 1986), pp. 130, 132; Drinker 1: 399–401, 425, 2: 827, 885–86.

10. Doerflinger, *Vigorous Spirit of Enterprise,* pp. 36, 38–39, 68, 157–58, 342–43; Smith, *"Lower Sort,"* pp. 63, 66, 68, 84–91, 124–25; Nash, *Urban Crucible,* pp. 250, 252–54, 257–59; Sharon V. Salinger, "Artisans, Journeymen, and the Transformation of Labor in Late Eighteenth-Century Philadelphia," *WMQ,* 3d ser., 40, no. 1 (Jan. 1983): 69–74; Schweitzer, "Spatial Organization," pp. 43–52; Bruce Laurie, *Working People of Philadelphia, 1800–1850* (Philadelphia: Temple University Press, 1980), pp. 11–13; Blumin, *Emergence of the Middle Class,* pp. 3, 14–16; Drinker 2: 851; Watson I, 204, 209.

11. James Mease, *The Picture of Philadelphia,* continued by Thomas Porter (Philadelphia: Robert DeSilver, 1831), p. vii; Donna J. Rilling, *Making Houses, Crafting Capitalism: Builders in Philadelphia, 1790–1850* (Philadelphia: University of Pennsylvania Press, 2001), p. 10.

12. Schweitzer, "Spatial Organization," pp. 45–47; Smith, *"Lower Sort,"* p. 21; Warner, *Private City,* pp. 13–14; Salinger, "Spaces," pp. 26, 28; *Soup Houses/Names of Soup Societies, Location of Soup Houses, Names of Officers, &c.,* broadside, Philadelphia, ca. 1865, LCP; W. E. B. DuBois, *The Philadelphia Negro: A Social Study* (1899; rpt. New York: Schocken, 1967), p. 37; Drinker 2: 1522.

13. [James Mease], "A Brief Sketch of the Origin and Present State of Philadelphia," *Port Folio* 5, no. 13 (Apr. 6, 1805): 98; Shammas, "Space Problem," p. 512; "Proceedings of Councils," *HRP* 13, no. 6 (Feb. 8, 1834): 85.

14. "Proceedings of Councils," p. 85; Rilling, *Making Houses,* pp. 164–65; Bernard L. Herman, *Town House: Architecture and Material Life in the Early American City, 1780–1830* (Chapel Hill: University of North Carolina Press for the Omohundro Institute of Early American History and Culture, 2005), pp. 195–97, 203–13.

15. Salinger, "Spaces," p. 24. Stuart M. Blumin calculated that in 1798 60 percent of Philadelphians lived in houses of 900 square feet or less. Assuming standard Anglo-American room sizes of 16-by-20 to 20-by-20 feet (320 to 400 square feet), this would mean that they had three rooms or fewer in their houses (Blumin, *Emergence of the Middle Class,* pp. 43–44).

16. Smith, *"Lower Sort,"* pp. 109, 181; Benjamin Loxley, "Memerandum Book, Made and Begun the 6th of January 1768—Concerning the Carpenters Co,s [*sic*] Interest and Buildings &ccc," Benjamin Loxley Papers, Uselma Clark Smith Collection, HSP, pp. 4–8; [Mathew Carey], *A Plea for the Poor* (3d ed. Philadelphia, 1836), pp. 2–15; "Misery," *Public Ledger,* Feb. 16, 1837 (reference courtesy of Shane White).

17. Helen Tangires, *Public Markets and Civic Culture in Nineteenth-Century America* (Baltimore: Johns Hopkins University Press, 2003), pp. 95, 108–17.

18. Mease, *Picture of Philadelphia,* p. 92; Elizabeth Gray Kogen Spera, "Building for Business: The Impact of Commerce on the Plan and Architecture of the City of Philadelphia, 1750–1800," Ph.D. diss., University of Pennsylvania, 1980, pp. 171–73; Alexander Mackay, *The Western World; or, Travels in the United States in 1846–47,* 2d ed. (London: Richard Bentley, 1849), 1: 140; Watson I, 205; Drinker 1: 694.

19. Oliver Evans Chapter, Society for Industrial Archaeology, *Workshop of the World: A Selective Guide to the Industrial Archaeology of Philadelphia* (Wallingford, Pa.: Oliver Evans Press, 1990), pp. 1–6; Philip Scranton, *Proprietary Capitalism: The Textile Manufacture at Philadelphia, 1800–1885* (Cambridge: Cambridge University Press, 1983), pp. 75–83, 95–96; Cynthia J. Shelton, *The Mills of Manayunk: Industrialization and Social Conflict in the Philadelphia Region, 1787–1837* (Baltimore: Johns Hopkins University Press, 1986), pp. 54–58.

20. New Orleans's institutions also hugged the fringes of the urbanized sector, although their placement was inflected by the city's distinctive topography.

21. For the vicissitudes of New Orleans's early plan, see Samuel Wilson, Jr., *The Vieux Carré, New Orleans: Its Plan, Its Growth, Its Architecture* (New Orleans: Bureau of Governmental Research for the City of New Orleans, 1968).

22. Peirce F. Lewis, *New Orleans: The Making of an Urban Landscape,* 2d ed. (Charlottesville: University of Virginia Press, 2003), pp. 22–34; Craig E. Colten, *An Unnatural Metropolis: Wresting New Orleans from Nature* (Baton Rouge: Louisiana State University Press, 2005), pp. 141–62.

23. John B. Rehder, *Delta Sugar: Louisiana's Vanishing Plantation Landscape* (Baltimore: Johns Hopkins University Press, 1999), pp. 55–57, 93; Richard Campanella, *Time and Place in New Orleans: Past Geographies in the Present Day* (Gretna, La.: Pelican, 2002), pp. 84–99.

24. Julien Poydras, *A Defence of the Right of the Public to the Batture of New Orleans* (Washington, 1809), pp. 10–11; *NOA* 2: 7–8; J. Richard Shenkel, Robert Sauder, and Edward R. Chatelain, *Archaeology of the Jazz Complex and Beauregard (Congo) Square, Louis Armstrong Park, New Orleans, Louisiana* (New Orleans: University of New Orleans, 1980), p. 27; NOCVb, 1: n.p. (Apr. 4, June 8, 1805); Wilson, *Vieux Carré,* pp. 60.

25. *An Account of Louisiana* (Philadelphia: John Conrad, 1803), p. 18; NOMP/T box 2, fol. 2 (June 15, June 22, July 20, 1805); Mayor James Mather to Julien Poydras, Oct. 14, 1809, John Minor Wisdom Collection, TUL, Batture Controversy, box 17; NOCVa, 1, n.p. (Apr. 6, 1811); Wilson, *Vieux Carré,* pp. 57–59; *NOA* 2: 10–11.

26. *Rélation de l'Incendie qu'a éprouvé la ville de la Nouvelle-Orléans, le 21 mars 1788* (Cap François: l'Imprimérie Royale, 1788); C. C. Robin, *Voyage to Louisiana by C. C. Robin, 1803–1805,* trans. Stuart O. Landry, Jr. (New Orleans: Pelican, 1966), pp. 90–91; George Morgan, New Orleans, to sister Rebecca Pile, Mar. 31, 1795, Pile Family Papers, 1793–1836, E-61, HSP; "Nouvelles étrangeres. Amérique septentrionale. De la Louisiane, le 22 juillet (3 thermidor). Suite de la lettre d'un colon de la Louisiane," *Gazette de France,* no. 1739 (Sept. 25, 1802), n. p., Berquin-Duvallon letters, TUL, M374.

27. NOMP/T, p. 943 (Aug. 22, 1812); *Historical Epitome of the State of Louisiana* (New Orleans, 1840), pp. 310–13.

28. Jay D. Edwards, "Cultural Identifications in Architecture: The Case of the New Orleans Townhouse," *Traditional Dwellings and Settlements Review* 5, no. 1 (1993): 17–32; Malcolm Heard, *French Quarter Manual: An Architectural Guide to New Orleans' Vieux Carré* (New Orleans: Tulane School of Architecture, 1997), pp. 21–23, 27–36, 38–41; John H. B. Latrobe, *Southern Travels: Journal of John H. B. Latrobe 1834*, ed. Samuel Wilson, Jr. (New Orleans: Historic New Orleans Collection, 1986), p. 48; Jay D. Edwards, "Cultural Syncretism in the Louisiana Creole Cottage," *Louisiana Folklore Miscellany* 4 (1976–80): 9–40; Jay D. Edwards, "The Origins of Creole Architecture," *Winterthur Portfolio* 29, nos. 2–3 (summer–autumn 1994): 155–89; John Michael Vlach, "The Shotgun House: An African Architectural Legacy," in *Common Places: Readings in American Vernacular Architecture,* ed. Dell Upton and John Michael Vlach (Athens: University of Georgia Press, 1986), pp. 58–77.

29. New Orleans Census, 1803, NOMP/T, box 6, fol. 14. An unsigned note on the document, probably by the copyist, objects that "this Census appears to be incorrect as by some unaccountable mistake the number of free People of Color in the Second Quarter are not included, and on the whole I think the Population underrated."

30. Thomas N. Ingersoll, *Mammon and Manon in Early New Orleans: The First Slave Society in the Deep South, 1718–1819* (Knoxville: University of Tennessee Press, 1999), pp. 248, 343.

31. [Charles Sealsfield], *The Americans as They Are* (London: Hurst, Chance, 1828), p. 161.

32. Anthony Lamarlère deposition, Oct. 3, 1816, HC, box VIII, fol. D, pt. 2; Joseph Roffignac, arrest warrant for Mulatto Tom, Jan. 12, 1822, Slavery in Louisiana Papers, HNOC, fol. 4; Madame Laroque deposition, Nov. 2, 1825, HC, box IX, fol. A, pt. 4; Salomon, slave, deposition, Slavery and Freedom in Louisiana Collection, University Archives, XUL.

33. Joseph Holt Ingraham, *The South-West. By a Yankee* (New York: Harper and Bros., 1835): 1: 159; Sylvia J. Pinner, "A History of the Irish Channel, 1840–1860," history honors thesis, Tulane University, 1954, pp. 1–2. In 1850, there were 20,200 Irish-born people in New Orleans, 11,220 German-born residents, and 7,522 "French" people, which may include those from the Francophone Caribbean (Pinner, "History of the Irish Channel," p. 1).

34. *New Orleans as It Is* (Utica, N.Y.: De Witt C. Grove, 1849), pp. 48–49; John F. Nau, *The German People of New Orleans, 1850–1900* (1954), p. 17; *NOA* 4: xiv, 25–36.

35. Louisiana State Legislature, *An Act to Consolidate the City of New Orleans* (1852); NOMP/T, box 2, fol. 2 (June 15, 22, 1805); Pinner, "History of the Irish Channel," pp. 4–6; R. Christopher Goodwin, with Paul C. Armstrong, Eric C. Poplin, David Moore, and Carol M. Poplin, *New Orleans Is Looking Forward to Its Past: An Archaeological Survey and Plan for Sections of New Orleans* (New Orleans: R. Christopher Goodwin and Associates for the Office of Cultural Development, Department of Culture, Recreation and Tourism, 1987), pp. 206–7; Jean Boze to Henri de St.-Gême, Oct. 1, 1829, SGP.

CHAPTER 2. **THE RELICS OF CIVILIZED LIFE**

1. Charles H. Haswell, *Reminiscences of an Octogenarian of the City of New York (1816 to 1860)* (New York: Harper and Bros., 1896), p. 12; Drinker 1: 425; Christine Meisner Rosen, "Noisome, Noxious, and Offensive Vapors, Fumes and Stenches in American Towns and Cities, 1840–1865," *Historical Geography* 25 (1997): 56–65; NOMP/T, box 2, fol. 17 (Apr. 25, 1812).

2. Edward H. Barton, *The Cause and Prevention of Yellow Fever at New Orleans and Other Cities in America,* 3d ed. (New York: H. Baillière, 1857), p. 266; *Phila. Ord.,* p. 129 (July 9, 1821); Min-

utes of the City Council, 1789–93, MS, Philadelphia City Archives, 97 (July 6, 1789), 101 (July 20, 1789); James Ronaldson, Philadelphia, letter to J[oseph] W[atson], Feb. 7, 1826, Dreer Collection, Alphabetical Series, HSP; Charles Dickens, *American Notes and Pictures from Italy* (Oxford: Oxford University Press, 1957), pp. 86–87.

3. "First Report of the Committee on Public Hygiene of the American Medical Association," *Transactions of the American Medical Association* 2 (1849): 433–34; Thomas Condie and Richard Folwell, *History of the Pestilence, Commonly Called Yellow Fever, Which Almost Desolated Philadelphia, in the Months of August, September & October, 1798* (Philadelphia: R. Folwell, 1799), pp. 6–7; *New Orleans as It Is* (Utica, N.Y.: De Witt C. Grove, 1849), p. 71.

4. Condie and Folwell, *History of the Pestilence*, p. 7; Drinker 1: 421.

5. Drinker 3: 1754, 2: 999, 1142; Condie and Folwell, *History of the Pestilence*, p. 8; Invoice of Stephen Bill, Mar. 30, 1831, Real Estate Accounts, 1817–1825, Stephen Girard Papers, ser. II, APS (also Drinker 3: 1631).

6. Drinker 2: 1067; Isaac Parrish, "Report on the Sanitary Condition of Philadelphia," *Transactions of the American Medical Association* 2 (1849): 462, 472–73; *Report of the Sub-Committee on Cleansing the City* (Philadelphia, 1849), p. 19; Shane White and Graham White, *The Sounds of Slavery: Discovering African American History through Songs, Sermons, and Speech* (Boston: Beacon, 2005), p. 156; Charles E. Rosenberg, *The Cholera Years: The United States in 1832, 1849, and 1866* (Chicago: University of Chicago Press, 1987), p. 17; "Annual Report of the New Orleans and Lafayette Board of Health, for the Year 1850," *Southern Medical Reports* 2 (1850): 60; James Mease, *The Picture of Philadelphia* (Philadelphia: B. and T. Kite, 1811), p. 125.

7. Condie and Folwell, *History of the Pestilence*, pp. 7–8; James Pitot, *Observations on the Colony of Louisiana from 1796 to 1802*, trans. Henry C. Pitot (Baton Rouge: Louisiana State University Press for the Historic New Orleans Collection, 1979), p. 110; *New Orleans Daily Picayune*, Oct. 8, 1854.

8. Laura L. Porteous, "Sanitary Conditions in New Orleans Under the Spanish Regime, 1799–1800: Translation of a Letter to the Cabildo from El Sindico Procurador General del Publico Dated January 24, 1800, in the Archives at the Cabildo, New Orleans," *LH* 15, no. 4 (Oct. 1932): 614; Cope, p. 574; Drinker 3: 1672; NOCVb, 9: 40 (Mar. 22, 1824); "Annual Report of the New Orleans and Lafayette Board of Health, for the Year 1850," p. 59; John Duffy, "Pestilence in New Orleans," in *The Past as Prelude: New Orleans, 1718–1968*, ed. Hodding Carter (New Orleans: Tulane University Press, 1968), p. 101.

9. NOMP/T, box 2, fol 3 (July 13, 1805); Mary Elizabeth Latrobe, "Memoir," in Latrobe, *Jnls.*, 3: 339; John H. B. Latrobe, *Southern Travels: Journal of John H. B. Latrobe 1834*, ed. Samuel Wilson, Jr. (New Orleans: Historic New Orleans Collection, 1986), p. 46; *New Orleans as It Is*, p. 22.

10. Latrobe, *Corr.*, 3: 497.

11. Latrobe, *Corr.*, 3: 497; "Modern Buildings," *New-York Mirror* 11 (Mar. 15, 1834): 295.

12. Complaints about cold were less frequent than were those about heat.

13. Luther F. Tower, Diaries, 1845–46, Louisiana and Lower Mississippi Valley Collection, Lousiana State University, Sept. 17, 1846; Drinker 2: 1058; "Excessive Heat," *Ladies Companion* 1, no. 3 (July 1834): 154; "Daguerreotypes Taken Coolly" (advertisement), *New-York Herald*, June 23, 1849, p. 3; "Bedbugs!" (advertisement), *New-York Daily Tribune*, May 23, 1849, p. 3; Harriet Martineau, *Retrospect of Western Travel* (London: Saunders and Otley, 1838), 1: 258; Latrobe, *Jnls.*, 3: 307; James Stuart, *Three Years in North America*, 3d ed. (Edinburgh: for Rob-

ert Cadell, 1833), 2: 196; Arthur Singleton, *Letters from the South and West* (Boston: Richardson and Lord, 1824), p. 129.

14. Charles W. Bradbury, New Orleans, draft letter to Sarah Bradbury, Cincinnati, Nov. 7, 1835, Bradbury Papers, SHC; Frank G. Johnson, *The Nicolson Pavement* (New York: W. C. Rogers, 1867), pp. 12, 82; Latrobe, *Jnls.*, 3: 300.; Albert J. Pickett, *Eight Days in New-Orleans* (Montgomery, Ala.: Albert J. Pickett, 1847), p. 19; Samuel Nicolson, *The Nicolson Pavement* (Boston: Dutton and Wentworth, 1855), p. 14; "Proceedings of Councils," *HRP* 8, no. 4 (July 23, 1831): 56; "Mac-Adamization," *New-York Mirror* 11 (Oct. 12, 1833): 119; "Wooden Pavement. From the New York Express," *Niles' Weekly Register* 51 (Sept. 3, 1836): 3; Daniel Bowen, *A History of Philadelphia* (Philadelphia: Daniel Bowen, 1839), pp. 82, 202; Benjamin Franklin Peters, Biographical Notes of Samuel J. Peters, MS, ca. 1850, McConnell Family Papers, TUL, box 1, fol. 7.

15. Stuart, *Three Years*, 1: 22; Mrs. Felton, *American Life. A Narrative of Two Years' City and Country Residence in the United States* (Bolton Percy, Eng.: for the authoress, 1843), p. 37; Drinker 3: 1667; NOMP/T, box 2, fol. 2 (June 26, 1805); Lang Syne [John Fanning Watson], "Auctions," *HRP* 2, no. 17 (Nov. 8, 1828): 261; *The Cries of Philadelphia* (Philadelphia: Johnson and Warner, 1810), pp. 24, 31; Latrobe, *Southern Travels,* p. 45.

16. Benjamin F. Butler, *Autobiography and Personal Reminiscences of Major-General Benj. F. Butler: Butler's Book* (Boston: A. M. Thayer, 1892), pp. 395–96.

17. Ibid.

18. [Alexander Graydon], *Memoirs of a Life, Chiefly Passed in Pennsylvania, within the Last Sixty Years* (Harrisburgh: John Wyeth, 1811), pp. 34–35.

19. Alexander Pope, "Epistle to Lord Burlington" (1731), in *Pope,* ed. Peter Levi (Harmondsworth: Penguin, 1974), p. 93; Joseph Addison, *Spectator,* no. 414 (June 25, 1712), in Joseph Addison, Richard Steele, et al., *The Spectator* (London: J. M. Dent, 1907), 3: 68. Stephen Carl Arch, "Writing a Federalist Self: Alexander Graydon's *Memoirs of a Life*," *WMQ*, 3d ser., 52, no. 3 (July 1995): 415–32.

20. James J. Gibson, *The Senses Considered as Perceptual Systems* (Boston: Houghton Mifflin, 1966), pp. 36, 51; José Luis Bermúdez, "Ecological Perception and the Notion of a Nonconceptual Point of View," in *The Body and the Self,* ed. José Luis Bermúdez, Anthony Marcel, and Naomi Eilan (Cambridge: MIT Press, 1995), p.162; Richard F. Thompson, *The Brain: A Neuroscience Primer,* 2d ed. (New York: W. H. Freeman, 1993), pp. 225–26.

21. George Butterworth, "An Ecological Perspective on the Origins of Self," in *Body and the Self,* p. 98; Andrew N. Meltzoff and M. Keith Moore, "Infants' Understanding of People and Things: From Body Imitation to Folk Psychology," in *Body and the Self,* pp. 48–51, 65.

22. Jacques Paillard, "Motor and Representational Framing of Space," in *Brain and Space,* ed. Jacques Paillard (Oxford: Oxford University Press, 1991), p. 164; Mallory Wober, "The Sensotype Hypothesis," in *Varieties of Sensory Experience,* pp. 31–32; R. Peter Hobson, "Through Feelings and Sight to Self and Symbol," in *The Perceived Self: Ecological and Interpersonal Sources of Self-Knowledge,* ed. Ulric Neisser (Cambridge: Cambridge University Press, 1993), pp. 254–79; Michael Tomasello, "On the Interpersonal Origins of the Self-Concept," in *Perceived Self,* pp. 174–83; David Jopling, "Cognitive Science, Other Minds, and the Philosophy of Dialogue," in *Perceived Self,* p. 300; Meltzoff and Moore, "Infants' Understanding of People and Things," p. 65.

23. Quassim Cassam, "Introspection and Bodily Self-Ascription," in *Body and the Self,* p. 311. Arch sees Graydon's central conceit as self*less*ness, but he means this in the social sense

that I call "personhood" (Arch, "Writing a Federalist Self," pp. 417–18). My point is that Graydon's journey to school recapitulated the human discovery of agency—"selfhood" in the sense that I used it in the Introduction.

24. Drinker 2: 1030.

25. Ulric Neisser, "Two Perceptually Given Aspects of the Self and Their Development," *Developmental Review* 11, no. 3 (Sept. 1991): 198.

26. Latrobe, *Southern Travels,* pp. 40–44.

27. Ulric Neisser, "Five Kinds of Self-Knowledge," *Philosophical Psychology* 1, no. 1 (1988): 41–45; Latrobe, *Southern Travels,* p. 43.

CHAPTER 3. **THE SMELL OF DANGER**

1. Theodore Clapp, *Autobiographical Sketches and Recollections, During a Thirty-Five Years' Residence in New Orleans* (Boston: Phillips, Sampson, 1857), p. 207.

2. Richard F. Thompson, *The Brain: A Neuroscience Primer,* 2d ed. (New York: W. H. Freeman, 1993), pp. 16–18; Martin Sarter and Hans J. Markowitsch, "Involvement of the Amygdala in Learning and Memory: A Critical Review, with Emphasis on Anatomical Relations," *Behavioral Neuroscience* 99, no. 2 (Apr. 1985): 369; Rachel S. Herz and Gerald C. Cupchik, "An Experimental Characterization of Odor-Evoked Memories in Humans," *Chemical Senses* 17, no. 5 (Oct. 1992): 519, 527; Harry T. Lawless, "Olfactory Psychophysics," in *Tasting and Smelling,* ed. Gary K. Beauchamp and Linda Bartoshuk (San Diego: Academic Press, 1997), pp. 128, 152–54; Eric Halgren, "The Amygdala Contribution to Emotion and Memory: Current Studies in Humans," in *The Amygdaloid Complex,* ed. Yehezkel Ben-Ari (Amsterdam: Elsevier/North-Holland Biomedical Press, 1981), p. 395; Michael Davis, "The Role of the Amygdala in Fear and Anxiety," *Annual Review of Neuroscience* 15 (1992): 353, 359, 361.

3. Daniel J. Boorstin, *The Lost World of Thomas Jefferson* (Boston: Beacon, 1948), pp. 111–16, 140–51; George Rosen, "Political Order and Human Health in Jeffersonian Thought," *Bulletin of the History of Medicine* 26 (1952): 38–40; Charles A. Miller, *Jefferson and Nature: An Interpretation* (Baltimore: Johns Hopkins University Press, 1988), pp. 58, 92; Jacquelyn C. Miller, "An 'Uncommon Tranquility of Mind': Emotional Self-Control and the Construction of a Middle-Class Identity in Eighteenth-Century Philadelphia," *Journal of Social History* 30, no. 1 (fall 1996): 131, 137; Ernst Cassirer, *The Philosophy of the Enlightenment* (Princeton: Princeton University Press, 1951), p. 18; J. Worth Estes, "Introduction: The Yellow Fever Syndrome and Its Treatment in Philadelphia, 1793," in *A Melancholy Scene of Devastation: The Public Response to the 1793 Yellow Fever Epidemic,* ed. J. Worth Estes and Billy G. Smith (Canton, Mass.: Science History Publications/USA, 1997), pp. 8–9; Michal McMahon, "Beyond Therapeutics: Technology and the Question of Public Health in Late-Eighteenth-Century Philadelphia," in *Melancholy Scene of Devastation,* pp. 104–5; Jacquelyn C. Miller, "Passions and Politics: The Multiple Meanings of Benjamin Rush's Treatment for Yellow Fever," in *Melancholy Scene of Devastation,* pp. 79–95.

4. William P. C. Barton, *A Treatise Containing a Plan for the Internal Organization and Government of Marine Hospitals, in the United States,* 2d ed. (Philadelphia: for the author, 1817), pp. 52–53; Mathew Carey, *A Short Account of the Malignant Fever, Lately Prevalent in Philadelphia,* 4th ed. (Philadelphia, Jan. 16, 1794), p. 80; Mary Elizabeth Latrobe, "Memoir," in Latrobe, *Jnls.,* 3: 335; NOCVb, 6:37.

5. Carey, *Short Account,* pp. 18, 21, 79; Drinker 1: 497; I. Bernard Cohen, *Benjamin Franklin's Science* (Cambridge: Harvard University Press, 1990), p. 119.

6. On miasma theory, see Carlo M. Cippola, *Miasmas and Disease: Public Health and the Environment in the Pre-Industrial Age* (New Haven: Yale University Press, 1992); John Duffy, *The Sanitarians: A History of American Public Health* (Urbana: University of Illinois Press, 1990), pp. 20–23; Erwin H. Ackerknecht, "Anti-Contagionism Between 1821 and 1867," *Bulletin of the History of Medicine* 22 (Sept.–Oct. 1948): 562–93; Laura L. Porteous, "Sanitary Conditions in New Orleans Under the Spanish Regime, 1799–1800: Translation of a Letter to the Cabildo from El Sindico Procurador General del Publico Dated January 24, 1800, in the Archives at the Cabildo, New Orleans," *LH* 15, no. 4 (Oct. 1932): 616; Edward H. Barton, *The Cause and Prevention of Yellow Fever at New Orleans and Other Cities in America*, 3d ed. (New York: H. Baillière, 1857), pp. 33, 35, 37–38.

7. Michel Halphen, M.D., *Observations sur la choléra-morbus qui a régné à la Nouvelle-Orléans en 1833 et en 1834* (Paris: J. B. Baillière, 1835), p. 172; [Charles Sealsfield], *The Americans as They Are* (London: Hurst, Chance, 1828), p. 193; Latrobe, *Jnls.*, 3: 313; Academy of Medicine of Philadelphia, *Proofs of the Origin of the Yellow Fever* (Philadelphia: Thomas and Samuel F. Bradford, 1798), p. 5; William Darby, *A Geographical Description of the State of Louisiana* (Philadelphia: John Melish for the author, 1816), pp. 227–29; *Proceedings of the College of Physicians of Philadelphia, Relative to the Prevention of the Introduction and Spreading of Contagious Diseases* (Philadelphia: Thomas Dobson, 1798), p. 9; Adrien Armand Gros and Nicolas Vincent Auguste Gerardin, *Rapport fait à la Société Médicale sur la fièvre jaune qui a regné d'une manière épidémique pendant l'été de 1817* (New Orleans: J. D. de St. Romes, 1818), p. 8; Drinker 3: 1862; Barton, *Cause and Prevention*, p. viii.

8. Darby, *Geographical Description*, p. 235; Ackerknecht, "Anti-Contagionism," p. 568; Duffy, *Sanitarians*, p. 20; Barton, *Cause and Prevention*, p. 17.

9. Barton, *Cause and Prevention*, p. 266.

10. Estes, "Introduction," pp. 1–17; McMahon, "Beyond Therapeutics," pp. 97–117; Thomas Condie and Richard Folwell, *History of the Pestilence, Commonly Called Yellow Fever, Which Almost Desolated Philadelphia, in the Months of August, September & October, 1798* (Philadelphia: R. Folwell, 1799), p. 7; James Pitot, *Observations on the Colony of Louisiana from 1796 to 1802*, trans. Henry C. Pitot (Baton Rouge: Louisiana State University Press for the Historic New Orleans Collection, 1979), p. 110; "First Report of the Committee on Public Hygiene of the American Medical Association," *Transactions of the American Medical Association* 2 (1849): 437, 439; Pierre-Frédéric Thomas, *Essai sur la fièvre jaune d'Amérique* (New Orleans: J.-B. Baillière, 1823), pp. 12–13, 23; Barton, *Cause and Prevention*, p. ix; "Annual Report of the New Orleans and Lafayette Board of Health, for the Year 1850," *Southern Medical Reports* 2 (1850): 59–60; "Health of Towns," *Illustrated Magazine of Art* 4 (1854): 286; Timothy Dwight, *Travels in New York and New England*, ed. Barbara Miller Solomon (Cambridge: Harvard University Press, 1969), 2: 260; Duffy, *Sanitarians*, pp. 40–41; Charles E. Rosenberg, "Disease and Social Order in America: Perceptions and Expectations," *Milbank Quarterly* 64, supp. 1 (1986): 52.

11. "Importance of Warm Bathing in Cholera Times," *New-York Daily Tribune*, June 11, 1849, p. 2; Drinker 2: 1149.

12. "First Report of the Committee on Public Hygiene," p. 437; Duffy, *Sanitarians*, pp. 40–41; Rosenberg, "Disease and Social Order," p. 52; Drinker 2: 956, 957, 1063, 1069; "Ordinance Additional to the Ordinance Relative to the Public Health," NOCVb, 6:37 (Mar. 17, 1821); Carey, *Short Account*, p. 79.

13. Barton, *Cause and Prevention*, p. 11.

14. Pitot, *Observations*, p. 110; Gros and Gerardin, *Rapport*, p. 8; *Report of the College of Physicians of Philadelphia . . . on Epidemic Cholera* (Philadelphia: Thomas Desilver, Jr., 1832), p. 25; Miller, "'Uncommon Tranquility of Mind,'" pp. 135, 138–40; Philadelphia Board of Health, *On Cholera* [Philadelphia, 1832], pp. 11–12; Daniel Walker Howe, *Making the American Self: Jonathan Edwards to Abraham Lincoln* (Cambridge, Mass.: Harvard University Press, 1997), pp. 5–6.

15. Robert J. Trumbull, *A Visit to the Philadelphia Prison* (Philadelphia: Budd and Bartram, 1796), p. 33; *New Orleans as It Is* (Utica, N.Y.: De Witt C. Grove, 1849), p. 23; Gros and Gerardin, *Rapport*, p. 8; Barton, *Treatise*, p. 78; Carey, *Short Account*, p. 61.

16. Carey, *Short Account*, p. 61; *Report of the College of Physicians*, p. 23; *New Orleans as It Is*, pp. 20–21; Charles E. Rosenberg, *The Cholera Years: The United States in 1832, 1849, and 1866* (Chicago: University of Chicago Press, 1987), pp. 5, 40, 43–45. Nineteenth-century readers would have read the word *shanty* as an allusion to the Irish.

17. "Domestic Items," *Home Journal*, June 21, 1853, p. 3; W. W. Montgomery, Boston, to Mayor Joseph Roffignac, New Orleans, Aug. 31, 1822, New Orleans Miscellaneous Documents, 1817–24, fol. 4, item 87–39-L, HNOC; Gros and Gerardin, *Rapport*, p. 7; NOMP/T, box 3, fol. 15 (June 19, 1819); *Rapport publié au nom de la Société médicale de la Nouvelle-Orléans, sur la fièvre jaune* (New Orleans: James M'Karaher, 1820), p. 35.

18. A[bsalom] J[ones] and R[ichard] A[llen], *A Narrative of the Proceedings of the Black People During the Late Awful Calamity in Philadelphia, in the Year 1793* (Philadelphia: for the authors, by William W. Woodward, 1794); Carey, *Short Account*, p. 63. A recent statistical analysis showed that both black and white death rates rose during yellow fever epidemics, although the black increase was less than the white, perhaps because African Americans already died at higher rates owing to systemic factors such as neglect by masters and poor nutrition (Susan E. Klepp, "Seasoning and Society: Racial Differences in Mortality in Eighteenth-Century Philadelphia," *WMQ*, 3d ser., 51, no. 3 [July 1994]: 480–87, 490–91).

19. Carey, *Short Account*, pp. 61, 63; Drinker 2: 1574; *Proceedings of the College of Physicians of Philadelphia*, p. 23.

20. Carole Shammas, "The Space Problem in the Early United States," *WMQ*, 3d ser., 57, no. 3 (July 2000): 525; Duffy, *Sanitarians*, p. 79; "Proceedings of Councils," *HRP* 5, no. 8 (Feb. 20, 1830): 334–35.

21. College of Physicians of Philadelphia, *Additional Facts and Observations Relative to the Nature and Origin of the Yellow Fever* (Philadelphia: Thomas Dobson, 1806), p. 21; "Laurens Street, New York," *Niles' Weekly Register* 46 (June 28, 1834): 303.

22. *Minutes of the Proceedings of the Committee, Appointed . . . to Attend to and Alleviate the Sufferings of the Afflicted with the Malignant Fever* (Philadelphia: R. Aitken and Son, 1794); Drinker 1: 496, 2: 1533–34, 1541, 1571, 1581, 1589; Academy of Medicine of Philadelphia, *Proofs of the Origins of the Yellow Fever*, pp. 5–6, 8, 38; Carey, *Short Account*, p. 61.

23. Barton, *Cause and Prevention*, pp. 185–89.

24. Benjamin F. Butler, *Autobiography and Personal Reminiscences of Major-General Benjamin F. Butler: Butler's Book* (Boston: A. M. Thayer, 1892), p. 400.

25. Barton, *Cause and Prevention*, pp. viii, 100.

CHAPTER 4. **NOISE AND GABBLE**

1. Frank G. Johnson, *The Nicolson Pavement* (New York: W. C. Rogers, 1867), p. 12; Albert J. Pickett, *Eight Days in New-Orleans* (Montgomery, Ala.: Albert J. Pickett, 1847), pp. 19, 27.

2. Johnson, *Nicolson Pavement*, p. 82.

3. Shane White and Graham White, *The Sounds of Slavery: Discovering African American History Through Songs, Sermons, and Speech* (Boston: Beacon, 2005), p. 152; Mark M. Smith, *Listening to Nineteenth-Century America* (Chapel Hill: University of North Carolina Press, 2001), p. 54; Drinker 2: 853; H[enry] Didimus, *New Orleans as I Found It* (New York: Harper and Bros., 1845), p. 17.

4. James J. Gibson, *The Senses Considered as Perceptual Systems* (Boston: Houghton Mifflin, 1966), pp. 75, 87; David Howes, "Sensorial Anthropology," in *The Varieties of Sensory Experience: A Sourcebook in the Anthropology of the Senses*, ed. David Howes (Toronto: University of Toronto Press, 1991), p. 171; Max Mathews, "The Ear and How It Works," in *Music, Cognition, and Computerized Sound: An Introduction to Psychoacoustics*, ed. Perry R. Cook (Cambridge: MIT Press, 1999), pp. 2–3; Drinker 1: 610, 2: 853, 3: 2005.

5. James Stuart, *Three Years in North America*, 3d ed. (Edinburgh: Robert Cadell, 1833), 2: 206; Latrobe, *Jnls.*, 3: 212; Jean Boze, "Nouvelles diverses," Sept. 17, 1832, SGP, fol. 195.

6. Edmund Burke, *A Philosophical Enquiry into the Sublime and Beautiful and Other Pre-Revolutionary Writings* (London: Penguin, 1998), p. 123; Rodney Needham, "Percussion and Transition," *Man*, n.s. 2 (1967): 606–10; Howes, "Sensorial Anthropology," p. 171.

7. Philip Hone, Diary, July 2, 1840, copy of MS at Metropolitan Museum of Art; "Wooden Pavements," *New-York Mirror* 17 (Nov. 2, 1839): 151; Johnson, *Nicolson Pavement*, p. 81.

8. Stuart, *Three Years*, 1:32; Drinker 3: 1677; Joseph Holt Ingraham, *The South-West. By a Yankee* (New York: Harper and Bros., 1835), 1: 100.

9. *The Cries of Philadelphia* (Philadelphia: Johnson and Warner, 1810), pp. 31–32.

10. Ibid., p. 22.

11. *New Orleans Bee*, Dec. 26, 1827.

12. "Proceedings of Councils," *HRP* 5, no. 25 (June 19, 1830): 393.

13. J. Thomas Scharf and Thompson Westcott, *History of Philadelphia, 1609–1884* (Philadelphia: L. H. Evarts, 1884), 3: 1778; Ingraham, *South-West*, 1: 102–3; Eric Lott, *Love and Theft: Blackface Minstrelsy and the American Working Class* (New York: Oxford University Press, 1993), p. 56; Dena J. Epstein, *Sinful Tunes and Spirituals: Black Folk Music to the Civil War* (Urbana: University of Illinois Press, 1977), pp. 92, 189; John Page, Diary, Feb. 5, 1838, TUL/MS, coll. 858; Lydia Maria Child, "Letter from New York, Number 1 [1841], in *A Lydia Maria Child Reader*, ed. Carolyn L. Karcher (Durham: Duke University Press, 1997), p. 305.

14. Mathew Carey, *A Short Account of the Malignant Fever, Lately Prevalent in Philadelphia*, 4th ed. (Philadelphia, 1794), p. 18; Drinker 3: 1872 (Oct. 22, 1805); NOCVa, May. 18, 1810; Frederika Bremer, *The Homes of the New World*, trans. Mary Howitt (New York: Harper and Bros., 1854), 2: 206.

15. Drinker 2: 889, 1352; Margaret B. Tinkcom, "The New Market in Second Street," *PMHB* 82, no. 3 (Oct. 1958): 393.

16. "Life in St. Louis," *Frank Leslie's Illustrated Newspaper* 1, no. 7 (Feb. 2, 1856): 123.

17. Lady Emmeline Stuart Wortley, *Travels in the United States, etc. During 1849 and 1850* (New York: Harper and Bros., 1851), p. 78.

18. Edward S. Ely, *Visits of Mercy* (London, 1813), p. 83; Pickett, *Eight Days*, p. 27; Thomas Hamilton, *Men and Manners in America* (Edinburgh: William Blackwood, 1834), 2: 205; Kenneth Cmiel, *Democratic Eloquence: The Fight over Popular Speech in Nineteenth-Century America* (New York: William Morrow, 1990), pp. 14–15, 63–66; Child, "Letter from New York," p. 302.

19. *Seventh Annual Report of the Managers of the Society for the Reformation of Juvenile Delin-*

quents in the City and State of New-York (New York: Mahlon Day, 1832), p. 25; William Going, *Memoir of William Going, Formerly Keeper of the State Prison, Charlestown, Mass.* (Boston: for the author, 1841), pp. 8, 20–21.

20. A. F. B. Crofton, "The Language of Crime," *Popular Science Monthly* 50 (1897): 831; George W. Matsell, *Vocabulum; or, the Rogue's Lexicon. Compiled from the Most Authentic Sources* (New York: G. W. Matsell, 1859), pp. iii–v.

21. John H. B. Latrobe, *Southern Travels: Journal of John H. B. Latrobe 1834*, ed. Samuel Wilson, Jr. (New Orleans: Historic New Orleans Collection, 1986), p. 45; Benjamin Franklin Peters, "Biographical Notes of Samuel J. Peters," ca. 1850, MS, McConnell Family Papers, Personal Papers, box 1, fol. 7, TUL; Rollin Fillmore, New Orleans, to H. G. Fillmore, Dec. 1, 1847, TUL, MS M692.

22. Latrobe, *Jnls.*, 3: 174–75 (Jan. 14, 1819); Ingraham, *South-West*, 1: 101–2; Drinker 2: 1072.

23. Harriet Martineau, *Retrospect of Western Travel* (London: Saunders and Otley, 1838), 1: 271; William Darby, *A Geographical Description of the State of Louisiana* (Philadelphia: John Melish for the author, 1816), pp. 265–66; Peters, "Biographical Notes," n.p.; Bernard Marigny, *Bernard Marigny à ses concitoyens* (New Orleans, 1853), pp. 2–3; NOCVb, 7: 71 (June 15, 1822); Hamilton, *Men and Manners*, 2: 207–8.

24. James Pierpont, letter to the City Recorder and Aldermen, June 29, 1821, HC, box IX, fol. A, pt. 1.

25. Depositions of Joseph Mason, David Shields, André Grégoire, and Jean-Baptiste Brisson, Feb. 5, 1811, HC, box VIII, fol. B, pt. 2.

26. "Esclave en marronage," advertisement, *l'Abeille de la Nouvelle Orléans*, Apr. 22, 1828.

27. Timothy Flint, *Recollections of the Last Ten Years* (Boston: Cummings, Hilliard, 1826), p. 347; White and White, *Sounds of Slavery*, pp. xvii, 20–23, 92–95; Ingraham, *South-West*, 1: 102–3

28. Anthony Synnott, "Puzzling Over the Senses: From Plato to Marx," in *Varieties of Sensory Experience*, pp. 61–76; Anne Carson, "The Gender of Sound," *Thamyris* 1, no. 1 (autumn 1994): 10–31; George Devereux, "Ethnopsychological Aspects of the Terms 'Deaf' and 'Dumb,'" in *Varieties of Sensory Experience*, pp. 43–45; *Fifth Annual Report to the Legislature, by the Pennsylvania Institution for the Deaf and Dumb* (Philadelphia: Board of Directors, 1826), p. 20; Lewis Weld, "Letter to Roberts Vaux," *HRP* 7, no. 1 (Jan. 1, 1831): 6; E. S. Abdy, *Journal of a Residence and Tour in the United States of North America* (New York: Negro Universities Press, 1969), 1: 225; Karin L. Calvert, *Children in the House: The Material Culture of Early Childhood, 1600–1900* (Boston: Northeastern University Press, 1992), pp. 19–27.

29. Mary P. Ryan, *Women in Public: Between Banners and Ballots, 1825–1880* (Baltimore: Johns Hopkins University Press, 1990), p. 22; Cmiel, *Democratic Eloquence*, pp. 13–14, 55–60; Lawrence W. Levine, *Highbrow Lowbrow: The Emergence of Cultural Hierarchy in America* (Cambridge: Harvard University Press, 1988), pp. 36–38, 46; Mary P. Ryan, *Civic Wars: Democracy and Public Life in the American City During the Nineteenth Century* (Berkeley: University of California Press, 1997), pp. 96–98, 111–12.

30. Cmiel, *Democratic Eloquence*, pp. 14, 16, 27, 56–60; Anthony P. Cohen, *Self-Consciousness: An Alternative Anthropology of Identity* (London: Routledge, 1994), pp. 42–50.

31. Fisher, p. 77.

32. Cope, pp. 574–75.

33. Kenneth S. Greenberg, "The Nose, the Lie, and the Duel in the Antebellum South," *Ameri-*

can *Historical Review* 95, no. 1 (Feb. 1990): 65; White and White, *Sounds of Slavery,* p. 157; Walt Whitman, "Song of Myself" [1855], in *Complete Poems and Selected Prose,* ed. James E. Miller, Jr. (Boston: Houghton Mifflin, 1959), p. 68.

34. Lydia Maria Child, "Letter from New York, Number 11" [1841], in *Lydia Maria Child Reader,* pp. 306–11.

35. Ibid., p. 312.

36. Carson, "Gender of Sound," pp. 12, 23; "Talking Women," *Godey's Lady's Book* 54 (June 1857): 561; "James Ronaldson," typescript "abstracted from Historical Catalogue of the St. Andrew's Society of Philadelphia, 1795–1907," Autograph Collection of the HSP, ca. 1907. Row houses were usually built as mirror images of one another, so that the doors were paired (see fig. 2).

37. Mary P. Ryan, *Mysteries of Sex: Tracing Women and Men Through American History* (Chapel Hill: University of North Carolina Press, 2006), pp. 86, 158–59, 162–63; Arthur Singleton, *Letters from the South and West* (Boston: Richardson and Lord, 1824), p. 16; William B. Davidson, Journal, 1825–25, MS, HSP, Nov. 22, 1825.

38. Cope, pp. 480–81, 501.

39. Cmiel, *Democratic Eloquence,* pp. 70–71; Madaline S. Edwards, *Madaline: Love and Survival in Antebellum New Orleans,* ed. Dell Upton (Athens: University of Georgia Press, 1996), pp. 36–38, 82, 118, 288; Ryan, *Women in Public,* pp. 19, 24, 31.

40. Fisher, p. 49; *A Memorial to the Honorable Senate and House of Representatives of the Commonwealth of Pennsylvania by the Colored Citizens of Philadelphia 1834* (Philadelphia, 1854; rpt. Philadelphia: Rhistoric Publications, 1969), pp. 1–2.

41. Deposition of Joseph Montégut, Jr., May 16, 1812, HC, box VIII, fol. C, pt. 1; J. Cornen, Plaquemines Parish, La., to Mayor Joseph Roffignac, New Orleans, May 12, 1826, NOMP/T, box 11, fol. 7; Deposition of Madame Veuve Robin, Oct. 12, 1813, HC, box VIII, fol. C, pt. 2; Deposition of Anthony Lamarlère, Oct. 3, 1816, HC, box VIII, fol. D, pt. 2.

42. White and White, *Sounds of Slavery,* pp. 148, 157–58; "Dixon," *New-York Herald,* May 17, 1839, p. 2:4.

43. Cohen, *Self-Consciousness,* pp. 71–78; Watson I, p. 479; White and White, *Sounds of Slavery,* p. 188.

44. William Mulder and A. Russel Mortensen, eds., *Among the Mormons: Historic Accounts by Contemporary Observers* (Lincoln: University of Nebraska Press, 1958), pp. 13–34, 67, 112, 114–15, 349, 361–62, 383.

45. Jacques Attali, *Noise: The Political Economy of Music,* trans. Brian Massumi (Minneapolis: University of Minnesota Press, 1999), pp. 6–7, 11; Michael Nyman, *Experimental Music: Cage and Beyond* (Cambridge: Cambridge University Press, 1999), p. 32; NOMP/T, box 5, fol. 4 (July 27, 1840); *Regulations for the Government of the Nightly Watch of the City of Philadelphia* [Philadelphia, 1823]; Drinker 1: 610 (Oct. 24, 1794); *Philadelphia in 1824* (Philadelphia: H. C. Carey and I. Lea, Aug. 1824), p. 169.

46. Cope, pp. 110–11.

47. Devereux, "Ethnopsychological Aspects of the Terms 'Deaf' and 'Dumb,'" pp. 44–45; Howes, "Sensorial Anthropology," pp. 188–89.

48. "Great Cities," *Putnam's Monthly Magazine* 5, no. 27 (Mar. 1855): 254–63.

49. "Editor's Drawer," *Harper's New Monthly Magazine* 9 (Aug. 1854): 421.

CHAPTER 5. **SEEING AND BELIEVING**

1. Walt Whitman, "Starting from Paumanok," in *Complete Poetry and Selected Prose,* ed. James E. Miller, Jr. (Boston: Houghton Mifflin, 1959), pp. 16, 23; Northern Star, "The Observer. The City of New-York," *New-York Mirror* 6 (Nov. 15, 1828): 147; "Editor's Drawer," *Harper's New Monthly Magazine* 9 (Aug. 1854): 421; George Templeton Strong Diary, copy of MS at Metropolitan Museum of Art, Aug. 24, 1845; "City Improvements. The New Custom-House," *New-York Mirror* 12 (Aug. 23, 1834), p. 57.

2. David Henkin, *City Reading: Written Words and Public Spaces in Antebellum New York* (New York: Columbia University Press, 1999), pp. 27–100; "New York Daguerreotyped. Group First: Business-Streets, Mercantile Blocks, Stores, and Banks," *Putnam's Monthly Magazine* 1, no. 2 (Feb. 1853): 358; "The Dry Goods Stores of Broadway," *Home Journal,* Oct. 27, 1849, p. 3; "Shopping in Broadway," *Holden's Dollar Magazine* 3, no. 5 (May 1849), p. 320.

3. "Sketchings. Broadway," *Crayon* 5 (Aug. 1858): 234; James Stuart, *Three Years in North America,* 3d rev. ed. (Edinburgh: for Robert Cadell, 1833), 2: 201; Latrobe, *Jnls.,* 3: 171.

4. Norbert Elias, *The Civilizing Process: The History of Manners* (New York: Pantheon, 1978), pp. 58–59, 115–16, 135–37; Richard L. Bushman, *The Refinement of America: Persons, Houses, Cities* (New York: Knopf, 1992), pp. xii–xiv; Cary Carson, "The Consumer Revolution in Colonial British America: Why Demand?" in *Of Consuming Interests: The Style of Life in the Eighteenth Century,* ed. Cary Carson, Ronald Hoffman, and Peter J. Albert (Charlottesville: University Press of Virginia for the United States Capitol Historical Society, 1994), p. 521; Barbara G. Carson, *Ambitious Appetites: Dining, Behavior, and Patterns of Consumption in Federal Washington* (Washington, D.C.: AIA, 1990), p. 15. The following account of gentility is particularly indebted to Bushman's work and to John Kasson, *Rudeness and Civility: Manners in Nineteenth-Century Urban America* (New York: Hill and Wang, 1990).

5. Drinker 2: 951.

6. Carson, "Consumer Revolution," p. 675; Daniel Walker Howe, *Making the American Self: Jonathan Edwards to Abraham Lincoln* (Cambridge: Harvard University Press, 1997), p. 114; Peter Lunt, "Psychological Approaches to Consumption: Varieties of Research—Past, Present and Future," in *Acknowledging Consumption: A Review of New Studies,* ed. Daniel Miller (London: Routledge, 1994), p. 249.

7. Charles Varlo, *Schemes Offered for the Perusal and Consideration of the Legislature, Freeholders, and Public in General* (London: J. Chapman, 1775), p. iii; Bryan S. Turner, *The Body and Society: Explorations in Social Theory,* 2d. ed. (London: Sage, 1996), pp. 22–29; James Deetz, *In Small Things Forgotten: An Archaeology of Early American Life,* rev. ed. (New York: Anchor, 1996), p. 35.

8. Anne Hollander, *Seeing Through Clothes* (New York: Avon, 1978), pp. xi–xii; Jennifer Craik, *The Face of Fashion: Cultural Studies in Fashion* (London: Routledge, 1994), pp. 2, 4, 5, 9.

9. George Lippard, *The Quaker City; or, the Monks of Monk Hall; A Romance of Philadelphia Life, Mystery, and Crime* [1845], ed. David S. Reynolds (Amherst: University of Massachusetts Press, 1995), pp. 154, 156.

10. Latrobe, *Jnls.,* 3: 190; [Robert Waln, Jr.], *The Hermit in America on a Visit to Philadelphia* (Philadelphia: M. Thomas, 1819–21), p. 91; Lippard, *Quaker City,* p. 156; [Asa Greene], *A Glance at New York* (New York: A. Greene, 1837), p. 81; Kasson, *Rudeness and Civility,* p. 127.

11. Edward T. Hall, *The Hidden Dimension* (Garden City, N.Y.: Anchor, 1966, 1969), pp. 7, 10, 66, 119; Naomi Eilan, Anthony Marcel, and José Luis Bermúdez, "Self-Consciousness and the Body: An Interdisciplinary Introduction," in *The Body and the Self,* ed. José Luis Bermúdez,

Anthony Marcel, and Naomi Eilan (Cambridge: MIT Press, 1995), p. 20; Celia A. Brownell and Claire B. Kopp, "Common Threads, Diverse Solutions: Concluding Commentary," *Developmental Review* 11, no. 3 (Sept. 1991): 297; John Campbell, "The Body Image and Self-Consciousness," in *Body and the Self,* p. 34; George Butterworth, "An Ecological Perspective on the Origins of Self," in *Body and the Self,* p. 101.

12. Anthony P. Cohen, *Self-Consciousness: An Alternative Anthropology of Identity* (London: Routledge, 1994), pp. 122–32; James J. Gibson, *The Senses Considered as Perceptual Systems* (Boston: Houghton Mifflin, 1966), pp. 18–19.

13. Marcel Kinsbourne, "Awareness of One's Own Body: An Attentional Theory of Its Nature, Development, and Brain Basis," in Bermúdez, Marcel, and Eilan, *Body and the Self,* p. 211; Ulric Neisser, "Five Kinds of Self-Knowledge," *Philosophical Psychology* 1, no. 1 (1988): 39–40; James J. Gibson, *The Ecological Approach to Visual Perception* (Boston: Houghton Mifflin, 1979), pp. 40–41; Jacques Paillard, "Motor and Representational Framing of Space," in *Brain and Space,* ed. Jacques Paillard (Oxford: Oxford University Press, 1991), p. 164.

14. Eleanor J. Gibson, "Ontogenesis of the Perceived Self," in *The Perceived Self: Ecological and Interpersonal Sources of Self-Knowledge,* ed. Ulric Neisser (Cambridge: Cambridge University Press, 1993), p. 33; Shaun Gallagher, "Body Image and Body Schema: A Conceptual Classification," *Journal of Mind and Behavior* 7, no. 4 (autumn 1986): 546, 548.

15. Hall, *Hidden Dimension,* p. 3; Butterworth, "Ecological Perspective," pp. 99, 101; Gallagher, "Body Image," p. 545.

16. "Jim Crow" lyrics at www.musicals101.com/lycrow.htm, downloaded Sept. 26, 2005; Eric Lott, *Love and Theft: Blackface Minstrelsy and the American Working Class* (New York: Oxford University Press, 1993), pp. 22–29; Cecelia Conway, *African Banjo Echoes in Appalachia: A Study of Folk Traditions* (Knoxville: University of Tennessee Press, 1995), pp. 95–102.

17. Gerilyn Tandberg, "Decoration and Decorum: Accessories of Nineteenth-Century Louisiana Women," *Southern Quarterly* 27, no. 1 (fall 1988): 22.

18. Sophie White, "'Wearing three or four handkerchiefs around his collar, and elsewhere about him': Masculinity and Ethnicity in French Colonial New Orleans," *Gender and History* 15, no. 3 (Nov. 2003): 531–35.

19. Carol Shammas, "The Space Problem in the Early United States," *WMQ,* 3d ser., 57, no. 3 (July 2000): 531–34; "The American Lounger—By Samuel Saunter, Esq.," *Port Folio,* ser. 4, 7, no. 4 (Apr. 1819): 325–26.

20. [William M. Bobo], *Glimpses of New-York City* (Charleston: J. J. McCarter, 1852), pp. 164–65.

21. Shane White and Graham White, *Stylin': African American Expressive Culture from Its Beginnings to the Zoot Suit* (Ithaca: Cornell University Press, 1998), pp. 45–53, 57; Charles Joseph Latrobe, *The Rambler in North America, MDCCCXXXII–MDCCCXXXIII* (New York: Harper and Bros., 1835), 2: 240; Roderick A. McDonald, *The Economy and Material Culture of Slaves: Goods and Chattels on the Sugar Plantations of Jamaica and Louisiana* (Baton Rouge: Louisiana State University Press, 1993), p. 149; Shane White and Graham White, "Slave Hair and African American Culture in the Eighteenth and Nineteenth Centuries," *Journal of Southern History* 61, no. 1 (Feb. 1995): 71–75; Louise Livingston Hunt, *Memoir of Mrs. Edward Livingston* (New York: Harper and Bros., 1886), p. 46; Joseph Holt Ingraham, *The South-West. By a Yankee* (New York: Harper and Bros., 1835), 1: 100; Tandberg, "Decoration and Decorum," p. 12.

22. Helen Bradley Foster, *"New Raiments of Self": African American Clothing in the Antebellum South* (Oxford, Miss.: Berg, 1997), p. 143; Douglas R. Egerton, *He Shall Go Out Free: The Lives*

of Denmark Vesey (Madison, Wis.: Madison House, 1999), pp. 99–100; Deposition of Etienne Mazureau, Dec. 18, 1813, HC, box VIII, fol. C, pt. 2.

23. [Francis J. Grund], *Aristocracy in America from the Sketch-Book of a German Nobleman* (London: Richard Bentley, 1839), p. 29.

24. Daniel H. Usner, Jr., "American Indians in Colonial New Orleans," in *Powhatan's Mantle: Indians in the Colonial Southeast*, ed. Peter H. Wood, Gregory A. Waselkov, and M. Thomas Hatley (Lincoln: University of Nebraska Press, 1989), p. 116; Daniel H. Usner, Jr., *Indians, Settlers, and Slaves in a Frontier Exchange Economy: The Lower Mississippi Valley Before 1783* (Chapel Hill: University of North Carolina Press, 1992), p. 45.

25. David I. Bushnell, "The Choctaw of St. Tammany Parish," *LH* 1, no. 1 (Jan. 1917): 15; Basil Hall, *Travels in North America, in the Years 1827 and 1828* (Edinburgh: for Cadell and Co., 1829), 3: 294–96; Arthur Singleton, *Letters from the South and West* (Boston: Richardson and Lord, 1824), p. 123; Henri Berquin-Duvallon, ed., *Vue de la colonie espagnole du Mississipi, ou des provinces de Louisianie et Floride Occidentale, en l'année 1802* (Paris: imprimérie Expéditive, 1803), p. 193; Latrobe, *Rambler*, 2: 241; Fredrika Bremer, *The Homes of the New World*, trans. Mary Howitt (New York: Harper and Bros., 1854), 2: 214.

26. Amos Stoddard, *Sketches, Historical and Descriptive, of Louisiana* (Philadelphia: Mathew Carey, 1812), pp. 299–300.

27. Elizabeth Johns, *American Genre Painting: The Politics of Everyday Life* (New Haven: Yale University Press, 1991), pp. xii–xiii, 12–22.

28. Edgar Allan Poe, "The Man of the Crowd" (1840; rev. 1845), in *Selected Writings of Edgar Allan Poe*, ed. Edward H. Davidson (Boston: Houghton Mifflin, 1956), pp. 131–39.

29. Herman Melville, *The Confidence Man: His Masquerade* (1857; rpt. New York: Holt Rinehart and Winston, 1964); Karen Halttunen, *Confidence Men and Painted Women: A Study of Middle-Class Culture in America, 1830–1870* (New Haven: Yale University Press, 1982), chap. 1.

30. Howe, *Making the American Self*, pp. 5–8, 21–22; E. S. Abdy, *Journal of a Residence and Tour in the United States of North America* (London: John Murray, 1835), 1: 74–75; James Flint, *Letters from America* (Edinburgh: W. and C. Tait, 1822), p. 39.

31. Carson, *Ambitious Appetites*, pp. 56–57; Katherine C. Grier, *Culture and Comfort: People, Parlors, and Upholstery, 1850–1930* (Rochester, N.Y.: Margaret Woodbury Strong Museum, 1988), pp. 6–7; "Clark's Broadway Tailoring" (advertisement), *Home Journal*, May 3, 1851, p. 3.

32. "The Petition and Memorial of the Subscribers, Licenced Inn and Tavern-Keepers," Jan. 12, 1804, McAllister Coll./LCP Coll., HSP; "Ardent Spirits," *HRP* 3, no. 6 (Feb. 7, 1829): 96; Marcia Carlisle, "Disorderly City, Disorderly Women: Prostitution in Ante-Bellum Philadelphia," *PMHB* 110, no. 4 (Oct. 1986): 564; George G. Foster, *New York by Gas-Light and Other Urban Sketches*, ed. Stuart G. Blumin (1850; rpt. Berkeley: University of California Press, 1990); Matthew Hale Smith, *Sunshine and Shadow in New York* (Hartford, 1868).

33. Lippard, *Quaker City*, pp. 46–49; David S. Reynolds, *Quaker City*, pp. xvi–xviii, xxxii–xxxvii; David S. Reynolds, *Beneath the American Renaissance: The Subversive Imagination in the Age of Emerson and Melville* (New York: Knopf, 1988), pp. 204–10.

34. Lippard, *Quaker City*, p. 553.

35. Cope, p. 581; [George Lippard], *Life and Adventures of Charles Anderson Chester, the Notorious Leader of the Philadelphia "Killers"* (Philadelphia, 1850); [George Lippard], *The Killers*

(Philadelphia: Hankinson and Bartholomew, 1850); George Lippard, *The Bank Director's Son* (Philadelphia: E. E. Barclay and A. R. Orton, 1851).

36. [Lippard], *Killers*, pp. 9, 13, 21, 32; [Lippard], *Life and Adventures of Charles Anderson Chester*, pp. 25–27.

37. [Lippard], *Life and Adventures of Charles Anderson Chester*, pp. 26–27.

38. Lippard, *Quaker City*, pp. 230, 243.

39. R. Peter Hobson, "Through Feeling and Sight to Self and Symbol," in *Perceived Self*, pp. 254–55, 266, 268; Michael Tomasello, "On the Interpersonal Origins of the Self-Concept," in *Perceived Self*, pp. 174–83; David Jopling, "Cognitive Science, Other Minds, and the Philosophy of Dialogue," in *Perceived Self*, pp. 290–309.

CHAPTER 6. **THE GRID AND THE REPUBLICAN SPATIAL IMAGINATION**

1. Thomas M. Doerflinger, *A Vigorous Spirit of Enterprise: Merchants and Economic Development in Revolutionary Philadelphia* (Chapel Hill: University of North Carolina Press for the Institute of Early American History and Culture, 1986), pp. 251–52; Richard G. Miller, "The Federal City, 1783–1800," in *Philadelphia, a 300-Year History*, ed. Russell F. Weigley (New York: Norton, 1982), p. 166; Sam Bass Warner, Jr., *The Private City: Philadelphia in Three Periods of Its Growth*, 2d ed. (Philadelphia: University of Pennsylvania Press, 1987), p. 100; Philadelphia City Council, Minutes, 1789–93, p. 1 (Act of Incorporation), meetings of Apr. 24, June 29, 1789.

2. "Petition to the Common Council from Some Citizens," n.d. (1790s), Philadelphia General Petitions, 1692–1799, Society Miscellaneous Collection, HSP, box 42, fol. 9. Like most contemporary historians, early-nineteenth-century Philadelphians erroneously associated the "Instructions" with the famous Penn-Holme map and with the plan of their own city. The work of Gary Nash and especially Hannah Benner Roach, published in the 1960s but unaccountably overlooked, has shown that the green country town was meant to be a rural township; it was modified by Penn and his surveyor Holme when they learned that neither the topography nor the legalities of existing landholdings would permit such a settlement to be established (Gary B. Nash, "City Planning and Political Tension in the Seventeenth Century: The Case of Philadelphia," *Proceedings of the American Philosophical Society* 112, no. 1 [Feb. 1968]: 54–63; Hannah Benner Roach, "The Planting of Philadelphia: A Seventeenth-Century Real Estate Development," *PMHB* 92, no. 1 [Jan. 1968]: 3–47 and 92, no. 2 [Apr. 1968]: 143–94). Roach says explicitly, "No longer valid is the premise that the 'green Country Towne,' first envisaged by Penn, was in any way related to the city depicted in Thomas Holme's *Portraiture of a City*, or that the *Portraiture* itself was a final and immutable picture of the city in fact" (Roach, "Planting," p. 5).

3. Roach, "Planting," p. 28; Martin P. Snyder, *City of Independence: Views of Philadelphia Before 1800* (New York: Praeger, 1975), pp. 16–22.

4. Watson II, 1: 169–70.

5. Warner, *Private City*, p. 52; Penn, *Papers*, 2: 121.

6. *To the Select and Common Councils . . . the Memorial and Remonstrance of the Subscribers* (Philadelphia, 1851), p. 3; "Petition to the Common Council from Some Citizens," n.d. (1790s), Philadelphia General Petitions, 1692–1799, Society Miscellaneous Collection, HSP, box 42, fol. 9; Watson II, 1: 405–7; Cope, pp. 459–60.

7. David M. Scobey, *Empire City: The Making and Meaning of the New York City Landscape*

(Philadelphia: Temple University Press, 2002), pp. 1–3; Jon A. Peterson, *The Birth of City Planning in the United States, 1840–1917* (Baltimore: Johns Hopkins University Press, 2003), pp. xv, 5–18; John W. Reps, *The Making of Urban America: A History of City Planning in the United States* (Princeton: Princeton University Press, 1965), p. 294; Edward K. Spann, "The Greatest Grid: The New York Plan of 1811," in *Two Centuries of American Planning*, ed. Daniel Schaffer (Baltimore: Johns Hopkins University Press, 1988), p. 11.

8. Peter Marcuse, "The Grid as City Plan: New York City and Laissez-Faire Planning in the Nineteenth Century," *Planning Perspectives* 2, no. 3 (Sept. 1987): 297; Spann, "Greatest Grid," p. 14, 16; Hendrik Hartog, *Public Property and Private Power: The Corporation of the City of New York in American Law, 1730–1870* (Chapel Hill: University of North Carolina Press, 1983), p. 158; Elizabeth Blackmar, *Manhattan for Rent, 1790–1850* (Ithaca: Cornell University Press, 1989), pp. 96–99.

9. Spiro Kostof, *The City Shaped: Urban Patterns and Meanings Through History* (Boston: Little, Brown, 1991), pp. 209–11, 232–35; John W. Reps, *Tidewater Towns: City Planning in Colonial Virginia and Maryland* (Williamsburg, Va.: Colonial Williamsburg Foundation, 1972), pp. 117–40; Reps, *Making of Urban America*, pp. 240–62, 264–75, 314–19; Frederick Gutheim, *Worthy of the Nation: The History of Planning for the National Capital* (Washington, D.C.: Smithsonian Institution Press, 1977), pp. 24–36; Thomas Jefferson, "Proceedings to be Had under the Residence Act," Nov. 29, 1790, in *Thomas Jefferson and the National Capital*, ed. Saul K. Padover (Washington, D.C.: Government Printing Office, 1944), p. 31; Evelyn Martindale Thom, *Baton Rouge Story: An Historical Sketch of Louisiana's Capital City* (Baton Rouge: Baton Rouge Foundation for Historical Louisiana, 1967), pp. 12, 14–16; Snyder, *City of Independence*, pp. 198–201.

10. Marcuse, "Grid," p. 228; Christine Boyer, *Manhattan Manners: Architecture and Style, 1850–1900* (New York: Rizzoli, 1985), p. 9.

11. Reps, *Making of Urban America*, p. 321; Spann, "Greatest Grid," p. 21.

12. Reps, *Making of Urban America*, p. 294; Spann, "Greatest Grid," p. 25; Alexander Mackay, *The Western World; or, Travels in the United States in 1846–47*, 2d ed. (London: Richard Bentley, 1849), 1: 133; Jacques-Pierre Brissot de Warville, *New Travels in the United States of America* (Dublin: W. Corbet, P. Byrne, et al., 1792), p. 315; Basil Hall, *Travels in North America, in the Years 1827 and 1828* (Edinburgh: for Cadell and Co., 1829), 2: 367.

13. Constance D. Sherman, "A French Artist Describes Philadelphia," *PMHB* 82, no. 2 (Apr. 1958): 207; Brissot de Warville, *New Travels*, p. 315; Hall, *Travels*, 2: 367; James Stuart, *Three Years in North America*, 3d rev. ed. (Edinburgh: for Robert Cadell, 1833), 1: 366; Thomas Hamilton, *Men and Manners in America* (Edinburgh: William Blackwood; London: T. Cadell, 1834), 1: 329, 336–37; Jefferson, "Proceedings," p. 31; Charles Dickens, *American Notes and Pictures from Italy* (Oxford: Oxford University Press, 1957), p. 98.

14. Timothy Dwight, *Travels in New York and New England*, ed. Barbara Miller Solomon (Cambridge: Harvard University Press, 1969), 1: 353; Cope, pp. 65–66.

15. Cope, pp. 65, 373; Job Tyson to Roberts Vaux, July 24, 1829, VP.

16. Dwight, *Travels*, 1: 355.

17. Watson I, appendix, p. 73.

18. Tyson to Vaux, July 24, 1829.

19. Spann, "Greatest Grid," p. 26; Paul Groth, "Street Grids as Frameworks for Urban Variety," *Harvard Architectural Review* 2 (spring 1981): 68–75.

20. David Hume, *An Enquiry Concerning Human Understanding and A Letter from a Gentleman to His Friend in Edinburgh* (Indianapolis: Hackett, 1977), pp. 31, 112; Frederick Copleston, *A History of Philosophy*, vol. 5: *Modern Philosophy: The British Philosophers; part II, Berkeley to Hume* (Garden City: Image, 1964), pp. 73, 99–100; Frederick Copleston, *A History of Philosophy*, vol. 6: *Modern Philosophy; part II: Kant* (Garden City: Image, 1964), pp. 50–51, 175; Leo Salingar, "Coleridge: Poet and Philosopher," in *The New Pelican Guide to English Literature*, vol. 5: *From Blake to Byron*, rev. ed., ed. Boris Ford (Harmondsworth: Penguin, 1982), p. 287; William Flint Thrall, Addison Hibbard, and C. Hugh Holman, *A Handbook to Literature*, rev. ed. (New York: Odyssey, 1960), p. 235; Samuel Taylor Coleridge, *Biographia Literaria: or, Biographical Sketches of My Literary Life and Opinions [1817]*, in *Selected Poetry and Prose of Coleridge*, ed. Donald A. Stauffer (New York: Modern Library, 1951), pp. 184–85, 263.

21. Nash, "City Planning," pp. 61, 70; Roach, "Planting," pp. 36, 38–39, 157; Edwin B. Bronner, "Quaker Landmarks in Early Philadelphia," in *Historic Philadelphia, from Its Founding Until the Early Nineteenth Century* (Philadelphia: American Philosophical Society, 1953, 1980), pp. 210–11.

22. Ernst Cassirer, *The Philosophy of the Enlightenment*, trans. Fritz C. A. Koelln and James C. Pettigrove (Princeton: Princeton University Press, 1951), pp. vii, 9; J. L. Heilbron, "Introductory Essay," in *The Quantifying Spirit in the Eighteenth Century*, ed. Tore Frängsmyr, J. L. Heilbron, and Robin E. Rider (Berkeley: University of California Press, 1990), p. 2; John E. Lesch, "Systematics and the Geometrical Spirit," in *Quantifying Spirit*, pp. 73–111.

23. John C. Greene, *American Science in the Age of Jefferson* (Ames: Iowa State University Press, 1984), pp. 37–59; Brooke Hindle, *The Pursuit of Science in Revolutionary America 1735–1789* (Chapel Hill: University of North Carolina Press, 1956), pp. 64–65, 114–17, 127–45; Simon Baatz, "Philadelphia Patronage: The Institutional Structure of Natural History in the New Republic, 1800–1833," *Journal of the Early Republic* 8, no. 2 (summer 1988): 123, 134, 138.

24. Hindle, *Pursuit of Science*, pp. 11–58; Brooke Hindle, "Charles Willson Peale's Science and Technology," in Edgar P. Richardson, Brooke Hindle, and Lillian B. Miller, *Charles Willson Peale and His World* (New York: Abrams, 1982), p. 115; I. Bernard Cohen, *Science and the Founding Fathers: Science in the Political Thought of Jefferson, Franklin, Adams, and Madison* (New York: Norton, 1995), p. 44; Lesch, "Systematics," pp. 74–88; Greene, *American Science*, pp. 48–52, 202, 204; Pennsylvania Hospital Board of Managers, Minutes, 4: 410, APH; Elizabeth McLean, "Town and Country Gardens in Eighteenth-Century Philadelphia," *Eighteenth-Century Life*, n.s. 8, no. 2 (Jan. 1983): 138, 142–45; Cope, pp. 160, 184.

25. Manasseh Cutler, in *Passing Through: Letters and Documents Written in Philadelphia by Famous Visitors*, ed. Clive E. Driver (Philadelphia: Rosenbach Museum and Library, 1982), p. 33; Cope, p. 160; Charles W. Thomson, "Diarium Desultorum, or a Journal of Passing Events," MS, NYHS, vol. 4, July 20, 1820, n.p.

26. Cohen, *Science and the Founding Fathers*, pp. 45–47; Vernon Pratt, "Foucault and the History of Classification Theory," *Studies in the History and Philosophy of Science* 8, no. 2 (1977): 163–71; Lesch, "Systematics."

27. Thomas Jefferson, *Notes on the State of Virginia*, ed. Thomas Perkins Abernethy (1780; New York: Norton, 1964); Greene, *American Science*, p. 198.

28. Hindle, *Pursuit of Science*, p. 346; J. L. Heilbron, *Elements of Early Modern Physics* (Berkeley: University of California Press, 1982), pp. 44–45, 61–62; Pratt, "Foucault," p. 167; Cohen, *Science and the Founding Fathers*, pp. 20, 41–43; I. Bernard Cohen, *Benjamin Franklin's Science*

(Cambridge: Harvard University Press, 1990), pp. 19, 27, 40–60; Frederick B. Tolles, *Meeting House and Counting House: The Quaker Merchants of Colonial Philadelphia, 1682–1763* (New York: Norton, 1963), pp. 181, 214, 217, 219; Greene, *American Science*, p. 20.

29. Joyce O. Appleby, *Capitalism and a New Social Order: The Republican Vision of the 1790s* (New York: New York University Press, 1984), p. 33; Tolles, *Meeting House and Counting House*, p. 103.

30. Roger North, *The Gentleman Accomptant*, 2d. ed. (London: E. Curll, 1715), pp. 1, 2, 17–18, 57–58, 62, 201.

31. Patricia Cline Cohen, *A Calculating People: The Spread of Numeracy in Early America* (Chicago: University of Chicago Press, 1982), pp. 27–28; R. Campbell, *The London Tradesman* (London, 1747), p. 284; Appleby, *Capitalism*, pp. 28, 39–50; Glenn Porter and Harold C. Livesay, *Merchants and Manufacturers: Studies in the Changing Structure of Nineteenth-Century Marketing* (Baltimore: Johns Hopkins University Press, 1971), pp. 7–9.

32. Appleby, *Capitalism*, p. 33; Daniel Walker Howe, *Making the American Self: Jonathan Edwards to Abraham Lincoln* (Cambridge: Harvard University Press, 1997), pp. 12, 28; Ronald Schultz, "The Small Producer Tradition and the Moral Origins of Artisan Radicalism in Philadelphia, 1720–1810," *Past and Present*, no. 127 (May 1990): 101–2; Cohen, *Science and the Founding Fathers*, p. 33.

33. Cohen, *Calculating People*, pp. 41, 44, 116–17, 127, 150–73; Heilbron, "Introductory Essay," p. 13; Clement Biddle, *The Philadelphia Directory* (Philadelphia: James and Johnson, 1791), pp. v–ix.

34. Hayden White, *Tropics of Discourse: Essays in Cultural Criticism* (Baltimore: Johns Hopkins University Press, 1978), pp. 81–100, 121–34; Lesch, "Systematics," pp. 79, 85–86, 88–89, 103.

35. Peale, *Papers*, 1: 448, 464; Hindle, *Pursuit of Science*, pp. 260–62; Greene, *American Science*, pp. 52–57; Robert E. Schofield, "The Science Education of an Enlightened Entrepreneur: Charles Willson Peale and His Philadelphia Museum, 1784–1827," *American Studies* 30, no. 2 (fall 1989): 21; Hindle, "Charles Willson Peale," pp. 110–11, 113, 129, 134; Edgar P. Richardson, "Charles Willson Peale and His World," in *Charles Willson Peale and His World*, pp. 98–99; Charles Coleman Sellers, *Mr. Peale's Museum: Charles Willson Peale and the First Popular Museum of Natural Science and Art* (New York: Norton, 1980), pp. 193, 214.

36. Peale, *Papers*, 1: 448, 516; Schofield, "Science Education," pp. 24, 26–27, 35–36; "A Guide to the Peale Museum," *Port Folio* 4, no. 19 (Nov. 7, 1807): 294; *Philadelphia in 1824* (Philadelphia: H. C. Carey and I. Lea, 1824), p. 101.

37. Peale, *Papers*, 1: 483–84; "Guide to the Peale Museum," p. 293; Sellers, *Mr. Peale's Museum*, p. 162; Hindle, "Charles Willson Peale," p. 154; Greene, *American Science*, p. 282; Schofield, "Science Education," p. 37.

38. Hindle, "Charles Willson Peale," p. 123–26; Pratt, "Foucault," pp. 168–70.

39. Joyce Appleby, *Liberalism and Republicanism in the Historical Imagination* (Cambridge: Harvard University Press, 1992), p. 298; Robert E. Shalhope, "Toward a Republican Synthesis: The Emergence of an Understanding of Republicanism in American Historiography," *WMQ*, 3d ser., 29, no. 1 (Jan. 1972): 49–80; Robert E. Shalhope, "Republicanism and Early American Historiography," *WMQ*, 3d ser., 39, no. 2 (Apr. 1982): 334–56; Daniel T. Rodgers, "Republicanism: The Career of a Concept," *Journal of American History* 79, no. 1 (June 1992): 11–38; Howe, *Making the American Self*, p. 12; Appleby, *Capitalism*, pp. 14–15.

40. Cohen, *Calculating People*, pp. 127–29, 133.

41. Schultz, "Small Producer Thought," p. 128; [Samuel Blodget], *Thoughts on the Increasing*

Wealth and National Economy of the United States of America (Washington, D.C.: Way and Groff, 1801), p. 15; Alexander Hamilton, "On the Establishment of a Mint," May 5, 1791, in *Reports of the Secretary of the Treasury of the United States* (Washington, D.C.: Duff Green, 1828–51), 1:132–56.

42. John Dorsey to William Jones, president of the Second Bank of the United States, n.d. [ca. 1818], William Jones Papers, Uselma Clark Smith Collection, HSP.

43. [Blodget], *Thoughts*, pp. 7–10, 24.

44. "Petition of Residents and Owners of Property in [the] Western Part of the City, for Improving Penn Square," MS, Jan. 20, 1827, LCP Coll., HSP.

45. Gutheim, *Worthy of the Nation*, p. 25; John M. Bryan, "Robert Mills: Public Architecture in South Carolina, 1820–1830," in *Robert Mills, Architect*, ed. John M. Bryan (Washington, D.C.: American Institute of Architects Press, 1989), p. 75.

46. Gutheim, *Worthy of the Nation*, p. 25.

47. Arthur Singleton, *Letters from the South and West* (Boston: Richardson and Lord, 1824), p. 6; Brissot de Warville, *New Travels*, p. 315.

48. Kostof, *City Shaped*, p. 132.

49. Latrobe, *Corr.*, 2: 45.

50. Hamilton, *Men and Manners*, 1: 330, 336.

51. Dickens, *American Notes*, p. 98.

52. Boyer, *Manhattan Manners*, p. 9; Spann, "Greatest Grid," pp. 11–39; Snyder, *City of Independence*, pp. 198–205; Carole Shammas, "The Space Problem in the Early United States," *WMQ*, 3d ser., 57, no. 3 (July 2000): 523.

53. Hartog, *Public Property*, p. 163.

54. D. B. Lee and W. Beach, "Lighting the City by Towers," *HRP* 13, no. 4 (Jan. 25, 1834): 55–56.

55. Martha A. Zierden and Jeanne A. Calhoun, "Urban Adaptation in Charleston, South Carolina, 1730–1820," *Historical Archaeology* 20, no. 1 (1986): 35; Samuel Wilson, Jr., *The Vieux Carré, New Orleans: Its Plan, Its Growth, Its Architecture* (New Orleans: Bureau of Governmental Research for the City of New Orleans, 1968), p. 13.

56. Walter Muir Whitehill, *Boston: A Topographical History*, 2d ed. (Cambridge: Harvard University Press, 1975), pp. 1–46; John W. Reps, *The Making of Urban America: A History of City Planning in the United States* (Princeton: Princeton University Press, 1965), pp. 147–50; Berthold Fernow, ed., *The Records of New Amsterdam from 1653 to 1674 Anno Domini* (New York: Knickerbocker, 1897), 1: 33, 36–37.

57. Watson II, 1: 233; Roach, "Planting," pp. 22–24, 33–37.

58. Watson II, 1: 364–66; Thomas Condie and Richard Folwell, *History of the Pestilence, Commonly Called Yellow Fever, Which Almost Desolated Philadelphia, in the Months of August, September & October, 1798* (Philadelphia: R. Folwell, 1799), pp. 6–7; Michal McMahon, "'Publick Service' versus 'Man's Properties': Dock Creek and the Origins of Urban Technology in Eighteenth-Century Philadelphia," in *Early American Technology: Making and Doing Things from the Colonial Era to 1850*, ed. Judith A. McGaw (Chapel Hill: University of North Carolina Press for the Institute of Early American History and Culture, 1994), pp. 114–47.

59. Edward F. Heite and Louise B. Heite, "Town Plans as Artifacts: The Mid-Atlantic Experience," *Quarterly Bulletin of the Archaeological Society of Virginia* 41, no. 3 (Sept. 1986): 143.

60. Whitehill, *Boston*, pp. 60–63, 73–94; Dwight, *Travels*, 1: 356.

61. Stuart, *Three Years*, 1: 21; Hartog, *Public Property*, p. 160; Blackmar, *Manhattan*, p. 99; Latrobe, *Corr.*, 1: 517.

62. Watson II, 1: 232–35.

63. C. C. Robin, *Voyage to Louisiana by C. C. Robin, 1803–1805,* trans. Stuart O. Landry, Jr. (New Orleans: Pelican, 1966), pp. 31–32.

64. NOCVa, Apr. 4, 1805, Apr. 20, 1805; NOMP/T, box 2, fol. 6, Mar. 23, 1811.

65. Biddle, *Philadelphia Directory,* p. xii.

66. "Proceedings of Councils," *HRP* 5, no. 25 (June 19, 1830): 390; Howard Gillette, Jr., "The Emergence of the Modern Metropolis: Philadelphia in the Age of Its Consolidation," in *The Divided Metropolis: Social and Spatial Dimensions of Philadelphia, 1800–1975,* ed. William W. Cutler and Howard Gillette, Jr. (Westport, Conn.: Greenwood, 1980), p. 11; John L. Zieber, *Change: A Song of the Present Times* (Philadelphia: John L. Zieber, n.d. [ca. 1857]), broadside at LCP.

67. Mackay, *Western World,* 1: 24–25; Albert Fossier, *New Orleans, the Glamour Period, 1800–1840* (New Orleans: Pelican, 1957), pp. 39–40; NOMP/T, box 2, fol. 2 (June 15, 1805); NOMP/T, box 3, fol. 2 (Mar. 18, 1818); Whitehill, *Boston,* pp. 74–78; Lee H. Nelson, *The Colossus of 1812: An American Engineering Superlative* (New York: American Society of Civil Engineers, 1990), pp. 19–23; "A Statistical Account of the Schuylkill Permanent Bridge," *Port Folio,* n.s., 5, no. 11 (Mar. 12, 1808): 168–71; 5, no. 12 (Mar. 19, 1808): 182–87; 5, no. 13 (Mar. 26, 1808): 200–4; 5, no. 14 (Apr. 2, 1808): 222–24.

68. Latrobe, *Corr.,* 1: 111–25; Benjamin Henry Latrobe, *The Engineering Drawings of Benjamin Henry Latrobe,* ed. Darwin H. Stapleton (New Haven: Yale University Press for the Maryland Historical Society), 1980, pp. 28–36, 183, 196; Jane Mork Gibson, "The Fairmount Waterworks," Philadelphia Museum of Art, *Bulletin* 84, nos. 360–61 (summer 1988): 2–11; Warner, *Private City,* pp. 102–9.

69. Dell Upton, "Inventing the Metropolis: Civilization and Urbanity in Antebellum New York," in *Art and the Empire City: New York, 1825–1861,* ed. Catherine Hoover Voorsanger and John K. Howat (New York: Metropolitan Museum of Art, and New Haven: Yale University Press, 2000), pp. 10–11.

70. Sherman, "French Artist," p. 207.

CHAPTER 7. **GRIDDING CONSUMPTION**

1. *Philadelphia in 1830–1* (Philadelphia: E. L. Carey and A. Hart, 1830), p. 221; *An Act to Incorporate the Stockholders of the Philadelphia Arcade* (Philadelphia, 1829), pp. 7–8; Franklin Fire Insurance Company of Philadelphia, Survey of the Arcade, Mar. 31, 1830, copy in PHC Arcade file; Johann Friedrich Geist, *Arcades: The History of a Building Type* (Cambridge: MIT Press, 1985), pp. 69, 536, 538; Brooke Hindle, "Charles Willson Peale's Science and Technology," in Edgar P. Richardson, Brooke Hindle, and Lillian B. Miller, *Charles Willson Peale and His World* (New York: Abrams, 1982), p. 145.

2. "Articles of Association of the Philadelphia Arcade Company," broadside, Oct. 20, 1825, Edward Shippen Burd Papers, HSP (all unpublished Arcade documents can be found in the Burd Papers unless otherwise indicated); Matthew Eli Baigell, "John Haviland," Ph.D. diss., University of Pennsylvania, 1965, p. 18; "To the Honorable Senate and House of Representatives of the Commonwealth of Pennsylvania," n.d. (ca. 1828); *Act to Incorporate the Stockholders,* p. 1; Richard Webster, *Philadelphia Preserved: Catalog of the Historic American Buildings Survey,* 2d ed. (Philadelphia: Temple University Press, 1981), p. 64; Watson II, 1: 376–77.

3. Geist, *Arcades,* pp. 12, 35–37, 39.

4. Neil McKendrick, John Brewer, and J. H. Plumb, *The Birth of a Consumer Society: The Commercialization of Eighteenth-Century England* (Bloomington: Indiana University Press, 1982), pp. 112, 121–22; Eliza Ripley, *Social Life in Old New Orleans* (New York: D. Appleton, 1912), p. 60.

5. Policy nos. 482/483 (Nov. 15, 1795), 122 (Oct. 25, 1785), MAC, pp. 304–6, 92–93.

6. Policy nos. 316 (Apr. 12, 1792); 296 (Dec. 6, 1791); 86–88 (May 5, 1785), MAC, pp. 215–16, 199–200, 60–62.

7. Policy nos. 294 (Dec. 3, 1791), 104–5 (Aug. 1, 1785), MAC, pp. 196–97, 75–76.

8. Watson II, 1: 240.

9. Edward Chappell, "Beyond the Pale: Architectural Fieldwork for Colonial Williamsburg," *Fresh Advices: A Research Supplement to the Colonial Williamsburg Interpreter* 4, no. 6 (Nov. 1983): iii.

10. Alan Powers, *Shop Fronts* (London: Chatto and Windus, 1989), p. 3; "An Act for regulating, Pitching, Paving and Cleansing the Highways, Streets, Lanes, and Alleys," Feb. 18, 1769, *Phila. Ord.*, p. 20; Watson II, 1: 221–22.

11. Watson II, 1: 221; Drinker 2: 1337; Leonard S. Marcus, *The American Shop Window* (London: Architectural Press, 1978), p. 15.

12. Watson II, 1: 222; Policy nos. 388–89 (Dec. 11, 1793), MAC, pp. 252–53.

13. James Mease, *The Picture of Philadelphia*, continued by Thomas Porter (Philadelphia: Robert DeSilver, 1831), 1: 92; Franklin Fire Insurance Co. survey no. 1534, 1834, PHC.

14. Watson II, 1: 222.

15. Daniel Walker Howe, *Making the American Self: Jonathan Edwards to Abraham Lincoln* (Cambridge, Mass.: Harvard University Press, 1997), pp. 107, 122–26.

16. Ulric Neisser, "Five Kinds of Self-Knowledge," *Philosophical Psychology* 1, no. 1 (1988): 39; James J. Gibson, *The Senses Considered as Perceptual Systems* (Boston: Houghton Mifflin, 1966), p. 19; Richard L. Bushman, *The Refinement of America: Persons, Houses, Cities* (New York: Knopf, 1992), pp. 69–72.

17. Geist, *Arcades*, p. 319; M. Veronica Stokes, "The Lowther Arcade in the Strand," *London Topographical Record* 23 (1974): 127; "Explanations, Rules and Regulations of the New York Arcade and Free Halls of Exhibition," *Frank Leslie's Illustrated Newspaper* 3, no. 55 (Dec. 27, 1856): 63.

18. Peter A. Browne to Edward S. Burd, Dec. 26, 1827; Watson III, 3: 190.

19. Russell Lewis, "Everything Under One Roof: World's Fairs and Department Stores in Paris and Chicago," *Chicago Historical Review* 12 (fall 1983): 29–43; [Edward Shippen Burd], Committee Report to Arcade Managers, July 1, 1826.

20. Haviland originally designed a two-story building but added the third before construction began when the museum agreed to move to the Arcade. The managers noted that the redesign would reinforce the building's contribution to the street, for a third floor would "give juster proportions to the building; have a tendency to increase its architectural beauty, and render it decidedly more ornamental to our City" ([Burd], Committee Report to Arcade Managers). See John Haviland, "Specifications of several Kinds of Artificers Work with a description of the Kind quality, and dimensions of the materials to be used and the manner of executing the Workmanship contained in the formation of a third Story to the Phiᵃ Arcade, agreeable to the accompanying Plans, Elevation and sections," July 182[6?], HP, 1: 134–137. The drawings mentioned in the title do not survive.

21. Geist, *Arcades*, pp. 3–4, 17, 35, 54, 69.

22. Alexander Mackay, *The Western World; or, Travels in the United States in 1846–47,* 2d ed. (London: Richard Bentley, 1849), 1: 25, 140; Ripley, *Social Life in Old New Orleans,* pp. 58, 161; Wilson, *Vieux Carré,* p. 78; [William M. Bobo], *Glimpses of New-York City* (Charleston: J. J. McCarter, 1852), pp. 115–16; Madisonian, "Sketches of the Metropolis. The Streets of New-York. Broadway—Chatham-Street," *New-York Mirror* 16 (Apr. 13, 1839): 329–30; "Economy" (advertisement), *New-York Evening Post,* Oct. 22, 1832, p. 4; "A Card" (advertisement), *Morning Courier and New-York Enquirer,* Nov. 1, 1832, p. 1; "Astor's Park Hotel," *Atkinson's Casket* 10 (Apr. 1835): 217; Watson II, 1: 226, 239.

23. Watson I, 203–5, 208.

24. Arthur Hobson Quinn, "The Theatre and the Drama in Old Philadelphia," in *Historic Philadelphia, from Its Founding Until the Early Nineteenth Century* (Philadelphia: American Philosophical Society, 1953, 1980), pp. 315–16; Watson II, 1: 375.

25. Daniel Bowen, *A History of Philadelphia* (Philadelphia: Daniel Bowen, 1839), p. 157.

26. Robert L. Alexander, "The Arcade in Providence," *JSAH* 12, no. 3 (Oct. 1953): 13; *NOA* 2: 70–71.

27. [John Gibson], *Gibson's Guide and Directory of the State of Louisiana, and the Cities of New Orleans and Lafayette* (New Orleans: John Gibson, 1838), pp. 320–21; *NOA* 2: 182–83; *New Orleans Picayune,* Jan. 31, 1847, p. 3:2.

28. [Gibson], *Gibson's Guide,* p. 320; *New Orleans Picayune,* Jan. 11, 1844, p. 2: 1.

29. [Gibson], *Gibson's Guide,* p. 320.

30. Burd Tax Book, 1847, Burd Papers; lease, Burd to John Finn and Thomas Winter, Apr. 4, 1823, Burd Papers; Fisher, p. 215.

31. Clipping attached to lithograph "The Pagoda and Labyrinth Gardens," Prints and Photographs Coll., HSP.

32. John Summerson, *Georgian London,* rev. ed. (Harmondsworth: Penguin, 1978), pp. 121–23.

33. William Parker Foulke [or Edward Haviland?], John Haviland obituary, MS, Apr. 14, 1852, Foulke Papers; James Elmes and Thomas Hosmer Shepherd, *Metropolitan Improvements; or, London in the Nineteenth Century* (London: Jones, 1827); Donald J. Olsen, *Town Planning in London: The Eighteenth and Nineteenth Centuries,* 2d ed. (New Haven: Yale University Press, 1982), pp. 99–125, 144–55; Summerson, *Georgian London,* pp. 177–90.

34. [John Haviland], "Buildings Designed by Jno: Haviland Esquire," MS, n.d. (ca. 1841), William Parker Foulke Papers, APS; Matthew Baigell, "John Haviland in Philadelphia, 1818–1826," *JSAH* 25, no. 3 (Oct. 1966): 197–208; Matthew Baigell, "John Haviland in Pottsville," *JSAH* 26, no. 4 (Dec. 1967): 306–9.

35. Bushman, *Refinement of America,* pp. 157–59, 356.

36. Haviland had worked on the interior decoration of the rebuilt theater (Baigell, "John Haviland," p. 293).

37. Geist, *Arcades,* pp. 310–12.

38. Agnes Addison Gilchrist, *William Strickland, Architect and Engineer, 1788–1854* (Philadelphia: University of Pennsylvania Press, 1950), pp. 50–51; *Philadelphia in 1824* (Philadelphia: H. C. Carey and I. Lea, 1824), pp. 193–95.

39. Charles Sellers, *The Market Revolution: Jacksonian America, 1815–1846* (New York: Oxford University Press, 1991), pp. 81, 151; Stuart Bruchey, *The Roots of American Economic Growth, 1607–1861: An Essay in Social Causation* (New York: Harper, 1968), pp. 107, 119–20, 125–27.

40. *Philadelphia in 1830–1,* p. 221; Peter A. Browne to Edward S. Burd, Oct. 3, 1827; Norman O. Brown, *Hermes the Thief: The Evolution of a Myth* (New York: Vintage, 1947, 1969), pp. 7, 34, 45, 79–83; Edward Tripp, *Crowell's Handbook of Classical Mythology* (New York: Thomas Y.

Crowell, 1970), pp. 299–302; G. M. Kirkwood, *A Short Guide to Classical Mythology* (New York: Holt, Rinehart and Winston, 1959), p. 55.

41. "To the Honorable Senate and House of Representatives"; Elva Tooker, *Nathan Trotter, Philadelphia Merchant, 1787–1853* (Cambridge, Mass.: Harvard University Press, 1955), pp. 158–59.

42. Alfred D. Chandler, Jr., *The Visible Hand: The Managerial Revolution in American Business* (Cambridge: Harvard University Press, 1977), pp. 8, 16; "To the Honourable Senate and House of Representatives."

43. "To the Honourable Senate and House of Representatives"; Morton J. Horwitz, *The Transformation of American Law, 1780–1860* (Cambridge: Harvard University Press, 1977), pp. 109–22; Bruchey, *Roots of American Economic Growth*, pp. 128–33.

44. *Act to Incorporate the Stockholders*, p. 5; "To the Honourable Senate and House of Representatives."

45. Browne to Burd, Jan. 29, 1828.

46. Watson I, pp. 219–20.

47. Browne to Burd, Nov. 8, 1827; Browne to Burd, Sept. 4, 1827; Browne to Managers of the Arcade, n.d.

48. Franklin Fire Ins. Co. 1830 survey, addendum of Aug. 27, 1844; "Arcade Hotel" flyer, July, 1855, LCP Print Collection no. (6)1322.F.130A; Franklin Fire Ins. Co. Survey no. 22311, Apr. 2, 1855; Watson III, 3: 190–91; Nicholas B. Wainwright, *Philadelphia in the Romantic Age of Lithography* (Philadelphia: Historical Society of Pennsylvania, 1958), p. 191.

49. Mackay, *Western World*, 1: 140; *Act to Incorporate the Stockholders*, p. 6; Watson III, 3: 190.

50. Glenn R. Conrad, ed., *A Dictionary of Louisiana Biography* (New Orleans: Louisiana Historical Association, 1988), pp. 35–36, 870.

51. *Act to Incorporate the Stockholders*, pp. 5–6.

52. *Act to Incorporate the Stockholders*, pp. 5–6. Emphasis in the original.

53. *Memorial of Sundry Merchants, Manufacturers, &c. of Baltimore. January 19, 1824* (Washington, D.C.: Gales and Seaton, 1824), p. 4.

54. Thomas M. Doerflinger, *A Vigorous Spirit of Enterprise: Merchants and Economic Development in Revolutionary Philadelphia* (Chapel Hill: University of North Carolina Press, 1986), pp. 18, 142–46; Watson I, 221; Mary Lorrain Peters, Diary 1837–39, MS, NYHS, p. 16; Cope, p. 139.

55. Haviland to John Branch, ca. 1830, HP, 2: 103–5.

56. Cope, pp. 211, 169; Watson I, pp. 220–21.

57. Ronald Schultz, *The Republic of Labor: Philadelphia Artisans and the Politics of Class, 1720–1830* (New York: Oxford University Press, 1993), pp. 6–7; Memorial of Sundry Merchants, Manufacturers, &c. of Baltimore, p. 4.

58. Watson I, 220–21; Watson II, 1: 240–1; "Mercantile Drumming," *Atkinson's Casket* (Graham's), 8 (Sept. 1833): 405; Tooker, *Nathan Trotter*, pp. 60, 137–38.

59. Watson I, p. 221; [Asa Greene], *A Glance at New York* (New York: A. Greene, 1837), pp. 110–11; Herbert G. Gutman, *Work, Culture and Society in Industrializing America: Essays in American Working-Class and Social History* (New York: Vintage, 1977), p. 60.

60. "Philadelphia Arcade; Joseph Moore Dealer in fancy & staple dry goods . . . ," Childs & Inman lithograph, Philadelphia, ca. 1830, HSP Society Print Collection—Small Stores and Factories—Dry Goods.

61. William Earl Dodge, "A Great Merchant's Recollections of Old New York, 1818–1880," in

Henry Collins Brown, ed. *Valentine's Manual of Old New York* n.s., 5 (New York: Valentine's Manual, 1921), p. 154; "Stewart's Temple," *Morris's National Press (Home Journal)* 1 (Apr. 18, 1846): 2; "Architecture," *Broadway Journal* 1, no. 12 (Mar. 22, 1845): 188–89; "The Wife's Error," *Godey's Lady's Book* 46 (June 1853): 495; "The Dry Goods Stores of Broadway," *Home Journal*, Oct. 27, 1849, p. 3; Alice B. Neal, "The Flitting," *Godey's Lady's Book* 54 (Apr. 1857): 331–39; "Employment for Females," *New-York Mirror* 12 (Dec. 20, 1834): 199; "Broadway in the Panic," *Ballou's Pictorial Drawing-Room Companion* 13, no. 24 (Dec. 12, 1857): 381; Michael Zakim, *Ready-Made Democracy: A History of Men's Dress in the American Republic, 1760–1860* (Chicago: University of Chicago Press, 2003), p. 124.

62. Watson II, 2: 591.

CHAPTER 8. **PERMUTATIONS OF THE PIGEONHOLE: ARCHITECTURE AS MEMORY**

1. R. Campbell, *The London Tradesman* (London: T. Gardner, 1747), pp. 292–93, 283; Patricia Cleary, "'She Will be in the Shop': Women's Sphere of Trade in Eighteenth-Century Philadelphia and New York," *PMHB* 119, no. 3 (July 1995): 181–202. Throughout the first part of this chapter my summary descriptions of the shape of business life depend on Glenn Porter and Harold C. Livesay, *Merchants and Manufacturers: Studies in the Changing Structure of Nineteenth-Century Marketing* (Baltimore: Johns Hopkins University Press, 1971); Alfred D. Chandler, Jr., *The Visible Hand: The Managerial Revolution in American Business* (Cambridge: Harvard University Press, 1977); and Thomas M. Doerflinger, *A Vigorous Spirit of Enterprise: Merchants and Economic Development in Revolutionary Philadelphia* (Chapel Hill: University of North Carolina Press, 1986), unless otherwise stated.

2. Elva Tooker, *Nathan Trotter, Philadelphia Merchant, 1787–1853* (Cambridge: Harvard University Press, 1955), p. 179.

3. "An Account of Peter A. Browne's Rent, Jan.–Dec. 1837," Society Coll., case 19, box 19, HSP.

4. Robert Greenhalgh Albion, with the collaboration of Jennie Barnes Pope, *The Rise of New York Port (1815–1860)* (New York: Scribner's, 1939), pp. 260–62; Chandler, *Visible Hand*, p. 37; Page Talbott, "The Office in the 19th Century," in *Wooton Patent Desks: A Place for Everything and Everything in Its Place*, ed. J. Camille Showalter and Janice Driesbach (Indianapolis and Oakland: Indiana State Museum and Oakland Museum, 1983), pp. 14–16; Ralph Edwards, "Bureaux, Bureau Tables and Writing Cabinets (Escritoire, Scriptor, Scrutoire, Secretaire, Secretary, etc.)," in *The Dictionary of English Furniture* (rev. ed.; London: Country Life, 1954), 2: 123–61; Barry A. Greenlaw, *New England Furniture at Williamsburg* (Williamsburg: Colonial Williamsburg Foundation, 1974), pp. 112–27.

5. Thomas Dilworth, *The Young Book-Keeper's Assistant* (12th ed.; Philadelphia: Benjamin Johnson, 1794), n.p.

6. JoAnne Yates, *Control Through Communication: The Rise of System in American Management* (Baltimore: Johns Hopkins University Press, 1989), pp. 26–28; Brooke Hindle, "Charles Willson Peale's Science and Technology," in *Charles Willson Peale and His World*, by Edgar P. Richardson, Brooke Hindle, and Lillian B. Miller (New York: Abrams, 1982), pp. 115–16.

7. Yates, *Control Through Communication*, pp. 28–31; Talbott, "Office in the 19th Century," p. 16.

8. Chandler, *Visible Hand*, p. 3.

9. National Park Service, *Independence: A Guide to Independence National Historical Park* (Washington, D.C.: Department of Interior, National Park Service, 1982), pp. 12–13; L. D. Ingersoll, *A History of the War Department of the United States* (Washington, D.C.: Francis B.

Mohun, 1879), p. 103; Gaillard Hunt, *The Department of State of the United States, Its History and Functions* (New Haven: Yale University Press, 1914), pp. 14–15.

10. Watson II, 1: 423; Hunt, *Department of State*, pp. 427–28, 49–51.

11. Chalmers M. Roberts, *Washington, Past and Present: A Pictorial History of the Nation's Capital* (Washington, D.C.: Public Affairs Press, 1949), pp. 140–41; Thomas Froncek, ed., *The City of Washington: An Illustrated History* (New York: Knopf, 1985), pp. 71, 86; Hunt, *Department of State*, p. 429; Ingersoll, *History of the War Department*, p. 109; George S. Hunsberger, "The Architectural Career of George Hadfield," Columbia Historical Society, *Records*, 51–52 (1951–52): 53.

12. Ingersoll, *History of the War Department*, p. 65; Alexander Mackay, *The Western World; or, Travels in the United States in 1846–47* 3d ed. (London: Richard Bentley, 1849), 1: 170; Graham H. Stuart, *The Department of State: A History of Its Organization, Procedure, and Personnel* (New York: Macmillan, 1949), p. 132; Frederick H. Seward, *Seward at Washington as Senator and Secretary of State* (New York: Derby and Miller, 1891), 2: 519.

13. Figures based on U.S. Department of State, *A Register of Officers and Agents, Civil, Military, and Naval, in the Service of the United States* (Washington, D.C.: Jonathan Elliott, 1816 and subsequent years) [hereafter *ROA* (year)]; Superintendent and Architect of Public Buildings, *Report to Accompany Bill H.R. No. 311, 27th Congress, 2d Session, H.R. Report no. 460, Mar. 29, 1842*, p. 1 [hereafter, H.R. Rep. 460]

14. *ROA* 1841; Hunt, *Department of State*, pp. 203–4, 211–12. Of course, the State Department also employed ambassadors, consuls, and representatives in other locations. However, this discussion concerns only the organization and disposition of office space in the seat of government (New York, Philadelphia, or Washington), and my figures for all the departments refer only to staff resident there.

15. Mills, *Guide*, pp. 13–14; "Reorganization of the Treasury Department," *House of Representatives Report no. 740, Reports of Committees, 24th Congress, 1st Session* (Washington, 1836), June 7, 1836, p. 11.

16. William Quereau Force, *Picture of Washington and Its Vicinity for 1845* (Washington, D.C.: William Q. Force, 1845), p. 35; Mills, *Guide*, pp. 13, 15; Ingersoll, *History of the War Department*, p. 117.

17. Based on *ROA*; "Reorganization of the Treasury Department," pp. 2–3, 13–15; P. G. Washington, "On Simplifying the System of Public Accounts," *House of Representatives, Executive Documents No. 71, 24th Congress, 2d Session, Jan. 6, 1837*, pp. 1, 4.

18. Robert Mills, "Plan of the 2nd floor of the Treasury Office, with the Fire Proof Wing Attached, as It Stood Previous to the Fire," Apr. 6, 1833; Mills, "Plan of the Attic or Garret Story as it stood previous to the Fire," both in National Archives, RG121, copies in Mills Papers. For the remainder of this discussion of the Treasury Building, all manuscript sources are cited from copies contained in the Mills Papers unless otherwise noted.

19. H. M. Pierce Gallagher, *Robert Mills, Architect of the Washington Monument, 1781–1855* (New York: Columbia University Press, 1935), p. 60; personal communication from Richard C. Cote, Office of the Curator, Department of the Treasury, May 29, 1996; *Reports of the Secretary of the Treasury of the United States* (Washington, D.C.: Duff Green, 1828–51), 3: 385.

20. Sara E. Wermeil, *The Fireproof Building: Technology and Public Safety in the Nineteenth-Century American City* (Baltimore: Johns Hopkins University Press, 2000), pp. 15–36; Talbot Hamlin, *Benjamin Henry Latrobe* (New York: Oxford University Press, 1955), pp. 153–54; Latrobe, *Corr.*, 2: 31–32, 62–69, 73.

21. Jeffrey A. Cohen, "Fireproof Wings to Pennsylvania Statehouse," in James F. O'Gorman, Jeffrey A. Cohen, George E. Thomas, and G. Holmes Perkins, *Drawing Toward Building: Philadelphia Architectural Graphics, 1732–1986* (Philadelphia: University of Pennsylvania Press for the Pennsylvania Academy of the Fine Arts, 1986), pp. 60–62; Gene Waddell, "Robert Mills's Fireproof Building," *South Carolina Historical Magazine* 80, no. 2 (Apr. 1979): 105–35; William H. Pierson, Jr., *American Buildings and Their Architects*, vol. 1: *The Colonial and Neoclassical Styles* (New York: Oxford University Press, 1970, 1986), pp. 387–93; Kenneth Severens, *Charleston: Antebellum Architecture and Civic Destiny* (Knoxville: University of Tennessee Press, 1988), pp. 28–33.

22. Department of the Treasury, Curator's Office [CO], Treasury Building Fact Sheet, ca. 1988; Denys Peter Myers, "The Treasury Building after Mills," *JSAH* 29, no. 3 (Oct. 1970): 266.

23. Robert Mills to Thomas Corwin, n.d., CO; H.R. Rep. 460, p. 9.

24. John Harris, *Sir William Chambers, Knight of the Polar Star* (University Park: Pennsylvania State University Press, 1970), p. 96; L. M. Bates, *Somerset House, Four Hundred Years of History* (London: Frederick Muller, 1967), p. 125.

25. Sergio Villari, *J. N. L. Durand (1760–1834): Art and Science of Architecture*, trans. Eli Gottleib (New York: Rizzoli, 1990), pp. 60–61.

26. Levi Woodbury, "Report from the Secretary of the Treasury, On the Re-Organization of the Treasury Department," Dec. 8, 1834, *Public Documents Printed by Order of the Senate of the United States, 23d Congress, 2d Session* (Washington, D.C.: Duff Green 1834), 1: 6.

27. The key documents of the controversy—the congressional memos, the reports of the architectural consultants, and Mills's response—are contained in Senate Report No. 435 to accompany bill No. 304, 25th Cong., 2d session, Apr. 17, 1838 [hereafter referred to as Sen. Rep. No. 435], Mills Papers.

28. Bulfinch to Hall, May 1, 1838. Walter's report was included in Sen. Rep. No. 435 and published independently, possibly at his own expense, as Thomas U. Walter, *Report on the New Treasury Buildings and Patent Office at Washington* (Philadelphia: L. R. Bailey, 1838).

29. George Watterston, *A New Guide to Washington* (Washington, D.C.: Robert Farnham; New York: Samuel Colman, 1842), p. 63; Sen. Rep. No. 435, pp. 14–15; see R. P. French, Commissioner of Public Buildings, to R. McClelland, Apr. 4, 1855 (containing a synopsis of Zadock Pratt's speech to Congress in favor of demolishing the Treasury Building, June 8, 1838), CO.

30. Mills to William Noland, Apr. 9, 1842; Mills to HCPB, Feb. 21, 1838; E. M. Huntington to Walter Forward, Secretary of the Treasury, Feb. 5, 1842, CO.

31. H.R. Rep. No. 460, p. 8; Sen. Rep. No. 435, pp. 23–24.

32. Mills, *Guide,* p. 3; Mills, Draft report to HCPB, spring 1838; Bulfinch to Hall, May 1, 1838.

33. Huntington to Forward, Feb. 5, 1842; Penrose to Forward, Feb. 10, 1842, CO.

34. James William McCulloh to Forward, June 11, 1842, CO; [Thomas L. Smith] to Forward, Feb. 4, 1842, CO; Thomas U. Walter to Sen. R. M. T. Hunter, Jan. 10, 1854, in Walter Letterbook, Jan.–Mar. 1854, Walter Pap.

35. [Smith] to Forward, Feb. 4, 1842; Huntington to Forward, Feb. 5, 1842; Penrose to Forward, Feb. 10, 1842; McCulloh to Forward, June 11, 1842; Mills to Noland, Apr. 9, 1842.

36. Washington, "On Simplifying the System of Public Accounts," p. 2; Reports of the Secretary of the Treasury, 4: 252; "Memorial of the Chamber of Commerce of New York," Apr. 20, 1846, *Public Documents Printed by Order of the Senate of the United States, 29th Congress, 1st Session* (Washington, D.C.: Ritchie and Heiss, 1846), vol. 5, no. 303; William Archer to Franklin Pierce, Mar. 22, 1855, CO.

37. Pierson, *American Buildings*, 1: 407.

38. Sen. Rep. No. 435, p. 15; French to McClelland, Apr. 4, 1855; Jane B. Davies, "Six Letters by William P. Elliot to Alexander J. Davis, 1834–1838," *JSAH* 26, no. 1 (Mar. 1967): 73; *Report of the Secretary of the Treasury . . . for the Year Ending June 30, 1863* (Washington, D.C.: Thomas H. Ford, 1863), p. 135; *Report of the Secretary of the Treasury . . . for the Year 1870* (Washington, D.C.: Government Printing Office, 1870), p. 244. He repeated the recommendation in 1872 (*Report of the Secretary of the Treasury . . . for the Year 1872* [Washington, D.C.: Government Printing Office, 1872], pp. 396–97); Mary Clemmer Ames, *Ten Years in Washington* (Hartford: A. D. Worthington, 1873), p. 304; *Report of the Secretary of the Treasury . . . for the Year 1870*, p. 244; Gallagher, *Robert Mills*, p. 63.

CHAPTER 9. **GRIDDING THE GRAVEYARD**

1. Jean Boze to Henri de St. Gême, Nov. 25, 1830, SGP; Madaline S. Edwards, *Madaline: Love and Survival in Antebellum New Orleans*, ed. Dell Upton (Athens: University of Georgia Press, 1996), p. 193; J. G. Dunlap, New Orleans, to Beatrice A. Dunlap, Augusta, Ga., Nov. 4, 1844, Dunlap Correspondence, 1827–69, TUL, box 1, fol. 3; A. Oakey Hall, *The Manhattaner in New Orleans* (1851; rpt. Baton Rouge: Louisiana State University Press, 1976), p. 109; John H. B. Latrobe, *Southern Travels: Journal of John H. B. Latrobe 1834*, ed. Samuel Wilson, Jr. (New Orleans: Historic New Orleans Collection, 1986), p. 53; Untitled item, *New Orleans Daily Picayune*, Nov. 2, 1844, 2: 1; Jean Boze to Henri de St. Gême, Dec. 1, 1829, SGP.

2. Dunlap to Dunlap; Boze to St. Gême, Dec. 1, 1829; Hall, *Manhattaner*, p. 110; Boze to St. Gême, Nov. 25, 1830.

3. Latrobe, *Southern Travels*, pp. 53–54.

4. Untitled item, *New Orleans Daily Picayune*, Nov. 1, 1844, 2: 2.

5. Joseph Holt Ingraham, *The South-West. By a Yankee* (New York: Harper and Bros., 1835), 1: 153–55; Edwards, *Madaline*, p. 207; Fredrika Bremer, *The Homes of the New World*, trans. Mary Howitt (New York: Harper and Bros., 1854), 2: 214; Hall, *Manhattaner*, p. 108. On the early history of New Orleans's cemeteries, I follow *NOA*, vol. 3, and Samuel Wilson, Jr., and Leonard V. Huber, *The St. Louis Cemeteries of New Orleans*, 20th ed. (New Orleans: St. Louis Cathedral, 1988).

6. David Lee Sterling, ed., "New Orleans, 1801: An Account by John Pintard," *LH* 34, no. 3 (July 1951): 230; Latrobe, *Southern Travels*, pp. 49, 53; James Pitot, *Observations on the Colony of Louisiana from 1796 to 1802*, trans. Henry C. Pitot (Baton Rouge: Louisiana State University Press for the HNOC, 1979), p. 110; Timothy Flint, *Recollections of the Last Ten Years* (Boston: Cummings, Hilliard, 1826), p. 312.

7. NOCVa, roll 45, July 22, 1806; Sterling, "New Orleans, 1801," pp. 230–31.

8. "Iron Coffins," *Port Folio*, ser. 4, 11, no. 1 (Mar. 1821): 119–24.

9. Jean Boze to Henri de St. Gême, SGP, Nov. 25, 1830; [John A. Elkinton], *The Monument Cemetery of Philadelphia (Late Pere La Chaise)* (Philadelphia: John A. Elkinton, 1837), p. 7; Blanche Linden-Ward, *Silent City on a Hill: Landscapes of Memory and Boston's Mount Auburn Cemetery* (Columbus: Ohio State University Press, 1989), p. 17.

10. Allan I. Ludwig, *Graven Images: New England Stonecarving and Its Symbols, 1650–1815* (Middletown, Conn.: Wesleyan University Press, 1966), p. 55.

11. John L. Cotter, Daniel G. Roberts, and Michael Parrington, *The Buried Past: An Archaeological History of Philadelphia* (Philadelphia: University of Pennsylvania Press, 1992), p. 202; "Central Presbyterian Church," *HRP* 13, no. 9 (Mar. 1, 1834): 143.

12. Latrobe, *Jnls.*, 3: 242.

13. John Michael Vlach, *The Afro-American Tradition in Decorative Arts* (Cleveland: Cleveland Museum of Art, 1978), pp. 139–47; Mechal Sobel, *The World They Made Together: Black and White Values in Eighteenth-Century Virginia* (Princeton: Princeton University Press, 1987), pp. 19, 218–19; Robert L. Hall, "African Religious Retentions in Florida," in *Africanisms in American Culture*, ed. Joseph E. Holloway (Bloomington: Indiana University Press, 1990), pp. 112–13; Daniel R. Roediger, "And Die in Dixie: Funerals, Death, and Heaven in the Slave Community 1700–1865," *Massachusetts Review* 22 (1981): 163–83.

14. Ludwig, *Graven Images*, pp. 60–62; Cotter, Roberts, and Parrington, *Buried Past*, p. 199; Gary Laderman, *The Sacred Remains: American Attitudes Toward Death, 1799–1883* (New Haven: Yale University Press, 1996), pp. 41–43, 52; Lawrence Stone, *The Family, Sex and Marriage in England, 1500–1800* (New York: Harper and Row, 1977), pp. 655–58; Edward Shorter, *The Making of the Modern Family* (New York: Basic Books, 1975), pp. 227–34; Daniel Walker Howe, *Making the American Self: Jonathan Edwards to Abraham Lincoln* (Cambridge: Harvard University Press, 1997), pp. 108–10; Colleen McDannell, "The Religious Symbolism of Laurel Hill Cemetery," *PMHB* 111, no. 3 (July 1987): 301; Latrobe, *Jnls.*, 3: 246; Linden-Ward, *Silent City*, p. 170; [Elkinton], *Monument Cemetery*, p. 6.

15. David Charles Sloane, *The Last Great Necessity: Cemeteries in American History* (Baltimore: Johns Hopkins University Press, 1991), p. 20; Linden-Ward, *Silent City*, p. 155; James Deetz, personal communication; Christopher Moore, "New York's Eighteenth-Century African Burial Ground in History," in *Reclaiming Our Past, Honoring Our Ancestors: New York's Eighteenth-Century African Burial Ground & the Memorial Competition*, ed. Edward Kaufman (New York: African Burial Ground Competition Coalition, 1994), p. 5.

16. Sloane, *Last Great Necessity*, p. 24; Michael Parrington, "Cemetery Archaeology in the Urban Environment: A Case Study from Philadelphia," in *Living in Cities: Current Research in Urban Archaeology*, ed. Edward Staski (Pleasant Hill, Calif.: Society for Historical Archaeology, 1987), pp. 56, 63; Cotter, Roberts, and Parrington, *Buried Past*, pp. 284–86.

17. Drinker 2: 932–33, 1523, 3: 1656.

18. Parrington, "Cemetery Archaeology," p. 57; Ingraham, *South-West*, 1: 156; John Duffy, *The Sanitarians: A History of American Public Health* (Urbana: University of Illinois Press, 1990), p. 74; Cotter, Roberts, and Parrington, *Buried Past*, p. 201; Richard A. Etlin, *The Architecture of Death: The Transformation of the Cemetery in Eighteenth-Century Paris* (Cambridge: MIT Press, 1984), p. 5.

19. Steven Robert Wilf, "Anatomy and Punishment in Late Eighteenth-Century New York," *Journal of Social History* 22, no. 3 (spring 1989): 509; Linden-Ward, *Silent City*, p. 152; Ithiel Town, Fayetteville, N.C., to Roger S. Baldwin, New Haven, Conn., Jan. 29, 1824, Baldwin Family Papers, General Correspondence, ser. 1, box 15, fol. 178, Yale University Manuscripts and Archives.

20. Ingraham, *South West*, 1: 157; Thomas Hamilton, *Men and Manners in America* (Edinburgh: William Blackwood; London: T. Cadell, 1834), 2: 215; Edwards, *Madaline*, p. 127; Bennett Dowler, *Researches upon the Necropolis of New Orleans* (New Orleans: Bill and Clark, 1850), p. 7.

21. Ingraham, *South-West*, 1: 157.

22. Latrobe, *Jnls.*, 3: 241–42. I have found no description of fours earlier than the senior Latrobe's, and the earliest extant examples seem to date from the early nineteenth century.

23. Latrobe, *Southern Travels,* p. 49; *New Orleans as It Is* (Utica, N.Y.: De Witt C. Grove, 1849), p. 59.

24. St. Louis Cemetery No. 2 Interment Book, 1877-1880, NOPL, p. 306.

25. NOCVb, 6: 96 (Aug. 11, 1821), 7: 93 (Aug. 3, 1822), 96 (Sept. 10, 1822); Leonard V. Huber and Guy F. Bernard, *To Glorious Immortality: The Rise and Fall of the Girod Street Cemetery, New Orleans's First Protestant Cemetery, 1822–1957* (New Orleans: Alblen, 1961); *NOA* 3: 18–19.

26. Timothy Dwight, *Travels in New York and New England* [1821–22], ed. Barbara Miller Solomon (Cambridge: Harvard University Press, 1969), 1: 137; Stanley French, "The Cemetery as a Cultural Institution: The Establishment of Mount Auburn and the 'Rural Cemetery' Movement," *American Quarterly* 26, no. 1 (Mar. 1974): 43; Sloane, *Last Great Necessity,* pp. 30–31; Linden-Ward, *Silent City,* pp. 136–41.

27. Sloane, *Last Great Necessity,* p. 31; Barbara Rotundo, "Mount Auburn: Fortunate Coincidences and an Ideal Solution," *Journal of Garden History* 4, no. 3 (Sept. 1984): 261; French, "Cemetery as a Cultural Institution," p. 43.

28. Dwight, *Travels,* 1: 137.

29. Dwight, *Travels,* 1: 138; Edward Augustus Kendall, *Travels Through the Northern Parts of the United States* (New York: I. Riley, 1809), 1: 254.

30. Dwight, *Travels,* 1: 137; Linden-Ward, *Silent City,* pp. 139–41.

31. B. Edwards, "The Burial Ground at New-Haven," Sept. 1833, 202–3. This article, included in the Metropolitan Museum of Art's *Art and the Empire City* 1833 research notebook, was published in a periodical that I have not been able to identify.

32. Kendall, *Travels,* 1: 256; ibid., p. 202.

33. Dwight, *Travels,* 1: 132; Algernon Sydney Roberts, Diary, 1826, 1831, n.p. (Aug. 2, 1831), MS, Algernon Sydney Roberts Papers, HSP; Fisher, p. 82 (Aug. 30, 1839); Rudy J. Favretti, "The Ornamentation of New England Towns: 1750–1850," *Journal of Garden History* 2, no. 4 (Oct.–Dec. 1982): 331–32; Sloane, *Last Great Necessity,* p. 32. The short-lived Lombardy poplars in many parts of the United States quickly fell victim to the "poplar worm" (Watson I, 202). Those in the New Burying Ground began to die by 1815.

34. Petition of Residents and Owners of Property in [the] Western Part of the City, for Improving Penn Square, Jan. 20, 1827, MS Coll. of the LCP, HSP.

35. "James Ronaldson," typescript "abstracted from Historical Catalogue of The St. Andrew's Society of Philadelphia, 1794–1907," ca. 1907, Autograph Collection of the HSP—Ronaldson; Gordon M. Marshall III, "James Ronaldson (1769–1841)," in *Philadelphia: Three Centuries of American Art* (Philadelphia: Philadelphia Museum of Art, 1976), p. 238.

36. [James Ronaldson], *Banks and Paper Currency: Their Effects upon Society* (Philadelphia, 1832); [James Ronaldson], *Reasons for Importing the Grain and Implements Enumerated at the End of this Address* (Philadelphia, 1841); James Ronaldson, *Memorial to the Senate and House of Representatives of the Commonwealth of Pennsylvania, on the Subject of Stephen Girard's Legacy* (Philadelphia, 1835); James Ronaldson, Philadelphia, to Thomas Cadwalader, near Wilmington, Del., Sept. 29, 1814, Cadwalader Coll., Thomas Cadwalader Section, box 23, HSP.

37. *Southwark, Moyamensing, Weecacoe, Passyunk, Dock Ward for Two Hundred and Seventy Years* (P: Quaker City, 1892), p. 35; Watson III, 3: 137; "James Ronaldson."

38. Watson III, 3: 136–37; *Philadelphia Cemetery: Copy of the Deeds of Trust, Charter, By-Laws,*

and List of Lot-Holders (Philadelphia: Mifflin and Parry, 1845), p. 2; "Men and Things," unidentified clipping, June 10, 1909, Campbell Coll., HSP, 19: 137.

39. *Philadelphia Cemetery: Copy of Deed of Trust* (Philadelphia, 1827), pp. 4, 11; *Philadelphia Cemetery* (1845), p. 1; *Philadelphia Cemetery, Ninth and Shippen Streets. Established by James Ronaldson,* 1827, broadside, May 10, 1859, Society Miscellaneous Coll., HSP, box 7c, fol. 5.

40. *Philadelphia Cemetery* (1827), p. 1; *Philadelphia Cemetery: Copy of Deed of Trust for the Triangular Piece of Land Added to It, by Which It Is Rendered Square* (Philadelphia: Henry Young, 1831); *Philadelphia Cemetery* (1845), p. 2.

41. "Won't Sell Cemetery," unidentified newspaper clipping, Aug. 6, 1918, Campbell Coll., 19: 170, HSP; Parrington, "Cemetery Archaeology," p. 57; *Philadelphia Cemetery* (1827), pp. 6–8.

42. J. Thomas Scharf and Thompson Westcott, *History of Philadelphia, 1609–1884* (Philadelphia: L. H. Everts, 1884), 1: 620.

43. William Cullen Bryant, "Thanatopsis" (1821); Madaline S. Edwards, "The Grave Yard," Feb. 4, 1844, Writing Book 1, MS, Charles W. Bradbury Papers, SHC, p. 23.

44. Edgar Allan Poe, "The Fall of the House of Usher," in *Introduction to Poe: A Thematic Reader,* ed. Eric W. Carlson (New York: Scott, Foresman, 1967), pp. 233–34.

45. Hall, *Manhattaner,* p. 110; Cope, p. 499.

46. Edwards, *Madaline,* p. 127.

47. Pierre-Frédéric Thomas, *Essai sur la fièvre jaune d'Amérique* (New Orleans and Paris: J.-B. Ballière, 1823), p. 23; Edward H. Barton, *The Cause and Prevention of Yellow Fever at New Orleans and Other Cities in America,* 3d ed. (New York: H. Baillière, 1857), p. 144.

48. Dwight, *Travels,* 2: 260; Sloane, *Last Great Necessity,* pp. 34–38; French, "Cemetery as a Cultural Institution," p. 42; David Schuyler, "The Evolution of the Anglo-American Rural Cemetery: Landscape Architecture as Social and Cultural History," *Journal of Garden History* 4, no. 3 (Sept. 1984): 293; Linden-Ward, *Silent City,* pp. 155–58, 358.

49. Drinker 2: 1421; Lady Emmeline Stuart Wortley, *Travels in the United States, etc. During 1849 and 1850* (New York: Harper and Bros., 1851), p. 126.

50. Draft of anonymous open letter to Marguilliers de l'Église St.-Louis, New Orleans, ca. 1832, Arnous-Lessassier Family Papers, Correspondence, 1832–33, TUL, box 1, fol. 4; Jean Boze, "Nouvelles diverses," SGP, Jan. 27, 1833; *NOA* 3: 27–42; E. D. Fenner, "General Report on the Medical Topography and Meteorology of New Orleans, with an Account of the Prevalent Diseases During the Year 1849," *Southern Medical Reports* 1 (1849): 25–26.

51. On the early history of Mount Auburn, see Jacob Bigelow, *A History of the Cemetery of Mount Auburn* (Boston: James Munroe, 1860); Linden-Ward, *Silent City;* and Shary Page Berg, *Mount Auburn Cemetery Master Plan 1993,* vol. 2: *Historic Landscape Report* (Cambridge, Mass.: Shary Page Berg for the Trustees of Mount Auburn Cemetery, 1993).

52. Kendall, *Travels,* 1: 254.

53. Linden-Ward, *Silent City,* pp. 178, 199; Andrew Jackson Downing, "Public Cemeteries and Public Gardens," in *Rural Essays,* ed. George William Curtis (New York: George P. Putnam, 1853), p. 156; French, "Cemetery as a Cultural Institution," p. 48.

54. Linden-Ward, *Silent City,* p. 178.

55. Ibid., pp. 358–59 n. 13; Sloane, *Last Great Necessity,* p. 55; Downing, "Public Cemeteries," p. 154.

56. Bryant, "Thanatopsis"; Bigelow, *History of the Cemetery of Mount Auburn,* p. 13; Schuyler, "Evolution of the Anglo-American Cemetery," p. 303; Sloane, *Last Great Necessity,* p. 76; Thomas Bender, "The 'Rural' Cemetery Movement: Urban Travail and the Appeal of Na-

ture" [1974], rpt. in *Material Life in America, 1600–1860,* ed. Robert Blair St. George (Boston: Northeastern University Press, 1988), pp. 505–18.

57. Colleen McDannell, *Material Christianity: Religion and Popular Culture in America* (New Haven: Yale University Press, 1995), pp. 103–31; Fisher, p. 10; Watson III, 3: 137; Aaron V. Wunsch, "Laurel Hill Cemetery," HABS No. PA-1811, Historic American Buildings Survey, National Park Service, U.S. Department of the Interior, 1999, pp. 3, 16–17; Constance M. Greiff, *John Notman, Architect, 1810–1865* (Philadelphia: Athenaeum of Philadelphia, 1979), pp. 18–19, 53–60.

58. Watson II, 1: 244; [John Jay Smith], *Guide to Laurel Hill Cemetery* (Philadelphia: C. Sherman, 1844), p. 48.

59. [Smith], *Guide,* pp. 11–15; Wunsch, "Laurel Hill," p. 18.

60. [Smith], *Guide,* p. 12.

61. *Regulations of the Laurel Hill Cemetery* (Philadelphia: A. Waldie, 1837).

62. Ann Douglas, *The Feminization of American Culture* (New York: Avon, 1977), p. 252, pp. 240–59.

63. Downing, "Public Cemeteries," p. 156n.

64. Daniel Bowen, *A History of Philadelphia* (Philadelphia: Daniel Bowen, 1839), pp. 108–9.

65. McDannell, "Religious Symbolism," p. 286; Douglas, *Feminization,* p. 252; David Schuyler, *The New Urban Landscape: The Redefinition of City Form in Nineteenth-Century America* (Baltimore: Johns Hopkins University Press, 1986), p. 54; Linden-Ward, *Silent City,* pp. 296–321; Blanche Linden-Ward, "Strange But Genteel Pleasure Grounds: Tourist and Leisure Uses of Nineteenth-Century Rural Cemeteries," in *Cemeteries and Gravemarkers: Voices of American Culture,* ed. Richard E. Meyer (Logan: Utah State University Press, 1992), pp. 293–328; Downing, "Public Cemeteries," p. 157.

66. Wunsch, "Laurel Hill," pp. 10–16; Aaron V. Wunsch, "Woodlands Cemetery," HALS No. PA-5, Historic American Landscapes Survey, National Park Service, U. S. Department of the Interior, 2003–4, pp. 45–46.

67. [Elkinton], *Monument Cemetery,* pp. 5–6, 9; Bowen, *History of Philadelphia,* p. 103; Robert W. Torchia, "No Strangers to the Ravages of Death: John Neagle's Portrait of Dr. John Abraham Elkinton," *Nineteenth Century* 18, no. 2 (fall 1998): 12–19.

68. [Elkinton], *Monument Cemetery,* pp. 5–7; *Act of Incorporation, By-Laws, Rules and Regulations, Officers and Members of the Monument Cemetery of Philadelphia* (Philadelphia, 1838), pp. 7, 9, 13; Bowen, *History of Philadelphia,* p. 105.

69. *NOA* 3: 27.

70. Edwards, *Madaline,* pp. 126–31.

71. Ibid., pp. 125, 131.

CHAPTER 10. **GRIDDED UTOPIAS**

1. The term "therapeutic" is David J. Rothman's, from *The Discovery of the Asylum: Social Order and Disorder in the New Republic* (Boston: Little, Brown, 1971).

2. In recent decades historians, notably David J. Rothman and Michel Foucault, have recognized the links among these institutions (Rothman, *Discovery of the Asylum;* Foucault, *History of Madness,* ed. Jean Khalfa, trans. Jonathan Murphy and Jean Khalfa [London: Routledge, 2006]; Foucault, *Discipline and Punish: The Birth of the Prison,* trans. Alan Sheridan [New York: Vintage, 1977]).

3. Norman Johnston with Kenneth Finkel and Jeffrey A. Cohen, *Eastern State Penitentiary:*

Crucible of Good Intentions (Philadelphia: Philadelphia Museum of Art for the Eastern State Penitentiary Task Force of the Preservation Coalition of Greater Philadelphia, 1994), pp. 58, 69; James Stuart, *Three Years in North America*, 3d ed., rev. (Edinburgh: for Robert Cadell, 1833), 1: 87; Gershom Powers, *A Brief Account of the Construction, Management, & Discipline, &c. &c. of the New-York State Prison at Auburn* (Auburn: U. F. Doubleday, 1826), p. 2.

4. Mathew Carey, *Essays on the Public Charities of Philadelphia,* 4th ed. (Philadelphia: J. Clarke, 1829), pp. 14, 17.

5. Samuel L. Knapp, *The Life of Thomas Eddy* (New York: Conner and Cooke, 1834), pp. 10–14, 42–54, and passim; [John Frost], *Lives of American Merchants, Eminent for Integrity, Enterprise and Public Spirit* (New York: Saxton and Miles, 1844), pp. 71–82; Latrobe, *Corr.,* 2: 862 n. 5.

6. Roderick N. Ryon, "Moral Reform and Democratic Politics: The Dilemma of Roberts Vaux," *Quaker History* 59, no. 1 (spring 1970): 3–14; Hugh Barbour and J. William Frost, *The Quakers* (New York: Greenwood, 1988), pp. 373–74; Gary B. Nash, *First City: Philadelphia and the Forging of Historical Memory* (Philadelphia: University of Pennsylvania Press, 2002), p. 183. Although Vaux corresponded extensively with Eddy he seems never to have met him, and he told a mutual acquaintance that he knew little of Eddy's personal character (Knapp, *Life of Thomas Eddy,* p. 16).

7. Knapp, *Life of Thomas Eddy,* pp. 192, 197; [Thomas Eddy], *An Account of the State Prison or Penitentiary House, in the City of New-York* (New York: Isaac Collins and Son, 1801), p. 6.

8. Michael Meranze, *Laboratories of Virtue: Punishment, Revolution, and Authority in Philadelphia, 1760–1835* (Chapel Hill: University of North Carolina Press, 1996), p. 294.

9. Meranze, *Laboratories of Virtue,* pp. 219–27; Roberts Vaux, *Notices of the Original, and Successive Efforts, to Improve the Discipline of the Prison at Philadelphia, and to Reform the Criminal Code of Pennsylvania* (Philadelphia: Kimber and Sharpless, 1826), p. 3.

10. Johnston, *Eastern State Penitentiary,* pp. 31, 36; [Thomas B. McElwee], *A Concise History of the Eastern Penitentiary of Pennsylvania* (Philadelphia: Neall and Massie, 1835), 1: 6–7; John Bender, *Imagining the Penitentiary: Fiction and the Architecture of Mind in Eighteenth-Century England* (Chicago: University of Chicago Press, 1987), pp. 21–22, 216, 218; [George Lippard], *The Killers* (Philadelphia: Hankinson and Bartholomew, 1850), p. 19; Anthony Vidler, *The Writing of the Walls: Architectural Theory in the Late Enlightenment* (Princeton: Princeton Architectural Press, 1987), pp. 77–78.

11. John Haviland, *A Description of Haviland's Design for the New Penitentiary, Now Erecting Near Philadelphia* (Philadelphia: Robert Desilver, 1824), p. 11.

12. Negley K. Teeters, *The Cradle of the Penitentiary: The Walnut Street Jail at Philadelphia, 1773–1835* (Philadelphia: Pennsylvania Prison Society, 1955), pp. 58–62; Haviland, *Description,* p. 4.

13. Bender, *Imagining the Penitentiary,* pp. 19–20, 201, 206.

14. John Howard, *The State of the Prisons in England and Wales* (Warrington, Eng.: William Eyres, 1777); William Bradford, *An Enquiry into How Far the Punishment of Death is Necessary in Pennsylvania* (Philadelphia: T. Dobson, 1793); Vaux, *Notices;* Pieter Spierenburg, "From Amsterdam to Auburn: An Explanation for the Rise of the Prison in Seventeenth-Century Holland and Nineteenth-Century America," *Journal of Social History,* spring 1987, pp. 440–42; Michael Ignatieff, *A Just Measure of Pain: The Penitentiary in the Industrial Revolution, 1750–1850* (London: Penguin, 1972), pp. 11–13, 53.

15. Ignatieff, *Just Measure of Pain*, pp. 44–75; Michael Meranze, "The Penitential Ideal in Late Eighteenth-Century Philadelphia," *PMHB* 108, no. 4 (Oct. 1984): 419–50; Bradford, *Enquiry*, pp. 3–7; Louis P. Masur, *Rites of Execution: Capital Punishment and the Transformation of American Culture, 1776–1865* (New York: Oxford University Press, 1989), pp. 50–70.

16. "An Act to Reform the Penal Laws of the State," 1790, in James T. Mitchell and Henry Flanders, *The Statutes at Large of Pennsylvania from 1682 to 1807* (Harrisburg: Harrisburg Publishing, 1896), 511–28; Teeters, *Cradle*, pp. 17–19.

17. Bradford, *Enquiry*, pp. 80–82; Robert Turnbull, *A Visit to the Philadelphia Prison* (Philadelphia: Budd and Bartram, 1796), pp. 4–6, 16–18.

18. [Thomas Eddy], *A View of the New-York State Prison in the City of New-York* (New York: T. and J. Swords, 1815), pp. 11–15; *An Account of the Massachusetts State Prison* (Charlestown: Samuel Etheridge, 1806); Harold Kirker, *The Architecture of Charles Bulfinch* (Cambridge: Harvard University Press, 1969), pp. 211–13.

19. U. R. Q. Henriques, "The Rise and Decline of the Separate System of Prison Discipline," *Past and Present*, no. 54 (1972): 61–93; Ignatieff, *Just Measure of Pain*, p. 61; Randall McGovern, "The Well-Ordered Prison: England, 1780–1865," in *The Oxford History of the Prison: The Practice of Punishment in Western Society*, ed. Norval Morris and David J. Rothman (New York: Oxford University Press, 1998), pp. 77–78; Gustave de Beaumont and Alexis de Tocqueville, *On the Penitentiary System in the United States*, trans. Francis Lieber (Philadelphia: Carey, Lea, and Blanchard, 1833; rpt. Carbondale: Southern Illinois University Press, 1964), p. 55; Bradford, *Enquiry*, pp. 81–82; "Act to Reform the Penal Laws of the State," sec. VII, in Mitchell and Flanders, *Statutes at Large*, p. 515; [Eddy], *Account*, p. 32.

20. Gershom Powers, *Report of Gershom Powers, Agent and Keeper of the State Prison, at Auburn* (Albany: Croswell and Van Benthuysen, 1828), pp. 9–11; Beaumont and Tocqueville, *On the Penitentiary System*, pp. 40, 58; Knapp, *Life of Thomas Eddy*, pp. 76, 244, 285, 286; Basil Hall, *Travels in North America, in the Years 1827 and 1828* (Edinburgh: for Cadell and Co., 1829), 1: 54; *A Brief Statement of the Causes Which Have Led to the Abandonment of the Celebrated System of Penitentiary Discipline, in some of the United States of America* (Liverpool: Harris, 1827), p. 35; Powers, *Brief Account*, p. 32.

21. Medicus, "On the Penitentiary System of Pennsylvania," *Port Folio*, ser. 4, 13, no. 1 (Jan. 1822): 106, 108; Roberts Vaux, *Reply to Two Letters of William Roscoe* (Philadelphia: Jesper Harding, 1827); Roscoe, *Brief Statement*; Roberts Vaux, *Letter on the Penitentiary System of Pennsylvania* (Philadelphia: Jesper Harding, 1827); Vaux to Governor George Wolf, Nov. 8, 1831, Wolf Papers, sec. V, HSP; Thomas Eddy to William Roscoe, Apr. 24, 1823, in Knapp, *Life of Thomas Eddy*, pp. 310–11; S. G. Howe, *An Essay on Separate and Congregational Systems of Prison Discipline* (Boston: William D. Ticknor, 1846), pp. vii, 20–27. On the Pennsylvania-Auburn debate, see Rothman, *Discovery of the Asylum*, pp. 81–88; Adam Jay Hirsch, *The Rise of the Penitentiary: Prisons and Punishment in Early America* (New Haven: Yale University Press, 1992), pp. 65–66, 88–91; and Meranze, *Laboratories of Virtue*, pp. 256–62. In fact, Beaumont and Tocqueville gave mixed reviews to both the Pennsylvania and Auburn systems.

22. Roscoe, *Brief Statement*, p. 13; [W. A. Coffey], *Inside Out; or, an Interior View of the New-York State Prison* (New York: for the author, 1823), p. 19; John Reynolds, *Recollections of Windsor Prison*, 3d ed. (Boston: A. Wright, 1839), p. 16; Beaumont and Tocqueville, *On the Penitentiary System*, p. 81; Edward Livingston, *A System of Penal Law, for the State of Louisiana* (Philadelphia: James Kay, Jr., and Brother, 1833), pp. 43, 309–10.

23. Livingston, *System of Penal Law*, pp. 309–10.

24. Ibid., p. 315; Beaumont and Tocqueville, *On the Penitentiary System*, p. 55.

25. Johnston, *Eastern State Penitentiary*, pp. 32, 40, 57; [McElwee], *Concise History*, 1: 13–14; Beaumont and Tocqueville, *On the Penitentiary System*, p. 57; Daniel Bowen, *A History of Philadelphia* (Philadelphia: Daniel Bowen, 1839), p. 181.

26. Beaumont and Tocqueville, *On the Penitentiary System*, p. 41; [Lippard], *Killers*, p. 19; William White, "Penitentiary System," *HRP* 1, no. 3 (Jan. 19, 1828): 47; Reynolds, *Recollections*, pp. 16–17; Gershom Powers, *Brief Account*, p. 37.

27. Howe, *Essay*, p. 27; Mease, *Picture of Philadelphia*, p. 82; Gershom Powers, *Letter of Gershom Powers, Esq.* (Albany: Croswell and Van Benthuysen, 1829), p. 16; Charles Dickens, *American Notes and Pictures from Italy* (Oxford: Oxford University Press, 1957), p. 100.

28. Powers, *Letter*, pp. 12–13; Powers, *Brief Account*, pp. 4–5; Francis Lieber, New York City, to Roberts Vaux, Philadelphia, Feb. 5, 1833, VP, reporting Dwight's statement.

29. Powers, *Letter*, pp. 13–14.

30. Knapp, *Life of Thomas Eddy*, p. 94; *Philadelphia in 1830–1* (Philadelphia: E. L. Carey and A. Hart, 1830), p. 133; Livingston, *System of Penal Law*, p. 708; Harriet Martineau, *Retrospect of Western Travel* (London: Saunders and Otley, 1838), 1: 128; *My First Fourteen Months in the Ohio Penitentiary* (Columbus: for the author, 1859), p. 13; Beaumont and Tocqueville, *On the Penitentiary System*, p. 83.

31. Thomas Hamilton, *Men and Manners in America* (Edinburgh: William Blackwood, 1834), 1: 340–41; Dickens, *American Notes*, p. 100; McElwee, *Concise History*, 1: 13, 15; Martineau, *Retrospect*, 1: 128.

32. Powers, *Brief Account*, p. 7; Mease, *Picture of Philadelphia*, p. 85; Haviland, *Description*, p. 4; Hall, *Travels*, 2: 347; *Second Annual Report of the Board of Managers of the Prison Discipline Society, Boston, June 1, 1827* (Boston: T. R. Marvin, 1827), p. 122.

33. Jeremy Bentham, *The Panopticon Writings*, ed. Miran Božovič (London: Verso, 1995), p. 43; Constance D. Sherman, "A French Artist Describes Philadelphia," *PMHB* 82, no. 2 (Apr. 1958): 212; Hamilton, *Men and Manners*, 1: 343; Knapp, *Life of Thomas Eddy*, p. 192; *State Prisons and the Penitentiary System Vindicated* (Charlestown, Mass.: S. Etheridge, 1821), p. 20; Committee of the Society for the Improvement of Prison Discipline, *Remarks on the Form and Construction of Prisons* (London: J. and A. Arch, Cornhill, etc., 1826), pp. 19, 20, 27; J. von S. Havilland [sic] to Joseph Adshead, Esq., Manchester, Dec. 13, 1845, William Parker Foulke Papers, APS.

34. John Haviland to I. Louis Tellkampf, Schenectady, N.Y., Oct. 11, 1842, HP, 6: 95.

35. Howe, *Essay*, p. 21; Knapp, *Life of Thomas Eddy*, p. 90; Stuart, *Three Years*, 1: 99; *Second Annual Report of the Board of Managers*, pp. 58–59.

36. [Eddy], *Account*, p. 65; [Coffey], *Inside Out*, p. 20; Vaux, *Notices*, p. 53; Vaux to Governor George Wolf, Nov. 4, 1831, Wolf Papers, sec. V, HSP; D. L. Dix, *Remarks on Prisons and Prison Discipline in the United States*, 2d ed. (1845; rpt. Montclair, N.J.: Patterson Smith, 1967), p. 27; Roscoe, *Brief Statement*, p. 5; Vaux, *Letter*, p. 11.

37. Ignatieff, *Just Measure of Pain*, pp. 59–67; Turnbull, *Visit*, p. 33.

38. Dell Upton, "Architecture in Everyday Life," *New Literary History* 33, no. 4 (autumn 2002): 719–20; Howe, *Essay*, p. 21.

39. Sherman, "French Artist," p. 212; John Haviland, "Explanation of a Design for a Penitentiary by John Haviland Archt," n.d., MS, HP, 1: 21–22, 24; Mease, *Picture of Philadelphia*, p. 86; Hamilton, *Men and Manners*, 1: 343.

40. Haviland, *Description*, pp. 4, 5; Haviland, "Explanation of a Design," pp. 19–29; Howe, *Essay*, p. 21.

41. Roscoe, *Brief Statement*, p. 35; Howe, Essay, p. 27; *Second Annual Report of the Board of Managers*, p. 60; R. S. M'Ewen, *The Mysteries, Miseries, and Rascalities of the Ohio Penitentiary* (Columbus, Ohio: John Geary, 1856), p. 60; Powers, *Brief Account*, p. 4.

42. Powers, *Brief Account*, p. 4; M'Ewen, *Mysteries*, p. 61; Fredrika Bremer, *The Homes of the New World*, trans. Mary Howitt (New York: Harper and Bros., 1854), 2: 607; Roscoe, *Brief Statement*, p. 35; Martineau, *Retrospect*, 1: 124; Shane White and Graham White, *Stylin': African American Expressive Culture from Its Beginnings to the Zoot Suit* (Ithaca: Cornell University Press, 1998), pp. 92–96.

43. Howe, *Essay*, p. 26.

44. "Eastern Penitentiary. Report upon the Eastern Penitentiary, House of Refuge, and Institution for the Deaf and Dumb," *HRP* 13, no. 18 (May 3, 1834): 284; Dickens, *American Notes*, p. 53; *My First Fourteen Months*, p. 17; Powers, *Brief Account*, p. 3; [Coffey], *Inside Out*, p. 79.

45. Powers, *Brief Account*, pp. 3–4.

46. Ibid.

47. Ibid., p. 29; *Account of the Massachusetts State Prison*, p. 36; Reynolds, *Recollections*, p. 15; William C. Sneed, *A Report on the History and Mode of Management of the Kentucky Penitentiary* (Frankfort: Yeoman Office, 1860), p. 24.

48. Jeremy Bentham, *A View of the Hard-Labour Bill* (London: for T. Payne and Son, T. Cadell and P. Elmsly, and E. Brooke, 1778), p. 60; Livingston, *System of Penal Law*, pp. 712–13.

49. *Thirteenth Annual Report of the Board of Managers of the Prison Discipline Society, Boston, May, 1838* (Boston: at the Society's Rooms, 1838), pp. 221, 231; *State Prisons and the Penitentiary System Vindicated*, p. 28.

50. Howe, *Essay*, pp. 42–43; Michael Stephen Hindus, *Prison and Plantation: Crime, Justice, and Authority in Massachusetts and South Carolina, 1767–1878* (Chapel Hill: University of North Carolina Press, 1980), p. 171.

51. Dickens, *American Notes*, p. 53; Committee of the Society for the Improvement of Prison Discipline, *Remarks on the Form and Construction of Prisons*, p. 42.

52. "Description of the Tread Mill, Recommended by the Society for the Improvement of Prison Discipline," *Port Folio*, ser. 4, 14, no. 5 (Nov. 1822): 429–31; Richard Peters, Belmont, to Roberts Vaux, Sept. 10, 1822, Vaux Papers; Peters to Vaux, Nov. 15, 1822; [Stephen Allen], *Reports on the Stepping or Discipline Mill, at the New-York Penitentiary* (New York: Van Pelt and Spear, 1823), p. 21; James Hardie, A. M., *The History of the Tread-Mill* (New York: Samuel Marks, 1824), pp. 16–20 (emphasis added).

53. Hall, *Travels*, 1: 62.

54. *Philadelphia in 1824* (Philadelphia: H. C. Carey and I. Lea, 1824), p. 144; *Second Annual Report of the Board of Managers*, p. 77; "On the Ventilation and Warming of Prison and other Buildings," *Pennsylvania Journal of Prison Discipline and Philanthropy* 1 (1845): 339; *The First Annual Report of the Inspectors of the Philadelphia County Prison* (Harrisburg: J. M. G. Lescure, 1848), p. 8; Dickens, *American Notes*, p. 84.

55. [McElwee], *Concise History*, 1: 26.

56. "A Statement of the Criminal Business of the Circuit Court of the United States for the Eastern District of Pennsylvania . . . ," *HRP* 8, no. 16 (Oct. 15, 1831): 251.

57. Dix, *Remarks*, p. 14; Powers, *Brief Account*, p. 15; Martineau, *Retrospect*, 1: 124; [Allen], *Reports on the Stepping or Discipline Mill*, p. 21; Hardie, *History of the Tread-Mill*, p. 27.

58. Howe, *Essay*, p. 28; Martineau, *Retrospect*, 1: 123.

59. *Second Annual Report of the Board of Managers*, p. 122; "On the Ventilation and Warming," pp. 338–39; Hamilton, *Men and Manners*, 1: 343.

60. Bradford, *Enquiry*, p. 4.

61. Horace Lane, *Five Years in State's Prison*, 5th ed. (New York: for the author, 1835); Reverend John Luckey, *Life in Sing Sing State Prison* (New York: N. Tibbals, 1860), p. 17; Roscoe, *Brief Statement*, p. 5; Dix, *Remarks*, p. 13; Powers, *Letter*, p. 14.

62. Bowen, *History of Philadelphia*, p. 181; [McElwee], *Concise History*, 1: 16–17; [Coffey], *Inside Out*, pp. 78–81.

63. [McElwee], *Concise History*, 1: 18–19; Dix, *Remarks*, pp. 13–14.

64. [McElwee], *Concise History*, 1: 17–18; Reynolds, *Recollections*, p. 65; James Bradley Finley, *Memorials of Prison Life* (Cincinnati: L. Swormstedt and A. Poe, 1855; rpt. New York: Arno, 1974), p. 26; M'Ewen, *Mysteries*, p. 28; *Memorandum of a Late Visit to the Auburn Penitentiary* (Philadelphia: J. Harding, 1842), pp. 4–5; Martineau, *Retrospect*, 1: 125.

65. [McElwee], *Concise History*, 1: 18, 42–43, 125–30, 2: 22–24.

66. Ibid., 1: 44–45, 2: 22–24, 30–31, 50–51.

67. Powers, *Brief Account*, p. 61.

68. William Roscoe, *Observations on Penal Jurisprudence, and the Reformation of Criminals* (London: T. Cavell, W. Davies, and J. and A. Arch, 1819), p. 152.

69. Vaux, *Notices*, p. 3; Livingston, *System of Penal Law*, p. 316.

70. *Fourth Annual Report of the Board of Managers of the Prison Discipline Society, Boston, 1829* (Boston: T. R. Marvin, 1829), pp. 54–55.

71. Dell Upton, "Lancasterian Schools, Republican Citizenship, and the Spatial Imagination in Early Nineteenth-Century America," *JSAH* 55, no. 3 (Sept. 1996): 238–53; Bentham, *Panopticon Writings*, p. 77.

CHAPTER 11. **ON THE WATERFRONT**

1. Richard Campanella, *Time and Place in New Orleans: Past Geographies in the Present Day* (Gretna, La.: Pelican, 2002), pp. 16–18, 45; Donald W. Davis, "Historical Perspective on Crevasses, Levees, and the Mississippi River," in *Transforming New Orleans and Its Environs: Centuries of Change*, ed. Craig E. Colten (Pittsburgh: University of Pittsburgh Press, 2000), pp. 85–91; Craig E. Colten, *An Unnatural Metropolis: Wresting New Orleans from Nature* (Baton Rouge: Louisiana State University Press, 2005), pp. 26–28.

2. Caroline Hale to Mary Hale and Alice L. March, Mar. 14, 1844, TUL; Edward Livingston, *Address to the People of the United States, on the Measures Pursued by the Executive with Respect to the Batture at New-Orleans* (New Orleans: Bradford and Anderson, 1808), p. i.

3. Charles Joseph Latrobe, *The Rambler in North America, MDCCCXXXII–MDCCCXXXIII* (New York: Harper and Bros., 1835), 2: 238; John G. Clark, *New Orleans 1718–1812: An Economic History* (Baton Rouge: Louisiana State University Press, 1970), pp. 299–330; Michael Zakim, *Ready-Made Democracy: A History of Men's Dress in the American Republic, 1760–1860* (Chicago: University of Chicago Press, 2003), p. 48.

4. Thomas Jefferson, *The Proceedings of the Government of the United States, in Maintaining the Public Right to the Beach of the Missisipi, Adjacent to New-Orleans* (New York: Ezra Sargeant, 1812), p. 71; James A. Padgett, ed., "Some Documents Relating to the Batture Controversy in New Orleans," *LH* 23, no. 3 (July 1940): 687.

5. Padgett, "Some Documents," pp. 683, 700–4, 707 and passim; *Pièces probantes à l'appui des*

droits des habitans de la cité d'Orléans et de ses faubourgs, sur la batture en face du faubourg Sainte-Marie (New Orleans: chez Jean Renard, 1807), pp. 4, 6; undated council order, John Minor Wisdom Collection, Batture Controversy, box 17, TUL.

6. New Orleans, Conseil de Ville, Resolutions and ordinances of the Conseil de Ville, 1, 1805–1815, NOPL, orders of June 22, July 13, 1805; petition of Jean Baptiste Arpin, Aug. 31, 1808; Pierre A. C. B. Derbigny, *Mémoire à consulter, sur la réclamation de la Batture, située en face du Faubourg Sainte-Marie à la Nouvelle-Orléans* (New Orleans: chez Jean Renard, 1807), pp. 3–4; typed translation of city council minutes, Manuscripts Department, TUL, box 2, fol. 10 (Aug. 5, 1812).

7. Hendrik Hartog, *Public Property and Private Power: The Corporation of the City of New York in American Law, 1730–1870* (Chapel Hill: University of North Carolina Press, 1983), pp. 44–68.

8. Jefferson, *Proceedings*, pp. 9, 19.

9. Thomas W. Tucker, "The King Is Lost Upon the Batture, or How Edward Livingston Seized the Altered Notion of Sovereignty to Settle His Batture Controversy, and the Havoc Bestowed Thereby," in *Louisiana: Microcosm of a Mixed Jurisdiction,* ed. Vernon Valentine Palmer (Durham, N.C.: Carolina Academic Press, 1999), p. 139 n. 15.

10. Edward Livingston, *Address,* p. xi; Jefferson, *Proceedings,* pp. 17–19.

11. Livingston, *Address,* pp. xii–xv; Jefferson, *Proceedings,* pp. 17–19; George Dargo, *Jefferson's Louisiana: Politics and the Clash of Legal Traditions* (Cambridge: Harvard University Press, 1975), p. 84; NOCVa, 1, Nov. 7, 1814; Tucker, "King Is Lost," pp. 136–37 n. 12.

12. *Morgan v. Livingston et al., 6 Mart.* (O.S.) 19 (1819); *Delabigarre v. Second Municipality of New Orleans, 3 La. Annual* 23 (1848); Tucker, "King Is Lost," pp. 129, 141–61.

13. Dargo, *Jefferson's Louisiana,* pp. 13–14, 84. Throughout this passage, I follow Dargo's exposition of the differences between the civil- and common-law traditions (*Jefferson's Louisiana,* pp. 11–17).

14. Tucker, "King Is Lost," p. 134 n. 11; Hartog, *Public Property,* p. 23.

15. Julien Poydras, *Speech of Julien Poydras . . . in Support of the Right of the Public to the Batture in Front of the Suburb St. Mary* (Washington, D.C.: A. and G. Way, 1810), pp. 20–24; Jefferson, *Proceedings,* pp. 71–72.

16. Poydras, *Speech,* p. 23; Julien Poydras, *Further Observations in Support of the Right of the Public to the Batture of New Orleans* (Washington, D.C.: A. and G. Way, 1809), p. 12; J. B. S. Thierry, *Reply to Mr. Duponceau* ([New Orleans], 1809), p. 47; Malone, *Jefferson,* p. 61; Jefferson, *Proceedings,* p. 18.

17. Peter Stephen Du Ponceau, *A Review of the Cause of the New Orleans Batture* (Philadelphia: Jane Aitken, 1809), pp. 32–33, 39–41; Livingston, *Address,* p. iii–iv, xxx.

18. John Locke, *The Second Treatise of Government,* ed. Thomas P. Peardon (Indianapolis: Bobbs-Merrill, 1952), pp. 17 (sec. 26), 20 (sec. 33), 71 (sec. 127); C. B. Macpherson, *The Political Theory of Possessive Individualism: Hobbes to Locke* (New York: Oxford University Press, 1962), pp. 197–222; Livingston, *Address,* p. xxx; Du Ponceau, *Review,* p. 41; Joyce Oldham Appleby, *Economic Thought and Ideology in Seventeenth-Century England* (Princeton: Princeton University Press, 1978), pp. 3–4, 52–63.

19. Du Ponceau, *Review,* p. 7; Dargo, *Jefferson's Louisiana,* pp. 74, 83, and passim; Douglas Hay, "Property, Authority, and the Criminal Law," in Douglas Hay, Peter Linebaugh, John G. Rule, E. P. Thompson, and Cal Winslow, *Albion's Fatal Tree: Crime and Society in Eighteenth-Century England* (New York: Pantheon, 1975), pp. 18–19, 26.

20. Gary Kulik, "Dams, Fish, and Farmers: The Defense of Public Rights in Eighteenth-Century Rhode Island," in *The New England Working Class and the New Labor History*, ed. Herbert G. Gutman and Donald H. Bell (Urbana: University of Illinois Press, 1987), pp. 187–213; Christine Meisner Rosen, "Noisome, Noxious, and Offensive Vapors, Fumes and Stenches in American Towns and Cities, 1840–1865," *Historical Geography* 25 (1997): 49–82; Dargo, *Jefferson's Louisiana*, pp. 6–7, 23; Norman K. Risjord, *Jefferson's America, 1760–1815* (Madison, Wis.: Madison House, 1991), pp. 253–56; Benjamin Franklin Peters, "Biographical Notes of Samuel J. Peters," ca. 1850, MS, McConnell Family Papers, Personal Papers, box 1, fol. 7, TUL/MS, n.p.; Bernard Marigny, *Bernard Marigny à ses concitoyens* (New Orleans, 1853), p. 2.

21. Julien Poydras, *A Defence of the Right of the Public to the Batture of New Orleans* (Washington, D.C.: for the author, 1809), p. 16; Thierry, *Reply*, p. 47.

22. *Morgan v. Livingston et al.*, 6 Mart. (O.S.) 19 (1819) at pp. 35–36 and passim; Thierry, *Reply*, p. 60; Michael Warner, *The Letters of the Republic: Publication and the Public Sphere in Eighteenth-Century America* (Cambridge: Harvard University Press, 1990), p. 61; Dargo, *Jefferson's Louisiana*, p. 83.

23. J. B. S. Thierry acknowledged that "all the best disposed, the wealthiest and the oldest inhabitants of the city, were present at that meeting [on Sept. 15, 1807], to protest against the spoliation of a public property" (*Reply*, p. 61).

24. Bernard Marigny, *Memoir of Bernard Marigny* [1822], trans. Olivia Blanchard (New Orleans: Survey of Federal Archives in Louisiana, WPA, 1939), p. 29; Pauline Maier, "Popular Uprisings and Civil Authority in Eighteenth-Century America," *WMQ*, 3d ser., 27, no. 1 (Jan. 1970): 3–35; E. P. Thompson, "The Moral Economy of the English Crowd in the Eighteenth Century," *Past and Present*, no. 50 (Feb. 1971): 76–136; Roy Porter, *English Society in the Eighteenth Century* (Harmondsworth: Penguin, 1982), pp. 115–18; Paul A. Gilje, *The Road to Mobocracy: Popular Disorder in New York City, 1763–1834* (Chapel Hill: University of North Carolina Press, 1987), pp. vii, 16–18, 30–31, 99; Thierry, *Reply*, p. 61; Dargo, *Jefferson's Louisiana*, p. 210 n. 29.

25. Samuel Wilson, Jr., *The Vieux Carré, New Orleans: Its Plan, Its Growth, Its Architecture* (New Orleans: Bureau of Governmental Research for the City of New Orleans, 1968), p. 90; Boze, "Suite au bulletin," Mar. 28, 1836, SGP, fol. 248; NOMP/T, box 1, fol. 3 (Mar. 14, 1808), box 2, fol. 5 (Feb. 16, 1811); Hartog, *Public Property*, pp. 104–10.

26. Tucker, "King Is Lost," pp. 153–56.

27. Penn, *Papers*, 2: 573–74.

28. Mathew Carey, *A Short Account of the Malignant Fever* (Philadelphia: by the author, Jan. 16, 1794), p. 67; Academy of Medicine of Philadelphia, *Proofs of the Origin of the Yellow Fever* (Philadelphia: Thomas and Samuel F. Bradford, 1798), pp. 6, 9.

29. Thaddeus Brown, *An Address in Christian Love, to the Inhabitants of Philadelphia* (Philadelphia: for the author, by R. Aitken, 1798), p. 38; [Paul Beck, Jr.], *A Proposal for Altering the Eastern Front of the City of Philadelphia* (Philadelphia: William Fry, 1820), pp. 3–4.

30. Henry Simpson, *The Lives of Eminent Philadelphians, Now Deceased* (Philadelphia: William Brotherhead, 1859), pp. 37–48; *The Biographical Encyclopaedia of Pennsylvania of the Nineteenth Century* (Philadelphia: Galaxy, 1874), pp. 201–2.

31. Francis Sheppard, *London 1808–1870: The Infernal Wen* (Berkeley: University of California Press, 1971), pp. 110–12; Gavin Weightman and Steve Humphries, *The Making of Modern London, 1815–1914* (London: Sidgwick and Jackson, 1983), pp. 18, 20, 76–77; Walter Muir Whitehill, *Boston: A Topographical History*, 2d ed. (Cambridge: Harvard University Press,

1968), pp. 84–88; Harold Kirker, *The Architecture of Charles Bulfinch* (Cambridge: Harvard University Press, 1969), pp. 188–93.

32. [Beck], *Proposal,* pp. 5–6; Sheppard, *Infernal Wen,* 285–86.

33. Hartog, *Public Property,* p. 62; Watson I, 211; Brown, *Address,* p. 38; [Robert Waln, Jr.,] *The Hermit in America on a Visit to Philadelphia* (Philadelphia: M. Thomas, 1819–21), 1: 69.

34. [Paul Beck, Jr.], "A Proposal for Altering the Eastern Front of the City of Philadelphia . . . ," *Collections of the Historical Society of Pennsylvania* 1, no. 6 (Nov. 1853): 385. This is a reprint of Beck's pamphlet with Girard's letter appended.

35. Stephen Girard, "Remarks on the intended Congregation of the Mariner's Church," MS, Miscellaneous Personal Papers: Politics, Pressure Groups and Public Service, 1794–1831, n.d. Stephen Girard Papers, APS. Microfilm 1967 825mf ser. II, R482.

36. "Proceedings of Councils," *HRP* 8, no. 12 (Sept. 17, 1831): 181.

37. "The Memorial of Stephen Girard," Miscellaneous Personal Papers: Politics, Pressure Groups and Public Service, 1794–1831, Sept. 26, 1831, Girard Papers, microfilm 1967 825mf ser. II, R482; Morton J. Horwitz, *The Transformation of American Law, 1780–1860* (Cambridge: Harvard University Press, 1977), pp. 42–53.

38. "Proceedings of Councils," *HRP* 8, no. 13 (Sept. 24, 1831): 203; 8, no. 14 (Oct. 1, 1831): 224; 8, no. 19 (Nov. 5, 1831): 292; 8, no. 21 (Nov. 19, 1831): 326.

39. Roberts Vaux to George Wolf, Jan. 14, 1832, Wolf Papers, V, HSP.

40. [Stephen Girard], *The Will of the Late Stephen Girard, Esq. . . . with a Short Biography of His Life* (Philadelphia: Lydia R. Bailey, 1839), pp. 1–2, 14–36.

41. [Girard], *Will,* pp. 30–35.

42. *Phila. Ord.,* pp. 183–85, 190; *Picture of Philadelphia* (Philadelphia: E. L. Carey and A. Hart, 1835), sig. U. Girard's will was reprinted in full in the city ordinances (ibid., pp. 419–39).

43. Simpson, *Lives of Eminent Philadelphians,* p. 44; editor's headnote to Beck, "Proposal," p. 382; [Girard], *Will,* pp. 32–33.

CHAPTER 12. **IN PUBLIC WALKS**

1. Jacques-Pierre Brissot de Warville, *New Travels in the United States of America* (Dublin: W. Corbett, P. Byrne, A. Grueber, et al., 1792), pp. 155–56.

2. "Letters from an Englishman in the United States to His Friend in Great Britain," *Port Folio,* ser. 4, 12, no. 2 (Dec. 1821): 305; Cope, p. 484; John H. B. Latrobe, *Southern Travels: Journal of John H. B. Latrobe 1834,* ed. Samuel Wilson Jr. (New Orleans: Historic New Orleans Collection, 1986), pp. 43, 45; Baron de Montlezun, *Voyage fait dans les années 1816 et 1817, de New-Yorck à la Nouvelle-Orléans* (Paris: Librairie de Gide fils, 1818), 1: 307; "Smoking," *Home Journal,* Sept. 14, 1850, p. 3; Fredrika Bremer, *The Homes of the New World,* trans. Mary Howitt (New York: Harper and Bros., 1854), 2: 605.

3. Alexander Mackay, *The Western World; or, Travels in the United States in 1846–47* (London: Richard Bentley, 1849), 1: 150–51; "Suppose," New York *Daily Times,* June 29, 1853, 8: 1.

4. Fisher, p. 113; Charles Dickens, *American Notes and Pictures from Italy* (New York: Oxford University Press, 1966), p. 112; E. S. Abdy, *Journal of a Residence and Tour in the United States of North America* (New York: Negro Universities Press, 1969), 2: 61–62; "Editor's Easy Chair," *Harper's New Monthly Magazine* 7 (Nov. 1853): 845.

5. Edward Augustus Kendall, *Travels Through the Northern Parts of the United States* (New York: I. Riley, 1809), 1: 317.

6. Charles Sellers, *The Market Revolution: Jacksonian America, 1815–1846* (New York: Oxford

University Press, 1991), pp. 354–58; Arthur M. Schlesinger, Jr., *The Age of Jackson* (Boston: Little, Brown, 1945), pp. 218–20, 313; Anthony Gronowicz, *Race and Class Politics in New York City Before the Civil War* (Boston: Northeastern University Press, 1998), pp. 59–85; Amy Bridges, *A City in the Republic: Antebellum New York and the Origins of Machine Politics* (Ithaca: Cornell University Press, 1984), pp. 26–27; Harry L. Watson, *Liberty and Power: The Politics of Jacksonian America* (New York: Hill and Wang, 1990), pp. 192–93.

7. Schlesinger, *Age of Jackson,* pp. 224–26; Watson, *Liberty and Power,* pp. 37–38.

8. "Customs of New-York," *New-York Mirror* 5 (July 5, 1828): 23; George Templeton Strong, Diary, Sept. 5, 1839, copy of MS at Metropolitan Museum of Art.

9. "Street Smoking," *Philadelphia Saturday Bulletin,* Oct. 15, 1831.

10. Cope, p. 298; William B. Davidson, Journal, 1824–25, MS, HSP, n.d.

11. Mary P. Ryan, *Civic Wars: Democracy and Public Life in the American City During the Nineteenth Century* (Berkeley: University of California Press, 1997), p. 61.

12. "Croton Water Works. Celebration of the Introduction of the Croton Water into the City of New York on the 14th Instant," *Niles' Weekly Register* 63 (Oct. 22, 1842): 127; Edward Wegmann, *The Water-Supply of the City of New York, 1658–1895* (New York: John Wiley and Sons, 1896), p. 46; E. Porter Belden, *New-York: Past, Present, and Future,* 2nd ed. (New York: G. P. Putnam, 1849), p. 41; "The Croton Celebration," *New World* 5 (Oct. 8, 1842): 238.

13. "The Atlantic Cable Festivities," *Harper's Weekly* 2 (Sept. 11, 1858): 586; "Broadway at Night," *Frank Leslie's Illustrated Newspaper,* Sept. 11, 1858, pp. 226–27; "Tiffany & Co." (advertisement), *Harper's Weekly* 2 (Sept. 4, 1858): 576.

14. Ronald L. Grimes, *Symbol and Conquest: Public Ritual and Drama in Santa Fe, New Mexico* (Ithaca: Cornell University Press, 1976), pp. 62–70; "Croton Celebration," 268.

15. Marshall Sahlins, *Islands of History* (Chicago: University of Chicago Press, 1985), pp. 92–95; Rhys Isaac, *The Transformation of Virginia, 1750–1790* (Chapel Hill: University of North Carolina Press, 1982), pp. 19–20; Grimes, *Symbol and Conquest,* p. 65.

16. Belden, *New-York,* p. 40; "Croton Water Works," p. 126; "Croton Celebration," 269.

17. "Croton Celebration," 269; Victor Turner, *The Ritual Process: Structure and Anti-Structure* (Ithaca: Cornell University Press, 1969), pp. 131–32.

18. Turner, *Ritual Process,* pp. 132–33; "Croton Celebration," 269.

19. Mary Ryan, "The American Parade: Representations of the Nineteenth-Century Social Order" in *The New Cultural History,* ed. Lynn Hunt (Berkeley: University of California Press, 1988), p. 137; "Croton Celebration," 268–69; Strong Diary, Oct. 14, 1842; "Croton Water Works," pp. 124–27; Belden, *New-York,* p. 39; Turner, *Ritual Process,* p. 132.

20. Susan G. Davis, *Parades and Power: Street Theatre in Nineteenth-Century Philadelphia* (Philadelphia: Temple University Press, 1986), pp. 27–28, 164, 172; Ryan, "American Parade," pp. 134, 137.

21. Strong Diary, Apr. 10, 1841.

22. Ryan, "American Parade," pp. 139–46, 148–52.

23. Mary P. Ryan, *Mysteries of Sex: Tracing Women and Men Through American History* (Chapel Hill: University of North Carolina Press, 2006), pp. 152–60; Ryan, "American Parade," pp. 139–46, 148–52; Bridges, *City in the Republic,* pp. 1, 125–31; Daniel Bowen, *A History of Philadelphia* (Philadelphia: Daniel Bowen, 1839), p. 87; *Francis Hopkinson's "Account of the Grand Federal Procession Philadelphia, 1788,"* ed. Whitfield J. Bell, Jr. (Boston: Old South Association, 1962), p. 9.

24. Ryan, "American Parade," p. 133; Simon P. Newman, *Parades and the Politics of the Street:*

Festive Culture in the Early American Republic (Philadelphia: University of Pennsylvania Press, 1997), pp. 7, 40.

25. Davidson, Journal, July 4, 1825.

26. Davis, *Parades and Power,* pp. 73–111; Shane White and Graham White, *Stylin': African American Expressive Culture from Its Beginnings to the Zoot Suit* (Ithaca: Cornell University Press, 1998), pp. 95–97; Drinker 2: 1347; Anneliese Harding, *John Lewis Krimmel: Genre Artist of the Early Republic* (Winterthur, Del.: Winterthur, 1994), pp. 211, 213–14, 216–18.

27. Grimes, *Symbol and Conquest,* p. 65; Shane White, "'It Was a Proud Day': African Americans, Festivals, and Parades in the North, 1741–1834," *Journal of American History* 81, no. 1 (June 1994): 13–50; White and White, *Stylin',* pp. 95–97, 101–2, 120–213.

28. Luther F. Tower, Diaries, 1845–46, MS, Louisiana and Lower Mississippi Valley Collection, Louisiana State University, Feb. 5, 1845; Albert J. Pickett, *Eight Days in New-Orleans* (Montgomery, Ala.: Albert J. Pickett, 1847), p. 31.

29. Joseph Holt Ingraham, *The South-West. By a Yankee* (New York: Harper and Bros., 1835), 1: 211; Cope, p. 29; White and White, *Stylin',* pp. 108, 110–14, 123.

30. Ryan, *Mysteries of Sex,* pp. 156–58; Bruce Dorsey, *Reforming Men and Women: Gender in the Antebellum City* (Ithaca: Cornell University Press, 2002), pp. 8, 12–13, 18–19.

31. Ryan, *Mysteries of Sex,* pp. 84–88; John Davis, *Travels of Four Years and a Half in the United States of America,* ed. A. J. Morrison (New York: Henry Holt, 1909), p. 355; "Chit-Chat or Table Talk of the Day," *Ladies Companion* 1, no. 2 (June 1834): 106.

32. Christine Stansell, "Women, Children, and the Uses of the Streets: Class and Gender Conflicts in New York City, 1850–1860," *Feminist Studies* 8 (summer 1982): 309–35; Dorsey, *Reforming Men and Women,* pp. 12–13.

33. Fisher, p. 19; "Ladies' Fairs," *Niles' Weekly Register* 40 (June 4, 1831): 237.

34. Mary Lorrain Peters, Diary, 1837–39, MS, New-York Historical Society, B.V. sec. Peters; Richard L. Bushman, *The Refinement of America: Persons, Houses, Cities* (New York: Knopf, 1992), pp. 81–83.

35. Mackay, *Western World,* 1: 200–202.

36. David Scobey, "Anatomy of the Promenade: The Politics of Bourgeois Sociability in Nineteenth-Century New York," *Social History* 17, no. 2 (May 1992): 203–27; Elizabeth Blackmar, *Manhattan for Rent, 1790–1850* (Ithaca: Cornell University Press, 1989), pp. 128–33; Cope, p. 240; Strong Diary, Jan. 1, 1844; Mrs. C. M. Kirkland, "New York," *Sartain's Magazine,* Sept. 1851, n.p.; "Sketches of New-York," *New Mirror* 1, no. 6 (May 13, 1843): 85.

37. Fisher, p. 153; Cope, p. 400.

38. Eliza Ripley, *Social Life in Old New Orleans* (New York: D. Appleton, 1912), pp. 62–63.

39. John Kasson, *Rudeness and Civility: Manners in Nineteenth-Century Urban America* (New York: Hill and Wang, 1990), p. 131–32; Mackay, *Western World,* 1: 216; Abdy, *Journal,* 1: 69; William Biddle Shepard to Ebenezer Pettigrew, Apr. 18, 1817, in Sarah McCulloh Lemmon, ed., *The Pettigrew Papers, 1, 1685–1818* (Raleigh, N.C.: State Department of Archives and History, 1971), p. 563.

40. [Francis J. Grund], *Aristocracy in America from the Sketch-Book of a German Nobleman* (London: Richard Bentley, 1839, 1: 29–30); "Chestnut Street," *Godey's Magazine and Lady's Book* 46 (Mar. 1853): 282; Madaline S. Edwards, *Madaline: Love and Survival in Antebellum New Orleans,* ed. Dell Upton (Athens: University of Georgia Press, 1995), pp. 204, 237.

41. "Advice to Ladies," *New Orleans Bee,* May 29, 1854.

42. "Old and New Times," *DeSilver's Philadelphia Directory and Stranger's Guide* (Philadelphia:

Robert de Silver, 1830), pp. 3–4; Bryan S. Turner, *The Body and Society: Explorations in Social Theory,* 2d. ed. (London: Sage, 1996), p. 14.

43. William W. Sanger, *The History of Prostitution* (New York: Harper and Bros., 1859), pp. 584–85.

44. Mary P. Ryan, *Women in Public: Between Banners and Ballots, 1825–1880* (Baltimore: Johns Hopkins University Press, 1990), pp. 3–4, 130–46.

45. Benjamin F. Butler, *Private and Official Correspondence of Gen. Benjamin F. Butler* (Norwood, Mass.: Plimpton, 1917), 1: 490, 530, 2: 35–36, 497–501, 3: 32; Sarah Morgan, *The Civil War Diary of Sarah Morgan,* ed. Charles East (Athens: University of Georgia Press, 1991), pp. 76–77; Ryan, *Women in Public,* p. 144; unidentified newspaper clipping enclosed in envelope labeled "General Butler's Order" and addressed from Headquarters, Department of the Gulf, New Orleans, June 30, 1862; S. L. Levy to My Dear Martha & Emma, July 24, 1862, and S. L. Levy to My Dear Martha, July 30, 1862, all in Phillips-Myers Papers, SHC, fol. 2.

46. Harriet Martineau, *Retrospect of Western Travel* (London: Saunders and Otley, 1838), 1: 258.

47. David Lee Sterling, ed., "New Orleans, 1801: An Account by John Pintard," *LH* 34, no. 3 (July 1951): 231; Thomas Ashe, *Travels in America* (London: for Richard Phillips, 1809), p. 315.

48. James Stuart, *Three Years in North America,* 3d rev. ed. (Edinburgh: for Robert Cadell, 1833), 2: 203; Martineau, *Retrospect,* 1: 262; William Darby, *A Geographical Description of the State of Louisiana* (Philadelphia: John Melish, 1816), p. 187; Ingraham, *South-West,* 1: 90.

49. Fisher, p. 18; "Things in New York," *Brother Jonathan* 4, no. 9 (Mar. 4, 1843): 250; "Park Row," *New-York Mirror* 8, no. 5 (Aug. 7, 1830): 33.

50. Draft petition to City Commissioners of Philadelphia on plans assigned for cab stands, Feb. 7, 1842, Edward Shippen Burd Papers, HSP.

51. Scobey, "Anatomy of the Promenade," p. 222.

52. Strong Diary, July 7, 1851; George G. Foster, "The Boys in the Street," *Home Journal,* Jan. 26, 1850, p. 3.

53. "Letters from an Englishman," p. 305; Lady Emmeline Stuart Wortley, *Travels in the United States, etc. During 1849 and 1850* (New York: Harper and Bros., 1851), pp. 46–47.

54. Martineau, *Retrospect,* 1: 262–63.

55. "Diary of Town Trifles," *New Mirror* 3, no. 7 (May 18, 1844): 104.

56. [William M. Bobo], *Glimpses of New-York City* (Charleston: J. J. McCarter, 1852), pp. 164–65; Henry Collins Brown, ed., *Valentine's Manual of the City of New York for 1916–7,* n.s. (New York: Valentine's Manual, 1916); "Facts and Opinions of Literature, Society, and Movements of the Day," *Literary World,* no. 206 (Jan. 11, 1851): 32.

57. [Bobo], *Glimpses,* pp. 164–65.

58. Bruce Laurie, "Fire Companies and Gangs in Southwark: The 1840s," in *The Peoples of Philadelphia: A History of Ethnic Groups and Lower-Class Life, 1790–1840,* ed. Allen F. Davis and Mark H. Haller (Philadelphia: Temple University Press, 1973), pp. 78–82; Bruce Laurie, *Working People of Philadelphia, 1800–1850* (Philadelphia: Temple University Press, 1980), pp. 58–61, 151, 153–57; Cope, pp. 436, 467, 517, 576, 581; Ryan, *Mysteries of Sex,* pp. 156–57; Fisher, p. 122.

59. *Phila. Ord.,* p. 248 (June 18, 1840); Wortley, *Travels,* p. 46; Mackay, *Western World,* 1: 27; [Bobo], *Glimpses,* p. 182; Richard C. Wade, *Slavery in the Cities: The South, 1820–1860* (New York: Oxford University Press, 1964), pp. 108, 181.

60. Mackay, *Western World*, 1: 152.

61. [Grund], *Aristocracy in America*, 1: 19.

62. E. E., "Letters Descriptive of New-York, Written to a Literary Gentleman in Dublin, No. III," *New-York Mirror and Ladies' Literary Gazette* 4 (Jan. 13, 1827): 195; Watson I, 352, 483; J. Thomas Scharf and Thompson Westcott, *History of Philadelphia, 1609–1884* (Philadelphia: L. H. Everts, 1884), 3: 1845–46; *Philadelphia in 1831* (Philadelphia: E. L. Carey and A. Hart, 1830), p. 145. On the origins of promenading in America and of landscaping to accommodate it, see Rudy J. Favretti, "The Ornamentation of New England Towns: 1750–1850," *Journal of Garden History* 2, no. 4 (Oct.–Dec. 1982): 325–42.

63. "Supplement to the Report of the Horticultural Society: Public Squares," *HRP* 7, no. 7 (Feb. 12, 1831): 128; *Phila Ord.*, 159 (May 8, 1828).

64. Samuel Wilson, Jr., *The Vieux Carré, New Orleans, Its Plan, Its Growth, Its Architecture* (New Orleans: Bureau of Governmental Research for the City of New Orleans, Dec. 1968), pp. 59, 90; Ashe, *Travels*, p. 310; Ingraham, *South-West*, 1: 88; Latrobe, *Corr.*, 3: 1061; James Edwards, New Orleans, to Eliza [Edwards], Cincinnati, Jan. 8, 1842, James Edwards Letters, 1841–42, Manuscripts Dept., TUL, M343.

65. NOMP/T, box 3, fol. 12 (Feb. 13, 20, 1819), fol. 13 (Mar. 13, 20, 1819); box 8, fol. 8 (Aug. 11, 1820); Latrobe, *Corr.*, 3: 1028, 1029n–30n; Leonard V. Huber, *Jackson Square Through the Years* (New Orleans: Friends of the Cabildo, 1982), pp. 36–39.

66. A. Oakey Hall, *The Manhattaner in New Orleans* (1851; rpt. Baton Rouge: Louisiana State University Press, 1976), pp. 89–90.

67. Leonard V. Huber and Samuel Wilson, Jr., *Baroness Pontalba's Buildings: Their Site and the Remarkable Woman Who Built Them,* 2d ed. (New Orleans: New Orleans Chapter of the Louisiana Landmarks Society and Friends of the Cabildo, 1966), pp. 36–47; Wilson, *Vieux Carré,* pp. 88–89; Huber, *Jackson Square,* pp. 63–68.

68. Elizabeth Blackmar and Roy Rosenzweig, *The Park and the People: A History of Central Park* (Ithaca: Cornell University Press, 1992), pp. 6–7, 238–51.

CONCLUSION

1. James Anthony Froude, *Thomas Carlyle: A History of the First Forty Years of His Life* (London: Longmans, Green, 1882), 2: 207.

2. *The First Annual Report of the Inspectors of the Philadelphia County Prison* (Harrisburg: J. M. G. Lescure, 1848); John Ely to Roberts Vaux, June 4, 1817, VP.

3. David J. Rothman, *The Discovery of the Asylum: Social Order and Disorder in the New Republic* (Boston: Little, Brown, 1971), pp. 237–38; Lawrence W. Levine, *Highbrow Lowbrow: The Emergence of Cultural Hierarchy in America* (Cambridge: Harvard University Press, 1988), esp. pp. 29–30, 178–200; "Fine Arts in New York," *United States Magazine,* 4 (Apr. 1857): 413–14; "Taste in New-York," *New York Quarterly,* 4 (1855): 56, 59.

4. "Turning Grain Elevators into Prisons?" *Urban Land,* Jan. 1990, p. 28; "New Jails Breaking Down Old Habits," *New York Times,* Jan. 8, 1992, p. A7.

5. Charles V. Bagli, "Public Plaza, Private Stage: A Hotel's Residents on Fifth Avenue Battle CBS at Its Doorstep," *New York Times,* Dec. 17, 2002, p. A31; Kathy Sheehan, "Curbing the Vendors: Sidewalk Posts Will Limit Number of Lunch Wagons," Philadelphia *Daily News,* Apr. 12, 1988, p. 6; Thomas Turcol, "Burrell unveils vendor bill; Plan is greeted with criticism," Philadelphia *Inquirer,* Sept. 27, 1990, pp. 1B, 4B.

6. Henry Weil, letter to the editor, *New York Times*, June 9, 2007.

7. Rick Bragg, "A Time for the Blues as the Quarter Cracks Down," *New York Times*, Nov. 12, 2002, p. A14.

8. Richard Longstreth, "Washington and the Landscape of Fear," *City and Society* 18, no. 1 (2006): 7–30.

Brown, Thaddeus, 295, 298

Browne, Peter A., 166–68, 170, 171, 172, 174, 181; and Pagoda Gardens, 165; and Philadelphia Arcade, 145, 158, 163, 181; urban systematizer, 166

Bryant, William Cullen, 225, 231

Bulfinch, Charles, 140, 245, 253, 296; and Treasury Building, 197, 299

Bulk (bay) windows, 151–53

Burd, Edward Shippen, 165, 170, 171, 325

Burial, premature, 226–27

Burke, Edmund, 66

Butler, Benjamin F., 49, 63; Gen. Order No. 28 ("Woman Order"), 321–22, *12.3*

Cabs, 324–25

Caldwell, James H., 172

Campbell, R., 180

Carey, Mathew, 55, 58, 60, 244

Carpenters' Company of the City and County of Philadelphia, 26, *1.5*

Carson, Anne, 77

Cemeteries: Boston, 210, 212; and city, 221, 225; and epidemics, 57, 228; family plots, 219–21; gravemarkers, 220–21; intramural, 210, 228; and miasma, 227; New York City, 210; as property, 218–19, 225, 234–35; reformed, 203, 205, 212–15, 228–29; removals, 210–12; rural, 205, 229–41; and systematic city, 221; traditional, 205–10; as urban places, 221. *See also names of individual cemeteries*; New Orleans; Philadelphia

Chambers, William, 194

Chandler, Alfred D., 184

Charleston, S.C., 139, 316

Child, Lydia Maria, 76

Cholera, 56

Cigars, 55, 99, 306, 308, 327, 328

Civic celebrations, 310–16

Civilization, 1, 2, 7

Claiborne, William C. C., 33, 284, 286, 288

Clapp, Theodore, 54, 240

Classification: natural history, 130; in republican spatial imagination, 134; and separation, 136; urban, 135, 336

Clay, Edward W., *Philadelphia Fashions, 1837,*

100, 104, *5.2*; *Promenade in Washington Square*, 96, *5.8*; *The Smokers*, 93, 207–10, 316, 326, *12.1*

Cmiel, Kenneth, 74

Coates, Benjamin, 276

Cohen, Anthony, 2, 94

Cohen, Patricia Cline, 129

Coleridge, Samuel Taylor, 122

Communitas, 312–13

Community, urban, 288, 289

Competency, 174–75

Competitive landscape, 178–79

Constitution: bodily, 55; epidemic, 57; moral, 55; political, 55

Consumption, 335; and selfhood, 157

Contagion, 57–58; moral, 256

Convicts, 259–60, 267–70, 271, 275

Cook, Joseph, 28

Cope, Thomas Pym: on Boston street pattern, 121; business losses, 174; contemplates suicide, 174; on New York street pattern, 120; on premature burial, 227; on smoking, 306; on women's speech, 78, 80

Corporation Pie, 42

Corridors, double-loaded, 187

Costume. *See* Dress

Countinghouses, 181, *8.1, 8.2*

Cries, vendors', 48, 67–68

Cries of Philadelphia, 67

Crime, 256–57

Criminality: among blacks, 269–70; among poor, 325–26; as disease, 256–57, 262

Cultural landscape, 10, 14

Dakin, James, 4

Dandies, 91, 100, 266, *5.4*

Dargo, George, 288, 290, 291

Dearborn, H. A. S., 229

Death, 208, 225–26

Derbigny, Pierre, 288

Desks, 182, *8.3*

Dickens, Charles: on Philadelphia plan, 120, 137, on prison life, 258, 260, 266

Dilworth, Thomas, 183–84

Disease, 55–56, 58–61; and crime, 256–57, 262